BETWEEN GIANTS

OSPREY

PUBLISHING

DEDICATION

For Dan

BETWEEN GIANTS

THE BATTLE FOR THE BALTICS
IN WORLD WAR II

PRIT BUTTAR

First published in Great Britain in 2013 by Osprey Publishing,
PO Box 883, Oxford, OX1 9PL, UK
PO Box 3985, New York, NY 10185-3985, USA
E-mail: info@ospreypublishing.com

OSPREY PUBLISHING IS PART OF THE OSPREY GROUP

ISBN: 978 1 4728 0749 6
e-book ISBN: 978 1 4728 0288 0
PDF ISBN: 978 1 4728 0287 3

Index by Alan Thatcher
Cartography by Tom Houlihan
Typeset in Trajan and Adobe Caslon Pro
Originated by PDQ Digital Media Solutions, UK
Printed in China through Wai Man Book Binding

15 16 17 18 19   10 9 8 7 6 5 4 3 2 1

Front cover image: German soldiers during a break in fighting near Smolensk, September 1941. (akg-images)

Osprey Publishing is supporting the Woodland Trust, the UK's leading woodland conservation charity, by funding the dedication of trees.

www.ospreypublishing.com

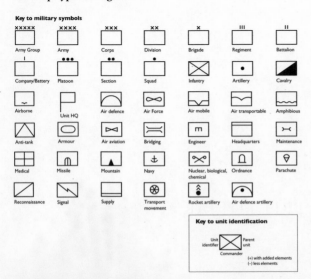

CONTENTS

LIST OF ILLUSTRATIONS

LIST OF MAPS

AUTHOR'S NOTE

Inevitably, a book such as this is only possible as a result of the generous help of many people.

My good friend David Clarke kindly loaned me several books, which I would otherwise have struggled to obtain. Indeed, David was responsible many years ago for first introducing me to Operations *Doppelkopf* and *Cäsar*, my first steps on the road that led to this book. Tom Houlihan, of www.mapsatwar.us, provided invaluable help and showed great patience when working with me on the maps. I am also hugely grateful to Irina Dovbush, who helped me find many of the Soviet sources that I used.

My agent, Robert Dudley, was as always a source of professional advice and personal encouragement. The staff at Osprey, particularly Kate Moore, Marcus Cowper and Emily Holmes, were as professional and as helpful as anyone could wish.

As usual, my family showed huge forbearance with me as I worked on this book, and I am eternally grateful to them.

DRAMATIS PERSONAE

Baltic States

Juozas Ambrazevičius – appointed as acting prime minister of Lithuania after the German invasion in 1941.

Oskars Dankers – appointed by the Germans in July 1941 as the leader of the future Latvian administration.

Augusts Kirhenšteins – government leader in Latvia following the Soviet invasion in June 1940.

Petras Kubiliūnas – appointed by the Germans in July 1941 as General Counsel in Lithuania, implementing German policies, particularly involved in recruiting Lithuanians for German forces.

Hjalmar Mäe – appointed by the Germans in July 1941 to run a directorate in Estonia implementing German policies.

Antanas Merkys – prime minister of Lithuania in 1939; removed in June 1940.

Vincas Mickevičius – Lithuanian Foreign Minister following the 1940 Soviet invasion; he remained in post for less than a month.

Ladas Natkevičius – Lithuanian ambassador to Moscow in 1939.

Justas Paleckis – leader of Lithuania following the 1940 Soviet invasion.

Konstantin Päts – Estonia's head of state on the outbreak of war in 1939; he was forced to resign in mid-July 1940.

Karl Selter – Estonian Foreign Minister in 1939.

Antanas Smetona – leader of Lithuania on the outbreak of war in 1939; in June 1940 he fled to Germany, and onwards to the United States.

Kārlis Ulmanis – Latvia's head of state in 1939; he was forced to resign in mid-July 1940.

Juozas Urbšys – Lithuanian Foreign Minister from 1938 to 1940.

Johannes Vares – Estonian Prime Minister following the 1940 Soviet invasion.

German

General Clemens Betzel – commander of IV Panzer Division during 1944; he and his division played a key part in operations *Doppelkopf* and *Cäsar* and in the fighting for Courland from October 1944 to January 1945.

Generalmajor Erich Brandenberger – commander of 8th Panzer Division during Operation *Barbarossa*.

Generalfeldmarschall Walther von Brauchitsch – commander of the German Army in 1941.

Generaloberst (from July 1940), later Generalfeldmarschall (from February 1943) Ernst Busch – commander of 16th Army during Operation *Barbarossa*; commanded Army Group Centre during the fighting around Narva of January–April 1944.

Oberst Hans Christern – commander of the 4th Panzer Division's 35th Panzer Regiment; he took command of 4th Panzer Division during Betzel's temporary absence in December 1944.

Generaloberst Johannes Friessner – commander of Army Group North during July 1944, replacing Lindemann, but handing over to Schörner by the end of the month.

Generalmajor Rüdiger von der Goltz – German commander in Latvia in 1918–19.

Generaloberst Heinz Guderian – chief of staff at German Army High Command (OKH).

General Christian Hansen – commander of 16th Army in 1944.

Reinhard Heydrich – head of the *Reichssicherheitshauptamt* ('Reich Main Security Administration' *or RSHA)*.

Generaloberst Erich Hoepner – commander of 4th Panzer Group, Army Group North, during Operation *Barbarossa*.

Oberst Hermann Hoth – commander of 3rd Panzer Group, Army Group Centre, during Operation *Barbarossa*.

SS-Standartenführer Karl Jäger – commander of *Einsatzkommando 3* from summer 1941; he was appointed commander of the Security Police and *Sicherheitsdienst* ('security department,' or SD) in Lithuania at the same time, and remained in Lithuania for two years. He wrote the Jäger Report, a detailed account of the killings of the Jews in the Kaunas ghetto during the second half of 1941.

Generaloberst Georg von Küchler – commander of 18th Army during Operation *Barbarossa*. He commanded Army Group North after the dismissal of Leeb in December 1941, but was dismissed in January 1944, and replaced by Model.

Generalfeldmarschall Wilhelm Ritter von Leeb – commander of Army Group North, the main military command in the Baltic region, comprising 16th Army, 18th Army and 4th Panzer Group, at the start of Operation *Barbarossa*.

Generaloberst Georg Lindemann – commander of 18th Army from January 1942 to March 1944; from end March until July 1944 he led Army Group North.

General (from June 1940), later Generalfeldmarschall (from July 1942) Erich von Manstein – commander of LVI Panzer Corps during Operation *Barbarossa*.

Generalfeldmarschall Walter Model – commander of Army Group North from January 1944, when he succeeded Küchler; he was promoted to field marshal two months later. On 31 March 1944 he was moved to Army Group North Ukraine and replaced at Army Group North by Lindemann; in June, he assumed command of Army Group Centre following Operation *Bagration*. He was transferred to the Western Front in August 1944, and was followed as commander of Army Group Centre by Reinhardt.

General Georg-Hans Reinhardt – commander of XLI Panzer Corps at the start of Operation *Barbarossa*. Promoted to *Generaloberst*, he commanded 3rd Panzer Army during the fighting around Vilnius in July 1944. In August 1944 he replaced Model as commander of Army Group Centre.

Joachim von Ribbentrop – German Foreign Minister 1938–45; he negotiated the Molotov–Ribbentrop Pact with the Soviet Union.

Alfred Rosenberg – a leading National Socialist, with a strong interest in racial theory; strongly anti-Semitic and anti-Bolshevik, he was highly influential in the development of Nazi racial ideology, and his ideas played a significant part in *Generalplan Ost*. From 1941 he was chief of the newly created *Reichsministerium für die besetzten Ostgebiete* ('Reich Ministry for the Occupied Eastern Territories') or *Ostministerium*.

General Dietrich von Saucken – commander of the newly reconstituted XXXIX Panzer Corps in summer 1944. He took command of *AOK Ostpreussen* in April 1945.

General Ferdinand Schörner – Appointed commander of Army Group North in July 1944, replacing Friessner. He had a reputation for imposing iron discipline, and was popular with Hitler. He served with Army Group North until January 1945, when 16th and 18th Armies became part of the newly designated Army Group Courland, under the command of Vietinghoff.

Friedrich Werner von der Schulenburg – German ambassador to Moscow in 1939.

Franz Walter Stahlecker – a lawyer who rose to high rank in the *Sicherheitsdienst* ('Security Administration' or SD); he commanded *Einsatzgruppe A* during Operation *Barbarossa*. He wrote a detailed report showing how his group operated in Lithuania following the German invasion.

SS-Obergruppenführer Felix Steiner – commander of III (Germanische) SS Panzer Corps from May 1943 to October 1944.

Generaloberst Heinrich von Vietinghoff – commander of the newly designated Army Group Courland from January to March 1945.

Soviet

Marshal of the Soviet Union Ivan Khristorovich Bagramian – as deputy Chief of Staff of the South-western Front at the start of Operation *Barbarossa*, Bagramian survived the defeat of the front in the Western Ukraine. He later rose to command first 16th Army, then 11th Army, before being appointed commander of 1st Baltic Front, in which role he played a key part in Operation *Bagration* in 1944. He was heavily involved in the fighting for the Courland region, and later wrote a detailed account of his experiences.

Lavrenti Beria – head of the NKVD, or Russian secret police.

General Ivan Danilovich Cherniakhovsky – commander of 28th Tank Division during Operation *Barbarossa*. He was promoted to command the 3rd Belarusian Front during 1944–45, and fought skilfully during Operation *Bagration*.

Colonel-General Ivan Mikhailovich Chistiakov – commander of 6th Guards Army from 1943 to the end of the war; he and his men played an important part in Operation *Cäsar* and in the fighting for Courland during October 1944.

Vladimir Georgievich Dekanozov – a Deputy Commissar for Foreign Affairs sent by the Soviet Union to organise a new government in Lithuania after the removal of Antanas Smetona in June 1940; in November 1940, he became Soviet ambassador to Berlin.

Leonid Alexandrovich Govorov – commander of the Leningrad Front from April 1942. In January 1945, following the disbanding of the Leningrad Front, he replaced Yeremenko as commander of 2nd Baltic Front.

Fyodor Isidorovich Kuznetsov – commander of the Baltic Special Military District, the first line of defence of Leningrad during Operation *Barbarossa*.

Maxim Maximovich Litvinov – Soviet Commissar for Foreign Affairs for most of the 1930s, but dismissed by Stalin in 1939, partly because of his Jewish ancestry.

Kirill Afanasevich Meretskov – commander of the Volkhov Front in January 1944.

Vyacheslav Mikhailovich Molotov – became Soviet Commissar for Foreign Affairs in 1939, on the dismissal of Litvinov by Stalin. Along with Stalin, he negotiated the Molotov–Ribbentrop Pact of 1939, which came to an end with the German invasion of the Soviet Union in June 1941.

Lieutenant General Petr Petrovich Sobennikov – commander of 8th Army at the start of Operation *Barbarossa*, he replaced Kuznetsov as Commander of the Baltic Special Military district following the fighting of June 1941.

Colonel-General Vasili Timofeevich Volskii – commander of 5th Guards Tank Army during the fighting in the Courland area of October 1944.

Marshal of the Soviet Union Andrei Ivanovich Yeremenko – commander of 2nd Baltic Front which joined the fighting in the Baltic during summer 1944.

Ivan Zotov – the Soviet ambassador in Latvia in 1940.

PREFACE

A quote often attributed – possibly incorrectly – to Josef Stalin is that 'the death of one person is a tragedy; the death of one million is a statistic'. Such a statement could certainly be said to apply to the Baltic States. The destruction and suffering endured by many nations during the Second World War are beyond question, but often the scale of the numbers involved can reduce their impact. The German atrocities in the Soviet Union, followed by Soviet atrocities in Germany, are well known and widely documented, but in terms of the proportion of the population lost, the countries caught between these powerful protagonists – Poland, Lithuania, Latvia and Estonia – suffered far more than any other. Whilst the deaths in Poland are relatively well known, the suffering in the Baltic States is rarely mentioned, even though their population loss, at roughly 20 per cent, was higher than that of any country other than Poland.

These terrible casualties were brought about by the unique circumstances of these three nations, which suffered three occupations in quick succession – the first Soviet occupation in 1939, the German occupation in 1941 and the second Soviet occupation in 1944–45, which would last nearly half a century. But in contrast to the situation in Poland, many of the deaths of Baltic citizens, particularly in Lithuania and Latvia, were at the hands of their fellow Balts, as the occupying powers ruthlessly exploited divisions within these countries. And, unlike Poland, the three nations were forced by their unique situation to offer support, albeit limited and reluctant, to Germany, leaving them unable to claim the backing of the victorious Allies in the post-war settlement.

This book does not attempt to judge the decisions made by the leaders and people of the Baltic States, who struggled to reconcile the situation in which they found themselves with their own aspirations; it seeks to give an account of the terrible destruction and bloodshed that had such a devastating effect on this corner of Europe, the consequences of which are still felt today.

INTRODUCTION

For several hundred years, the people of the Baltic States were little more than pawns in the wars fought by foreign rulers on their lands. During this period, their own aspirations – even those of the relatively small numbers of more affluent Balts – were of no consequence. Eventually, this led to the rise of nationalist movements in the late 18th century, and the series of wars that brought independence in the wake of the First World War. But despite their similar histories during these wars, and the Second World War that followed, the origins of the three nations were very different, resulting in three very distinct countries.

Lithuania, the most southerly of the Baltic States, was the first of the three to form a national entity when Mindaugas was crowned as its first king in 1253. Ten years later, his country began a long conflict with the crusading Teutonic Knights from neighbouring Prussia. In 1385, Lithuania formed a union with Poland and embraced Christianity for the first time; the two nations now cooperated against their shared enemy in Prussia, and won a decisive victory over the Teutonic Knights at Tannenberg or Grunwald in 1410. As the Prussian threat declined, many Lithuanian nobles sought to break the union with Poland, but the rising power of the Grand Duchy of Muscovy forced Poland and Lithuania into ever-closer cooperation. The resultant commonwealth lasted until it was dismembered during the First Partition of Poland in 1772. Thereafter, Lithuania became part of the Russian Empire.

Latvia, immediately to the north of Lithuania, was peopled by similar tribes to the original Lithuanians. They slowly merged into five distinct groupings, and resisted attempts by missionaries to introduce Christianity in the late 12th century. Like the tribes of Estonia, the Latvians were separated from the depths of Russia by dense forests and swamps, and until the advent of seaborne trade from the west they enjoyed a relatively isolated, if hard and frugal, existence. The traders who accompanied the Christian missionaries established a series of ports along the Baltic coast to facilitate the growing trade with northern Europe, and many of these ports became part of the Hanseatic

League, a trading network of independent cities that originated in the German port of Lübeck. The resistance of the local people to Christianity attracted the attention of the German crusading orders, for whose members a crusade in the pagan Baltic region was regarded as spiritually equivalent to the much harder task of fighting to recapture the Holy Land; it had the added benefit of being much closer to home, and was therefore far easier – and cheaper – to organise. The sons of several kings of Western Europe served short spells in the Baltic Crusades, and were able to join the fighting orders and return home within a year. In 1202, the Bishop of Riga, whose post had only been in existence for a year, established a new order of knights, the Brotherhood of the Sword, which rapidly conquered the territory known as Livonia. In 1236, the knights of the order raided the territory of the Samogitians, one of the larger local tribes. As they returned home, they found their way blocked by a force of Samogitian warriors near the small settlement of Saule, today known as Šiauliai. In the fighting that followed, nearly the entire Christian army, which numbered 3,000, was killed, including up to 60 knights. Volkwyn, the Master of the Order, was amongst the dead. Tribes to the south of the River Daugava, who had been laboriously conquered by the Sword Brothers, rose up in revolt. In order to survive, the remaining knights were transformed into the Livonian Order, formally a branch of the Teutonic Knights of Prussia, though the presence of Lithuania between the territories controlled by the two crusading orders helped prevent a merging of their strength. As the power of the crusading orders declined, Latvian territory was annexed by its neighbours, with southern parts coming under Lithuanian and Polish control while Sweden occupied northern Livonia. Eventually, like Lithuania, Latvia was absorbed into the Russian Empire.

Estonia was culturally different from its two southern neighbours, with its language having far more in common with Finnish. It was the last part of the region to embrace Christianity, coming under the influence of the Teutonic crusaders from 1208 onwards. Shortly after, Denmark took an interest in the area, occupying the northern parts of the country. Local people rose up against Danish rule in 1343, and not long afterwards the Danes sold their interest in the region to the Livonian Order; an ecclesiastical state called *Terra Mariana* was then established under Livonian control. It was perhaps typical of the history of the region that various factions – the Livonian Knights, the ecclesiastical authorities and local secular Baltic German interests – fought a series of civil wars for control of Estonia, with little or no regard for the local people, other than as a source of manpower for their forces. When the Livonian Order was finally defeated in 1345, the various factions agreed to put aside their differences and formed the Livonian Confederation. In the 16th century, the Danes took a renewed interest in Estonia, before Sweden gained control of the northern part of the country. A series of wars between Sweden on the one hand, and the Lithuanian-Polish Commonwealth on the other, followed. Eventually, the Swedes gained complete control of the territory of modern Estonia, and forced the German landowners to grant greater autonomy to the Estonian peasantry, but in 1710, the region came under Russian control as a result of the Great Northern War. For the Estonians, this was more than the replacement of one foreign ruler by another; the Russians revoked the limited reforms that the Swedes had initiated, restoring serfdom and the dominance of the Baltic German nobility.

These different histories, with a common end point, left the three nations with distinct differences as well as similarities. Because of its association with Poland, Lithuania was a largely Catholic country, and its nobility had close family links with the Polish aristocracy. Estonia and Latvia, by contrast, had an ethnically German ruling and landowning class, who formed the bulk of the population of the larger towns and cities, and both countries followed much of Germany and Scandinavia in embracing Lutheran Christianity. In return for the restoration of their rights over the local peasantry, the Baltic German families provided the Russian Empire with many of its finest administrators, diplomats and army officers; inevitably, this resulted in great hostility between the ethnic Estonians and Latvians, and their Baltic German overlords. The roots of the Baltic antipathy to Russia that played such a big part in the region's history in the 20th century therefore stretched back several hundred years.

The reimposition of serfdom proved to be short-lived, and was reversed in Estonia and parts of Latvia by 1819. Whatever the intention of this step, it proved to be of little value to the local peasants, as land remained in the control of the German landowning families, and the newly liberated former serfs lacked the financial resources to purchase land of their own. It was only in the middle of the 19th century that a limited degree of land reform occurred. At the same time, relaxation of laws relating to compulsory membership of trading guilds resulted in more Latvians and Estonians moving from the countryside into the large coastal cities; the population of Tallinn was over 50 per cent Estonian by 1871, and grew further to over 67 per cent Estonian by 1897. During the same period, the Latvian population of Riga grew from 23 to 42 per cent.

Religion was another field in which cultural differences provided ample opportunities for conflict. Competition between the established churches in the Baltic States – the Lutheran church in Latvia and Estonia and the Roman Catholic church in Lithuania – and the Russian Orthodox church led to an increase in publications in Estonian, Latvian and Lithuanian, and to a rapid increase in literacy – by the end of the century, almost the entire population of the Baltic States was literate.[1] A common feature in all three countries during the 19th century was an attempt by Russia to impose Russian culture upon the region. In addition to the efforts of the Orthodox Church, all school education was compulsorily in Russian, and in Lithuania the publication of Latin alphabet books in Lithuanian was banned until 1904. Catholics in Lithuania were barred from local government posts in 1894, a move which resulted in a tight association in the region between nationalist sentiment and the Catholic Church. Russian efforts were undermined by the presence of a substantial Lithuanian population in nearby East Prussia, where material continued to be published in Lithuanian and smuggled across the border. Unlike Latvia and Estonia, Lithuania was comparatively untouched by the industrial revolution, and remained a largely agricultural state. Consequently, much of its growing population emigrated to the New World rather than to the industrial cities, as was the case in the two northern countries.

The 20th century started with widespread turmoil across the Russian Empire. In 1905, nationalists convened assemblies in Tallinn, Riga and Vilnius, while in the countryside of Estonia and Latvia, the unrest targeted the unpopular German aristocracy. Some 200 country manors were set ablaze, and about 300 people were killed. Some of the victims were rich landowners, others were Latvians and Estonians who in the opinion of their neighbours were sympathetic to the Baltic Germans. A few were targeted for the flimsiest of associations with the landowning aristocracy, as was the case of an elderly parson in the town of Jelgava, or Mitau:

> His chief delight had been the collection of Lettish [Latvian] songs, riddles, proverbs and legends. Over this labour he had gone blind … Suddenly the peasants attacked his parsonage, shot his sexton, threatened his daughter, burned his library, smashed his china, trampled on his harpsichord, and made a bonfire of his furniture in the garden, kindling it with his manuscripts.[2]

In Lithuania, by contrast, there was much less civil disturbance, with a few attacks on Russian teachers and the Orthodox clergy. The Russian response varied in accord with the intensity of the trouble: in Lithuania, there was limited repression, while in Tallinn and Riga the Russian Army fired on protestors, killing over 150 and wounding hundreds more. About 400 Estonians were killed in the countryside as Russian troops put an end to attacks on landowners' property; in Latvia, the nationalists gained control of considerable areas of countryside, and several expeditions were mounted before Russian control was restored, leaving over 1,100 dead. Many more were deported to Siberia.[3]

The First World War brought further conflict to the region. Initially, Russian armies advanced into East Prussia, but were decisively defeated at Tannenberg and the Masurian Lakes in 1914. In the following months, most of Latvia and Lithuania were occupied by German forces, but Estonia remained under Russian control. The collapse of Imperial Russia and Lenin's seizure of power in 1917 led to further anarchy as the remnants of the Russian Army withdrew. Faced with a potentially protracted civil war, the Bolsheviks opened peace negotiations with Germany, Austria-Hungary and Turkey in December 1917, in the city of Brest-Litovsk, in an attempt to secure peace with the Central Powers, so that the Red Army could concentrate its efforts against the White Russians.

It was, according to those present, a most remarkable set of negotiations. Germany and the Austro-Hungarian Empire were represented by aristocratic diplomats and senior army officers from patrician families, while the Bolshevik delegation was made up of dedicated revolutionaries. Prince Leopold of Bavaria found himself seated at dinner next to Anastasia Bizenko, who was described by the German Foreign Minister, Richard von Kühlmann, as looking like an elderly housekeeper. During the dinner, Bizenko told Leopold how she had shot General Sakharov, a city governor who she earnestly described as 'an evil man'. At the beginning of the conference, the head of the Bolshevik delegation was Adolf Joffe, a longstanding supporter of Trotsky who had been in exile in Siberia until earlier that year. The leader of the Austro-Hungarian delegation, Graf Ottokar Czemin von und zu Chudenitz, was astonished to hear Joffe's view that a universal application of self-governance to all nations, along the lines of the Bolshevik Revolution, would be followed by the people of those nations learning to love one another and to live in peace. It was the intention and ambition of the Bolsheviks, Joffe told his dinner-table neighbour, to export the revolution first to the rest of Europe, and then to the rest of the world. The war had not gone well for the Austro-Hungarian Empire; its initial invasion of Serbia had been a complete disaster, and a mixture of incompetent High Command, confusion brought about by the multitude of ethnicities and languages in the Empire, and intractable supply problems had prevented the Austro-Hungarian Army from contributing significantly to the German effort. Indeed, by 1916, the German military had frequently likened their alliance with the Habsburg Empire as like being shackled to a corpse. Now, with widespread unrest throughout the Empire and open mutiny in its demoralised armies, Chudenitz reacted with horror to Joffe's comments:

> I pointed out to him that we should not ourselves undertake any imitation of the
> Russian methods, and did not wish for any interference with our own internal

affairs; this we must strictly forbid. If he persisted in endeavouring to carry out this Utopian plan of grafting his ideas on ourselves, he had better go back home by the next train, for there could be no question of making peace. Mr Joffe looked at me in astonishment with his soft eyes, was silent for a while, and then, in a kindly, almost imploring tone that I shall never forget, he said: 'Still, I hope we may yet be able to raise the revolution in your country too.'[4]

Negotiations foundered in February 1918, when Leon Trotsky, who was now head of the Bolshevik delegation, decided that further progress was impossible, as the Germans were insisting on territorial concessions, while the Bolshevik position was to concede no territory, nor agree to any financial reparations to the Central Powers. There was a resumption of hostilities, which proved disastrous to the Russian position, with German troops pushing into Estonia, and when negotiations resumed a month later, the Bolsheviks were forced to accept far worse terms than those originally offered. Russia renounced any claim to Finland, Estonia, Latvia, Lithuania, Belarus, the Ukraine and Poland. In the words of the treaty, Germany and Austria-Hungary would determine the future fates of these territories in agreement with their populations. The reality of the situation was that the Germans would seek to establish client states, based upon whatever minority support they could gain.

Just as it seemed that German dreams of an empire in Eastern Europe that would allow it to rival the British Empire were about to be realised, the abdication of the Kaiser and the collapse of the German Empire in late 1918 changed the situation entirely. As the German army began to withdraw from the Baltic States, the Soviet leadership saw an opportunity to regain territory that had been conceded in the Treaty of Brest-Litovsk. From their perspective, the treaty had been imposed upon them when they were at their weakest, and as the successors to the Czar they regarded themselves entitled to the same territories that Czarist Russia had controlled. There also appeared to be some prospect of exporting the Bolshevik Revolution into the heart of Europe, and the establishment of new Soviet Socialist Republics in the Baltic States, Poland, and even Germany would see the dream outlined by Joffe during the Brest-Litovsk talks beginning to come true. Therefore, intent on reclaiming territory that many Russians regarded as rightly theirs, and seeking an opportunity to spread Bolshevism to the west, Soviet forces began to move against the Baltic region. Although this has been described as the Soviet Westward Offensive, and according to one source was given the codename *Target Vistula*, it seems that there was no central planned offensive.[5] Rather, a series of uncoordinated movements occurred in the same region, with little if any overall coordination. In addition to geopolitical considerations, the animosity of the Soviet leadership towards the Baltic States certainly played a part in the development of events. Lenin told his staff, 'Cross the frontier somewhere, even if only to the depth of a kilometre, and hang 100–1,000 of their civil servants and rich people.'[6]

If the war that followed had been limited to the invading Bolshevik forces and the fledgling nationalist armies of the three states, it would have been over in early 1919, with an almost complete victory for the Red Army. But there were many parties involved in the struggle, each with its own agenda. At the heart of these conflicting agendas lay the fundamental conundrum posed by the three states: was it feasible for them to exist as independent nations, or would they be forced to sacrifice some degree of independence to secure the support of one of their powerful neighbours?

The Bolshevik vision of the future of these states has already been mentioned. The Germans developed their ideas of the shape of Eastern Europe as the First World War progressed. The concept of *Mitteleuropa* as a German empire was first proposed in detail by Friedrich Naumann in 1915, in his book of the same name.[7] He suggested that a new constellation of states could be created from the western parts of the Russian Empire; these states would gradually become more German as a result of settlement, and by providing an area for German economic exploitation *Mitteleuropa* would serve as a counterbalance to the British Empire's colonies. Moreover Austria-Hungary and Turkey, both allies of Germany, would become increasingly dependent economically upon Germany and its vassal states, and would eventually become little more than vassal states themselves.

Several different levels of autonomy were proposed for the new states. Estonia, Latvia and Lithuania would be semi-autonomous, with almost complete control of government functions by Germany. They would be early targets for German colonisation, and consequently it was not expected they would remain even semi-autonomous for a prolonged period.[8] It is important to bear in mind how the German concept of colonies differed from that of the British or French. Whilst Britain ensured that there was almost no autonomy in the non-white parts of the British Empire, there was no real intention to settle these areas with sufficient numbers of white British citizens to create a British majority. The Germans, in contrast, intended to 'Germanise' their colonies in full, and regarded all non-Germans, regardless of their skin colour, as inferior to Germans. In the German protectorate of South West Africa – modern-day Namibia – the forcible seizure of land from local people for German settlers, in an attempt to create an 'African Germany', led to an uprising by the Herero people.[9] The German response was a genocidal war, resulting in the deaths of tens of thousands of Herero.[10] This attitude to colonies persisted long after the fall of the Kaiser, and strongly influenced the behaviour of Nazi Germany towards occupied parts of Eastern Europe. Indeed, many of the key figures of the Nazi era had links with the Herero War; Hermann Goering's father was one of the German officers involved in the genocides.

The Treaty of Brest-Litovsk effectively gave Germany permission to create *Mitteleuropa*, and even though the treaty was renounced by Lenin shortly afterwards, on the grounds that it had been forced upon the Soviet Union, the Germans did not abandon their dream of an East European empire. The fall of the Kaiser was a huge setback, but, despite this, German policy in the Baltic States appears to have been one of trying to establish dominance of the area through client states, thus creating a pro-German status quo that would survive any final peace settlement with the Western Powers. Large numbers of German troops assembled as volunteer formations, known as the *Freikorps*, and played an important part in the independence wars in the Baltic States. Whilst their assistance in driving back the Bolshevik forces was invaluable, they had no intention of helping to create truly independent states; rather, they often worked to further the German vision of puppet regimes, either under direct German control, or dominated by the Baltic German aristocracy. It should be stressed that this was particularly the case in Latvia; Baltic Germans in Estonia were largely strong supporters of Estonian nationalism, and helped raise some of the first military units that fought for Estonian independence.

The Polish vision of the future of those parts of Europe caught between Germany and Russia was not entirely dissimilar to the German vision. The Poles wished for a constellation of independent states collectively known as *Międzymorze* ('Between the seas', referring to the belt of land running from the Baltic coast to the Adriatic Sea). These states would – of course – be dominated by Poland, which would be the largest member of the confederation. In addition, the Polish vision saw no possibility of an independent Lithuania. Instead, the old commonwealth between the two nations would be recreated, with Lithuania reduced to a semi-autonomous part of Poland. Whilst the Lithuanian nationalists welcomed the involvement of Poland in the war against the Bolshevik forces, they were less enthusiastic about what they perceived as Polish interference in Lithuania itself, including an attempted coup and the seizure of the Lithuanian capital, Vilnius.

There was a further armed faction in the area, with a completely different vision of how matters should be arranged. The White Russians, still embroiled in their civil war against the Bolsheviks, were committed to a restoration of the Russian Empire, in which they were prepared to grant the Baltic States a limited degree of autonomy. The Germans sought to cooperate with the White Russians in the hope of creating a restored Russian Empire that would then support Germany against the British and

French; the British and French, by contrast, were anxious to support the White Russians against the Bolsheviks, but tried to reconcile this with supporting the Baltic States in their bid for independence.

Whilst the end of the First World War brought peace to the west, turmoil continued in the east, with fighting among groups of different nationalities and loyalties on the territory of all three Baltic States, in the three Baltic wars of independence, though the interactions among these three wars make it almost impossible to look at any of them in isolation. As the nationalist movements of Lithuania, Latvia and Estonia struggled to raise their own forces, they received aid of varying reliability from other countries. Estonia's strong links with Finland resulted in several hundred Finns volunteering to fight for Estonian independence. A British light cruiser squadron delivered munitions and weapons, and also prevented the Soviet fleet based in Petrograd from making any significant foray into the Baltic. The Red Army units that invaded the three states were badly led, poorly trained and supplied in only the most haphazard of ways. Once the initial momentum of the Bolshevik invasion ceased, the Estonian nationalist government – with substantial support from Finland, the British cruisers and White Russian forces – swiftly regained control of its territory. Latvia was almost completely overrun by the Red Army, but the Baltic Germans and the *Freikorps* under the command of Rüdiger von der Goltz managed to retain control of a small bridgehead around the port of Liepāja, and in conjunction with other German forces in northern Latvia, Goltz's units and the small Latvian nationalist army retook Riga. Thereafter, as Goltz tried to establish a pro-German government in place of the nationalist administration, there was confused fighting between the Germans and the Latvians, with Estonian forces aiding the latter, ultimately resulting in the expulsion of the *Freikorps* from Latvia.

In Lithuania, the relationship with both Germany and Poland played a major part in the course of the country's war of independence, and also helped shape its fate in the years that followed. During the Brest-Litovsk negotiations, the Germans had made an offer to Lithuania: Germany would recognise Lithuania's independence in return for permanent federation with Germany, with matters such as defence, foreign affairs, and currency being controlled by Berlin. The Vilnius Conference, a body of Lithuanian nationalists, considered this offer, and responded that it would accept it, provided that Lithuania could retain autonomy over both its internal affairs and foreign policy. This latter point was incompatible with the German requirement for alignment on military issues, and Germany rejected the proposal. Nevertheless, on 11 December 1917, the Vilnius Council voted to accept the German offer subject to the conditions it had already stipulated, and accordingly made what amounted to a limited announcement of independence. This proved to be a controversial move, and was criticised by Lithuanians both at home and in exile, who felt that the concessions to Germany were too great. It also attracted the ire of the Entente Powers, who were still at war with Germany. In January 1918, the Vilnius Council attempted to modify its announcement, adding an additional stipulation that Lithuania should be granted a national assembly of regional constituents. The Germans, who had already made clear their opposition to the council's previous conditions, rejected this latest requirement. The council now found itself facing hostility from all quarters, and many of its members threatened to resign. On 16 February, it agreed to issue a new announcement of Lithuanian independence, but this time without any reference to a permanent alliance with Germany. The German occupying forces prevented any publication of this announcement within Lithuania, though it was widely reported in the German press, and news inevitably spread back into Lithuania itself.

In March 1918, following the signing of the Treaty of Brest-Litovsk, Germany announced that it recognised Lithuanian independence on the terms that the Vilnius Council had announced on 11 December. Wrangling over the precise nature of this independence continued, and in June, the council invited the Count of Württemberg to become monarch of Lithuania. This placed an intolerable strain on the council, and several members resigned. In any event, the German government refused to accept this arrangement, and prevented the would-be King Mindaugas II from travelling to his new country.[11] The frustrated members of the Vilnius Council found that Germany blocked almost every attempt they made to formulate policy, a deadlock that continued until the collapse of Germany in November. At this stage, the council revoked its invitation to the Count of Württemberg. It also expanded its membership to include Jewish and Belarusian members, in an attempt to increase its popular appeal with these two communities; at first, the Jewish community was offered two seats, but this was declined, with the Jewish leaders demanding that their membership should be proportional to the Jewish population within Lithuania. Consequently, they were offered a third seat. A new Lithuanian government was proclaimed, with Augustinas Voldemaras as prime minister. Antanas Smetona, who had chaired the council when it first formed, became President.

Lithuania found itself in a chaotic state. Groups of German soldiers, often refusing to follow the orders of their officers, crossed the country in a steady stream towards Germany. The new government had no means of collecting taxes, and consequently was unable to carry out any significant functions. Voldemaras announced that Lithuania did not intend to threaten its neighbours, and therefore concluded that there was no urgency to create an army. Unfortunately for Voldemaras, the Bolsheviks had a very different attitude, and swiftly overran the eastern parts of Lithuania. On 5 January 1919, they reached Vilnius.

The historical capital of Lithuania was a multi-ethnic city. A German census in 1916 suggested that half of the city's population was Polish, and a substantial part of the remaining population was Jewish, leaving the Lithuanians in a very small minority; however, other surveys suggested that the population of the surrounding area was predominantly Lithuanian.[12] Indeed, the Jewish population of Vilnius had earned the city the appellation of the 'Jerusalem of the North' from Napoleon. Such a multi-ethnic mix was bound to create additional tensions, which could be exploited by any outside power that chose to do so. Belatedly, the Lithuanian nationalist government started to raise troops, but these were in no position, either tactically or in terms of their strength, to defend Vilnius; the most active defenders were pro-Polish partisans, but they were unable to prevent the Red Army from seizing the city. From here, the Bolshevik troops gradually advanced west, but their drive ran out of momentum as their almost non-existent supply lines failed to replenish the troops. The Lithuanians had also succeeded in raising German volunteers to fight for them, particularly in Saxony, and these veteran soldiers proved to be a formidable force.

Another army that was operating in the area was that of Poland. Already at war with Russia, the Poles launched a major offensive against the Red Army in the spring of 1919. Józef Piłsudski, the Polish head of state, planned the operation with his customary meticulous attention to detail, launching diversionary attacks on Lida, Navahrudak and Baranovichi. His main objective, though, was Vilnius, with a force of 800 cavalry, 2,500 infantry and artillery assigned to the task. Rather than wait for the slower infantry to arrive, the Polish cavalry commander, Colonel Wladyslaw Belina-Prazmowski, decided to attack with his horsemen on 18 April. He swept around the city and attacked from the east, taking the Soviet garrison by surprise and overrunning the suburbs. As the Bolshevik forces rallied, the Polish infantry began to arrive, and with their support – and aided by Polish partisans from Vilnius – Belina slowly gained the upper hand, clearing the city of Russian forces by the end of 21 April.[13]

By the end of June, the Red Army had been driven out of almost all of Lithuania, and negotiations now began about the border between Poland and Lithuania. This proved to be a difficult business, not least because Piłsudski did not wish to see the creation of an independent Lithuania, favouring the restoration of the former Polish-Lithuanian Commonwealth. Deadlocked over the future status of the Vilnius region – claimed by both countries, but occupied by Polish troops – the Lithuanians and Poles asked the Conference of Ambassadors of the Entente Powers to intervene. At this stage, the difference in diplomatic status between Lithuania and Poland became starkly apparent. Poland had been recognised by the Entente Powers, and was even specifically mentioned in one of Woodrow Wilson's famous Fourteen Points:

> An independent Polish state should be erected which should include the territories inhabited by indisputably Polish populations, which should be assured a free and secure access to the sea, and whose political and economic independence and territorial integrity should be guaranteed by international covenant.[14]

By contrast, Lithuania had not yet received international recognition. In many circles, particularly those that favoured a restoration of the Russian Empire, Lithuania's independence was distinctly unwelcome. It can therefore have been of little surprise to anyone when the Conference of Ambassadors chose not to return Vilnius and the surrounding area to Lithuania.

Although he was opposed to Lithuanian independence, Piłsudski was acutely aware that any future commonwealth could only succeed with the agreement of the Lithuanian people, and he made every effort to persuade the Lithuanians to cooperate with his plans. He and his subordinates proposed that the fate of the Vilnius region be decided in a plebiscite, but the Lithuanians rejected this. But the Bolsheviks were not quite finished. In 1920, a revitalised Red Army once more invaded, driving the Poles out of Vilnius. Shortly after, Soviet Russia and Lithuania agreed a peace treaty, as part of which the Vilnius region was assigned to Lithuania. Such an arrangement was unacceptable to the Poles, and in October the Polish general Lucjan Żeligowski apparently mutinied and marched on Vilnius, taking the city on 9 October. He then declared the creation of the Republic of Central Lithuania, which merged with Poland in 1923. It later transpired that Żeligowski's mutiny was nothing of the sort, and had actually been ordered by the Polish head of state, Piłsudski. Vastly outnumbered, the Lithuanian army could do nothing to counter this seizure of the region, and the Vilnius question remained a source of severe friction between the two countries throughout the inter-war years, preventing any possible cooperation between Poland and Lithuania. The Baltic wars of independence were therefore a manifestation of the conflict between two alternative visions: on the one hand, the three states had strong nationalist aspirations, while on the other hand, their more powerful neighbours – Soviet Russia, Germany and even Poland – regarded them as too small and weak to survive without being part of a larger power bloc. This question would be subjected to even more brutal inspection in the Second World War, and the resolution of the issue would take over 70 years and cost millions of lives before independence was finally achieved towards the end of the century.

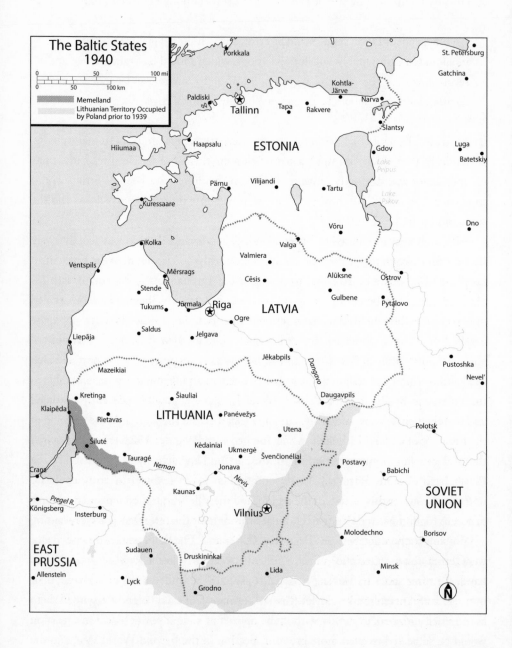

The Baltic States
1940

0   50   100 mi
0   50   100 km

Memelland
Lithuanian Territory Occupied
by Poland prior to 1939

Porkkala

St. Petersburg

Gatchina

Kohtla-
Järve

Paldiski

Narva

Tallinn   Tapa   Rakvere

Slantsy

ESTONIA

Luga

Hiiumaa   Haapsalu   Gdov

Batetskiy

Lake
Peipus

Pärnu   Vilijandi   Tartu

Lake
Pskov

Kuressaare

Võru

Dno

Kolka   Valga

Valmiera

Ventspils   Mērsrags   Alūksne   Ostrov

Stende   Cēsis

Gulbene   Pytalovo

Tukums   Jūrmala   Riga   LATVIA

Saldus   Ogre

Jelgava

Liepāja

Jēkabpils

Pustoshka

Mazeikiai   Dangavo   Nevel'

Kretinga   Daugavpils

Klaipēda   Šiauliai   Panévežys   Polotsk

Rietavas   LITHUANIA

Šiluté   Utena

Tauragé   Kédainiai   Ukmergé   Švenčionéliai   Postavy   Babichi

Cranz   Neman   Jonava   Nevis

Pregel R.   Kaunas   SOVIET
UNION

Königsberg   Insterburg   Vilnius

Molodechno   Borisov

EAST
PRUSSIA   Sudauen   Druskininkai

Allenstein   Lida   Minsk

Lyck   Grodno

Chapter 1

MOLOTOV, RIBBENTROP AND THE FIRST SOVIET OCCUPATION

The decade that preceded the Second World War saw major changes in all three Baltic States. Originally created as republics, they all adopted totalitarian rule. Estonia's head of state, Konstantin Päts, used a threatened coup by hard-line anti-Soviet and anti-parliamentary nationalists to declare rule by decree in 1934. In the same year, the Latvian leader, Kārlis Ulmanis, also dismissed his parliament, partly as a response to the worldwide economic situation. In the case of Lithuania, a military coup in 1926 – triggered by growing criticism of the government for its attempts to negotiate with the Soviet Union – abolished parliament and placed Antanas Smetona in command of the country. It is noteworthy that in all three cases, a powerful motivation behind the unrest that led directly or indirectly to dictatorship was growing anti-Bolshevik sentiment. Much of this was due to persisting concerns that the Soviet Union might one day attempt to restore Russian control of the region. At the same time, resentment at German attempts to establish hegemony in the region in the aftermath of the First World War remained strong. Consequently, the people of the Baltic States, and their leaders, watched developments between their powerful neighbours with concern. The Molotov–Ribbentrop Pact, announced on the eve of the German invasion of Poland in 1939, came as a shock to the Western Powers, and an even greater shock to the Baltic States, appearing to confirm that neither neighbour was remotely interested in the ongoing independence of the three nations. But the background to the Pact was that despite their dramatic ideological differences, the two nations had attempted to define non-aggression treaties for many years.

In the aftermath of the First World War, Weimar Germany signed two treaties with the Soviet Union. The first was the Treaty of Rapallo in 1922, in which the two powers renounced any territorial or financial claims against each other. This was followed four years later by the Treaty of Berlin, which declared a five-year pact of non-aggression, and neutrality by either power should the other be involved in a conflict. In 1931, an extension to the latter treaty was agreed, but almost immediately relations between the two countries deteriorated, a process that accelerated after Hitler came to power in 1933. Persecution of the German Communist Party, overt hostility in diplomatic arenas and the publication of the second volume of *Mein Kampf*, calling for German expansion into Russian territory and equating communists with Jews, all played a part.

Maxim Maximovich Litvinov, the Soviet Commissar for Foreign Affairs for most of the 1930s, regarded Nazi Germany as the greatest threat to the Soviet Union. His preferred policy to contain the German threat was to build strong links with France and Britain, but Stalin's insistence that any such alliance had to include the right of the Soviet Union to station troops in Estonia and Latvia made agreement almost impossible, given the role that France and Britain had played in helping Estonia drive the Red Army from its territory during the wars of independence. For Stalin, the proximity of the border between the Soviet Union and the Baltic States – particularly Estonia – and key locations, such as Leningrad, made a Soviet military presence in the three states a defensive necessity. In 1936, the NKVD (*Narodnyy Komissariat Vnutrennikh Del* or 'People's Commissariat for Internal Affairs', the Soviet Secret Police) reported that there were growing links between many Estonian government officials and Germany. In addition, the NKVD report continued, the Estonian government believed that the Latvians were already 'completely in the service of Germany'. By contrast, the ordinary people of the two countries were reported to be pro-Soviet.[1]

To a considerable extent, this report almost certainly was written with foreknowledge of what Stalin wished to hear, and its content was designed to ensure that the writer did not offend his superiors. Nevertheless, intelligence from other sources appeared to confirm the views of the Germans and the Soviets that the three states would be forced to choose a side. In March 1937, a Finnish envoy to the region reported:

The territory of Lithuania is situated between Germany, the Soviet Union and Poland. If there is a clash between these states, it will threaten the existence of Lithuania. Such a frightening prospect obliges Lithuania to seek the safest position. It is axiomatic that [the Lithuanian government] seeks the protection of Great Britain and France – in vain, as they are far away. Neutrality? But in practice, neutrality means complete isolation. Thus, Lithuania has to choose between Poland, Germany and the Soviet Union, and Lithuania ... [will choose] the latter.

The essential difficulties in the relationship of Lithuania with Germany and Poland, do not exist in the relationship between the Soviet Union and Lithuania.[2]

Negotiations between the Soviet Union and Germany were hamstrung by Litvinov's Jewish ancestry, and this was one of the reasons for his dismissal by Stalin in May 1939.[3] After the Munich Agreement of 1938, Stalin felt that there was little prospect of the capitalist powers containing Hitler, and he started to consider direct negotiations. Litvinov's dismissal came during the era of Stalin's widespread purges of the army and other organisations, and it was perhaps unsurprising that the sacking of the commissar was accompanied by the arrival of large numbers of NKVD troops at the Commissariat of Foreign Affairs; many of Litvinov's aides were arrested and interrogated in a vain attempt to secure incriminating evidence against their leader.

Litvinov's replacement was Vyacheslav Mikhailovich Molotov, who had been a Bolshevik almost from the start of the Communist Party. Born with the surname Scriabin, he adopted the name Molotov, derived from the Russian word *molot*, meaning hammer, for his political work. Many of his contemporaries preferred the nickname 'Stone Arse', on account of his long hours of work. It was characteristic of his reputation for pedantry that he often corrected colleagues, pointing out that Lenin had originally referred to him as 'Iron Arse'. He was far less keen on reminding people of the occasion that Lenin had condemned him for being the author of 'the most shameful bureaucratism, and the most stupid'.[4] He owed his rise more to his consistent loyalty to Stalin than to any political excellence, and had a reputation for brutality; he played a leading role in the wave of arrests and executions that did so much harm to the Soviet Union during the 1930s. As soon as he was appointed, Stalin instructed him to purge the Commissariat of Foreign Affairs of Jews, using the phrase 'Clean out the "Synagogue."'[5] Molotov later recalled this order: 'Thank God for these words! Jews formed an absolute majority in the leadership and among the ambassadors. It was not good.'[6] The fact that Molotov's wife was Jewish appeared to make little difference to his enthusiasm for following his leader's instructions.

Tentative moves towards negotiations between Germany and the Soviet Union started in April 1939, but although economic measures were agreed, at least in outline, during July, there was little progress on serious diplomatic talks until several weeks after Litvinov's dismissal. Tensions had been raised during the summer when Latvia, under pressure from Germany, agreed to sign a non-aggression pact; Latvian diplomats joked lugubriously that 'Germany can now sleep in peace: Latvia will not attack it.'[7] Stalin and Molotov feared that they might find themselves with the unwelcome presence of German troops within easy striking distance of major Soviet cities, particularly after Nikitin, the Soviet ambassador in Tallinn, reported that German and Estonian officials had met to discuss collaboration in the construction of a major road from the Estonian–Latvian border to the north[8]; consequently, the Soviets increased their own diplomatic approaches to Berlin. Despite this, progress remained slow, not least because the agendas of the two countries diverged considerably.

Stalin's requirements from a treaty with Germany were more than simply a non-aggression pact. In order to ensure that Leningrad could be defended, it was highly desirable for the Soviet Union to be given a free hand to place troops in Estonia. Although the border with Latvia was a little further away from vital locations, and the land route from this border into the Soviet interior was a difficult one, as the Wehrmacht would discover in 1941, a similar argument could be made for Latvia as for Estonia. The Western Powers had steadfastly refused to countenance granting the Soviet Union such freedom of action, and although an Anglo-French delegation travelled to Moscow in August 1939, there was little prospect of an agreement that would satisfy Stalin. Hitler, by contrast, about to invade Poland, was anxious to secure an agreement with the Soviet Union, and had no compunction about agreeing spheres of influence with his large eastern neighbour. On 15 August, the German ambassador to Moscow, Graf Friedrich Werner von der Schulenburg, informed Molotov that the German Foreign Minister, Joachim von Ribbentrop, wished to have a meeting, and that matters such as a non-aggression pact and a division of Eastern Europe into spheres of influence could be settled to the mutual advantage of the two powers. On 17 August, Kliment Voroshilov, the Commissar for Defence, proposed to the Anglo-French delegation a treaty of mutual military assistance, which would require Poland and Rumania to allow the passage of Soviet troops in the event of a German attack. When the British representative replied that he had no authority to agree such a deal, Stalin lost patience and decided to cement arrangements with Germany.[9]

Two days later, Molotov summoned Schulenburg and presented him with a draft non-aggression pact. On 21 August, the Anglo-French delegation was dismissed, even as Ribbentrop prepared to travel to Moscow. The German Foreign Minister arrived on 23 August, and met Stalin and Molotov that afternoon. The broad outline of a deal was agreed within hours, and the pact, designed to last ten years, was signed at 0200hrs on 24 August.

The treaty became public on the same day, and was greeted with shock throughout the world, by both allies and potential foes of Germany and the Soviet Union. Ambassador Nikitin in Tallinn reported with great satisfaction that the bewilderment of the Estonians was complete, and that the government was totally disoriented by this new development.[10] Neither of the signatories had any illusions about the pact. On the very day that the pact was signed, Stalin joined his closest associates on a duck hunt, telling them: 'Of course it's all a game to see who can fool whom. I know what Hitler's up to. He thinks he's outsmarted me but actually it's I who's tricked him.'[11]

Hitler, too, regarded the treaty as merely a temporary expedient. As preparations for the invasion of Poland progressed, he gave his views to his followers: 'There is no time to lose. War must come in my lifetime. This pact was only meant to stall for time, and, gentlemen, to Russia will happen what I have practised with Poland – we will crush the Soviet Union.'[12]

Caught between the two powers, the Baltic States struggled to adapt to the sudden change in their world. For several years, they had been pressured, often overtly, by Germany and the Soviet Union to choose which they would support. Suddenly, the two opposed powers were friends. They struggled to make sense of this dramatic shift and its effect on their own status, unaware that a protocol to the Molotov–Ribbentrop Pact had already decided their fate. The text of the protocol, secret at the time and denied by Moscow until the fall of the Soviet Union, gave Stalin his desired territorial gains to protect the approaches to Leningrad:

> In the event of a territorial and political rearrangement of the regions making up the Baltic States (Finland, Estonia, Latvia, Lithuania) the northern frontier of Lithuania will simultaneously serve as the frontier of the spheres of interest of Germany and the USSR. In this, Lithuania's interest in connection with the Vilnius District is recognised by both parties.[13]

Given longstanding German claims to Estonia and Latvia, based on historical involvement in the area, the ease with which Germany conceded these territories to the Soviet Union is indicative of how keen Hitler was to secure a deal with Stalin, but nothing less would have appeased the Soviet leader, who regarded the deployment of the Red Army in the two countries as an essential requirement for the defence of Leningrad. At first, the Germans requested that their sphere of influence should include Courland, the western part of Latvia, but Stalin responded that the entire region had been part of the Russian Empire, and that the USSR therefore had an overriding claim to the territories.

As war between Germany and Poland drew ever closer, the German envoy to Lithuania, Erich Zechlin, informed the Lithuanian government on 29 August that in the event of war, Berlin would require Lithuania to observe total neutrality; should this not occur, Germany would have to take whatever steps were required to safeguard its interests. In an attempt to sway Lithuanian sentiment, the Germans hinted that any conflict between Germany and Poland could result in territorial realignment, including the Vilnius region, currently part of Poland, and that the Lithuanians should take steps to seize the region once war began. It was clear that the German concept of 'strict neutrality' was somewhat different from what the words might have been taken to mean. The Lithuanians now found themselves under pressure from other quarters: the British and French pressed the Lithuanian government not to attack Poland, even within the disputed Vilnius region.

German forces invaded Poland on 1 September. Polish refugees flowed into Lithuania, which proclaimed its intention to remain strictly neutral; to the disappointment of the Germans, Lithuania made no attempt to seize Vilnius and the surrounding area. On 17 September, Soviet forces entered Poland from the east. As it was clear that the Red Army would seize Vilnius – the city itself fell to Soviet troops on 19 September – Berlin ordered Zechlin to stop encouraging the Lithuanians from making any move of their own.

With the entire Vilnius region in Soviet hands, Stalin found himself in a strong position with regard to both Germany and Lithuania. Molotov put off discussions with either nation about Vilnius, though he hinted to the Lithuanians that Vilnius would be part of a general settlement of issues in the area.[14] Meanwhile, Ribbentrop informed the Lithuanian Foreign Minister, Juozas Urbšys, that Germany was prepared to offer a treaty in which Lithuania would fall under the protection of Germany, with Lithuanian troops coming under the command of the Wehrmacht. To the irritation of the Germans, the Lithuanians informed both the British and the Soviets of the German offer, and Ribbentrop cancelled a proposed meeting with his Lithuanian counterpart.

If Germany was having some difficulty in securing its share of the Baltic States, the Soviet Union appeared to have no such handicaps. The first move came against Estonia, aided by an incident involving a Polish submarine. The *Orzeł*, deployed in the Baltic Sea, reached Tallinn on 14 September, where the ship's captain was hospitalised with a serious illness. The Hague Convention required Estonia to intern the submarine, and, after German demands for action, Estonian forces duly boarded the vessel. The crew of the *Orzeł* had other ideas, and slipped out of the harbour on 18 September, taking advantage of foggy conditions. They left two Estonian sailors who had been aboard the submarine on the Swedish coast, together with clothing and sufficient money for them to return to Estonia, and escaped to Britain, eventually reaching the naval base in Rosyth. On 24 September, Molotov informed Karl Selter, the Estonian Foreign Minister, who happened to be in Moscow to discuss trade agreements, that the '*Orzeł* incident' demonstrated that Estonia was not acting as a true neutral state, and that the Estonian authorities must have collaborated with the Polish submarine crew during their escape. As its neutrality was now in question, Estonia had to accept a military alliance or mutual assistance agreement with the Soviet Union. Selter was also informed that some 160,000 Soviet troops were deployed along the Estonian border, and that they would take whatever action was required to ensure that Estonia fulfilled its obligations. The Estonians were given little time to agree to what amounted to an ultimatum. A tentative approach to Germany was rebuffed by Berlin – the Germans added that they would block any arms shipments to Estonia from the west.[15] The Soviet Air Force sent its planes sweeping low over Tallinn to intimidate Päts' government, and on 27 September, Selter was summoned to the Bolshoi Ballet, where Stalin and Molotov were watching a production of Swan Lake. During the interval at the end of the first act, they met Selter in the lobby of the theatre. Molotov insisted on an immediate agreement stationing 35,000 Soviet troops in Estonia. Stalin generously offered to reduce this to a mere 25,000, but in any event Estonia had no option but to acquiesce, not least because the entire strength of the Estonian armed forces amounted to only 16,000 men.[16] The agreement was signed the following day, allowing 25,000 Soviet troops to be stationed on two islands and in the port of Paldiski.[17]

With Estonia out of the way, Soviet attention turned to Latvia. On 30 September, Moscow invited the Latvian government to send plenipotentiaries to the Soviet capital for discussions. On 2 October, Molotov informed the Latvian delegation that the Soviet Union intended to bring its relations with Latvia into line with its new arrangements with Estonia. Like Päts in Estonia, Ulmanis knew that Latvia could not stand alone against the Soviet Union. The lack of reaction by Germany to the Soviet 'agreement' with Estonia confirmed widely held suspicions about the existence of the secret protocol to the Molotov–Ribbentrop Pact, and on 4 October, Latvia caved in to Soviet pressure. Around 30,000 Soviet troops moved into Latvia over the next few days.

The issue of Lithuania was far more complex, and Germany and the Soviet Union continued to haggle over the spoils of war. In addition to agreeing spheres of influence in the Baltic States, the secret protocol had outlined a demarcation line in Poland between the two nations. On 25 September, Stalin suggested that the existing agreement should be altered. German forces had seized the area around Lublin, which according to the secret protocol should have passed to the Soviet Union; Stalin now suggested that Germany should retain control of Lublin, and instead the Soviet Union should gain Lithuania. After all, he pointed out, the Red Army was already in

Vilnius, and a resolution of the Vilnius question would be far easier if there were no need for a complex set of negotiations involving Germany, Lithuania and the Soviet Union. After a short delay, the Germans agreed on 28 September, though with the proviso that parts of south-west Lithuania would pass to Germany.

Two days before, the Lithuanian Communist Party – which had no links with Moscow – had issued a proclamation that Germany was intending to occupy Lithuania, and that Lithuania should look to the Soviet Union for its salvation. The day after Germany and the Soviet Union had agreed to divide Lithuania between them, the Lithuanian representative in Moscow, Ladas Natkevičius, was summoned to the Kremlin. Here, Molotov informed him that Stalin wished the Lithuanians to send a senior minister to Moscow for talks. Molotov also stated that Germany would agree to whatever arrangements were made between Lithuania and the Soviet Union, effectively confirming that Lithuania's two large neighbours had already agreed that Lithuania would be within the Soviet sphere of influence. As had been the case with Estonia and Latvia, it was made clear that time was of the essence, and the meeting concluded with the words of Mikhail Kalinin, the titular Soviet head of state, that the time for a 'platonic' relationship was over: 'To whom are you closer: the Germans or us?'[18]

Natkevičius returned to Kaunas for discussions, and in early October headed back to Moscow, followed by the Lithuanian Foreign Minister, Juozas Urbšys. The Germans were becoming nervous that their planned seizure of south-west Lithuania would be perceived as part of a predatory carve-up of a small nation (which is of course exactly what was intended), and asked the Soviet side to avoid discussing the matter with the Lithuanians until after the Soviet Union had already sent troops into Lithuania. They hoped that when the Red Army sent its troops into Lithuania, the south-west portion would be left free of occupying troops, and the Wehrmacht would then be able to secure the area, if necessary claiming that this was to prevent a complete Soviet takeover.

However, this request came too late; Stalin had met Urbšys on 3 October and informed him that Lithuania had three choices. The first was a mutual assistance pact, in line with the agreements with Estonia and Latvia. The second, not mutually exclusive with the first, was a treaty to return the Vilnius region to Lithuania. The third was a treaty that would result in south-west Lithuania being surrendered to Germany. Urbšys was genuinely shocked by the third suggestion, and declared that any surrender of Lithuanian territory to Germany would be 'the greatest injustice that one could imagine'.[19] Lithuanian suggestions that their declaration of neutrality was sufficient to protect Soviet interests were dismissed. Soviet troops would have to be deployed in Lithuania, insisted Stalin and Molotov. However, Lithuanian independence would be respected. Stalin even suggested that the Soviet troops in Lithuania would be ordered to suppress any communist rising if required.

Discussions then turned to the Vilnius question. The Lithuanians discovered that they were being offered a far smaller piece of territory than they had expected. Stalin made it clear that any return of territory to Lithuania was dependent on Moscow's goodwill. The talks concluded without agreement. Lithuania had been forced to return the city of Klaipėda – Memel to the Germans – to Germany earlier in the year, and Urbšys complained that Lithuania now faced even further territorial losses. Stalin's response showed how skilfully he and Molotov had manoeuvred events: 'Germany tears away your territory. We, to the contrary are giving to you. What comparison can there be!'[20]

On 4 October, Molotov told Schulenburg, the German ambassador, that the question of German occupation of south-west Lithuania had already been raised with the Lithuanian delegation. In a desperate attempt to catch up with events, Berlin now informed the Lithuanians that the return of Vilnius to Lithuania had been at the insistence of Germany, and that the cession of south-west Lithuania to Germany was a small price to pay for this. On 7 October, discussions resumed in Moscow. The Lithuanians were prepared to accept a mutual assistance pact, but did not want Soviet troops on their soil. Molotov responded that Lithuania had to accept the same terms as Estonia and Latvia. His deputy, Vladimir Potemkin, commented that 'Lithuania is showing no enthusiasm for recovering Vilnius'.[21] The linkage of the Vilnius question and Soviet troop deployments was thus made explicit. The Lithuanian delegation paused briefly for private discussions. It was clear that Soviet troops would enter Lithuania regardless of what they did, but at least they would gain Vilnius if they accepted the Soviet pact, so they agreed to sign the treaty establishing a mutual assistance pact, the deployment of 20,000 Soviet troops in Lithuania, and the return of Vilnius.

It is not clear whether Stalin had always intended to control Lithuania, or whether he merely took advantage of events on the ground, particularly the unwillingness of the Lithuanians to seize Vilnius themselves. In any event, the Soviet leadership demonstrated adept and ruthless opportunism and skill in their manoeuvrings. During all of the complex negotiations with Germany, Estonia, Latvia and Lithuania, Molotov and Stalin formed a very effective team; Molotov repeatedly acted as the 'hard man', while Stalin made conciliatory gestures, such as reducing the numbers of troops to be deployed in the Baltic States. Isolated from the west and denied support from Germany, the three Baltic governments ultimately had no choice but to agree to Stalin's demands.

As Soviet garrison troops began to settle into their new billets – in the first months of their stay, they were ordered to keep a low profile – Moscow's attention turned to Finland. The details of the Winter War[22] are beyond the scope of this book, but the protracted fighting and the poor performance of the Red Army left Stalin and his associates fully occupied for the moment. Far too late, the three Baltic States held tentative talks about cooperation, though they were too anxious about Soviet reactions to take any significant military steps. Some of Latvia's and Estonia's gold reserves were sent to Britain and the United States, and some of the ambassadors in the west were given powers to assume the role of head of state, should the governments in the home countries be unable to continue to function. Meanwhile, the Baltic States attempted to tiptoe a neutral line in the diplomatic arena. They refused to join western condemnation of the Soviet Union's attack on Finland in the League of Nations, and abstained in the vote that expelled the Soviet Union from the organisation.

For Lithuania, there was the added problem of trying to assimilate the Vilnius region. The head of state, Antanas Smetona, was anxious to take credit for the return of the 'historic capital' to Lithuania; opponents of the government wished to prevent this, and promoted the idea that Lithuania should be grateful to the Soviet Union rather than to Smetona for the territorial adjustment. Whatever the reaction of most of Lithuania, attitudes in Vilnius itself were far from universally in favour of reunion with Lithuania. The minority status of Lithuanians in Vilnius had actually worsened since the city was seized by Poland, with many Poles migrating into the city and its surrounding area. In addition, Jewish refugees fleeing from the German advance into Poland had further increased its non-Lithuanian population. For the Jews, the choice between German dominance and Soviet dominance was a simple one, and from the very start, Jews in both Latvia and Lithuania were amongst those who were the warmest supporters of the Soviet troops. Even if they regarded the Soviet Union as the lesser of two evils, they were well aware of the treatment of Jews in Germany and Poland by the Germans. Nevertheless, despite this, the attitude of the Jewish population was varied. Undoubtedly, the most vociferous and visible part of the community was composed of those who supported the presence of Soviet troops; however, it seems that they were outnumbered by more conservative elements, who simply wished to be left in peace, though they were conscious that this was far more likely to happen under Soviet control than German. As this conservative majority remained relatively silent, the public perception of Jewish hostility to the Lithuanian state was clearly established in the minds of the Lithuanian population throughout the country.

There were also significant food shortages in Vilnius, and on 31 October, allegations that Jewish shopkeepers were hoarding bread resulted in an eruption of anti-Jewish violence. Many Jewish shops were looted, and several Jews were badly beaten, but elsewhere there were demonstrations in favour of the Soviets and against the Lithuanians. Much of the violence against Jews came from the Polish community, and continued for several days. The Jewish community was critical of the recently arrived Lithuanian police force in the city, which intervened late and often ineffectively; their task was not helped by the fact that few police officers spoke Yiddish or Polish, or by their poor grasp of the layout of the city.

The Latvian Jewish community was also coming under increasing suspicion. At the outset of the Bolshevik Revolution, the industrialised heartland of Latvia was a fertile recruiting ground for communism, and Latvians formed a disproportionally large proportion of the Soviet Communist Party, partly due to the large numbers of ethnic Latvians who lived inside Russia itself. In the late 1930s, Stalin's paranoia of any he regarded as having questionable loyalty to the Soviet Union – and to himself in particular – led to a series of 'national operations' by the NKVD. The Latvian Operation resulted in thousands of ethnic Latvians being deported to Siberia, and over 16,000 were executed. Despite this, the Soviets encouraged Latvian Jews, as well as ethnic Russians in Latvia, to regard the Soviet troops as their best protection against both the Germans and the Latvians themselves. The Ulmanis government policy of 'Latvia for Latvians' was unequivocally nationalistic, but it was also combined with strong measures to prevent violence against Jews. Nevertheless, Soviet agitators now set to work, persuading large parts of the Jewish community that Latvia was only marginally less anti-Semitic than Germany.

In February 1940, the Red Army finally began to get the upper hand over its tough Finnish opponents, and with a satisfactory end to the Winter War in sight, Stalin returned his attention to the Baltic States. The Soviet envoys to the three states attended a conference in Moscow, where they were instructed to increase political activity.[23] Of the three states, Estonia represented the fewest opportunities for the Soviet agitators to play one ethnic group against another. Whilst the policy of forcing the Baltic States to accept mutual assistance treaties in the autumn of 1939 had started with Estonia and had then moved south, there were good reasons for further progress occurring in the opposite direction. Firstly, there were far more opportunities to set different ethnic communities against each other in Latvia and Lithuania, and secondly, securing the southern countries first would create a barrier to any refugee traffic.

In Latvia, the Soviet ambassador Ivan Zotov had for several years sent a steady stream of reports back to Moscow about the pro-Soviet sentiment not only of Jews, but of other urban dwellers, particularly the Russian and Belarusian minorities. To a large extent, these reports were influenced as much by what Zotov thought Stalin wished to hear as by the reality on the ground.[24] The urban working classes were in favour of closer cooperation and even union with the Soviet Union, Zotov stated in several telegrams; and he claimed that the rural population, too, was unhappy with the Ulmanis regime.[25] Zotov was not alone in sending misleading information. One of his colleagues, Ivan Cechaev, sent a report detailing the possibilities of establishing a communist underground movement in eastern Latvia, and sought to portray the Ulmanis government as a fascist dictatorship that held the Latvians back from their desire to join the Soviet Union. Colonel Vasiliev, the military attaché to the Soviet Embassy in Riga, reported in May 1939: 'The workers are of the opinion that the Red Army will enter the territory in the near future. The intelligentsia think thus: better the Soviet forces than the Germans ... the majority of the workers support a direct union of Latvia to the Soviet Union.'[26]

The reality was very different. For a few brief months during the Latvian war of independence, much of Latvia had been under Bolshevik control, and there had been widespread arrests and killings, usually with minimal or no judicial process, of those perceived as hostile to the Bolsheviks. Although large numbers of Latvians had originally been supporters of the Bolsheviks, many of these changed their opinion after these killings, while other Bolshevik sympathisers chose to leave Latvia as the Red Army retreated. The policies of Ulmanis following his victory in the post-war elections and during his years of dictatorial rule during the 1920s and 1930s had resulted in a remarkable increase in living standards throughout Latvia, further undermining support for radical changes. In particular, the land reforms introduced by Ulmanis during the 1920s were an effective answer to many of the long-held grievances of the rural population, and in any event, Soviet attempts to introduce collectivised farming in those parts of the Baltic States that the Bolsheviks had controlled during the wars of independence were not remembered with any fondness.

How much Stalin was aware of the exaggeration and – on some occasions – complete fabrication of information from Latvia and the other Baltic States is open to question. The experience of the Latvians during their war of independence had certainly left strong anti-German feelings, but this was matched by an equally strong anti-Soviet sentiment. However, there were still large bodies of communist sympathisers, despite the banning of the Latvian Communist Party. Significantly, Jews formed a disproportionately large percentage of these sympathisers. A report of the Latvian Ministry of the Interior in 1929 stated that 50 per cent of the membership of the banned Communist Party and 60 per cent of the Latvian youth organisation *Komjautnatne*, equivalent to the Soviet *Komsomol*, were Jewish.[27] The Soviet authorities were keen to exploit any tension between the nationalist Ulmanis regime and minority populations, both Jewish and Russian, and even as the Riga government was being forced into accepting a mutual assistance treaty, Zotov reported to Moscow:

> The dreadful poverty of the Jewish residents is striking. About a third of the Jewish population depend on voluntary organisations ... in recent times, Jews have been increasingly subject to legal proceedings on negligible evidence. The state machinery promotes anti-Semitism in the workplace ... for economic and political reasons and [out of a sense of] national humiliation, the Jewish workers follow the development of the USSR with interest and affection. They express their sympathy for a land with no nationalistic hatreds or differences, and where the brotherhood of workers is an everyday fact.[28]

As time passed, there were frequent pro-Soviet demonstrations in Latvian cities and towns, but it is questionable how well these represented the sentiments of the majority. There were particularly large demonstrations in the summer of 1940 in Riga, but it seems that the majority of those involved were either ethnic Russians or Jews.[29]

The situation in Lithuania was particularly complicated. The Anglo-French alliance, which had ostensibly declared war on Germany to protect Poland, was unable to accept the transfer of the Vilnius region to Lithuania. In an attempt to avoid embarrassment, the French asked the Lithuanians not to mention the issue, and in return did not raise it themselves. Although the Lithuanian leadership hoped for and expected a victory by the Western Powers over Germany, they were constantly reminded by Moscow that Vilnius had been returned to Lithuania by the Soviets on two occasions, the first at the end of the Lithuanian war of independence, the second following the fall of Poland. By contrast, Molotov maintained, the Western Powers had done nothing to help Lithuania. Throughout the winter of 1939–40, the Soviets repeatedly obstructed Lithuanian government attempts to establish better trade links with the Western Powers and encouraged closer cooperation with Germany, whilst simultaneously stating, both publicly and in private, that they were not meddling with Lithuanian affairs. Such a policy reflected the attitude of Moscow to the arrangements with Germany: whilst Stalin and others might regard the Pact as a temporary expedient, they behaved – in trade matters, at least – as if they intended to respect it fully. Speaking to the Supreme Soviet at the end of October, Molotov stressed that the pacts with the three Baltic States did not constitute any interference in internal matters. The resolution of the Vilnius question, he stressed, demonstrated the noble principles of Soviet foreign policy. Shortly after, Molotov wrote to Nikolai Pozdniakov, the Soviet ambassador to Lithuania, forbidding all Soviet officials from getting involved in any political activity within Lithuania: 'The least effort of any of you to mix into the internal affairs of Lithuania will incur the strictest punishment of the guilty person ... it is necessary to reject gossip about the "Sovietisation" of Lithuania as provocative and harmful.'[30]

Publicly, Lithuanian officials made repeated favourable comments about the new relationship with the Soviet Union. In private, they were less certain of the future. From February 1940, Augustinas Povilaitis, the head of the Lithuanian security service, had regular secret meetings with a Gestapo agent, supplying the Germans with detailed information about the Soviet bases in Lithuania. Details of their discussions are controversial, as Povilaitis was extensively interrogated by the Soviets, and the account of this interrogation clearly shows a man who was increasingly desperate to placate his interrogators. As one Lithuanian historian commented, 'Povilaitis' interrogators just had to want it, and he would have confessed to having dug a tunnel from Kaunas to Vilnius.'[31]

Meanwhile, domestic problems abounded for all three Baltic States. Germany effectively blocked their lucrative pre-war trade with Britain and the west, while offering little in return. Responsibility for the costs of the Soviet garrisons had not been defined in the mutual aid pacts, and Soviet authorities frequently refused to pay bills for goods received by the garrisons, complaining that the amounts were exaggerated. In February 1940, the deteriorating economic situation led to a wave of strikes in Lithuania; although Smetona publicly blamed this on communist agitators, he was aware that in reality the Lithuanian Communist Party remained small and relatively weak, whereas the financial difficulties facing all Lithuanians were very real.

It is not known for certain when Stalin decided to act to occupy the Baltic States, but it seems likely that a firm decision was made in the spring of 1940, perhaps as late as the last week of May. By this time, German troops had already moved to occupy Denmark and Norway, The Netherlands had fallen, and German armour had reached the English Channel. Estonian diplomats in Moscow were convinced that events in Western Europe precipitated a move by the Soviet Union to secure complete control of the Baltic States before Hitler might choose to reconsider the previously agreed 'spheres of influence'.[32] Stalin had hoped that Hitler would become embroiled in a prolonged war in the west, greatly reducing his strength and ability to attack the Soviet Union. He was therefore alarmed by the inability of the Western Allies to put up significant resistance to the German advance, and concluded that he would have to take whatever measures were necessary to secure his own frontiers. The first inkling of coming events was when Soviet tanks stationed in the Vilnius region were ordered to move to Gaižūnai, closer to Kaunas – which had been the 'temporary capital' of Lithuania while Vilnius was under Polish control, and remained the seat of government despite its return – on 18 May. A week later, Molotov summoned the Lithuanian ambassador, Ladas Natkevičius, and handed him a note alleging that Lithuanians working for or with the protection of the Lithuanian government were luring Soviet soldiers into criminal activities. The nature of these activities was not given, though it was implied that two soldiers had been kidnapped. Molotov concluded that he was sure that the Lithuanian government would take appropriate measures, and that the Soviet government would not be forced to take further steps itself.

Earlier in the month, Natkevičius had informed the Soviet authorities about the suicide of a Soviet soldier in Lithuania, but he knew of no other incidents involving the Soviet garrisons in his country. Nor did anyone in Kaunas. On 27 May, Smetona's prime minister, Antanas Merkys, rejected the Soviet allegations as unfounded, but ordered the creation of a commission to investigate further.

The Lithuanian government now found itself drawn into an increasingly Kafkaesque world, in which it found itself unable to determine the exact nature of the charges it faced. Urbšys asked if the Lithuanian commission could speak to the Soviet soldiers involved in the allegations, but was told that they were not available, as they were undergoing treatment for the harm they had suffered. Even more surreal was Molotov's reaction to requests for more information about the exact nature of the allegations: he told the baffled Lithuanians that the Lithuanians could not expect the Soviet authorities to do their work for them, and should sort the matter out themselves. In early June, nearly 300 Lithuanians suspected of a variety of crimes around the Soviet garrison areas were arrested, but none were found to have been involved in anything that could be linked to the Soviet allegation. An attempt to increase security around the Soviet garrisons backfired; the Soviets now complained that the Lithuanians were harassing the garrisons, even preventing laundry from being collected and delivered. The Lithuanians were also accused of conspiring with the Latvians and Estonians to create an anti-Soviet alliance. It was certainly true that the three countries had discussed mutual defence in the winter, but the reality was that there were already more Soviet troops stationed on their territory than their combined armies. Any united anti-Soviet position was untenable.

On 4 June, Merkys was summoned to Moscow. On 7 June, Molotov informed him that the Soviet authorities believed that the Lithuanian Minister of the Interior, Kazys Skučas, and Augustinas Povilaitis were behind the anti-Soviet acts, which still remained nebulous. Povilaitis was of course the head of the Lithuanian security services, and had been holding regular meetings with a Gestapo agent. Talks continued, moving steadily away from the vague charges of interfering with the Soviet garrisons and towards Soviet demands for a restructuring of the Lithuanian government. Any attempt by the Lithuanians to return to the nature of the accusations was deflected by Molotov, who invariably responded by accusing the Lithuanians of anti-Soviet activity. Finally, late on 14 June, Molotov made his final demand. The only way to resolve the situation was for the Lithuanians to place Skučas and Povilaitis under arrest, and to create a new government that would be more friendly to the Soviet Union. Also, Lithuania would have to accept more Soviet troops on its territory. A deadline of 1000hrs the following day was given, with the threat that Soviet troops would then enter Lithuanian territory even in the absence of any agreement.

The immediate reaction of the Lithuanians was that they had no grounds to arrest Skučas and Povilaitis. Molotov replied that they should arrest them anyway, and find appropriate charges afterwards.[33] If they were unable to do so, he said, the Soviet authorities would help them find suitable charges. The Lithuanian government argued throughout the night. Smetona wanted to resist, even if such resistance served only a symbolic role, but he was in a minority. Finally, they came to the only conclusion possible: they would accept Soviet terms. Merkys resigned, Smetona announced that he would leave the country, and Stasis Raštikis was asked to form a new government.

When the Lithuanian Foreign Minister advised Molotov of these developments the following day, he was stunned by the Soviet response. Molotov rejected the suggestion that Raštikis should be the new prime minister, and told Urbšys that he would send Vladimir Dekanozov, a Deputy Commissar for Foreign Affairs, to Kaunas to supervise the creation of a new government. Soviet troops began to move into Lithuania later in the day. The arrival of Soviet troops in Kaunas was greeted by noisy demonstrations, mainly in support. Lithuanian historians have repeatedly maintained that these demonstrations were made almost entirely by the Jewish population, but Soviet accounts naturally maintained that many of those who greeted them with flowers were Lithuanians. Nevertheless, there was a widespread acceptance at the time that the Jews were more enthusiastic about Soviet occupation than they had ever been about Lithuanian nationalism. A report by the Lithuanian security service made observations that were shared by many others:

When the USSR army marched into Lithuania, the Jews began to express their arrogance. It happened that an irresponsible element of Jewish society, mostly youths, walked the streets of the cities and would not even yield the sidewalks for walking Lithuanians to pass. Also, there are Lithuanian complaints that the Jews are declaring in threatening form: 'Now we are the lords.'[34]

Smetona left Kaunas before the Soviets arrived. He issued himself a visa to Germany and crossed the border later that day; there was a moment of farce when Lithuanian border guards refused to allow him to leave Lithuania, and he finally entered Germany by wading through a shallow stream. He had repeatedly investigated the possibility of fleeing to Germany ever since the enforced mutual assistance treaty of the previous year, and left Lithuania with several important documents and a large amount of cash. Despite allegations that he siphoned off government funds, later investigation has suggested that the money was his own.[35] He eventually travelled on to the United States. He lived there until his death in a house fire in January 1944.

Even while Smetona and his ministers were holding their all-night meeting in Kaunas, Stalin had concluded that the Lithuanian issue was settled, and was moving against Latvia. A group of NKVD soldiers crossed the border into Latvia during the night and attacked a Latvian border post near the town of Masļenki. There was a brief exchange of fire, which left several Latvian soldiers dead or wounded, before the NKVD troops withdrew. They took with them ten Latvian soldiers and 27 civilians as prisoners.[36] The purpose of this raid was never made clear, but even as Latvian officials awoke to the news that neighbouring Lithuania was being occupied, they learned of the night's events in Masļenki. A day later, on 16 June, the Ulmanis government in Riga and the Päts government in Tallinn received ultimatums from Molotov. Citing the meetings of the three Baltic States during the winter, he accused them of plotting against the Soviet Union, and demanded that they allow the Red Army to enter their territory. The two countries also had to agree to create new Soviet-friendly governments, and were given barely eight hours to agree.

Both Estonian and Latvian ministers considered armed resistance. The Estonians were aware that their successes in their war of independence were only possible due to the support of both Finland and the Western Powers, and neither could be relied on in the current crisis; the Red Army was also a far more formidable force than it had been at the end of the First World War. Consequently, the Tallinn government concluded that fighting would be pointless. A few hours after Molotov's ultimatum, a further message reached Riga, warning that any signs of troop mobilisation would result in the bombing of Latvian cities. Attempts to request the sale of weapons from Germany, or even German diplomatic intervention, were in vain. The governments had no choice but to agree, and Soviet troops crossed into their territory within hours. Ulmanis made a radio announcement to his people even as Soviet tanks rolled into Riga, calling on them to remain calm: 'I remain in my place,' he told them, 'as you should in yours.'[37] His words were generally heeded. Nevertheless, noisy demonstrations in Riga by residents of the 'Moscow' suburb – an area dominated by

Jews and ethnic Russians and Belarusians – escalated into attacks on the Riga police. Shots were fired, leaving three demonstrators dead and 26 injured. Some 67 police officers were also injured before order was restored.[38] It later transpired that this incident had been deliberately contrived. Soviet agitators had encouraged the residents of the Moscow suburb to demonstrate energetically, whilst at the same moment Soviet military authorities were urging the police to ensure that strict order was maintained. The purpose of the exercise, it seems, was to increase tension between the 'downtrodden ethnic minorities' and the 'quasi-fascist state'. There were even reports of Soviet soldiers firing into the crowd from their armoured vehicles during the protests.[39] There was also violence in the port of Liepāja, though here the Latvian authorities were forbidden from intervening by the Soviet garrison.

Now that the three Baltic States had been swallowed, the process of assimilating them began. Stalin sent some of his most capable colleagues, Andrei Vyshinski and Andrei Zhdanov, to Riga and Tallinn respectively to supervise the creation of pro-Soviet governments. Smetona's departure from Lithuania was not greeted with universal dismay. Many had grown tired of his dictatorship, which had increasingly been dominated by his own personality cult, and even members of his government had been willing to accept the Soviet ultimatum as a means of getting rid of him. Nevertheless, Dekanozov left nothing to chance, declaring that as Smetona had left the country, he had effectively resigned as President. Although Prime Minister Merkys had resigned, he was now the acting President; Dekanozov had him dismissed. The new head of the government was Justas Paleckis, a left-wing journalist. At first, the government had only a minority of communists, but this increased over time. In any event, the power of the government was strictly curtailed. Dekanozov and his colleagues were effectively running the country.

At the same time, Vyshinski and Zhdanov presented the Ulmanis and Päts governments with lists of ministers for their new governments. Both Baltic leaders rejected the lists, resulting in further orchestrated demonstrations against the nationalist governments. In Tallinn, the protesters surged through police barracks, supported by Soviet troops, and there was a brief exchange of fire between them and the police.[40] Again, the governments bowed to the inevitable. Augusts Kirhenšteins became the new government leader in Latvia, and Johannes Vares became the Estonian prime minister. Ulmanis and Päts continued as heads of state until they were forced to resign in mid-July. By the end of the month, both had been taken to the Soviet Union. Ulmanis died in captivity in 1942; Päts, who was returned to Estonia after the war, was forced to receive psychiatric treatment on the grounds that he continued to insist that he was the President of Estonia, and was moved back to the Soviet Union as too many people in Estonia recognised him, even in hospital. He died in 1956. Other significant figures also disappeared into the Soviet Union. Antanas Merkys was arrested when he attempted to flee to Sweden, and was held in captivity until 1954. Although he was released, he was forbidden from returning to Lithuania, and died the following year. Juozas Urbšys, the Lithuanian Foreign Minister, was in Moscow for talks, and was simply detained there. He was sent to Siberia, and remained there for 13 years; however, he lived to see the restoration of Lithuanian independence, and died in 1991.

As the new administrations settled down to their tasks, the first to feel the wind of change were the senior officials, both military and civilian, who rapidly found themselves unemployed. The armies were reorganised along Soviet lines, and now included Institutes for Political Instruction. Those politicians who had thought that they might be able to establish a *modus vivendi* with the Soviet Union began to grow alarmed. The new Lithuanian Foreign Minister, Vincas Mickevičius, met Molotov on 30 June to express concern at how the Lithuanian government was being sidelined by Soviet officials. Molotov's reply left him in no doubt about what lay ahead: 'You must take a good look at reality and understand that in the future small nations will have to disappear. Your Lithuania along with the other Baltic nations, including Finland, will have to join the glorious family of the Soviet Union.'[41]

Mickevičius submitted his resignation on his return to Lithuania, and non-communist members of the three governments began to follow his lead. Meanwhile, it was announced that all three countries would hold new elections in mid-July. Candidates could only be nominated by 'legal' institutions; this effectively meant only the communist parties, which were now the only legal political parties. Admittedly, most of the candidates put forward were not members of the communist parties, but to a large extent this reflected their very limited membership. The three communist parties had all been illegal until the arrival of the Red Army the previous month, and in the case of Latvia, most Latvian communists had spent the inter-war years in the Soviet Union, where they were caught up in the Latvian Operation of the late 1930s. In Estonia, opposition groups managed to get 78 candidates nominated, but Zhdanov instructed the government to take steps to invalidate them. Most withdrew in the face of intimidation and violence, and although a few managed to make it to the ballot, their votes were then summarily discounted. Attempts to create lists of alternative candidates in Latvia and Lithuania were also blocked.

The Soviet authorities went to considerable lengths to pressurise people into taking part in the elections. Nevertheless, the turnout in Lithuania was so low that voting was extended by a day. As was usually the case with Soviet-controlled elections, the result was a foregone conclusion. The cynicism of the process was sometimes astonishing. In at least one case – in Estonia – election officials calculated how many votes were required to record a turnout of 99.6 per cent, and topped up the completed ballot papers with unused ones to achieve the total.[42] Nobody can have been surprised when it was announced that over 90 per cent of the votes in each country were in favour of the list of communist candidates. Documents found in Estonia after Soviet forces were driven out in 1941 showed that the Central Electoral Committee alone forged over 35,000 votes, presumably in addition to malpractice at lower levels.[43]

The three new People's Assemblies met on 21 July. Their first acts were to declare the creation of Soviet Socialist Republics, followed by application for membership of the USSR. This amounted to the total of their political activity. Delegates were dispatched to Moscow, where the Supreme Soviet received the applications for membership on 1 August. Within six days, it had accepted all three applications. The Baltic States had effectively ceased to exist as independent nations. As a final settlement of German and Soviet bargaining, Moscow paid Berlin $7.5 million in gold as compensation for Germany not receiving the south-west part of Lithuania. It was the culmination of an extraordinary series of events, in which the Soviet Union had effectively conquered the Baltic States with barely a shot fired. Heavily involved in fighting in the west, Hitler was in no position to intervene, even if he had wanted to.

Another feature of the agreement between Moscow and Berlin related to the fate of ethnic Germans in the Baltic States. Since 1938, Nazi Germany had pursued a policy known as *Heim ins Reich*, under which German communities living outside Germany were encouraged to return to their homeland. Even prior to the Soviet takeover of the Baltic States, treaties had been agreed with Latvia and Estonia to allow Baltic Germans to sell their possessions and return to Germany, where they would be used to repopulate the annexed portions of Poland. By spring 1940, nearly 14,000 Baltic Germans had left Estonia, and about 51,000 had left Latvia. Many Baltic Germans chose to stay in Estonia and Latvia, but over the next year the Soviet annexations of the three Baltic States made the majority think again. In addition, as German plans for an invasion of the Soviet Union developed, Berlin sought to remove as many Germans as possible from what it foresaw would become a war zone. Consequently, an additional 7,000 Baltic Germans now left Estonia, and 10,500 left Latvia. Like those who had departed the previous year, most went to what had been western Poland. When they arrived in Poland, they were carefully assessed according to their racial purity, before they were given Polish farms and businesses to replace those that they had left behind in Estonia and Latvia; the money from the sale of their previous possessions was kept by the German state.[44]

Full-scale Sovietisation of the Baltic States swiftly followed their annexation, with nationalisation of private firms, both small and large. The departure of the Baltic Germans, who despite the reforms of the 1920s and 1930s had remained major landowners, did a great deal to accelerate the process. Although workers received substantial pay rises, these lagged far behind galloping inflation, leaving almost everyone far worse off. But while these changes caused hardship, the most significant impact of the Soviet occupation was from a series of arrests, commencing at the time of the elections. Seen from a Soviet point of view, these mass arrests made perfect sense. Marxist doctrine stated that a primary purpose of any organisation is to perpetuate itself. Therefore, it was reasoned, organisations that had existed before Sovietisation would attempt to recreate themselves in their pre-Soviet shape. In order to ensure that all parts of society developed in line with Soviet thinking, it was necessary to carry out radical surgery to prevent any such process. And, of course, the widespread fear created by such radical surgery would guarantee that social control was maintained.

The number of arrests increased steadily through 1940, reaching an average of over 200 per week in Lithuania alone by the end of the year. Most of those arrested received only the most rudimentary legal process. Distinct categories were drawn up for the arrests, including members of any anti-Soviet political parties, jail guards, former Czarist and White Russian officers and former White Russian volunteers, men who had been officers in the armies of the Baltic nations, Polish officers who had sought refuge in Lithuania, people who had been expelled from the communist parties, clergy, former landowners and industrialists, high-ranking civil servants, and all those with foreign ties. This latter group included those with completely innocent links with the outside world, such as philatelists.[45] Even though the Soviets continued to try to exploit ethnic differences, being a Jew or an ethnic Russian was no protection against arrest if the individual conformed to one of the identified groups:

It has been discovered that the entire staff of the Jewish School in Liepāja is made up of reactionary elements, who were already working in the school during the Ulmanis era and had been put in place by the Ulmanis regime, while *Komsomol* members with education certificates and training were not taken on.[46]

At first, the NKVD found it difficult to identify people in these groups, as they had to rely on Lithuanian, Latvian and Estonian documents, and struggled with the language barriers they faced. Consequently, it was only in 1941, shortly before the German invasion, that mass arrests and deportations really gathered pace. The NKVD was long-practised in such activities, and it seems that planning started in detail in May, when Lavrenti Beria, the head of the NKVD, handed Stalin plans drawn up by one of his deputies, Vsevolod Merkulov, entitled 'An Operation to Cleanse the Lithuanian, Latvian and Estonian Soviet Socialist Republics of Anti-Soviet, Criminal and Socially Dangerous Elements'.[47] A few months earlier, communist party workers in the three countries had been exhorted to start identifying 'enemies of the people'. Late on 13 June, the arrests began. Thousands of people were rounded up and herded onto cattle trains, which rumbled off on the first stage of the long journey to Siberia. It is not known how many died before they reached their destination; some estimates put the figure as high as 40 per cent.[48] In some cases – particularly officers of the old nationalist armies – those arrested were simply shot on the spot. By 17 June, Merkulov was able to report to Stalin that 40,170 people had been rounded up in the three countries.

The effect of these deportations on the population of the three Baltic States was enormous. Combined with other losses – ethnic Germans had already left for Germany, and the June wave of arrests was merely the largest and latest in a process that had begun with the arrival of the Red Army in force the previous year – it is estimated that Estonia lost 60,000 citizens, Latvia 35,000, and Lithuania 34,000 before the departure of the Soviets in 1941.[49] The high figure for Estonia is probably due to the fact that it was the last area to be overrun by the Wehrmacht, and the Soviets therefore had additional time for further arrests, and for conscription into the Red Army after the German invasion began. However, it could have been worse. There are indications that a second wave of mass arrests was planned for late in June. One Lithuanian government official later claimed to have seen a document suggesting that up to 700,000 deportations were envisaged from Lithuania alone.[50] Although this seems a huge number, amounting to perhaps a quarter of the population, it is consistent with the scale of deportations seen within the Soviet Union, particularly in 1944 and after, when Stalin exacted a terrible revenge on the ethnic communities that he regarded as having been friendly to the Germans.

Whilst the deportations resulted in widespread terror in all three countries, they also hardened anti-Semitic feelings in Lithuania and Latvia. The Jews were widely seen as being pro-Soviet, and there was a general view that they had played a major part in the deportations. In some cases, events were remembered in a way that emphasised the role of the Jews in the Communist Party:

When they began to ship the people away [aboard the cattle trains], the tension between Jews and Lithuanians reached its peak. When the truck carrying Russian soldiers drove into the village to round people up, a young Jew came with them, wearing the red star. And one saw that the Russian soldiers were not to blame for what happened, that the leader and chief executioner was just this one.[51]

The bitter irony was that in many of the categories of those arrested, the Jews deported during June formed a greater percentage of deportees than Jews made up in the overall population – in other words, the Jewish communities suffered more in percentage terms than Lithuanians and Latvians. Moreover, many Jews did not welcome the annexation of Lithuania and Latvia by the Soviet Union, and tried to escape from the region. The Japanese Consul in Lithuania, Chiune Sugihara, collected information about German and Soviet moves for his government, using a number of Polish officers and officials who had fled to Lithuania after their country was overrun by its neighbours and had since avoided arrest. He used his position to grant them Japanese passports, and arranged for some to travel by rail to the Soviet Far East and from there to Japan. Over time, many Jews also contacted Sugihara, and several thousand escaped via the same route; they travelled on from Japan to Palestine and the United States.[52] Nevertheless, in other areas of life, too, there was huge resentment at the apparent advancement of Jews and ethnic Russians in preference to Baltic nationals. In Latvia, Jews played a prominent part in many media, such as the (state-controlled) press, films and radio. After the years of the Ulmanis regime's policy of 'Latvia for Latvians', when ethnic minorities were generally marginalised, even a relatively small increase in the presence of Jews in the media would have been immediately noticeable. Even Latvian members of the Communist Party were worried at the way things were developing; one recorded that 'The Russians are stirring up hatred between nationalities everywhere.'[53] It was inevitable that when the opportunity came, Lithuanians and Latvians would not be slow to take their revenge.

Chapter 2

ROSENBERG, *GENERALPLAN OST* AND PREPARATIONS FOR *BARBAROSSA*

Alfred Rosenberg was born in 1893 in Tallinn, which was then part of the Czar's empire. His parents were Baltic Germans, descendants of settlers who had come to the area during preceding centuries; his father was a businessman from Latvia, and his mother was from the Estonian community of Baltic Germans. He studied in Riga and Moscow, and left for Germany when the Bolsheviks seized power, having chosen to support the White Russian cause. He was an early adherent of the National Socialists, and together with his mentor, Erwin von Scheubner-Richter, he was one of those who planned the failed 'Beer Hall Putsch' of 1923. Scheubner-Richter was killed during the attempted putsch – he was shot while walking arm in arm with Hitler, and as he fell he dislocated Hitler's shoulder – and Rosenberg became leader of the National Socialists while Hitler was in prison. It was not a particularly successful appointment, and Hitler later suggested that he had deliberately chosen someone who would not be able to supplant him in the long term.[1] Given that there was no reason at the time to doubt that Rosenberg would do a competent job, and that Hitler cannot have known how long he would be incarcerated, this comment may well have been made with the benefit of hindsight.

As the Nazis rose to power, Rosenberg became increasingly interested in racial theory, particularly where it concerned Jews. He was strongly anti-Bolshevik, following his family's flight from Russia, and also an implacable anti-Semite. Indeed, he was one of the first to formulate the concept of 'Jewish Bolshevism', which came to dominate so much of German thinking about the Soviet Union, and it is likely that he was influential in Hitler's adoption of this term. It was inevitable that in the chaotic world of Nazi ideology, his views would have a major impact upon the development of German plans.

The historic desire to expand German culture to the east pre-dated the unification of Germany itself, with the settlement of large numbers of Germans in the Baltic States and beyond as part of the *Drang nach Osten* ('drive to the east'), a recurrent theme for centuries. Friedrich Ratzel coined the phrase *Lebensraum* at the beginning of the 20th century, and the concept was then developed by others, almost always with the view that the logical place for Germany to seek its new 'living space' was in Eastern Europe. Whilst almost all of these proposals were hostile to Poland and identified this as the first and easiest area for Germany to seize, there was a clear intention to proceed further east, even beyond the historic lands of the Teutonic and Livonian Knights. Despite the failure to establish *Mitteleuropa* in and after the First World War, German theorists continued to talk about possible future expansion eastward, and Hitler made clear in *Mein Kampf* that he regarded such a policy as an essential part of securing *Lebensraum* for Germany:

> Germany must find the courage to gather our people and their strength for an advance along the road that will lead this people from its present restricted living space to new land and soil, and hence also free it from the danger of vanishing from the earth or of serving others as a slave nation.[2]

This was in keeping with a widely held view in Germany that it was 'natural' in terms of social Darwinism for strong nations and civilisations to expand, while weaker ones faded away. Hitler was determined that Germany should be in the former group. It was typical of the selective and muddled thinking of the National Socialists that while they accepted the concept of social Darwinism, they – like Stalin – believed that their own society represented the ultimate peak of social evolution, and would not in turn be replaced by other societies.

It seems that several studies were undertaken during the 1930s about possible rearrangements of territory in Eastern Europe; during the Nuremberg Trials, Obergruppenführer Erich von dem Bach-Zelewski testified that Heinrich Himmler had overseen these discussions. In 1940, more detailed planning began, resulting in the creation of a set of documents that made up *Generalplan Ost*. It is difficult to determine the exact chain of events that led to the creation of *Generalplan Ost*, because many documents relating to the plan were deliberately destroyed in the final days of the war. Standartenführer Hans Ehlich stated at Nuremberg that he was responsible for drawing up the plan, and using his testimony and fragmentary documentation and letters, it has been possible to recreate most of the plan, though no copies of it survived the war.[3] In particular, a document entitled *Stellungnahme und Gedanken zum Generalplan Ost des Reichsführers-SS* ('Opinion and Ideas Regarding the General Plan for the East of the Reichsführer-SS') by Dr Erich Wetzel has proved vital. This critique of *Generalplan Ost* includes a great deal of information about the contents of the plan.

Rosenberg's personal thoughts played a large part in the development of the plan. He proposed that the former Czarist Empire be broken into several components, each of which would form a *Reichskommissariat*: Ostland, consisting of the Baltic States; Moskowien, stretching from Moscow to the Urals and the Barents Sea; Ukraine; and Caucasus. He also wished to create a fifth region, broadly stretching along the southern Soviet Union close to the borders with Iran and Afghanistan, but Hitler ordered him to abandon this in order to concentrate on the four regions in the western part of the Soviet Union. In many respects, Rosenberg was significantly past the peak of his influence by this stage. He had written a book in the early 1930s entitled *Der Mythus des 20. Jahrhunderts* (The Myth of the 20th Century), a lengthy exposition on racial theory, particularly with regard to the 'Jewish Question', but although the book sold well, few senior National Socialists could say that they had read the entire work, or regarded it as a useful contribution to their beliefs; Hitler dismissed it as 'stuff nobody can understand'.[4] In 1941, as plans for the German invasion of the Soviet Union reached a detailed level, Rosenberg was appointed chief of the newly created *Reichsministerium für die besetzten Ostgebiete* ('Reich Ministry for the Occupied Eastern Territories', often abbreviated to *Ostministerium*). The quality of its personnel was varied, to say the least:

> When ministries were summoned to supply their quotas of civil servants for the new *Führerkorps Ost* ... [they saw] in this call a welcome opportunity to rid themselves of personal enemies, obnoxious meddlers and incompetent chair-warmers ... [resulting in] a colourful and accidental conglomeration of Gauleiters, Kreisleiters, Labour Front officials, and a great number of SA [*Sturmabteilung* or 'Storm Detachment', the para-military wing of the Nazi Party before the war] leaders of all ranks, who assumed high positions in the civil administration after listening to a few introductory lectures delivered by Rosenberg's staff.[5]

Rosenberg's authority over this body was further weakened by the fact that many members of the *Ostministerium* remained loyal to their former patrons, and sought to undermine Rosenberg so that other senior members of the National Socialist movement – particularly Heinrich Himmler, Hermann Goering, Martin Bormann

(Party Minister of the National Socialist Party, Chief of the Party Chancellery, and later Hitler's personal secretary), and Erich Koch (Gauleiter of East Prussia) – could develop their own empires. Rosenberg protested to Hitler about being obstructed by these and other figures on several occasions, but was unable to prevent what he regarded as interference in his jurisdiction. This was a recurring theme in German administration during the war, as Hitler actively encouraged his subordinates to compete for power, believing that this would allow the strongest and best to rise to the top. The chaos and dislocation this policy caused was far greater than any benefits.

In April 1940, Rosenberg described in detail his vision of the development of the new territories of the east:

> The aim of our policy, therefore, appears to lie in this direction: to resume in an intelligent manner and sure of our aim, the aspirations to liberation of all these peoples and to give them shape in certain forms of states ... and to build them up against Moscow, so as to free the German Reich of the eastern nightmare for centuries to come.[6]

In other words, it was Rosenberg's intention to create a series of buffer states between Germany and the 'barbaric east'. This was at odds with Hitler's own vision of a German *Herrenvolk* supported by the remnants of the local population who had been reduced to slave status. Opposed to the creation of any form of buffer state, Hitler argued that any attempt to introduce self-government would inevitably start a nation down the road to full independence.[7] Rosenberg found himself in a very small minority with his views. Ironically, the only major National Socialist figure to think along similar lines – Joachim von Ribbentrop in the Foreign Ministry – was often at loggerheads with Rosenberg on other issues, as he perceived the latter as developing a sphere of influence that overlapped too much with his own, preventing them from making common cause. The input of the *Reichssicherheitshauptamt* ('Reich Main Security Administration' or RSHA, a section of the SS) into *Generalplan Ost* took a very different approach from Rosenberg to the four regions. There would be no room for any semi-independent states in the former Soviet Union, and all of the regions would remain tightly under Berlin's control. As has been discussed, German policy towards colonies was very different from that of Britain and France, and the whole concept of *Lebensraum* was to create areas populated mainly by Germans. Hitler consciously modelled his approach on the settlement of North America. As he told his followers, 'We eat Canadian wheat and don't think about the Indians.'[8] In keeping with this attitude, the plan called for the removal of all elements of the population who could not be 'Germanised'.

With so much of German manpower mobilised for war, there was a pressing need for agricultural imports into Germany to keep the nation fed. With memories of near-starvation as a result of the British naval blockade of the First World War, it was inevitable that Hitler would turn to the east as a source of these food supplies. In particular, the Ukraine, with its historically fertile land, was seen as the source of both industrial and agricultural resources that would allow Germany to avoid forever the threat of blockade.[9] During the years since the First World War, the Soviet urban population had grown by about 25 million. The elimination of these Soviet citizens would allow for the Ukrainian 'surplus' to be sent west.[10]

The alteration in the population of the four new territories was to be achieved by a variety of means, depending on the people involved. There was a clear intention from the start that Jewish communities would not be tolerated, and would simply be exterminated. German plans relating to the Jews went through several distinct phases. Initially, the intention was to establish a Jewish 'colony' in the conquered parts of Poland, but this proved to be impractical for several reasons. Firstly, there was a feeling that the proposed colony in and around Lublin was still too close to Germany. Secondly, after the conquest of Poland, it proved almost impossible to transfer Jews from Germany and the west to Poland, because the authorities in occupied Poland simply couldn't cope with the numbers involved. A second proposed solution to the 'Jewish Question' was to establish a Jewish colony on a distant island such as Madagascar. Although France, the European power that currently controlled Madagascar, had fallen to Germany, British domination of the oceans made any such plan impossible to execute. Instead, Germany attempted to persuade Stalin to accept several million Jews into the Soviet Union, where they could be settled in some remote part of Siberia or Soviet Central Asia; Stalin refused. Now, with planning for a German conquest of the Soviet Union at an advanced stage, a new solution arose, namely that the Jews would simply be worked to death, building new roads across the conquered territories of Russia. The Final Solution of mass extermination only became a formal policy when the rapid conquest of Russia failed to occur.

Other populations in the territories that would be conquered, such as Roma, would also have been treated the same way. Slavs were to be deprived of access to medical care, and their food supplies would be reduced, resulting in deaths through starvation. There were also proposals for mass sterilisation, to ensure that the current generation of 'undesirables' would be the last in the occupied territories. Others, including the bulk of the Soviet urban populations, would be driven east out of the new territories, into Western Siberia. Although the plans were not explicit about what would happen to them, it must have been clear that pushing so many people into an undeveloped wilderness would result in the swift deaths of most. Indeed, although the decollectivisation of Ukrainian agriculture might have had political advantages, by addressing one of the greatest resentments of the rural Ukrainian population, the Germans intended to preserve the collectivised system, as it would be easier for them to ensure that agricultural output went to their chosen destinations, thus ensuring the starvation of tens of millions of Soviet city dwellers. This was made explicit in a document known as the Hunger Plan, which was finalised during March 1941.[11]

Hitler made his views on the measures to be used abundantly clear in a conference in July 1940: 'While German goals and methods must be concealed from the world at large, all the necessary measures – shooting, exiling, etc. – we shall take and we can take anyway. The order of the day is: first, conquer; second, rule; third, exploit.'[12]

The numbers of people intended for removal from Eastern Europe were staggering. Only 15 per cent of Poles would be allowed to remain in Poland, while the figures for Belarus, the Ukraine, and Russia were 25 per cent, 35 per cent and 50 per cent respectively. Those who were allowed to stay would include a small number deemed worthy of Germanisation; the rest would be treated as slave labour. It was anticipated that over 45 million persons would be deported into Siberia. For the Baltic States, the deportations were intended to reduce the 'native' population of Estonia and Latvia by about 50 per cent, and that of Lithuania – which was 'contaminated' by its historical links with Poland – by 85 per cent. The suggestion that Stalin's purges would eventually have removed perhaps a quarter of the population of the Baltic States should be measured against these planned German deportations. *Generalplan Ost* originally intended for the Baltic States to become Germanised in about 25 years; Himmler altered this target to 20 years.[13]

Generalplan Ost would be implemented in two distinct phases. The first phase, known as the *Kleine Planung* ('small plan') would take place as soon as the relevant territory was overrun. The second phase, or *Grosse Planung* ('large plan') would then be put into effect over about 20 to 30 years. It was anticipated that the major expulsions would come during this phase. However, the diversion of food from 'undesirable' populations would occur as part of the *Kleine Planung*, and if this resulted in mass deaths through starvation, as was intended for the first winter following the expected German victory, it would reduce the amount of work required in the *Grosse Planung*.

The hostility of Germany towards the citizens of the Baltic States is worth closer examination. Attitudes towards Estonia, Latvia and Lithuania in Germany between the wars were influenced by two main factors. Firstly, there were significant numbers of former Baltic Germans, such as Rosenberg himself, who had left their homelands in difficult circumstances. The relationship between the Baltic Germans and the Baltic nationals had frequently been a prickly one; most of the aristocracy and landowners of Latvia and Estonia had been German, and, as has been discussed, these communities had been extensively involved in the wars of independence in attempts to prevent the nationalists from coming to power, particularly in Latvia. At the very least, the Baltic Germans were determined that any government of an independent Latvia would be a close ally of Germany, and their own interests as the major landowners would be protected. Secondly, those wars of independence had involved large numbers of German soldiers serving in the *Freikorps*. These volunteers had been made promises of large rewards for their service, including grants of land in the Baltic States, but by the end of the liberation wars, the *Freikorps* were fighting against the nationalist governments in a final attempt to establish pro-German puppet states, and few men received what they regarded as their fair rewards. Both these factors, against a historic background of long-term attempts by Germans to establish control over the area, led to a sense of entitlement to the Baltic coast as a German area. In the league tables of races in terms of which the National Socialists viewed the world, the Baltic peoples fell somewhere between the German *Herrenvolk* and the Slav *Untermensch*. There were even distinctions between the different nationalities. Estonians were perceived as being above the others, as they had strong historic (and therefore ethnic) links with the Finns and Swedes, who were seen as Aryans. The Lithuanians were regarded as the lowest, due to their historic association with the hated Poles.

The experiences of the Baltic people during the Soviet occupation shifted public opinion in the three states, at least amongst the non-Jewish and non-Russian sections, in favour of Germany. There was widespread hope and expectation that a war between the Soviet Union and Germany was coming, and as part of this war the Germans would restore Baltic independence. There would be a price to pay, but most Estonians, Latvians and Lithuanians were so traumatised by the experience of Soviet rule, particularly the deportations and mass arrests, that they were quite prepared to become allies of Germany. But in May 1941, Rosenberg issued a document to his staff entitled 'Instructions for a *Reichskommissar* in Ostland'. It made clear that whatever the future held for the Baltic States, there was no prospect of Germany restoring independence to the region:

The objective of a *Reichskommissariat* for Estonia, Latvia and *Weissruthenien* [the western and northern parts of Belarus] must be to strive for a form of German protectorate, and then through Germanisation of racially acceptable elements, colonisation by German people, and deportation of unwanted elements, to turn this region into a part of the Greater German Reich.[14]

In addition to those elements deemed 'unwanted' due to ethnicity, the Germans drew on their experiences in Poland. The intellectual elite of the three countries was to be deported, in an attempt to eliminate any residual spark of nationalism. Rosenberg anticipated that in Latvia alone this would add up to 40,000 to the number to be deported. But whilst there was general agreement within the German hierarchy about these policies, their implementation looked problematic. Himmler published detailed criteria that people in the occupied lands would have to satisfy to be deemed worthy of Germanisation, but some of his subordinates protested, pointing out that large portions of the population of Germany itself would not be able to satisfy these criteria. In view of this, many within the SS and the various bodies competing for the right to control the occupied territories favoured a model based on ancient Sparta: the Germans would be in the position of the Spartans, the Slavs would be reduced to slave Helots, and there would be room for a third category, the *Perioikoi*, free people without full citizen status, who would serve the Reich as loyal allies – in other words, much in line with Rosenberg's original proposals. The people of the Baltic States in particular were seen to be fit to play the role of *Perioikoi*. Rosenberg himself also saw such a role for the people of the Ukraine, whom he had rightly identified as being largely hostile to the Soviets. Hitler, though, rejected this out of hand. The Ukrainians were Slavs, and would be treated appropriately.

One of the problems that Germany would have faced was that of providing sufficient settlers to realise these grandiose dreams. The *Heim ins Reich* policy resulted in over 120,000 Baltic Germans moving to Germany, and after including ethnic Germans from other parts of Europe the total came to over 850,000. Most were settled in the western parts of Poland; for example, the German population of Poznań increased from 6,000 in 1939 to over 93,000.[15] But despite these measures, there were not enough settlers to Germanise Poland, let alone the vast territories further north and east. It was expected that the German population would grow steadily, not least due to the ban on abortions and lack of provision of birth control. These future generations, it was hoped, would provide the bulk of the settlers. Other, more extreme views were also considered. Goering and the head of the RHSA, Reinhard Heydrich, advocated extermination of the entire male population of the Ukraine, after which the SS would be given free rein to impregnate as many racially acceptable women as possible.

The overall military plans for *Barbarossa*, the German invasion of the Soviet Union, are beyond the scope of this book. The main military command in the Baltic area was Army Group North, commanded by Generalfeldmarschall Wilhelm Ritter von Leeb. Born in Bavaria in 1876, he saw service in China during the Boxer Rebellion, and served on both the Western and Eastern Fronts in the First World War. He remained in the Reichswehr in the inter-war years, playing a major part in suppressing Hitler's Beer Hall Putsch in 1923. Hitler was suspicious of him due to his well-known anti-Nazi opinions, and matters were not helped when Leeb was the only senior German officer to object to the plans to defeat Britain and France by attacking through Belgium. For the second time in the century, he maintained, the world would condemn Germany for attacking Belgium while it was a neutral country.[16] He was promoted to *Generalfeldmarschall* after his troops broke through the Maginot Line during the Battle of France, and now found himself commanding a powerful force on the northern flank of the German deployment. Despite his experiences in the west, he remained a cautious man, and in some respects failed to grasp the huge significance of the combination of armoured warfare and German tactical and operational doctrine, and how well suited one was to the other.

Leeb commanded two infantry armies and a panzer group – the appellation 'panzer army' was created after the onset of *Barbarossa*. 18th Army, under the Prussian Generaloberst Georg von Küchler, was on the left flank. Like all his generation, Küchler had seen service in the First World War, and had also fought in Latvia in the *Freikorps*, serving for a time as a staff officer to the German commander in the Baltic, Rüdiger von der Goltz. He had led his 18th Army across the Netherlands in 1940 and on to Paris, and now he and his men prepared to invade Lithuania. He had at his disposal I Corps, with five infantry divisions, and XXVI Corps, with four divisions. On his right flank was 16th Army, commanded by General Ernst Busch, a veteran of the Western Front in the First World War, who had commanded the army during the fighting in Belgium and France in 1940. His force consisted of II Corps with two divisions, and X Corps with five divisions.

The strike power of Leeb's army group was in Generaloberst Erich Hoepner's 4th Panzer Group. Widely known in the army as *Der alte Reiter* ('the old cavalryman'), Hoepner had been an early enthusiast for panzer warfare, and was assigned to the command of XVI Panzer Corps in 1938. After successful campaigns in Poland and France, he now found himself promoted to *Generaloberst*. His panzer group consisted of two motorised corps, with SS Division *Totenkopf* in reserve. XLI Panzer Corps, with two panzer divisions, a motorised infantry division, and a regular infantry division, was commanded by General Georg-Hans Reinhardt, who had led 4th

Panzer Division to Warsaw in 1939. Alongside him was LVI Panzer Corps, with one panzer division, one motorised infantry division, and a regular infantry division. Its commander was Erich von Manstein, who during the inter-war years had been the first to propose the creation of the *Sturmgeschütz* assault gun for close infantry support, as well as being one of the main architects of the successful German campaign through the Ardennes in 1940. He had commanded XXXVIII Corps during the Battle of France, and his men were the first to reach and cross the Seine. Now, he would have a chance to show what he could achieve with a panzer corps.

The panzer divisions had captured the imagination of the world in the opening campaigns of the war, but the bulk of the German army was composed of infantry divisions, which still marched and fought on foot. Their relative immobility compared to the motorised panzer divisions was a source of some concern, and even in the comparatively short Polish and western campaigns, the panzer divisions had often been left isolated while the infantry struggled to keep up. To an extent, panzer divisions had been organised with an awareness of this possibility, and contained sufficient engineering, maintenance and supply formations to allow them to function for extended periods without full contact with the rest of the Wehrmacht. The rapid advance of the panzer divisions and their resultant isolation in the west had not resulted in any significant setbacks, though the British counter-attack against the German armoured spearheads near the English Channel resulted in some anxious moments. In the vast spaces of the Soviet Union, the inability of the infantry to keep up with the panzer divisions would be ruthlessly exposed. The infantry divisions consisted of three infantry regiments, an artillery regiment, and one battalion each of reconnaissance, engineer, and anti-tank troops. The bulk of the artillery was horse-drawn, further limiting their mobility. The panzer divisions at this stage of the war had an infantry brigade, consisting of one or two infantry regiments, and in many cases a battalion of motorcycle-mounted infantry. The armoured element consisted of a panzer brigade, usually of two panzer regiments, with a total of up to four battalions of tanks between them. In addition, the division had reconnaissance, engineer and anti-tank battalions, as well as a regiment of artillery – in contrast to the infantry divisions, most of this artillery was either motorised or towed by half-tracks and trucks. The motorised infantry divisions had two motorised infantry regiments and a motorcycle battalion, an artillery regiment, and engineer and anti-tank battalions.

The tanks of the panzer divisions had led the way across Poland, Belgium and France, but were in many respects inferior to those of Germany's enemies. Most divisions still had large numbers of Pz.II tanks, which had first entered service in 1936. The 9-ton vehicles were armed with a 20mm gun, and their armour was originally intended to protect the crew only from light infantry weapons. Later versions had armoured enhancements up to 30mm, but this provided minimal protection against anti-tank guns. The Pz.III was numerically the main tank at the outset of *Barbarossa*. It was the first German tank specifically designed to engage other tanks, and was a substantially larger vehicle than the Pz.II, weighing 23 tons. Its armour was increased from an original specification of 15mm to 30mm, but this was still inadequate for engagement with other tanks. From the outset, the tank had been designed to carry a 50mm gun, but at the time it entered service, the Wehrmacht's anti-tank battalions were equipped with 37mm guns, and these were fitted to the Pz.III in the interests of standardisation. By the eve of *Barbarossa*, most Pz.III had been upgraded to 50mm guns, though most had shorter barrels than Hitler had decreed, resulting in lower muzzle velocity and less penetrative power. There were also large numbers of Pz.III chassis in use as assault guns. The *Sturmgeschütz* III was produced in response to a proposal from Manstein in 1935 for such a vehicle, in order to provide advancing infantry with heavy weapon support that could deal with bunkers and other fortifications. The vehicle could be fitted with a more powerful gun than the Pz.III, as it lacked a turret, and battalions of these vehicles were assigned as armour support for infantry divisions. In 1941, they were armed with a short-barrelled, low-velocity 75mm gun, reflecting their original role as infantry support. Later, they would be rearmed with high-velocity 75mm guns so that they could play an increasing role in anti-tank warfare.

The Pz.IV was Germany's heaviest tank in 1941, and originally had been intended as an infantry support weapon; however, the inadequacy of the Pz.III in tank-to-tank engagements led to a role reversal, with the Pz.IV being preferred in engagements against enemy armour and the Pz.III being used for infantry support. It weighed 25 tons and had 50mm frontal armour, and was armed with a variety of guns during its long life – it was the only German tank to remain in production throughout the war. In 1941, most Pz.IVs were armed with a short 75mm gun, and the low muzzle velocity of this weapon limited its efficacy in anti-tank combat.

In terms of preparation for war, the Wehrmacht in 1941 was in good shape; nearly all of the army officers and NCOs had experience of fighting in Poland and the west. The Luftwaffe, too, had a strong body of experienced men, but had not made good the losses suffered during the Battle of Britain. It now found itself committed to fighting a new war in the east, on a huge scale, while the RAF remained undefeated in the west. Perhaps the biggest weakness of the Wehrmacht was its logistic problems, partly due to a failure to plan for a prolonged war. In most respects, German equipment was not ordered with sufficient spare parts to allow for a sustained effort over a long time; for example, it was standard practice in Britain and the United States to order at least two aero engines per mounting, ensuring plentiful replacement engines and spare parts, whereas in Germany, the ratio was closer to 1:4. Stocks of spare parts had been badly depleted as a result of the fighting in France and the Battle of Britain, and unless the Wehrmacht won a quick victory, it would rapidly run into disabling shortages.

The operational orders for Army Group North called for Hoepner's panzers to advance along the Tilsit–Daugavpils axis, with 18th Army on the left, between Hoepner and the Baltic, and 16th Army on the right, providing contact with the northern elements of Army Group Centre. Once this initial objective had been achieved, 4th Panzer Group would continue to drive north across Latvia and Estonia to the southern tip of Lake Peipus, at Pskov. 18th Army would complete the conquest of the Baltic States, but it was anticipated that as Army Groups North and Centre advanced on diverging axes, 16th Army would find it increasingly difficult to retain contact with Army Group Centre. The plan therefore required that, having destroyed the bulk of Soviet forces in its path, Army Group Centre would provide aid on its flanks to both Army Group North and Army Group South, prior to a final drive on Moscow. Army Group North would move against its ultimate objective, Leningrad, prior to any drive against the Soviet capital – Hitler's directive of 18 December 1940, which first laid down the plans for *Barbarossa*, clearly stated this:

> Only after the accomplishment of offensive operations, which must be followed by the capture of Leningrad and Kronstadt [the Soviet naval base just outside Leningrad] are further offensive operations authorised, with the objectives of occupying Moscow, the important communications and armaments manufacturing centre.
>
> Only a surprisingly rapid collapse of the Russian ability to resist can justify an attempt to achieve both objectives simultaneously.[17]

There were many factors that combined to produce the stunning German victories of the early war years. Perhaps the key to German success was the coincidental development of armoured and mechanised warfare at the same moment that German military doctrine reached a particular stage of evolution, a process that had started in the wake of a crushing defeat in the early 19th century. After the Prussian army was soundly defeated by Napoleon at Jena and Auerstadt in 1806, the Prussians began a detailed analysis of why the French had prevailed. The result was the Prussian – later German – General Staff. This body championed the concept of something that became known as *Auftragstaktik*, a word perhaps best translated into English as 'mission-oriented tactics', although this expression was not explicitly used in German military writing. The intention was to create an army in which a commander would make a subordinate aware of his intentions, and would assign the subordinate a mission. A mixture of forces would be assigned to the subordinate, who was left to make detailed arrangements without interference from above. Maximum emphasis was placed upon subordinates showing initiative in interpreting their orders. In its extreme, *Auftragstaktik* allowed for the subordinate to ignore the mission that he had been assigned, so long as the actions that he took achieved the overall intentions of his superior. One of the clearest articulations of this concept was made by Helmuth von Moltke:

> The situations under which an officer has to act on the basis of his own view of the situation are diverse. It would be wrong if he had to wait for orders at times when no orders can be given. But his actions are most productive when he acts within the framework of his senior commander's intent.[18]

The movement began to gain pace after the Franco-Prussian War, and did not meet with universal approval. Indeed, those who preferred more traditional command and control, or *Normaltaktik*, were the very people who coined the expression *Auftragstaktik* to describe their opponents' principles. It was only by detailed management of all aspects of combat, they argued, that the tendency of increasing mobility and range of weapons could be controlled, to prevent complete fragmentation on the battlefield.

Auftragstaktik gained support throughout the First World War, and by the time the Germans mounted their final offensive on the Western Front in 1918, it was almost the norm for all German operations. It became commonplace for German officers and even NCOs to spend time with other arms – consequently, German commanders in the Second World War often had experience of working with infantry, artillery and armour. This resulted in excellent use of all components of the *ad hoc* battlegroups that were created for the fulfilment of missions.

In order for *Auftragstaktik* to be effective and successful, several factors needed to be combined. Firstly, all elements of the command structure had to understand its nature, and the importance of the overall intention of higher commands, rather than lower-level missions; the missions were merely a means to an end, to be altered or discarded if better means to the same end arose. Secondly, those entrusted with such tactical and operational freedom needed the skills and initiative to be able to react to changing circumstances effectively, so that any unexpected obstacles could be overcome, and any unexpected opportunities could be exploited. Thirdly, the extended command structure around any commander – the rest of the headquarters staff – had to be able to organise logistic and other matters in a flexible manner, allowing the commander himself to concentrate on battlefield developments. Finally, to allow for effective functioning in the event of casualties or other dislocation, every commander needed to be able to function up to two levels above his current command, and had to understand the objectives appropriate to those higher levels.

The advent of mechanised warfare, particularly in the form of the panzer division, occurred at a time when the German General Staff was particularly well adapted to *Auftragstaktik*. The panzer division, with its integration of tanks, artillery, infantry, and combat engineers, with dedicated support columns, was in many ways the ideal instrument for such a mode of operation. By the beginning of *Barbarossa*, many – though, as will be seen, not all – German officers had had time and opportunity to understand the new capabilities that such divisions offered, when combined with the prevailing operational doctrine within the Wehrmacht.

Generalplan Ost required its initial phase, the *Kleine Planung*, to be carried out in the wake of the advancing armies. Partly to achieve this, and partly to ensure the rapid establishment of order, the SS reactivated several *Einsatzgruppen* ('task forces'), which would follow in the wake of the Wehrmacht's three army groups. The precursor for such units was Reinhard Heydrich's *Einsatzkommando*, which had secured Austrian government buildings during the *Anschluss* of 1938. The *Einsatzgruppen* themselves were first formed during plans for the invasion of Czechoslovakia, but the Munich Agreement made the invasion unnecessary; nevertheless, the *Einsatzgruppen* repeated the role of securing government offices and documents, and also helped detain Czechoslovak government officials before they could quietly slip away. In preparation for the invasion of Poland, Heydrich once more resurrected his *Einsatzgruppen*, but on this occasion, their objectives were far more wide-ranging. They were given a free hand to execute anyone regarded as hostile to Germany, and using a special list of 'undesirable' Poles they sought out and killed Polish intelligentsia, clerics, and others who might be seen as being leaders of their communities, in addition to any other individuals who attracted their wrath. In many cases, their actions raised protests from the Wehrmacht, which feared that its own reputation would be damaged.[19]

By the end of October 1939, the *Einsatzgruppen*, functioning in eight groups, had killed an estimated 20,000 Poles. The groups saw brief service in Western Europe in 1940, reverting to their original role of securing government offices, and in preparation for *Barbarossa*, they were once more activated. In May 1941, Heydrich visited the German Border Police School, where the leaders of the *Einsatzgruppen* were undergoing training, and gave clear instructions that the groups were to kill Jews.[20] In order to prevent the friction seen during the Polish campaign, Heydrich met General Eduard Wagner, the First Quartermaster of the Wehrmacht, on 28 April 1941 and drew up an agreement for how the *Einsatzgruppen* would operate. In keeping with this agreement, Generalfeldmarschall Walther von Brauchitsch, commander of the German Army, issued instructions telling all army commanders that their units were to compile lists of Jews in the areas they seized, and that these lists were to be passed to the *Einsatzgruppen*. Although the orders did not specify what the *Einsatzgruppen* would do with these lists, there can have been little doubt in the minds of the commanders.

Heydrich would have been aware of the enmity between Latvians and Lithuanians on the one hand, and the Jewish populations of Latvia and Lithuania on the other, not least because German intelligence reports accurately commented on the growing anti-Semitism in the wake of the Soviet occupation. He therefore advised his subordinates to take advantage of this: 'No steps will be taken to interfere with any purges that may be initiated by anti-Bolshevik or anti-Jewish elements in the newly occupied territories. On the contrary, these are to be secretly encouraged.'[21]

Einsatzgruppe A was assigned to Army Group North, and began to assemble in Gumbinnen in East Prussia on the eve of *Barbarossa*. Its commander was Franz Walter Stahlecker, a lawyer who rose to high rank in the *Sicherheitsdienst* ('Security Administration' or SD). His command was divided into two *Sonderkommando* and five *Einsatzkommando*, each responsible for a different section of the front.

Facing the Wehrmacht was the Red Army, still recovering from the terrible purges of the 1930s. The scale of the purges was enormous; they had accounted for over 30,000 officers, stripping the Red Army of many of its best leaders. The officers who were left were either completely inexperienced, or those deemed politically acceptable, or both. In the aftermath of the purges, the army was under far stricter political control, and the political commissars attached to units at every level repeatedly interfered with training and deployment, challenging orders if they felt that they did not satisfy political doctrine.

In 1939, after forcing the Baltic States to accept the mutual assistance pacts, Stalin had turned his attention to Finland, the remaining state covered by the secret protocol to the Molotov–Ribbentrop Pact. As early as 1938, the Soviet Union had started to push the Finnish concept of neutrality, warning the Finns that the Red Army might seek to move troops through Finland in the event of a war between the Soviet Union and Germany. It was suggested that in order to facilitate this, Finland might wish to cede or lease some of its islands on the maritime approaches to Leningrad; having fought their own war of independence against Russia, which they had won with aid from Germany, the Finns refused. In 1939, Finland became aware of a steady build-up of Soviet troops on its borders, and commenced a precautionary mobilisation of its reserves under the guise of ongoing military training. In early October, Moscow sent Helsinki a demand for the cession of territory, including several Baltic islands and part of the mainland close to Leningrad. After lengthy debate, the Finns rejected the ultimatum. On 26 November, a Soviet border post came under shellfire; the shells were later proved to have been deliberately fired by a unit of the NKVD, but the Soviet authorities placed the blame on the Finns and demanded that the Finns withdraw from the border area.[22] At the end of the month, the Red Army invaded Finland.

The Winter War proved to be a stunning setback for the Red Army. Kliment Voroshilov, Stalin's close ally and People's Commissar for the Defence of the Soviet Union, had predicted a quick victory, but a combination of factors worked against the Soviets. The territory hugely favoured the defenders, and planning for the operation was inept and inadequate, based upon wildly optimistic assumptions of swift success. The weaknesses of the purged officer corps of the army were exposed in full as the determined and skilful Finnish defenders inflicted devastating losses on the Red Army. After 105 days of fighting, the Soviets were finally able to overcome the Finns and impose a treaty upon them; by then, they had lost over 320,000 casualties, compared to Finnish losses of about 70,000.

The Supreme Military Soviet convened a review of the performance of the Red Army, and Semon Konstantinovich Timoshenko, who had been sent to Leningrad by Stalin to take control of the Winter War and bring it to a successful conclusion, made wide-ranging recommendations for reform, covering topics as varied as clothing, radio equipment and operational tactics. However, many of these had not yet been implemented by the summer of 1941, while others had been watered down to preserve political control of the army. The Red Army would enter its most testing war in a poor shape.

Soviet armour was organised into mechanised corps, which had first been formed late in 1940. Each corps had two tank divisions and one motorised division, with a total strength of about 36,000 men and about 1,000 tanks.[23] The rifle divisions of the Red Army consisted of three infantry regiments, two artillery regiments, and a light tank battalion of 16 tanks. Although the paper strength of the division was over 14,000, most divisions had between 8,000 and 10,000 personnel, and their tank and artillery support was frequently non-existent. Each Soviet army was intended to possess one mechanised corps, three infantry corps each with two or three infantry divisions, and additional artillery and anti-tank units, but as was the case at lower levels, most armies had neither the men nor the equipment for all these army-level formations.

The equipment of the Red Army varied greatly in quality. In 1930, a Soviet delegation to Britain visited the Vickers factory and placed an order for a small number of Vickers Mk.E tanks, together with a licence to build them in Russia. The 6-ton tank was developed into the Soviet T26, which was then manufactured in vast numbers, with over 10,000 being produced over the years. Its original armament – machine guns in twin turrets, designed so that it could fire in both directions as it broke through enemy lines – was upgraded to a single 45mm gun, and its armour, and consequently its weight, also increased over time. Like the German Pz.II, it was essentially an obsolete design by 1941, lacking both the protection and firepower to survive on the battlefield, but it formed a large proportion of Soviet armoured forces.

Like all armies in the 1920s, the Red Army followed the concept of breakthrough tanks, which would force a breach in the enemy front line, and exploitation or cavalry tanks, lighter and faster vehicles that could exploit the resultant breach. The BT7 was a 14-ton vehicle with a 45mm gun, and perhaps 5,000 were built. Their light armour – only 22mm at the thickest point – left them vulnerable to enemy fire, and large numbers of the vehicles, more complex than the T26, were immobile at the start of *Barbarossa* due to a chronic shortage of spare parts.

The T26 was generally regarded as too light a vehicle to be an effective breakthrough tank, and several prototypes of larger vehicles were produced. Three prototypes were tested in combat during the Winter War, and the KV tank was selected as the best. Named after Kliment Voroshilov, it was produced in two forms, the 45-ton KV1 with a 76mm gun and (in smaller numbers) the 53-ton KV2, mounting a 152mm howitzer in a huge slab-sided turret. Heavier than any of its German opponents, its armour – over 70mm thick in places – rendered it almost immune to German anti-tank fire. But despite its good cross-country performance, it was not popular with tank crews. The fighting compartment was badly designed, and the gearbox was particularly difficult to use, often requiring the driver to hit it with a hammer.[24] Its weight prevented it from using many of the bridges in the Soviet Union, and it was expensive to build and difficult to maintain. Several hundred of these nevertheless formidable tanks were available to the Red Army's formations in the Baltic States.

The most famous Soviet tank of the Second World War was the T34. At first, the Soviet designers sought to design a new cavalry tank to replace the BT7, but its designer, Mikhail Koshkin, developed the concept into what became the T34. At 26 tons, and equipped with a powerful diesel engine and wide tracks, it was more manoeuvrable than any other Soviet tank of its day, and its powerful 76mm gun – the same weapon that was fitted to the more complex, heavier and more expensive KV1 – was capable of killing any German armour it might encounter. Its revolutionary sloping armour gave it excellent protection, and it was present in significant numbers at the start of the German invasion; but as with so many Soviet weapons, many T34s were inoperable due to mechanical problems and a lack of spares. Most Soviet tanks also lacked radios – only the commander's vehicle had a set, for communication with higher authorities, and even these sets were often faulty. All communication between the unit commander and his subordinate tanks was meant to be via flags waved from the turret, something that was hardly practical in the middle of an intense battle, and in any event likely to fail as the subordinate tanks would be too busy to keep an eye on any flags being waved from the command tank. Consequently, communication between commanders and their juniors was almost impossible once battle began, resulting in almost total inflexibility in their use; unable to contact their superiors, Soviet tank crews had little choice but to struggle on with their original battle plans, even if it was clear that these were not going to succeed.

The Red Army Air Force was, on paper at least, a formidable force, with nearly 19,000 combat aircraft. Although a large proportion of these were obsolescent or obsolete models, there were several squadrons of newer aircraft like the MiG3 and Il2. But the air formations were hamstrung by the same constraints as all other parts of the Soviet military machine. Firstly, spare parts shortages reduced the number of combat aircraft by about 15 per cent. Secondly, many pilots had very few hours' experience of flying their planes, particularly the newer models – training had been limited by the fear of crashes, which would have exposed commanding officers to charges of sabotage. Thirdly, tactical doctrine was based upon outdated concepts from the early 1930s about mass deployment of air power. Even if such concepts had not already been shown to be invalid, for example during the Battle of Britain, the Soviets lacked sufficient front-line airfields to allow such a mass deployment. This resulted in planes being crowded into a small number of airfields, making them easy targets should the Luftwaffe get the opportunity to attack first.[25]

The forces deployed in the Baltic States formed the Baltic Special Military District, the first line of defence of Leningrad. Commanded by Fyodor Isidorovich Kuznetsov, the Baltic District was probably the weakest of the three Soviet military districts along the border. It was made up of Lieutenant General Petr Petrovich Sobennikov's 8th Army in western Lithuania, Lieutenant General Vasili Ivanovich Morozov's 11th Army to the east, and 3rd and 12th Mechanised Corps. In reserve, Kuznetsov had 27th Army, commanded by Major General Nikolai Erastovich Berzarin. The numerical strength of the force was impressive, with nearly 370,000 men and over 1,500 tanks; by contrast, Army Group North possessed 655,000 men and nearly 1,400 tanks. Like all Soviet armoured forces, large numbers of the tanks in Kuznetsov's mechanised corps were disabled due to shortages of spare parts. By contrast, although the Wehrmacht too faced logistic problems, it would at least start the campaign with all of Army Group North's tanks operational. This, combined with the poor level of training in nearly every part of the Red Army, meant that the advantage lay hugely with the Germans.

Soviet plans for a possible war with Germany had been in existence for several years. The primary concern in the north was the defence of Leningrad, which was seen as a centre for the mass mobilisation of Soviet forces. Both Kuznetsov's Baltic Special Military District and the Leningrad Military District would seek to protect the city from early attack. Kuznetsov's forces were expected to contain any German attack and bring it to a standstill between the frontier and the River Daugava, while General Markhian Michailovich Popov's Leningrad Military District dealt with any incursion by the Finns. Once these initial objectives had been achieved, the two districts would seek to achieve air superiority over the attackers, and then stand ready to participate in centrally directed counter-offensives.[26] The plan assumed that it would take the Wehrmacht at least 15 days to prepare for a war, and that the Soviet Union would be aware of these preparations; the reality was that despite repeated warnings from a variety of sources, the Soviet leadership was taken completely by surprise by the start of *Barbarossa*. Kuznetsov's local plans were to use these 15 days to move his troops to the frontier – most divisions had only a single regiment on the border, with the rest of their personnel in peacetime billets some way to the rear. Once the fighting began, he intended to use his two mechanised corps to mount an early and decisive armoured counter-thrust to break up and destroy the advancing German spearheads. It does not appear to have occurred to anyone within the Soviet chain of command that they might not have the precious 15 days to prepare for war. In any event, the deficiencies in ammunition, fuel and spare parts could not possibly have been remedied in such a short time. The Red Army would enter a desperate struggle for survival with huge handicaps.

Soviet operational doctrine in 1941 was in a confused state. During the inter-war years, visionary officers like Mikhail Tukhachevsky perceived that the scale of modern war prevented the more traditional approach of seeking a single decisive battle:

> Since it is impossible, with the extended fronts of modern times, to destroy the enemy's army at a single blow, we are obligated to try to do this gradually by

operations which will be more costly to the enemy than to ourselves ... In short, a series of destructive operations conducted on logical principles and linked together by an uninterrupted pursuit may take the place of the decisive battle that was the form of engagement in the armies of the past, which fought on shorter fronts.[27]

As Soviet doctrine developed – often in the face of considerable resistance from more traditionally minded senior officers – the engagement and attrition of the enemy's forces as outlined by Tukhachevsky became combined with the concept of deep operations, devised and described in detail by contemporaries such as Georgi Isserson and Vladimir Triandaffilov, which required semi-independent mobile formations to operate against the enemy's supply and command lines, in order to disrupt and paralyse the enemy throughout the depth of his deployment.

Heavily involved in the restructuring of the Red Army in the early 1930s, Tukhachevsky developed airborne units, equipped with light armour and artillery, that were far ahead of their contemporaries. He was an outspoken proponent of combined arms formations, and his leading role in modernising the Red Army earned him promotion to field marshal in 1935. The following year, he formalised his views in *Vremmenyi Polevoi Ustav RKKA* ('New Field Service Regulations of the Red Army'). As a result of this document, he has often been credited with being the author of the 'deep operations' theories that were first articulated and developed by Isserson and Triandaffilov, which he attempted to build into future Red Army doctrine. Nevertheless, he had clearly given some thought to such concepts himself, writing in 1924:

> The setting up of a deep battle – that is the simultaneous disruption of the enemy's tactical layout over its entire depth – requires two things of tanks. On the one hand they must help the infantry forward and accompany it; on the other they must penetrate into the enemy's rear, both to disorganize him and to isolate his main forces from the reserves at his disposal. This deep penetration by tanks must create in the enemy's rear an obstacle for him onto which he must be forced back and on which his main forces must be destroyed. At the same time this breakthrough must destroy the enemy's artillery, cut his communications and capture his headquarters.[28]

Whilst his reputation as a ground breaking military theoretician has benefited from his incorporation of the ideas of others, there can be no question of his own revolutionary views, as can be seen in his observations about the future development of air warfare, written in 1931:

> The achievements in modern technology, which include automatic stabilisation of aircraft aloft, open new possibilities in conducting large-scale air operations even in adverse weather conditions. The combination of automatic stabilisers, television and the utilisation of infrared equipment will soon permit conducting complex operations, regardless of fog or cloud cover.[29]

In addition to understanding the developments that were changing the nature of each component of the military machine – air power, artillery, tanks, infantry weapons etc. – Tukhachevsky grasped the importance of integrating these different weapons together, in order to maximise their efficacy. Such integration, he argued, would require a mindset amongst officers that was not dissimilar to the German requirements for *Auftragstaktik*:

> The best results will be achieved in battle when all commanders, from the highest to the lowest, are trained in the spirit of bold initiative. *Personal initiative is of decisive importance*. Proper control on the part of the senior commander involves: a clear and succinct manner of setting forth missions; the proper selection of the direction of attack and the timely concentration of sufficiently strong forces for the purpose; provision for proper cooperation of units and for the greatest possible utilization of personal initiative; [and] support and exploitation of success at any particular point of the front.[30]

Unfortunately, Tukhachevsky was one of the first victims of Stalin's purges of the Red Army. He was arrested in 1937, and confessed under duress that he was working with German spies. It has been suggested that he had in fact contacted anti-Stalin groups during a visit to the west in 1936, but it seems that he was the victim of high-level plotting. Stalin was determined to purge the Red Army, which he regarded as the only institution capable of overthrowing him, and an agent working for the NKVD passed forged documents to the Germans implying that Tukhachevsky was plotting against Stalin. The Germans saw an opportunity to discredit a visionary and powerful Soviet senior officer, and forged further documents to implicate Tukhachevsky.[31] Found guilty of treason, he was executed on 11 June 1937, less than three weeks after his arrest.

The widespread purges that followed Tukhachevsky's execution effectively destroyed any possibility of the Soviet military command being able to show the sort of personal initiative so highly prized in the *Red Army Field Service Regulations*.

Initiative became a dangerous trait for any Soviet officer, and was replaced by a rigid adherence to orders from above. The Red Army would therefore respond to the German assault in an inflexible manner, with units at all levels struggling to carry out orders that had been rendered meaningless by the pace of the German advance. It would take the Red Army several years to relearn the importance of allowing its officers the freedom to improvise and show initiative.

A further setback was an imprecise understanding of the lessons of the Spanish Civil War and the Winter War against Finland. These conflicts raised doubts about the value of large mechanised formations, and as a result Soviet armour was reorganised into smaller divisions instead of large tank corps. These new divisions would prove to be far too weak to stand against their equivalent German opponents in 1941. In light of the German successes of 1939 and 1940, attempts were made to reverse this trend, but these were incomplete by the onset of *Barbarossa*. Indeed, Timoshenko did not anticipate that the process would be finished until mid-1942.[32]

The road to war was probably an inevitable one. Hitler clearly intended to attack the Soviet Union at some point, and preparations began over a year before the actual onset of hostilities. Meanwhile, at a political level at least, the Molotov–Ribbentrop Pact seemed to be working in the first few months. Moscow instructed communist parties across Europe to oppose the war, condemning the British and French as reactionary capitalists. Trade arrangements allowed Germany to escape the impact of any British attempts to enforce a blockade, but by the summer of 1940, the pact was showing signs of strain. Despite the explicit statements in the secret protocol about spheres of influence, the Germans were concerned about Soviet moves against Finland and the Baltic States, while the Soviet Union grew increasingly impatient with Germany's failure to keep up with payments for grain and raw materials. The fall of France left Stalin feeling that war with Germany might come sooner rather than later, and he found it difficult to retain a veneer of courtesy when complimenting Schulenburg on the German victory. At one stage, he complained to Molotov: 'Couldn't they put up any resistance at all? Now Hitler's going to beat our brains in!'[33]

However, the continued resistance of Britain appeared to reassure Stalin that Hitler would remain occupied in the west, at least for the time being, and there was a brief relaxation in tension. In November 1940, Molotov visited Berlin for talks about the areas of friction between the two powers, particularly Finland and the Balkans. The Germans were evasive when Molotov tried to pin them down on their intentions in Rumania and Bulgaria. During the visit, there was an air raid on Berlin. Ribbentrop tried to reassure Molotov that the British were finished. 'If that's so,' asked Molotov, 'why are we in this shelter and whose bombs are those falling?'[34]

Molotov's persistent probing about the Balkans might have triggered a final decision in Berlin. Hitler signed a directive authorising detailed planning for *Barbarossa* on 18 December 1940. Stalin was informed of this by his spies less than two weeks later. Although this galvanised the Soviet leader into a rearmament programme, he remained ambivalent, veering between fear of Germany and insistence that there would be no immediate war. At one stage, when Georgi Zhukov, who would become the greatest Soviet general of the war, tried to draw his attention to the German build-up in Poland, Stalin replied that the Germans had reassured him that this was merely a training exercise. Soviet and British measures in Yugoslavia resulted in the pro-German regime being overthrown, and rather than risk an invasion of the Soviet Union with a potentially hostile Yugoslavia to the rear, Hitler was forced to postpone *Barbarossa* while he sent troops into the Balkan nation. To Stalin's disappointment, Yugoslavia fell in less than two weeks. Any respite from the threat of invasion was a short one.

As 1941 wore on, the signs of impending hostilities were there for all to see. Unfortunately for Stalin, his own past record didn't help matters. The head of the NKVD's foreign department, Vsevolod Merkulov, and Filip Golikov, chief of military intelligence, were both acutely aware that they were in their posts because their predecessors had been executed by Stalin. Consequently, they were anxious not to bring Stalin's wrath upon themselves, and ensured that Stalin heard what they thought he wanted to hear. Schulenburg, the German ambassador in Moscow, who was opposed to a German invasion of the Soviet Union, tried to drop hints to Dekanozov, the Soviet official who had overseen the absorption of Lithuania and was now Soviet ambassador to Berlin. Dekanozov reported his conversation to Stalin, who dismissed it, suggesting that German disinformation was now even reaching the upper levels of the diplomatic service. Finally, on 12 May, Stalin agreed to mobilisation of 500,000 reserves and more troops being moved closer to the frontier, but continued to pour scorn on intelligence reports, including those that gave the actual date of the invasion. Aware that the Red Army needed more time to prepare for a war, Stalin continued to insist that there could therefore be no possibility of war, and refused to take proper measures for fear of triggering a conflict. Even on the eve of the invasion, with alarming news coming from all quarters – almost all of Germany's diplomats' families had left Moscow, German ships had left Soviet ports even before they had unloaded their cargo, and German deserters were giving detailed information about the timing of the attack – Stalin veered between accepting that a war was about to begin, and musing whether Hitler really would attack. After the bloody purges of the preceding years, even those who believed the reports were not prepared to act against Stalin's instructions, which remained the same right to the end: do nothing to provoke the Germans.

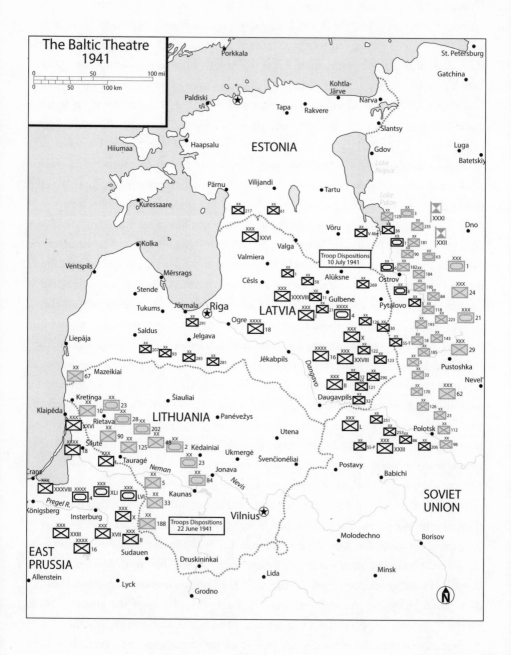

Chapter 3

THE WEHRMACHT IN FULL FLOOD

Shortly after 0300hrs on 22 June 1941, the Wehrmacht's artillery began to fire on Soviet border positions. In Army Group North's sector, the bombardment was relatively short, as there were few hard targets within close range of the border. *Luftflotte 1*, providing air support for the army group, sent nearly 400 aircraft north in its first strike as German troops began to move forward. The toughest resistance was due north of the former Lithuanian city of Klaipėda, now known as Memel. 291st Infantry Division ran into a stubbornly held strongpoint, where Leutnant Weinrowski became Army Group North's first confirmed casualty.[1]

Overhead, the Luftwaffe was in complete control. Wilhelm Lubbeck, a soldier in 58th Infantry Division, was a little distance from the front line, as his division was part of XXXVIII Corps, held in reserve. He was still close enough to the frontier to hear the initial moments of the war:

> A cascade of explosions reverberated around us. Our artillery unleashed a short but devastating bombardment of the enemy's positions, and the flashes of light from the explosions lit the entire eastern horizon. Then, as dawn broke, a ceaseless droning echoed in the sky above us. Wave after wave of planes were appearing – Heinkels and Junkers, Stukas and Messerschmits – all flying east.[2]

The initial German air strike accounted for over 100 Soviet aircraft before they could even get into the air. At 0715hrs, an optimistic order was sent to the Red Army Air Force, calling for immediate massed strikes against German positions to a depth of up to 90 miles. Only a few aircraft managed to get airborne, and fewer still reached the border zone. Their impact on the battle was negligible.

As the hot summer sun rose into a cloudless sky, German armoured forces poured forward almost unchecked. Even the infantry made swift progress; on the Baltic coast, 291st Infantry Division made up for time lost in overcoming the stubborn border defences, and pushed on to reach Latvian territory in mid-afternoon. Its spearheads covered a remarkable 41 miles by the end of the day, most of it on foot. When the division reached Liepāja – known as Libau to the Germans – on 23 June, heavy fighting broke out with Major General Nikolai Dedaev's 67th Rifle Division. It took the Germans nearly three days to take the town: 'The house and street battle was very bitterly fought. Enemy machine-gun fire spat from camouflaged firing points. Resistance could only be broken by heavy infantry guns firing from open positions, and the shells of heavy howitzers and mortars.'[3] Much of the Soviet 67th Rifle Division was wiped out. The remnants withdrew across Courland towards Riga. Dedaev was one of the dead.

8th Panzer Division, from Manstein's LVI Panzer Corps, demonstrated on the first day of *Barbarossa* the power of a panzer division, combined with the flexibilities of *Auftragstaktik*. The division's 10th Panzer Regiment was equipped with a mixture of Pz.II, Pz.III and Pz.IV tanks, but its most numerous tank was the Czech-designed Pz.38(t), a 10-ton vehicle with a long-barrelled 37mm gun. With only 30mm of armour, it was not a particularly well-armed or well-armoured vehicle, but it had an excellent maintenance record and was regarded by its crews as superior to the German Pz.I and Pz.II. Manstein's operational goal for the opening phase of the war was to advance as fast as possible to secure crossings over the River Daugava, widely regarded as the best defensive line available to the Red Army. If the bridges at Daugavpils could be captured intact, and a bridgehead established on the north-east bank, it would be almost impossible for the Red Army to prevent all of Lithuania and Latvia, as well as a substantial part of Estonia, from being overrun.

The task of Generalmajor Erich Brandenberger's division was to secure the bridges before they could be destroyed by the retreating Red Army. Brandenberger and his staff studied the maps of the terrain they would have to cover, carefully weighing up the limited options, given the poor road network over which they would be operating. They concluded that there were 37 waterways between them and their objective, seven of them at least 25 yards wide.[4] In order to help deal with these problems, the division requested – and was assigned – additional bridging units.

The initial objective was the River Dubysa, and Brandenberger divided his division into three battlegroups. On the right flank of the division was *Kampfgruppe Crisolli*, with the bulk of a motorised rifle regiment, a reinforced motorcycle battalion, a battalion of tanks, and a combat engineer company. On the left flank was *Kampfgruppe Scheller*, a more powerful group with a motorised rifle regiment, a battalion of tanks, a reinforced reconnaissance battalion, and combat engineers and additional forces.[5] *Kampfgruppe Bodenhausen* was ready to support either battlegroup, or exploit their successes. It was anticipated that the main breakthrough would be made by *Kampfgruppe Scheller*, which would be preceded in its advance by an infantry regiment from the neighbouring 290th Infantry Division – the infantry would overcome the Soviet border defences, after which the armour and mechanised troops would push forward rapidly. True to the principles of *Auftragstaktik*, Brandenberger positioned himself with Scheller's battlegroup.

Crisolli's first wave included his combat engineers, led by Hauptmann Hallauer. They rapidly cleared the road of Soviet mines, despite being under constant fire, and the waiting armour was rapidly unleashed. Hallauer was badly wounded during his mine-clearing operation, and was awarded the Knight's Cross; however, he died of his wounds two days later, before he could receive the decoration. The vehicles of Crisolli's battlegroup suddenly found themselves advancing through open country – the Soviet defences on their sector proved to be no more than the immediate frontier line. Before 0600hrs, Crisolli signalled division headquarters that he had reached the outskirts of Yubarkas, and minutes later a tank platoon rattled across the bridges over the River Mituva. In a brief fight, Crisolli proceeded to secure the town. Meanwhile, further to the north-west, 8th Panzer Division's reconnaissance elements which were moving forward in front of *Kampfgruppe Scheller* ran into tough resistance in dense woodland. Brandenberger immediately saw that the division's breakthrough – and therefore its axis of advance – probably lay with Crisolli rather than Scheller, and at 0734hrs he advised his headquarters that he was moving to accompany the more successful battlegroup.[6]

Crisolli pushed east under cloudless skies. Shortly after midday, the leading motorcycle company of his battlegroup reached Seredžius, a remarkable 40 miles east of Yubarkas. At about the same time, Generaloberst Hoepner, commander of 4th Panzer Group, visited division headquarters, where he was briefed on developments by Brandenberger's chief of staff. As with Brandenberger's own position with his lead elements, it was characteristic of German doctrine that Hoepner should visit his divisions in order to keep pace with developments. In a similar manner, Manstein visited 8th Panzer Division's headquarters shortly after, and added his approval of Brandenberger's plans, further urging that the division press on to reach Ariogala before the end of the day. He need not have worried. The division's diary recorded:

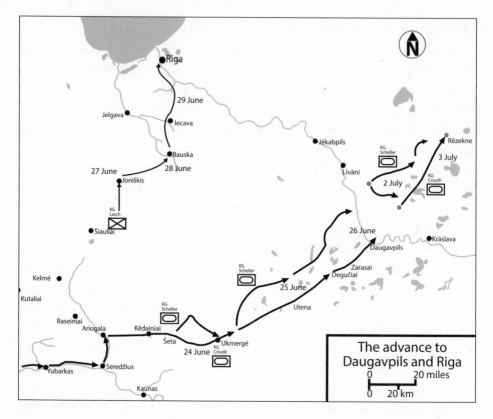

The bulk of *Gruppe A* [Crisolli's battlegroup] had meanwhile succeeded, without further fighting, in advancing to the Ariogala sector, where the flanking high ground was occupied by the enemy. The bridge from Ariogala was unusable by vehicles, but a ford with a firm bed, suitable for all vehicles, was discovered in close proximity to the road, across which the tanks rapidly began to cross, followed by the armoured personnel carriers, for deployment against the high ground at Ariogala.

This rapid thrust, which was certainly not expected by the enemy, succeeded in breaking enemy resistance, including armoured cars, and in capturing the high ground covering the ford.

At the same time, the assault on the main road bridge of Ariogala, which had been ordered by the division commander, supported by our artillery and the tank battalion, was carried out and completed successfully by 1725.[7]

A few minutes later, Manstein joined Brandenberger at the vital road bridge over the Dubysa that had just been captured. Crisolli's battlegroup had advanced over 48 miles from its start line, but there was still daylight. Within the limits of remaining fuel,

Brandenberger was ordered to press on with his tanks towards Kadainiai. Barely two miles from Ariogala, the German spearhead ran into troops that it mistakenly identified as elements of the Soviet 5th Tank Division, and was forced to halt at 2300hrs. In less than 20 hours, these leading German troops had covered 55 miles from their starting positions. 8th Panzer Division was admittedly dispersed over a large area, with *Kampfgruppe Scheller* still struggling through the border fortifications, but the day's objectives had been achieved with time to spare.[8]

Gustav Klinter, moving forward with the division's motorised infantry, remembered his first sight of Soviet dead:

The air had that putrefying and pervasive burnt smell reminiscent of the battle zone and all nerves and senses began to detect the breath of war. Suddenly, all heads switched to the right. The first dead of the Russian campaign lay before our eyes like a spectre – a Mongolian skull smashed in combat, a torn uniform and bare abdomen split by shell splinters. The column drew up and then accelerated ahead – the picture fell behind us. I sank back thoughtfully into my seat.[9]

The onset of hostilities had converted the Baltic region into the North-west Front; all along it, Kuznetsov's armies struggled to bring their infantry forward from their barracks. The regiments deployed along the border were scattered and annihilated during the morning, and many of the columns hurrying forward, harassed from the air, ran into the advancing German forces, which sent them reeling back in disarray. The Soviet 48th Rifle Division was spotted by German bombers and subjected to a sustained bombardment; it suffered heavy losses before it could even get into battle. Soviet commanders at all levels struggled to keep up with events. The few reports reaching them from the front line spoke of unimaginable disasters, and there was little or no information available from aerial reconnaissance. At the very highest levels, Stalin's subordinates argued about who should wake their leader and tell him what was happening. Some, like Georgi Maximilianovich Malenkov, Chairman of the Council of Ministers, even attempted to bully those telephoning Moscow to change their reports.[10] The Politburo met an hour after the German invasion started, and Stalin continued to refuse to authorise full-scale counter-attacks – it was possible, he argued, that the fighting was due to provocative action by German generals, acting without the knowledge or authority of Hitler. It was only after Schulenburg was summoned to the Kremlin, where he told Molotov that Berlin had been forced to take action because of Soviet troop concentrations near the border, that Stalin finally accepted that his nation was indeed at war.

Acting effectively in an intelligence vacuum, the Soviet People's Commissariat of Defence – essentially the defence ministry – sent Directive 3 to Kuznetsov:

> While firmly holding on to the coast of the Baltic Sea, deliver a powerful blow from the Kaunas region into the flank and rear of the enemy Suvalki grouping, destroy it in cooperation with the Western Front, and capture the Suvalki region by the end of 24 June.[11]

This order required Kuznetsov and his neighbouring Western Front to the south-east to cooperate in order to destroy what amounted to Hoepner's 4th Panzer Group, Busch's 16th Army, and parts of General Hermann Hoth's 3rd Panzer Group in the German Army Group Centre. Even without the losses already incurred, such an undertaking would have been beyond the power of the two Soviet fronts. In the circumstances, under hostile skies and with major casualties already reducing their strength, it was a ludicrous order. In any event, General Dmitri Gregorovich Pavlov's Western Front was in even worse shape than Kuznetsov's front, driven back in chaos by two German panzer groups. Kuznetsov received the order at 1000hrs on 23 June, by which stage he had already issued orders to his two mechanised corps to begin their counter-attacks. His pre-war plans called for these counter-attacks to be made against the main enemy concentration, but in the absence of clear information about German movements, he simply ordered the two corps forward according to pre-planned axes of advance into the area where the Germans appeared to have made the most progress: 12th Mechanised Corps would advance from Šiauliai and move south-east, while 3rd Mechanised Corps would attack from Kėdainiai towards the north-west.

12th Mechanised Corps was commanded by Major General Nikolai Mikhailovich Shestopalov, a former cavalryman. He dispatched his 23rd and 28th Tank Divisions towards the enemy, but the attack was doomed from the start. Ammunition and fuel shortages, combined with insufficient time to gather the various sub-units into an orderly whole, and a complete lack of knowledge of the whereabouts of German units, resulted in a piecemeal attack.

23rd Tank Division was deployed to the west of 28th Tank Division. Near Kutaliai, 23rd Tank Division encountered elements of the German 11th and 1st Infantry Divisions, and though it made some initial progress, a confused battle continued for a day before the exhausted Soviet division was forced back, abandoning many of its tanks as they ran out of fuel. A little to the east, the Soviet 28th Tank Division attacked south against the 1st and 21st Infantry Divisions; the two sides first encountered each other at dusk on 23 June:

Between 12 and 15 tanks drove down the road running south-east from Kaltinėnai. At the same moment, Gefreiter Hasse from 14 Coy, Inf.Reg.22, had brought his gun into position at the road fork a kilometre north of the Butkaičiai estate. The gunner shot up six of the rapidly advancing tanks at close range, even though the gun was almost overrun.[12]

Hasse was probably fortunate that the tanks he faced were either T26 or BT7 models; his 37mm gun would have been ineffective against the heavier Soviet armour.

The German axis of advance was towards the north-east, while the Soviet armour was attempting to attack southwards. Three days of fighting followed, with the increasingly bewildered Soviet units struggling to react to enemy movements. Through a mixture of enemy action, mechanical breakdowns and fuel shortages, the two Soviet divisions lost all but 45 of their original 749 tanks, and were driven back in a chaotic retreat.[13] For the commander of 28th Tank Division, Ivan Danilovich Cherniakhovsky, it was a chastening baptism of fire. He survived the setback, and eventually rose to command a front during 1944–45.

Kuznetsov's other major armoured formation, 3rd Mechanised Corps, was deployed north-west of Kaunas, and it too set off in its pre-planned counter-attack. Its commander, Alexei Vasileevich Kurkin, sent 5th Tank Division and 84th Motorised Division to support the hard-pressed units of 11th Army, struggling to hold back Busch's 16th Army on the approaches to Kaunas. The remaining unit of 3rd Mechanised Corps, 2nd Tank Division, drove north-west into the area where Hoepner's 4th Panzer Group was operating.

Meanwhile, Brandenberger was busy making preparations for the second day of combat. Much of 8th Panzer Division's firepower was now transferred to *Kampfgruppe Crisolli*, so that it could make the most of its remarkable breakthrough. But for most of 23 June, the battlegroup remained stationary near Ariogala. There were several reasons for this. Firstly, Brandenberger wished to bring forward other combat elements of his division, to avoid stops at a later stage for regrouping. Secondly, supplies had to be brought forward. The poor road network over which the Wehrmacht was operating hindered both of these factors; Scheller's battlegroup, hurrying to catch up with Crisolli, was ordered off the main road for two hours by corps-level traffic police while 3rd Motorised Infantry Division was given priority. But an additional factor was that German reconnaissance had spotted the impending attack of the Soviet 2nd Tank Division, and given that Crisolli's battlegroup at Ariogala was the closest German unit, it seemed likely that this was the intended target of the Soviet attack. Consequently, an order to advance swiftly to Kėdainiai was cancelled, and the German forces in Ariogala

– increasing in strength as more elements of 8th Panzer Division arrived – adopted a defensive posture. It was only in mid-afternoon that it became clear that the Soviet armoured force was headed for Raseiniai, and was completely oblivious to the presence of 8th Panzer Division; indeed, it seems that the Soviet High Command had lost all track of where the German division was.

As the axis of the Soviet attack became clear, Hoepner briefly debated whether he should divert 8th Panzer Division to join what was to become the battle of Raseiniai. After some deliberation, he decided that the division should press on towards its original objective. However strong the Soviet force was, the increasing dislocation caused by a swift advance to the Daugava was more important. Consequently, at 1700hrs, he ordered 8th Panzer Division to push on through Kėdainiai towards Šėta.[14] The German forces around Raseiniai would have to deal with the Soviet 2nd Tank Division on their own.

Immediately, Brandenberger dispatched his reconnaissance battalion towards Kėdainiai, followed by the rest of the division. The town was captured at 0330hrs on 24 June, with its vital bridge intact. The next objective was Šėta, about six miles further east. Relieved that the day spent waiting around Ariogala had not resulted in any apparent strengthening of the Soviet lines, Brandenberger pressed on. Remnants of the Soviet 5th and 33rd Rifle Divisions attempted to hold Šėta, to no avail. Although the nearest neighbouring German unit was 27 miles away, Brandenberger reaped the benefits of being right at the front of the thrust: he could see for himself the complete chaos brought about by his rapid advance. Sensing that a pause would probably be more dangerous than continuing the drive, he pressed on to Ukmergė, reaching the town towards the end of the day, an advance of 30 miles from Ariogala. Despite reports of Soviet forces approaching him from almost all points of the compass – even as Šėta was being captured, *Kampfgruppe Crisolli* beat off an attack by about 15 Soviet tanks, including the division's first encounter with a KV1 – and with some elements of his division still strung out over a distance of up to 36 miles, Brandenberger remained bullish about his prospects, and drove Crisolli forward an additional six miles from Ukmergė before calling a halt for the day.

Further to the north-west, though, the German armour around Raseiniai was having a far less comfortable time. Igor Nikolaevich Soliankin had commanded the Soviet 2nd Tank Division for a year. He had 300 tanks at his disposal, including 50 heavy KV1s, and a small number of KV2s. His division began to move north-west on 23 June, but did not encounter the enemy until late the following day. Meanwhile, XLI Panzer Corps was advancing north-east towards the town of Raseiniai. 6th Panzer Division had divided into two battlegroups. *Kampfgruppe Seckendorf* had a

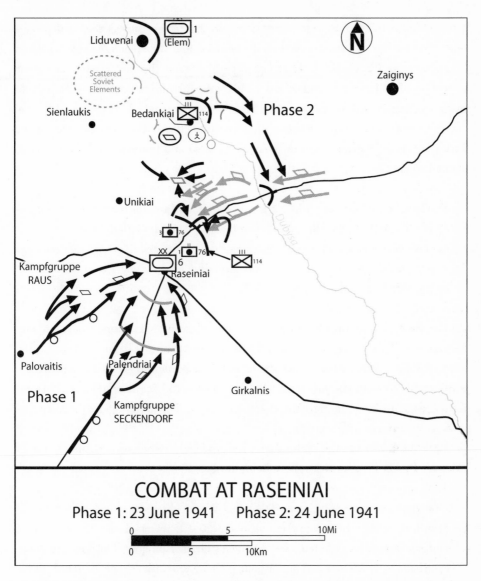

COMBAT AT RASEINIAI
Phase 1: 23 June 1941   Phase 2: 24 June 1941

rifle battalion, a motorcycle battalion, a tank battalion, and engineering, anti-tank and anti-aircraft support, and was tasked with pushing up to Raseiniai along the main road from the south, while *Kampfgruppe Raus*, a little further west, advanced on a converging axis, with a battalion each of infantry and tanks. The division's reconnaissance battalion moved ahead to seize crossings over the River Dubysa, to the north-east of Raseiniai. Although it is a small river, the steep sides of the Dubysa valley offered the retreating Red Army a potential defensive line, and Generalmajor Franz Landgraf, commander of 6th Panzer Division, was anxious to secure a substantial bridgehead as soon as possible.

At first, in the face of scattered and uncoordinated resistance, the battlegroups made good progress, rapidly securing Raseiniai while the reconnaissance battalion began to cross the Dubysa and set up a perimeter on the east bank. During the afternoon of 24 June, Seckendorf moved his units forward towards the bridges held by the reconnaissance battalion, while Raus set off northward, to secure additional crossings near Katauskiai. At about the same time, Soliankin's armour reached the perimeter of the German reconnaissance battalion, and immediately attacked with about 100 tanks:

> The battalion might have held out longer, had it not been for the monster tanks, whose 70-cm tracks literally ground everything in their path into the earth – guns, motorcycles, and men. There was not a single weapon in the bridgehead that could stop them. After the massacre, the tanks waded through the Dubysa, easily crawling up the 45-degree banks.[15]

As the Soviet tanks breasted the top of the western valley slope, they ran into Seckendorf's battlegroup, which was hastily deploying into a defensive line. To the horror of the Germans, they discovered that the heavyweight KV1s were almost invulnerable to German anti-tank fire. The mass of Soviet armour rolled forward relentlessly, breaking through the defensive line and penetrating to the division's artillery positions a little to the rear.

Both the KV1s and the even heavier KV2s seemed to be unstoppable. A courier from 1st Panzer Division witnessed the fighting:

> Our companies opened fire from 700 meters. We got closer and closer, but it didn't disturb the enemy. Soon we were only about 50–100 meters from each other. A fantastic engagement opened up – without any German progress. The Soviet tanks continued their advance and our armour-piercing projectiles simply bounced off. The Soviet tanks withstood point-blank range fire from both our 50mm and 75mm guns. A KV2 was hit more than 70 times, and not a single round penetrated. A very few of the Soviet tanks were immobilized and eventually also destroyed as we managed to shoot at their tracks, and then eventually brought up the artillery to hammer them at close range. Assault engineers then attacked by foot with satchel charges.[16]

Unfortunately for Soliankin's division, the limitations imposed by their lack of radios, poor training and outdated doctrine made themselves felt all too soon. The tanks diverged and set off on individual battles, rather than concentrating on a single objective. There was almost no infantry support, and the tanks soon began to run short of fuel and ammunition. Nevertheless, there were still difficult moments ahead for the Germans, who found themselves driven back most of the way to Raseiniai. A single tank – a KV1 in some accounts, a KV2 in others – succeeded in penetrating deep into the German position, shooting up a column of German trucks in the process, and stopped on a road across soft ground. Four 50mm anti-tank guns from 6th Panzer Division's anti-tank battalion engaged it, hitting it several times; the tank returned fire, knocking out each gun in turn. A heavy 88mm gun from the division's anti-aircraft battalion – the most potent anti-tank gun of its day – was laboriously manoeuvred behind the Soviet tank. It opened fire at about 800 yards range, but before it could score a hit, the KV1 knocked it out.

Under cover of darkness, German combat engineers crept up to the tank with satchel charges, which failed to destroy it, though they may have damaged its tracks. As it grew light on 25 June, German tanks fired on the Soviet behemoth from nearby woodland, while a second 88mm gun was brought around to attack the KV1 from behind. Several shots were fired, but only two penetrated the tank. As German infantry approached, the battered Soviet tank attempted to fight them off with machine-gun fire, but grenades thrown through its hatches finally brought its resistance to an end. In some accounts of the battle, the Germans showed their respect for such a brave foe by burying the crew with full military honours, while other accounts suggest that the crew escaped during the night after running out of ammunition.[17]

The exhausted Soviet tanks finally came to a halt immediately to the east of Raseiniai. Meanwhile, the Germans were swiftly regaining their composure. 6th Panzer Division was ordered to contain the Soviet thrust along its western and southern edges, with Seckendorf's badly mauled battlegroup playing a blocking role, and Raus' battlegroup moving along the Dubysa valley to the site of the initial battle between the reconnaissance battalion and Soliankin's tanks; 1st Panzer Division, which had crossed the Dubysa at Lyduvėnai, a little to the north of Raseiniai, abandoned its plans to continue its northerly advance and executed a sharp turn to the right. While 36th Motorised Infantry Division deployed in its place at the northern tip of the German advance, 1st Panzer Division followed Raus' battlegroup along the Dubysa, and then pushed further east and south, into the rear of Soliankin's division. The Soviet 11th Rifle Division, which had been too badly battered by 1st Panzer Division to make any offensive move of its own, could only watch helplessly as the Germans manoeuvred with impunity. 48th Rifle Division, already badly cut up by German air attacks, should have been supporting the Soviet armour, but after the heavy German air attacks of the previous day, was still struggling to organise itself. Many of its units were overrun by the German armour and routed. Barely a day after the start of the war, it had lost 70 per cent of its personnel, and all of its heavy equipment. Its commander, Major General Pavel Vasileevich Bogdanov, was taken prisoner. Later in the war, he appeared to join the German cause, becoming intelligence officer to the 1st Russian National SS Brigade. However, he deserted in 1943, and joined a local partisan unit, which promptly placed him under arrest. He was imprisoned until 1950, when he was condemned to death as a traitor and executed.

According to the war diary of 1st Panzer Division, its spearheads made contact with troops of 6th Panzer Division at Sokaiciai at 0838hrs on 25 June, completing the encirclement of the Soviet 2nd Tank Division. Fighting continued for another day, but the outcome was never in doubt. Almost all of Soliankin's 2nd Tank Division was within the encirclement, unable to retreat as its vehicles were out of fuel; only a single BT7 tank and 400 men escaped.[18] Soliankin died with his division, and the Germans counted over Soviet 200 tanks destroyed or abandoned. Their own losses were substantial, but importantly, they ended the battle in possession of the contested ground: their repair teams would eventually be able to return many of their vehicles to action.

The battle of Raseiniai resulted in a brief pause in the German advance, as 1st Panzer Division was forced to divert its forces for the encirclement. By its conclusion, Kuznetsov's front had no substantial armoured assets left, but the consequences of the action were far more widespread. Like other such engagements along the vast front line, it showed the Germans that their assumptions about the superiority of their armour were wildly optimistic. It was one of many battles that stimulated development of larger, heavier German tanks, though it would take nearly two years before these vehicles appeared in any significant numbers.

Elsewhere, German progress was far more straightforward. Lithuanian nationalists in Kaunas, part of the Lithuanian Activist Front, commenced their uprising on the first day of the war. There was sporadic fighting with the Soviet garrison, resulting in the deaths of about 200 insurgents, but the first decisive success for the Lithuanians came on 23 June when they seized a radio station, and later that day broadcast an appeal to the Germans to bombard the Soviet forces that were already leaving the city. At the same time, the radio station declared the creation of a provisional Lithuanian government. A day later, the reconnaissance battalion of 123rd Infantry Division reached Kaunas, followed by sections of the neighbouring 121st Infantry Division. Lithuanians lined the streets in large numbers to greet the German forces, hoping that they came as liberators rather than as conquerors. There were uprisings elsewhere against the Soviet forces, many – though not all – of them coordinated by the Lithuanian Activist Front. In some cases, entire companies of Lithuanian soldiers, whose units had been incorporated into the Red Army, either deserted *en masse* or actively turned against the Soviets.[19]

Whilst the bulk of the German troops invading Lithuania were part of Army Group North, the Vilnius area fell within the remit of Army Group Centre. 7th Panzer Division, part of 3rd Panzer Group, reached the town of Alytus at midday on 22 June, where two key bridges were seized over the River Niemen. As the division's tanks attempted to exploit their two bridgeheads, they ran into dug-in Soviet tanks on the high ground to the east, and suffered heavy losses. Repeated Soviet counter-attacks followed, but by dusk the two bridgeheads had coalesced and the Soviet forces were driven off.

After a night spent recovering and repairing damaged vehicles, 7th Panzer Division pushed on towards Vilnius the following morning, at first hindered more by burning woodland and fallen trees across the road than by Soviet resistance. Immediately to the west of Vilnius, the division's reconnaissance battalion ran into tougher resistance, but outflanked the Soviet defences and succeeded in seizing vital bridges required for a further advance. By the evening, elements of the reconnaissance battalion, reinforced by tanks, secured the high ground to the south-east of Vilnius, and as darkness fell armoured columns pushed north and seized the eastern parts of the city.[20]

Early the following morning, the division's motorcycle battalion captured the airfield outside Vilnius. As the division's tanks secured the eastern parts of the city, the infantry moved into the centre at first light:

> The city was decorated with Lithuanian flags, and the advancing troops were greeted with jubilation. Substantial materiel and food supplies were seized at the railway station, and about 50 aircraft were captured by German troops at the airfield. The infantry brigade, following the advance of the panzer regiment, took up positions south of the city. From the south, enemy armoured battlegroups launched repeated attacks on the division's columns and positions south of Vilnius; they were all beaten off.[21]

While Reinhardt's XLI Panzer Corps was delayed by the fighting around Raseiniai, its neighbouring formation, LVI Panzer Corps, continued to advance, aided greatly by the increasing dislocation in the Soviet front line: 8th Army was being driven north along the coast, while 11th Army found its line of retreat to the north cut off by the advancing German armour, and fell back to the east. In between, there were only scattered elements, and Manstein's corps was ideally positioned to take advantage of the gap that yawned ever wider in the Soviet lines. After a brief pause late on 24 June, to allow essential fuel and ammunition to be brought forward, Brandenberger once more organised his division's battlegroups. Crisolli was to advance on the right flank directly towards Daugavpils, with Scheller's battlegroup on the left; still lagging some distance behind, Scheller would join the advance as soon as he could, while Crisolli was to set off at first light on 25 June. After an advance of only nine miles, Crisolli was halted by determined Soviet resistance near Trakiniai. The Soviet forces fought a determined action to hold the line of yet another small river, and were only driven out when a group of German tanks made use of a nearby ford and outflanked them. By early afternoon, Brandenberger was with Crisolli's battlegroup as it motored into Utena, having advanced a further 33 miles, slightly halfway from its morning start line to its objective at Daugavpils.

Soviet artillery on high ground overlooking Utena subjected the German battlegroup to a short but heavy bombardment, and then Soviet light tanks, with infantry in support, attacked from the east. With more of his tanks arriving in a steady stream, Brandenberger deployed his armour to attack on a broad front either side of Utena, with support from whatever infantry was available. For the loss of one Pz.38(t) and one Pz.IV, his division captured or destroyed one Soviet tank, four armoured cars, and a variety of anti-tank guns and field guns. Pursuing the shattered Soviet troops, 8th Panzer Division's tanks pushed on to Degučiai.[22]

The vital bridges – the main road bridge, and a rail bridge about a mile to the west – over the Daugava at Daugavpils were now within striking range. In order to capture them, Brandenberger reinforced Crisolli's battlegroup to increase its strength to the bulk of his division's panzer regiment, four battalions of infantry (including one from 3rd Motorised Infantry Division), a motorcycle battalion, and an artillery battalion. But in order to maximise the chances of seizing the bridges intact on 26 June, Crisolli was also assigned 8 Company of the Brandenburg Regiment.

The Brandenburg Regiment was the Wehrmacht's 'special forces' unit, and owed its origins to a successful, if short-lived, battalion of Polish-speaking German soldiers who enjoyed conspicuous success in 1939, capturing and holding important road junctions in advance of the Wehrmacht. Under the aegis of the *Abwehr* – the military intelligence branch of the Wehrmacht – a new unit was raised after the end of the Polish campaign. In stark contrast to the racially selective policies of other German bodies such as the SS, the new unit specifically sought out soldiers who looked like, or actually were, Poles or Slavs. All recruits were required to be fluent in at least one language other than German, and were familiar with the customs and behaviour of the inhabitants of other countries. 8 Company, under the command of Oberleutnant Knaak, was made up of fluent Russian speakers. Dressed in Soviet uniforms, the company led the advance towards the bridges in two captured Red Army trucks.

The division's war diary described the advance to the Daugava:

10th Panzer Regiment set off in the early morning hours towards Daugavpils. After a short but tough fight, it succeeded in seizing the bridge at Zarasai in a surprise attack, breaking through the Russian defences there and pushing on to the Daugava bridges without halting.

With them was a detachment of 800th Regiment [the Brandenburgers] under the command of Oberleutnant Knaak, who had received a gunshot wound in a similar operation at Kėdainiai, but had stayed with his troops. The left group of 800th Regiment, which was sent against the railway bridge, drove past five enemy armoured cars and reached the bridge, where it encountered more enemy armoured cars, which it could not attack with its machine-guns. As a result, it pulled back to the main road to the south and took up positions near the road bridge. There, Feldwebel Krückeberg was able to cut through a cable, which he had guessed had been laid in preparation for demolition of the bridge.

The second group from 800th Regiment was deployed against the road bridge, with Oberleutnant Knaak in the leading vehicle. The Russian guards on the west side of the bridge, who were chatting to civilians, were taken completely by surprise and gunned down, and the group from 800th Regiment drove over the Daugava bridge to the other bank. Meanwhile, an anti-tank gun had been spotted there, and it fired on the leading vehicle, knocking it out and mortally wounding Oberleutnant Knaak. At the same time, a deadly fire started up from the Daugava bank, which was strongly occupied, and from all the houses on either side of the bridge.

It was thanks to the foresight of Oberstleutnant Fronhöfer that the tanks of 10th Panzer Regiment were following immediately behind the groups from 800th Regiment.

Although the tanks did not succeed in thrusting over the rail bridge to the east bank, as the enemy artillery fire had blown a large hole in the bridge and set off part of the demolition charge laid there, the tanks motored across the road bridge without pausing, destroyed the troops on the bank, engaged the Russians firing from the houses in an energetic firefight, and immediately thrust on into the inner part of the city, fighting everywhere with the Russians who were rushing up from all directions. Major Wendenburg sent a detachment along the east bank of the Daugava to the rear of the railway bridge, to secure it from behind.

These tanks too succeeded in rushing the railway bridge, which was thus secured by tanks at either end, and was in German hands ...

At the same time, the armoured personnel carrier company (1 Coy, 8th Rifle Regiment) under Oberleutnant von Flotow followed the tanks, and in further advance with the tanks, in heavy fighting, platoon alongside platoon, moved into the city.[23]

Fighting on the north-east bank of the Daugava was intense. The Soviet defenders – many of whom were identified by the Germans as 'tough Kirghizians' – attempted to disable the German tanks by rolling hand grenades under their tracks. At the same time, Soviet aircraft also attacked, but to no avail. The bulk of a German tank battalion, commanded by Major Wendenburg, broke through and secured the road running north-east from Daugavpils, and took up defensive positions to prevent any Soviet counter-attack. By mid-afternoon, with 8th Panzer Division's motorised infantry beginning to arrive, the balance tilted firmly in favour of Brandenberger's men. Some of the infantry were deployed to reinforce the defensive screen to the north-east, just in time to help intercept a determined Soviet counter-attack. A company of German tanks, led by Hauptmann Kühl, surged into the attacking Soviet forces, and claimed to have destroyed 20 light tanks, 20 field guns, and 17 anti-tank guns in a brief but fierce engagement, utterly disrupting the Soviet attack. One group of Soviet tanks succeeded in penetrating the German defences to the east, and accompanied by infantry, almost reached the road bridge before being brought to a halt by a German anti-tank battery that had only just crossed the river. By mid-evening, the Soviet attacks had all been repulsed.[24]

Further elements of 8th Panzer Division, including *Kampfgruppe Scheller*, continued to arrive throughout the night. On 27 June, units of 3rd Motorised Division also reached the Daugava, taking up positions to the right of 8th Panzer Division. Manstein's LVI Panzer Corps had advanced an astonishing 185 miles since crossing the border, and had completely dislocated Kuznetsov's defensive line. For their extraordinary achievements, Brandenberger, Crisolli and Fronhöfer were all awarded the Knight's Cross. The same award was granted posthumously to Knaak and Flotow; the latter, who led the armoured personnel carriers that crossed the road bridge immediately behind the tanks, was killed in the battle to secure the north-east bank.

In an attempt to restore the situation, STAVKA – the newly established Soviet High Command – ordered Berzarin's 27th Army, still in reserve, to fill the gap in the Soviet line, where Kuznetsov's two armies had retreated on diverging axes. To give it additional strength, Lelyushenko's 21st Mechanised Corps was attached to 27th Army, and 22nd Army was also dispatched to the area, to deploy around Kaunas and prevent further retreats by 11th Army. Berzarin was to establish a defensive line along the Daugava, but this would be of little benefit if 8th Panzer Division were able to exploit the bridgehead that it had already established. Both sides rushed troops to the area. The Red Army committed Lelyushenko's mechanised corps, supported by considerable air assets, to an attack against the bridgehead on 27 June, and heavy fighting erupted. German fighters of *Jagdgeschwader 54*, which had just deployed to the airfield in Daugavpils, found themselves engaged almost immediately in attempts to defend the city from Soviet aircraft. The confusion that reigned in Soviet circles is amply demonstrated by the arrival at the same airfield on the afternoon of 27 June of three Soviet reconnaissance aircraft, which were promptly captured by the Germans.[25]

Although the Soviet attempts to destroy the bridgehead across the Daugava continued until 29 June, the heaviest attacks were on the first day, and by 28 June, sufficient German forces had gathered for a resumption of the advance, with Soviet attacks restricted to the eastern part of the bridgehead. But in contrast to the opening days of *Barbarossa*, Brandenberger's immediate superiors – Manstein at LVI Panzer Corps and Hoepner at 4th Panzer Group – showed little appetite for another audacious surge forward. It seems that the sudden mood of caution originated at the headquarters of Army Group North. Generalfeldmarschall Wilhelm Ritter von Leeb had actually retired from active service in 1938 after 43 years in the army, and was a conservative figure, in every sense of the term. In 1938, he published a book entitled *Die Abwehr* ('Defence'), describing how the German army might deal with an attack from the west while German forces were committed in Poland. Unlike Hoepner and Manstein, he did not visit the front-line headquarters of his panzer forces, and was thus isolated from the confident mood that reigned there; similarly, he did not experience first-hand the sense of elation at the clear disintegration of the Soviet defences. Instead, he insisted that the forces on the Daugava hold their positions until the slow-moving infantry divisions of 16th Army arrived. An early advance, he insisted, would be too risky. Despite his own inclinations, Hoepner was forced to pass on these instructions to his corps commanders:

> The Commander in Chief of the Army Group is strongly influenced by the idea that given the existing situation, the Panzer Group alone cannot break enemy resistance between the Daugava and Leningrad and is taking measures to bring up the infantry armies closer yet to the Panzer Group.[26]

This appears to ignore the fact that a single division of the panzer group had completely disrupted Soviet resistance between the frontier and Daugavpils. On 29 June, Brandenberger interpreted his instructions to hold and enlarge the bridgehead as allowing him to probe forward, and pushed his division 20 miles further north, encountering only light Soviet resistance. Despite this, he was ordered to halt, and his division remained stationary for the next two days.

Although 8th Panzer Division was straining at its lead and was desperate to push on, German losses in the face of the Soviet assaults on Daugavpils were severe; *SS Division Totenkopf*, deployed from the German reserves, lost nearly a third of its combat strength, forcing the temporary disbandment of one of its regiments. But Soviet losses were heavier still. 21st Mechanised Corps lost 79 of its 107 tanks, and was unable to dislodge Manstein's bridgehead.[27] Gradually, even in the hard-contested eastern part of the bridgehead, the advantage tilted in favour of the Germans, who steadily levered the Soviet forces back. Exhausted and decimated, the Soviet divisions facing Manstein's corps – from west to east, 163rd, 46th, 185th, and 42nd Tank Divisions, with 112th Rifle Division at the eastern end of the line nearest Krāslava – were forced to concede defeat and withdrew north-east.

In any event, a prolonged defence along the line of the Daugava was now impossible. Moving up on Manstein's left flank, Reinhardt's XLI Panzer Corps reached the river on 28 June and took Jēkabpils that day, but another attempted *coup de main* by the Brandenburg Regiment failed to capture the bridge. In less than ten hours, German combat engineers built a pontoon bridge, while infantry crossed on rafts to secure the north bank. Two days later, 6th Panzer Division crossed the Daugava a little to the east at Līvāni. The Soviet unit in this sector, 202nd Rifle Division, had been in continuous action since the war had begun, and had lost most of its heavy equipment in the preceding days. It lacked the firepower or numbers to hold back the German armour.

Even as Reinhardt's panzer divisions were forcing their way across the Daugava, a mixed German battlegroup approached the Latvian capital, Riga. Colonel Otto Lasch led a force consisting of an infantry regiment from 1st Infantry Division, with a battalion of *Sturmgeschütz* assault guns and a company of anti-aircraft guns, to Joniškis late on 27 June. From here, he was ordered to press on towards Riga, in an attempt to cut off the Soviet forces in Courland. He set off at 0030hrs on 28 June, rushing forward to Bauska, where he beat off strong Soviet attacks from the west. With the bridges over two rivers near the town secured, Lasch continued to fight off Soviet counter-attacks, and the following night pressed on towards Riga itself.

As it grew light, Lasch found himself pressing forward through the retreating Red Army. Wherever he met resistance, he deployed and attacked, overrunning two motorised artillery batteries in the process. His line of march lay across a series of tributaries to the Daugava, and the bridges over these small rivers were vital to a rapid advance. In the confusion, his column rapidly captured the crossings at Iekava and Ķekava. At 1020hrs, Lasch's vanguard reached the western edge of Riga, and pushed on swiftly towards the vital bridges across the Daugava. As they approached the road bridge, the Germans ran into a Soviet column on foot, also making for the bridge. Immediately, a hectic fight erupted at close quarters; aboard the leading vehicle, Lasch personally shot at and silenced a quad machine gun mounted on a Soviet truck. Continuing his wild advance, Lasch sent five assault guns and supporting infantry racing over the road bridge, while he set up a defensive perimeter on the east bank. His combat engineers moved onto the railway bridge, where they found that demolition charges had already been prepared; they located and cut a command wire, but were unsure whether there might be others.

The German column had successfully seized the road bridge across the Daugava, but suddenly found itself assailed on all sides. In addition to the road and railway bridges, there was a pontoon bridge over the river, and within minutes of Lasch's spearhead reaching the east bank, there were two huge explosions as Soviet troops detonated the charges in the pontoon bridge and road bridge. The former was completely destroyed, the latter badly damaged. Soviet forces in the main part of Riga, on the east bank, now began to organise themselves for an assault on the small detachment that had crossed the river, while large numbers of Soviet troops that were retreating to Riga from the west launched a series of attacks on the main German contingent under Lasch's personal command. The fighting raged all day at close range, with repeated – though poorly coordinated – attempts by the Soviet troops to penetrate Lasch's lines and reach the bridges; in addition to wishing to destroy the German force, the Soviet soldiers were aware that German control of the bridges prevented their own escape to the east.

Knowing that the small contingent on the east bank was coming under heavy pressure, Lasch dispatched two assault groups from a motorcycle battalion to cross the railway bridge on foot, in order to reinforce the eastern bridgehead. The Soviet forces on the east bank spotted their movement, and poured a heavy fire onto the railway bridge; most of the German infantry was killed or wounded, and no soldiers reached the east bank. Meanwhile, during the early evening, there were two major assaults on the western bridgehead. Several tanks were destroyed on the western approach, and only a determined counter-attack on the south-west perimeter restored the defensive line. Shortly after, the German commander of the eastern bridgehead retreated back across the badly damaged road bridge, with three of his men. All were wounded, and they reported to Lasch that they were the only survivors of the force that had rushed across the bridge.

As the evening drew on, the Soviet units on the west bank launched further attacks. Lasch's men counted over 40 knocked-out tanks around their perimeter. With darkness came a pause in the fighting, but there were suddenly more loud explosions as the Red Army succeeded in blowing up parts of the railway bridge. For Lasch and his exhausted men, the worst was over. Reinforcements had been hurrying to catch up with them all day, and the first elements of 61st Infantry Division arrived before dawn. A final Soviet attempt to break up Lasch's bridgehead was beaten off at first light, and the battle for Riga was effectively over. Early the following day, 1 July, German infantry crossed the Daugava in boats and found that the Red Army had abandoned the city.[28]

Lasch was justifiably proud of the achievements of his men, and was awarded the Knight's Cross for his part in the battle. He claimed that his command had fought off most of the Soviet 8th Army; whilst his men certainly defeated several times their number, much of 8th Army actually succeeded in escaping beyond the Daugava by crossing further upstream. On 27 June, faced with catastrophe on all parts of the front, Kuznetsov had ordered 8th Army to retreat north into Estonia, while 11th and 27th Armies withdrew to the north-east. Prior to the deployment of 27th Army, the advance of Manstein's LVI Panzer Corps had opened a large gap in the centre of the Soviet lines, and now a new gap opened between the two axes of retreat, leading directly to Ostrov and Pskov and, beyond there, to Leningrad. Keen to exploit this, Hitler wanted all of 4th Panzer Group to press on to Ostrov. However, Leeb continued to insist that circumstances on the ground demanded a pause in the advance. With the infantry divisions still struggling to catch up with the panzers, he continued to resist pressure, from both above and below. Kuznetsov was grateful for the short time that he was granted by Leeb's caution, but even if he had been given more time, there were limits to what could be achieved. His armoured strength had fallen to 150 tanks, and his front had only 154 combat aircraft available.[29]

In any event, Stalin had run out of patience with Kuznetsov. He was removed from command, and replaced by Sobennikov, who had been commander of 8th Army. Unlike the unfortunate Dmitri Pavlov, the commander of the Red Army's Western Front at the beginning of the war, Kuznetsov survived his demotion.[30] He continued to be in command of armies and fronts until the end of the war. To stiffen the command structure of the North-west Front, Stalin dispatched Nikolai Fedorovich

Vatutin, First Deputy Chief of the General Staff, to become Sobennikov's chief of staff, with stern instructions to resist the German advance at all costs.

On 1 July, Manstein was finally given orders to advance again. He issued orders to Brandenberger's 8th Panzer Division to renew its advance early the following day, setting it the objective of reaching Kārsava, about 51 miles to the north-east. Early on 2 July, the brilliant sunshine that had lasted since the beginning of the campaign was replaced by heavy rain. The combination of deteriorating road conditions and determined Soviet defenders prevented an easy resumption of the rapid advance of earlier days. The main thrust on the right flank of 8th Panzer Division struggled to drive back the Soviet defences, and it was only when Brandenberger ordered his reconnaissance battalion, which was advancing with the left flank of the division, to attack east in order to outflank the Red Army units blocking the main thrust that significant gains were made. On 3 July, slowly overcoming the Soviet defences, the two battlegroups of 8th Panzer Division worked their way forward to Rēzekne, taking the town in the evening.

Hoepner's panzer group had been ordered to advance to Lake Peipus, and after securing the land corridor between the northern shore of the lake and the Baltic, to press on with the bulk of the panzer group from the southern end of the lake towards Leningrad; this order was then amended to stop the panzers at Pskov until the infantry could catch up. While Busch's 16th Army continued to spread out to cover the western flank of the army group, Küchler's 18th Army would advance into Estonia. After struggling through the mud for two days, Reinhardt's panzer corps reached Ostrov on 4 July. Early the same day, 8th Panzer Division rapidly advanced from Rēzekne to Kārsava, and from here was ordered to turn more to the east, to cover the right flank of the German advance. Further progress was hindered by a combination of poor roads and large numbers of abandoned Soviet vehicles, and then brought to a halt when the retreating Red Army blew the bridge at Golisevo, on the Soviet border; the withdrawing Soviet 227th Rifle Division had lost too many personnel and equipment in the hard fighting of the preceding days to be able to put up much resistance. The weather improved in the coming days, but the boggy ground around the Velikaia valley proved a considerable obstacle. Still, although much hard fighting lay ahead for the two panzer corps, they were now onto Russian territory.

Had 8th Panzer Division been allowed to advance immediately after the capture of Daugavpils, what might have been the outcome? Given the chaos and dislocation throughout the Soviet chain of command, it seems most unlikely that sufficient forces could have been concentrated to hold up the German division. The weather throughout the days that Brandenberger was left to fret on the north-east bank of the Daugava was sunny, unlike the rain that arrived almost as soon as the German advance was resumed, and at the very least, 8th Panzer Division would have enjoyed better conditions – in terms of a disorganised enemy and weather – than it endured during its advance to Kārsava. Had elements of Manstein's corps reached northern Latvia within a day or two of seizing Daugavpils, most of the Soviet forces attempting to escape from Riga and Courland would have been encircled and destroyed, thus facilitating a rapid German advance across Estonia. The wait at Daugavpils therefore probably resulted in even greater delays later in the campaign. In 1940, during the German drive towards the English Channel, the panzer divisions were halted for an entire day due to nervousness in Berlin and at Higher Command levels about the possible isolation of the German armour, and this short delay probably gave the British just enough time to retreat to Dunkirk. Similarly, the short delay at Daugavpils allowed the Red Army to escape from Riga and the surrounding area, and wasted several days of excellent campaigning weather. Whilst the blame for the hold-up lies with Leeb, he was not alone in showing such caution – similar considerations resulted in an even more wasteful pause in the German Army Group Centre's drive towards Moscow. It is debatable whether the ultimate outcome of the campaign might have been different; some have argued that the delay effectively cost the Germans their best opportunity to capture Leningrad at an early stage of the campaign.[31]

Further west, the German 18th Army advanced rapidly across northern Latvia. Rather than risk a further series of battles that would fragment the front line, the Soviet 8th Army, now commanded by Lieutenant General Fedor Sergeevich Ivanov, tried to pull back its front line in a coherent manner. The Soviet 10th Rifle Corps was closest to the coast, with three rifle divisions, while 11th Rifle Corps was further inland, with an additional three rifle divisions, together with what remained of the various mechanised corps that had been thrown into the battle. In practice, these rifle divisions – significantly below strength at the start of the campaign – were now in many places reduced to barely 2,000 men. By 9 July, Ivanov had pulled back into Estonia, and was attempting to defend a line from the coast at Pärnu to Lake Võrtsjärv, and thence to Lake Peipus, with one corps either side of Lake Võrtsjärv. At this stage of the campaign, several factors began to work in favour of the defenders. Firstly, reinforcements had begun to arrive, though many of these were poorly equipped and even more poorly trained. Secondly, the lengthening German lines of supply were beginning to impose checks on their rate of advance. Thirdly, the diverging German forces were no longer able to support each other so effectively, either directly or indirectly – breakthroughs by 4th Panzer Group earlier in the campaign had destabilised the Soviet forces along the entire front, but now the German armour was much further away from the Baltic coast, and in any event the presence of Lake Peipus effectively separated its area of operation from that of 18th Army. Also, the Luftwaffe was struggling to provide adequate air support over such a huge battlefield. Forward airfields, either captured from the retreating Soviets or improvised on open ground, were liable to turn to mud whenever it rained, and there simply weren't enough planes, with adequate supplies, to maintain support wherever the Wehrmacht demanded it.

As a consequence, the German 18th Army faced tougher resistance in its advance across northern Estonia than it had done in the entire campaign to date. As a further hindrance, Army Group North assigned the conquest of what remained of Estonia a relatively low priority: the main emphasis remained the thrust towards Leningrad, initially in an attempt to seize the city, and subsequently to isolate it and to link up with the Finns. In the second half of July, as 6th Panzer Division advanced towards Leningrad, east of Lake Peipus, 58th and 1st Infantry Divisions struggled to move forward in parallel, between the panzer division and the lake. Resistance steadily increased, while the German forces found themselves increasingly stretched to cover the vast expanses of front line.

In Latvia and Lithuania, the Germans had taken advantage of spontaneous uprisings against the Red Army, though they had rarely instigated such rebellions. The Estonians had maintained links with the Finns for many years, dating back to the Estonian war of independence, when Finnish volunteers had come to the aid of the struggling Estonian Army. Even after the pacts imposed by Stalin on the Baltic States in 1939, such contacts continued, though in secret. As a result, when the Soviet Union annexed Estonia in 1940, many Estonian officers and soldiers fled the short distance to Finland – some also travelled to Sweden – and these men were now formed into a volunteer battalion by the Germans. An attempt was made to land part of this battalion on the north Estonian coast on 5 July, but failed due to bad weather. Two days later, about 40 men were put ashore; it had been intended to land a larger group, but some of the transports were intercepted by Soviet warships and forced to turn back. The men who succeeded in returning to Estonia set up makeshift landing strips, where further men and supplies were flown in from Finland. They now provided the Germans with valuable intelligence, as well as harassing Red Army units when the opportunity arose.[32]

Elsewhere, Estonian guerrillas were operating against the Red Army. The Estonian *Omakaitse* ('Home Guard') was first created during the turbulent period between the departure of the Czar's armies and the arrival of the Germans in 1917. The following year, it was renamed the *Kaitseliit* ('Defence League') and remained in existence until

1940. Although it was suppressed during the Soviet occupation, many members started up a new underground *Omakaitse*, and this provided the nucleus for the creation of several large groups of anti-Soviet guerrillas after the onset of *Barbarossa*. One large group of guerrillas, led by Major Friedrich Kurg, moved to seize the city of Tartu, midway between Lakes Võrtsjärv and Peipus. The group had been planning such an operation for weeks, even before the German invasion began; there had been informal talks with Tartu University Hospital about treating casualties as early as June.

There were three crossings over the River Emajõgi in the town, the 'liberty bridge' in the western part of the city, an old stone bridge, and a pontoon bridge. The pontoon bridge was dismantled on 6 July, and two days later, Red Army engineers began preparations to blow up the stone bridge. On 9 July, a demolition charge destroyed the northern end of the bridge. Later the same day, a German reconnaissance patrol attempted to enter the town from the north-west, but was beaten off. The guerrillas decided to attack the small remaining Soviet garrison the following day.

On 10 July, fighting broke out around the town as the Estonian guerrillas moved to secure key buildings. Another German reconnaissance patrol, led by Hauptmann Kurt von Glasenepp, entered the town, and the German armoured cars provided welcome fire support for the guerrillas. By the end of the day, the western half of the town was under the control of the Estonians, but the German armoured cars now withdrew to refuel and rearm. Aware that they lacked the strength to prevent the Red Army from moving back across the 'liberty bridge' into the western parts of the city, the Estonians sent an urgent message to the Germans outside the city asking for help.

Later that night, the Soviet engineers destroyed the 'liberty bridge', but fighting flared up again as the Soviet 16th Rifle Division moved towards the city. At the same time, a German task force, consisting of two reconnaissance battalions and an infantry battalion, commanded by Generalmajor Karl Burdach, was ordered to secure the city, and more guerrillas, including Friedrich Kurg and other former Estonian army officers, also entered Tartu. Fighting continued for several days, with much of the southern part of the city reduced to rubble. Further German reinforcements were fed into the battle, which continued until the end of the month.[33]

After pausing to regroup, 18th Army resumed its drive into Estonia on 22 July. The reinforced 61st Infantry Division attacked and seized Põltsamaa, north of Lake Võrtsjärv. The following day, as 217th Infantry Division joined the attack at Türi, 61st Infantry Division moved against Jõgeva, in an attempt to isolate the Red Army forces near Tartu. To avoid this, the Soviet 48th and 125th Rifle Divisions, together with the remnants of 16th Rifle Division from Tartu, withdrew a little to the north, but they

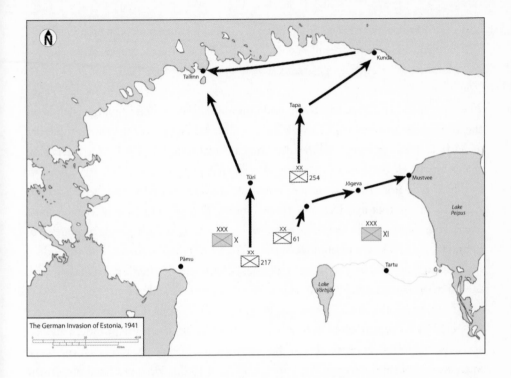

The German Invasion of Estonia, 1941

were too late; on 25 June, 61st Infantry Division reached Lake Peipus near Mustvee, cutting off the Soviet forces. Fighting continued until late July, but repeated Soviet attempts to break out were blocked. Finally, on 27 July, the remaining men – nearly 8,800 – were forced to surrender.

With the newly arrived XLII Corps on the left and XXVI Corps on the right, 18th Army pushed north again on 29 July. XXVI Corps made good progress, striking at the seam between the Soviet 10th and 11th Rifle Corps; 254th Infantry Division reached Tapa on 4 August, and arrived at the Baltic coast at Kunda three days later. The two Soviet rifle corps were separated, with 11th Rifle Corps forced to withdraw towards Narva while 10th Corps fell back on Tallinn. German forces followed swiftly towards Narva, but were held up by gunfire from Soviet destroyers near the coast. It was only with the deployment of a heavy coastal artillery battery on 13 August that the destroyers were driven off. The three divisions of XXVI Corps slowly closed in on Narva, and finally took the city on 16 August. Pursuing the retreating Soviet troops, elements of the German 291st Infantry Division seized bridgeheads across the River Narva:

The old borderlands were reached. From the top of Hermann Castle [a fortress held for many years by the Livonian Knights] the terrain to the east was flat and forested, it was like the beginning of another world. Estonia, with its blue-black-white banners and its friendly people, was behind us; Russia proper, exotic and unknown, lay before the soldiers.[34]

There remained the Soviet forces in and around Tallinn, and on the large islands off the western coast of Estonia. Outside Tallinn, General Walter Kuntze, the commander of XLII Corps, had three infantry divisions at his disposal. 254th Infantry Division was on the Baltic coast to the east of the Estonian capital, with 61st Infantry Division, freshly arrived from the destruction of Soviet forces south of Mustvee, to the south-east and 217th Infantry Division to the south. The western part of the German encirclement was made up of *Kampfgruppe Friedrich*, with a single regiment of infantry, and artillery and engineer elements of several formations. The defenders, the Soviet 10th Corps, had what remained of three rifle divisions, together with several battalions of naval infantry – a mixture of marines and sailors.

The battle for Tallinn began on 19 August. The approaches to Tallinn were protected by fortifications built by the Estonians during their war of independence, and subsequently strengthened, and the Germans made slow progress past the seven main strongpoints. Soviet warships operating close to the coast and from within the harbour added their firepower to the defence, but inexorably, the Germans advanced.

> Reval [Tallinn] was burning. Tracers flew back and forth at the edge of the city.
> The towers of the old Hanseatic town were black against the bright night sky. As
> the morning fog cleared on 27 August, the heavy air and artillery activity resumed.
> Russian cruisers and destroyers joined in the land battle from the harbour, and the
> earth trembled under the impact of 180mm shells.[35]

By the fifth day of the attack, the assault spearheads were within six miles of the city centre, and a day later, the fighting reached the main urban area. With no possible option of a breakout over land along the coast to the east, the Soviet forces began to make arrangements for a seaborne evacuation. The Germans were aware of these preparations, and in combination with Finnish forces, laid extensive minefields on the approaches to Tallinn; despite having considerable naval assets in the area, the Soviet Navy was unable to intervene, partly due to the weather. Luftwaffe air operations against the port area of Tallinn were increased, within the limits of availability of air support.

On 28 August, as the battle for Tallinn reached its peak and German troops pressed into the heart of the city, the Soviet naval evacuation began. Smokescreens were created in an attempt to hide the activity from the Germans, but heavy artillery fire killed perhaps 1,000 people waiting to embark on the ships. The first convoy, led by Captain Bogdanov, consisted of two destroyers, ten minesweepers and minelayers, five transports, and a number of smaller vessels. It left the port just before midday. Two hours later, two smaller convoys followed, with the main Soviet naval force, consisting of the cruiser *Kirov*, three destroyers, four submarines and an icebreaker, departing in mid-afternoon. German forces were waiting, and a torpedo boat flotilla of five vessels attempted to intercept the convoys. The German boats were driven off by the guns of the Soviet warships, but the minefields and repeated Luftwaffe attacks inflicted heavy losses. The first ship to strike a mine was the steamer *Ella*. Six destroyers, two submarines, four minelayers, and several transports were sunk, with a total loss of over 12,000 lives, during the two days it took for the Soviet vessels to reach Kronstadt. Nevertheless, some 28,000 people escaped to safety. In Tallinn, nearly 12,000 men had been left behind, and were forced to surrender to the Germans. Despite the intensity of the fighting, German losses were between 3,000 and 4,000 men, a far smaller number than that of the defenders.[36]

In order to complete their control of the Baltic, the Germans needed to seize the large islands off the Estonian coast, where a substantial Soviet garrison force had established itself. The German operation, codenamed *Beowulf*, commenced on 8 September, with landings by the reinforced 61st Infantry Division on Vormsi, Saaremaa and Muhu. Fighting continued until 5 October. On 12 October, elements of 61st Infantry Division landed on the last remaining island, Hiiumaa. The defenders fought on until 21 October. The Germans lost a little under 3,000 men; the entire Soviet garrison of over 23,000 men was lost, with nearly 5,000 killed and the rest captured.

The campaign to seize the Baltic States was over. With the exception of the Estonian islands, operations were complete with the fall of Tallinn at the end of August, barely two months after the beginning of hostilities. Stalin had seized the three states partly in order to protect Leningrad; this aim has to be seen as a failure. If Estonia, Latvia and Lithuania had continued as independent nations, it is likely that it would have taken the Wehrmacht at least as long to seize them, whether this were achieved by diplomatic pressure or by force of arms, and the Red Army could have used the intervening weeks to prepare itself better for battle. Instead, the frontier armies were annihilated, and the battered remnants would now have to fight on the outskirts of Leningrad itself. In the Baltic States, as the smoke and dust of battle dispersed, everyone – Estonians, Latvians, Lithuanians and their German occupiers – looked to see what the future held for the three countries.

Chapter 4
THE BALTIC HOLOCAUST

The nations involved in the Second World War entered the conflict at different points in time. In almost every case, the main emotions that the population felt on their entry into the war were fear or consternation. For many in the Baltic States, though, the initial reaction was very different, as one Lithuanian recorded: 'It struck Lithuania like a clap of thunder: WAR. What joy, WAR. People met and congratulated each other with tears in their eyes. Everyone felt that the hour of liberation was near.'[1]

As the Germans marched into Lithuania, they were greeted by jubilant crowds, and thousands of people who threw bunches of flowers to the men they regarded as their saviours from the Bolsheviks. One observer noted that red blooms were conspicuously absent from the bouquets.[2] But whilst many Lithuanians celebrated, the reaction of Lithuania's Jewish community was very different: 'Although crowds of Lithuanians greeted the Germans with flowers, it was no surprise that we closed our shutters, lowered our curtains, and locked ourselves up in our homes.'[3]

Neither of these reactions was particularly surprising, given the events that had occurred in the Baltic States; similar sentiments were evident in Latvia and to a lesser extent – not least due to the very small Jewish population – in Estonia. The reactions showed a fundamental difference between Jewish and non-Jewish communities in their response to the German invasion; but the differences between the two communities ran far deeper, and would be exploited ruthlessly by the Germans. A few weeks before the onset of *Barbarossa*, a farmer in the Lithuanian town of Plungė was heard to remark: 'The Germans only have to cross the border, and on the same day we will wade in the blood of Jews in Plungė.'[4]

The history of anti-Jewish pogroms is a long one, stretching back at least as far as the Alexandrian Empire. Throughout the 19th century, there were repeated attacks on Jews in most of Europe, and given the large concentration of Jews in Poland and the Russian Empire, it was inevitable that these areas would see the greatest number of aggressive incidents. Remarkably, given the large Jewish population of Latvia and Lithuania, there was relatively little anti-Jewish violence in the Baltic States, compared with other parts of the Czar's empire. In Lithuania, there was certainly widespread hostility at various levels, but this was little different from other Catholic countries, and violence to persons or property was unusual. The hostility towards Jews exemplified by the above quote, therefore, is all the more striking.

As has been discussed, there was a widespread perception in Lithuania and Latvia that the Jews were active supporters of the Soviet occupation. From the point of view of the Jews, there was little apparent choice. Whilst many – perhaps even most, given that Jews were strongly represented amongst the business classes – would have preferred to have been allowed to continue living their lives in Lithuania and Latvia as they had done for much of the century, the division of Europe into spheres of influence by Germany and the Soviet Union left no room for such dreams. If the Baltic States were to be forced into either the Soviet or the German camp, the Jews had to choose the former. Although the Final Solution had not yet been devised or implemented, the treatment of Jews in territories controlled by Germany was well known, and if there were any doubts, the flood of Jewish refugees from Poland into Lithuania in 1939 dispelled them. An additional factor that resulted in many Jews seeking employment with the new communist authorities was that before the Soviet occupation, most Jews worked in private firms. The nationalisation of these firms left many of them unemployed, and given the lack of job opportunities elsewhere, they took whatever employment they could get from the new governments. Nevertheless, in the interests of balance, it must be pointed out that the Jewish populations of Lithuania and Latvia formed a disproportionately large percentage of the membership of communist and pro-communist organisations even prior to the Soviet occupation.

Unfortunately for the Jewish population as a whole, some of those who worked for the Soviet regime during 1939–41 had a very prominent profile. Large parts of the communist administrations were made up of those perceived as foreigners – either Latvian and Lithuanian communists who arrived from the Soviet Union with the occupying forces, or Russians. Of the rest, although Jews formed a minority of the new administrations, they formed a larger proportion than Latvians and Lithuanians recruited from the local population. Consequently, many Lithuanians and Latvians grew to feel that the new regime favoured Jews above other groups. It became commonplace for people to tell each other that 'Under this regime, only the Jews live well', and to talk about 'the Jewish takeover of the regime'.[5]

Some of the pronouncements of the regime also raised anti-Semitic sentiment. Genrikas Zimanas, head of the Lithuanian Minorities Bureau, declared that the arrival of Soviet troops had dealt a mortal blow to anti-Semitism; the Soviet Union, he maintained, was the only state in the world free of anti-Semitism. Stalin himself had declared that anti-Semitism was a capital offence, and the Communist Party would never contemplate anti-Semitism, as this was equivalent to counter-revolutionary thinking.[6] Given the attitude of Stalin to Jews at the time, this seems an extraordinary statement; in any event, many Lithuanians interpreted it as further proof of the 'privileged status' of Jews.

It was into this volatile and increasingly polarised environment that the invading Germans brought their dreams of a New Order, requiring the subjugation or elimination of those deemed to be undesirable. The Jews were at the top of that particular list.

Prior to the invasion of the Soviet Union, Hitler made very clear to all his subordinates that the new war was to be like no other. On 30 March 1941, he addressed his senior officers on the nature of the coming conflict. Franz Halder, Chief of Staff of the army, recorded in his diary afterwards that the conflict would be a 'struggle between two ideologies'. Hitler condemned Bolshevism as being a form of 'antisocial criminality', and given the danger that communism represented for Germany, the war had to result in the 'extermination of Bolshevik commissars and of the communist intelligentsia'. When it came to officials of the Soviet Union, Hitler stated that 'Commissars and GPU [*Gosudarstvennoye Politicheskoye Upravlenie* or 'State Political Directorate', a part of the NKVD] personnel are criminals and must be treated as such. The struggle will differ from that in the west.'[7] At the beginning of June 1941, all units were informed that Bolsheviks, agitators, partisans, saboteurs, and Jews must all be treated as potential enemies. It was at this point that Wehrmacht units were told that it was their responsibility to compile lists of all Jews in their areas, and to hand these lists to the *Einsatzgruppen* that followed the front-line units. Although much of the Wehrmacht tried to behave as if fighting the Red Army was its sole function and attempted to leave implementation of Hitler's more extreme policies, and those required by *Generalplan Ost*, to other agencies such as the SS, there can be little doubt that almost every part of the German military machine had a role in the atrocities that followed the invasion.

The speed and scale of the killing of Jews in Lithuania and Latvia made the previous activities of German forces in Poland seem no more than a prelude. There were several components to these killings; some were carried out by the Wehrmacht, others by Lithuanians and Latvians, and many by the *Einsatzgruppen*. Whilst it is in some respects practical to consider these different agencies in turn, it should be remembered that all these groups were active in overlapping timescales.

Security in the rear areas was the responsibility of special security divisions, which as the war went on often found themselves forced into taking on a front-line role. Three such formations – 207th, 281st, and 285th Security Divisions – followed in the wake of Army Group North, while 403rd Security Division took control of the Vilnius region after Army Group Centre had moved on. These divisions came under the overall command of an officer with the title *Befehlshaber des Rückwärtigen Heeresgebietes* ('Commander of the Rear Army Areas', often abbreviated to *Berück*), a post held in the Army Group North area by General Franz von Roques. By coincidence, his cousin, Karl von Roques, held the equivalent command behind Army Group Centre. The son of a family that originated in the flight of Huguenot Protestants from France, he was not an enthusiastic advocate of Hitler's concept of a brutal, racial war. Although he ordered all Jews in his area to wear six-pointed yellow stars on their right breasts, his decrees regarding the creation of ghettos stated that such activity should not be regarded as a priority, and should only proceed when adequate resources had been made available.[8]

The commanders of the security divisions also displayed some reluctance to show the ruthlessness that Hitler desired. Roques' orders to the divisions – perhaps deliberately – did not make expressly clear how they were to operate. Generalleutnant Carl von Tidemann, commander of 207th Security Division, and Generalleutnant Friedrich Bayer, commander of 281st Security Division, explicitly ordered their men that 'shooting sections of the population purely on the grounds that they are members of the Communist Party or of other groups, for example Jews', was forbidden. Likewise, although the security divisions were to seize groups of Jews to be held as hostages, in an attempt to ensure the good behaviour of the rest of the population, they were not to hand these groups over to the SS, at least while the groups remained within the area defined as Rear Army Areas.[9]

The combat divisions in the front line also sometimes showed little appetite for following Hitler's orders regarding commissars and Jews. In an attempt to change this, General Hermann Hoth, commander of Army Group Centre's 3rd Panzer Group – which included 7th Panzer Division, the unit that seized Vilnius – issued an order as early as 28 June, less than a week after the beginning of *Barbarossa*, stating that any members of the Wehrmacht who allowed communist officials to escape would face court martial; the order warned soldiers to remain aware of 'the well-known Asiatic practices of murder, treachery, and perfidy'.[10] However, it seems that in many other cases there was little friction between the Wehrmacht and the SS. In

October 1941, Franz Walther Stahlecker, commander of *Einsatzgruppe A*, recorded that cooperation with the army was 'generally good, in a few cases, for instance with the 4th Panzer Group under Generaloberst Hoepner, very close, almost cordial'.[11] Stahlecker's report is a detailed description of his *Einsatzgruppe* in the early months of the war, and illustrates clearly how it functioned. It is therefore worthy of detailed attention.

Einsatzgruppe A crossed into Lithuania a day after the Wehrmacht invasion. Originally, it was intended that the *Einsatzgruppen* would function in areas handed over by the army as it advanced, but Stahlecker recorded that this proved unworkable for two reasons. Firstly, the rapid advance of the army led to delays in handing over rear areas; secondly, fighting partisans and suppressing communist activity was best done within the combat zone. This was because local paramilitary formations, which were used extensively by the Germans to carry out many of the killings of Jews and others, were frequently disarmed once the front line had moved on. If they were to be used to augment the work of the *Einsatzgruppen*, therefore, this would have to be before their weapons were confiscated. There was also a feeling that once a degree of normality had returned, it would be far harder to incite locals to 'spontaneous' attacks. In many cases, groups of Lithuanians and Latvians spontaneously organised themselves into paramilitary groups, but in order to help create as many local units as possible, *Einsatzgruppe* personnel accompanied the leading German units into Kaunas, Riga and Tallinn, and rapidly established 'volunteer detachments from reliable natives in all three Baltic provinces'. These detachments were an essential part of the plan to deal with the Jews:

… native anti-Semitic forces were induced to start pogroms against Jews during the first hours after capture, though this inducement proved to be very difficult. Following out orders, the Security Police was determined to solve the Jewish question with all possible means and most decisively. But it was desirable that the Security Police should not put in an immediate appearance, at least in the beginning, since the extraordinarily harsh measures were apt to stir even German circles. It had to be shown to the world that the native population itself took the first action by way of natural reaction against the suppression by Jews during several decades and against the terror exercised by the Communists during the preceding period.

… In view of the extension of the area of operations and the great number of duties which had to be performed by the Security Police, it was intended from the very beginning to obtain the co-operation of the reliable population for the fight against vermin – that is mainly the Jews and Communists. Beyond our directing of the first spontaneous actions of self-cleansing, which will be reported elsewhere, care had to be taken that reliable people should be put to the cleansing job and that they were appointed auxiliary members of the Security Police.[12]

The report then goes on to provide further information about these 'self-cleansing actions':

Considering that the population of the Baltic countries had suffered very heavily under the government of Bolshevism and Jewry while they were incorporated in the USSR, it was to be expected that after the liberation from that foreign government, they (i.e. the population themselves) would render harmless most of the enemies left behind after the retreat of the Red Army. It was the duty of the Security Police to set in motion these self-cleansing movements and to direct them into the correct channels in order to accomplish the purpose of the cleansing operations as quickly as possible. It was no less important in view of the future to establish the unshakable and provable fact that the liberated population themselves took the most severe measures against the Bolshevist and Jewish enemy quite on their own, so that the direction by German authorities could not be found out. In Lithuania this was achieved for the first time by partisan activities in Kaunas. To our surprise it was not easy at first to set in motion an extensive pogrom against Jews. Klimatis, the leader of the partisan unit … who was used for this purpose primarily, succeeded in starting a pogrom on the basis of advice given to him by a small advanced detachment acting in Kaunas, and in such a way that no German order or German instigation was noticed from the outside.[13]

Stahlecker had accompanied the leading units into Kaunas, and made his way to the offices of the Lithuanian State Security Department, which had been seized by members of the Lithuanian Activist Front. Here, he made a speech calling for a pogrom against the Jews, but was disappointed that there was little apparent enthusiasm for such an act. Instead, he turned to Algirdas Klimatis, who had organised a paramilitary group of about 600 individuals, and had taken part in fighting against the retreating Red Army. He had no allegiance either to the Lithuanian Activist Front or to the newly proclaimed provisional government, and proved to be a willing accomplice for the Germans. On 25 June, his men started attacking Jews in the suburb of Vilijampolė, and spread their activity from there to other parts of the city and the surrounding area. The exact number of victims of this pogrom is disputed. Stahlecker claimed that in three days, some 5,000 Jews were killed, but it has been suggested that Stahlecker may deliberately have exaggerated the number of killings.[14]

In many cases, the attacks on Jews were genuinely spontaneous, with little or no encouragement from the Germans – indeed, it seems that once the pogroms commenced, they spread rapidly to neighbouring areas. Dov Levin described how Lithuanians looted Jewish houses, attacking Jews and raping women. One Lithuanian waved several bloodstained passports at Levin as proof of the Jews he had already killed.[15] The Lithuanian partisans wore white armbands, and were widely known as *baltaraiščiai* ('white armbands'). Even within the ranks of the partisans, there was a perception that not all of those wearing armbands were actively fighting the Red Army:

> Some procured guns and took part in the fight for the Fatherland, while others broke into shops, private homes and abandoned houses, where they took every opportunity to steal and take away things, or bury them in the earth.[16]

Whilst not all partisans took part in anti-Jewish attacks, it seems that most of those who robbed, beat and killed Jews were wearing white armbands.[17] Some partisan leaders, such as Jurgis Bobelis in Kaunas, attempted to prevent such acts by their men; Bobelis threatened to execute any men found to be involved in random attacks. Others simply turned a blind eye to events. Many continued to make little distinction between Jews and communists, and encouraged their men to round up all those who fell into either category.

Stahlecker's *Einsatzgruppe* was divided into several *Einsatzkommando*, each with its area of operations. *Einsatzkommando 3* was under the command of Karl Jäger, who was born in the Swiss town of Schaffhausen in 1888. He served as an artilleryman in the First World War, and thereafter was a member of the so-called Black Reichswehr, a paramilitary grouping designed to circumvent the restrictions imposed on the size of German armed forces by the Treaty of Versailles. He was an early adherent of the National Socialist movement, and was enrolled into the ranks of the SS in 1936. He rose rapidly through the ranks, and by summer 1941 held the rank of *Standartenführer* (the equivalent army rank would be colonel). At this stage, he was ordered to form *Einsatzkommando 3*. When its 120 personnel gathered at their training base in the small town of Pretzch, Jäger learned that in addition to commanding the *Einsatzkommando*, he would also be the commander of the Security Police and *Sicherheitsdienst* ('Security Department' or SD) in Lithuania. Both at Pretzch and in a meeting in Berlin, Reinhard Heydrich, chief of the RSHA, made clear to Jäger and other similarly ranked SS officers that 'in the event of a war with Russia, all the Jews in the east will have to be shot'.[18]

Jäger arrived in Kaunas with his unit after the initial wave of killings of Jews by Klimatis and his men. The first section of *Einsatzgruppe A* to arrive in Kaunas was *Einsatzkommando 1*, which now handed over the area to Jäger's men. Jäger later noted that Jews were still moving about freely in the city – perhaps in keeping with Roques' instructions that the establishment of ghettos had a low priority – and he swiftly took measures to establish a ghetto and to restrict their movements and activities. The early killings were used as a justification for the establishment of the ghetto – only in this way, Jäger stated, could Jews be protected from further pogroms. This was a well-practised argument, and had been used during the 1930s in Germany itself.

The pretence of protecting Jews in the ghetto lasted barely a day. Two days after his arrival in the city, Jäger recorded that 463 Jews had been killed 'by Lithuanian partisans', a number that rose to over 2,500 within the next two days.[19] By December 1941, about 22,000 Jews had been executed, leaving about 15,000 Jews in the ghetto; the list of victims is chronicled in a report that Jäger wrote at the end of the year, listing with painstaking detail the locations, dates, and nature of the victims, dividing them into men, women and children.[20] The report also lists the killings in Vilnius and Minsk, and if these are added to those killed in Kaunas, the number exceeds 133,000. The report concludes with the words: 'Today I can confirm that our objective, to solve the Jewish problem for Lithuania, has been achieved by EK 3. In Lithuania there are no more Jews, apart from Jewish workers and their families.'[21]

These chilling sentences mean that between 22 June and 1 December, over 120,000 Lithuanian Jews had been killed. Jäger participated in some of the shootings himself, and ensured that all of his officers did so too. Those who showed reticence were threatened.[22] Jäger himself appears to have been affected by these experiences. He told Heinz Jost, who succeeded Stahlecker as Jäger's superior, that he couldn't sleep, and was haunted by visions of dead women and children.[23] None of these feelings seems to have interfered with his ability to continue with the killings. He remained in Lithuania for two years before being assigned a variety of administrative roles in Germany.

Outside the large cities of Lithuania, special measures were taken to facilitate the killing of Jews. One example was the *Rollkommando Hammann*, a mobile killing squad of less than a dozen German officers and about a hundred Lithuanians, mainly members of Bronius Norkus' *Tautinio Darbo Apsaugos* ('National Security') battalion. During the latter half of 1941, the *Kommando* was active in over

50 locations, in both Lithuania and southern Latvia, accounting for the deaths of over 9,000 Jews. The Jäger report describes in detail the preparations required for this unit to function:

> The implementation of such actions is primarily a question of organisation. The objective of systematically rendering every district free of Jews required thorough preparation of every individual task and investigation of the prevailing circumstances in the relevant district. Jews had to be assembled at one or more locations. On the basis of their number, locations for the required graves had to be identified and dug.[24]

In Vilnius, the German authorities rapidly introduced a series of measures for Jews to wear identifying symbols, such as six-pointed stars and armbands. These were changed frequently in the early stages of the occupation, causing panic amongst the Jews as they struggled to find material of the appropriate colour. Jews began to be moved to designated buildings in mid-July as the first phase of the creation of a ghetto; the formal establishment of the ghetto occurred in September. 403rd Security Division and *Einsatzkommando 9* both reported that they were working smoothly together, with the division stating that in August and September 1941 it executed 45 military commissars and 197 civilian communist officials; many of this latter group were Jews.[25] The *Einsatzkommando*, which arrived on 2 July, executed 321 Jews between 4 and 8 July, and later achieved figures of 500 killings per day. By 19 July, it had accounted for over 7,600 individuals.[26] Wolfgang Ditfurth, commander of 403rd Security Division, reported in mid-July that he had reduced rations to the Jewish part of the population by 50 per cent. He was aware of the shootings carried out by the *Einsatzkommando* and its Lithuanian auxiliaries, but requested that these were carried out in locations out of sight of his men.[27]

The experiences of the child Mascha Rolnikaite and her family in Vilnius are in many ways typical of Jews caught up in the German takeover. She was nearly 14 years old when the Germans arrived in Vilnius. She was the daughter of a Jewish couple; her father was a lawyer, who worked for the Soviet authorities. As the Red Army began to leave the city, he left his family to organise transport for them to leave. The family waited in vain for him to return, and watched the first German troops arrive. The following day, they learned that the new authorities had ordered shops and restaurants to reopen, but restaurants and cafes had to display a sign stating that entry of Jews was forbidden. When Rolnikaite attempted to return to school to collect documents that her mother thought would be important, she was shocked when a Lithuanian boy confronted her:

'What do *you* want here? Go, back the way you came!'

I asked him to let me past. But he snatched my cap from my head.

'Get away! And stop plaguing our school!'[28]

She feared the reaction of her teacher, but to her relief, he helped her recover her documents, and even accompanied her on her way home.

Perella Esterowicz was slightly younger than Mascha Rolnikaite, the only child of the local representative of the Hungarian firm Tungsram, as well as western battery and tyre manufacturers. Growing up in Vilnius in the 1930s, when the city was under Polish control, she remembered seeing anti-Semitic graffiti even as a small child. After the city was assigned to Lithuania by the Soviet Union, her father lost contact with his foreign suppliers, but established a new business. The communist authorities nationalised this the following year after the Soviet annexation of Lithuania, and as a 'bourgeois' family, the Esterowiczes had to give up a large part of their luxurious apartment. Despite being unemployed, her father managed to avoid deportation to Siberia, though her aunt and uncle only escaped by fleeing their house when the NKVD came to arrest them. Tragically, their escape indirectly led to their deaths; the Germans shot her uncle within a few weeks of their arrival, and her aunt died in the ghetto in 1943.

As German troops approached Vilnius, the communist official who had taken possession of the bulk of the Esterowicz apartment fled to the east. Perella's father was arrested on suspicion of signalling to Soviet aircraft by leaving his apartment light burning at night, and suddenly found himself facing a hostile group of German officials. When they realised he could speak excellent German, and that he had been a customer in a coffee house in Berlin where one of the Germans had worked, he was released. A Polish garage-owner, who had been Esterowicz's customer before the war, provided him with a document showing that he worked in the Polish garage which was now helping repair Wehrmacht vehicles, thus protecting him from further arrest.[29]

News spread by word of mouth through the Jewish community of attacks and pogroms. Soon, the Rolnikaite house was searched for radios and other forbidden items. There were repeated searches, and all items in the house were recorded in an inventory – except the best furniture, which was immediately removed. Jewish families were warned that if they attempted to sell any of their furniture, they would face severe punishment, even death. They were required to hand over all jewellery and cash in excess of 30 Reichsmarks. Later, there was a demand that all Jews pay an additional large sum of cash or face immediate arrest. This was almost impossible for many, who had already been robbed or had handed over their valuables; to the relief of the Rolnikaite family, Mascha's schoolteacher, Hendrikas Jonaitis, appeared at their house and gave her mother the required cash. Like a substantial minority of Lithuanians, he was prepared to risk his own life to help protect others.[30]

Restrictions continued to increase in both number and severity. Shortly after Rolnikaite's 14th birthday, a month after the invasion had begun, Jews were forbidden from walking on pavements. The day before the Vilnius ghetto was established, Rolnikaite ventured out on the streets in search of Jonaitis, her schoolteacher, without the obligatory insignia of a Jew. He looked after her overnight, but the following day, when she attempted to return to her family, she found that the ghetto had been established, with barbed wire across the streets. There were actually two ghettos, a small one and a large one, separated by a single road. Rolnikaite entered one of the ghettos, and when she couldn't find her family, succeeded in crossing to the other; she was fortunate that she recognised one of the guards as the schoolboy who had attempted to turn her away from her school, and managed to persuade him to let her pass. It was several days before the family was reunited in the crowded ghetto.[31]

Ghetto life was difficult in the extreme. Mascha Rolnikaite, her mother, and her three siblings had to sleep in a room with several others, squeezed into a space between two beds; there were barely enough beds for the elderly and children. The Esterowicz family was lucky, in that they had been driven from their apartment when the ghetto was first established, and being amongst the first arrivals, were able to secure a room for themselves and their extended family. As more and more people were crammed into the ghetto, the family was forced to allow others to join them, and their room, measuring 6ft by 24ft became home to 26.[32]

Most of the day-to-day running of the ghetto was in the hands of the *Judenrat* (Jewish council) and the ghetto police, which was headed by Jacob Gens, a former officer of the Lithuanian army. Both the ghetto police and the *Judenrat* were answerable to Standartenführer Franz Murer, who had been appointed Vilnius Commissar for Jewish Matters. Soon, those who had work were moved to one ghetto, while those without work were herded together into the smaller ghetto. There were repeated 'actions', a euphemism for the forcible round-up of a variable number of Jews, who were then taken away and executed. Various categories were selected – the infirm, the elderly, those without work. On other occasions, people were simply herded together regardless of their status. There was a pretence by the authorities that the infirm and elderly were being taken elsewhere so that they could receive better care, but those left behind had little doubt that they would never see their loved ones again. Rolnikaite described a typical 'action':

Once more an action. Not a big one, but an action nevertheless.

During the night, a taciturn troop of Lithuanian soldiers quietly slipped into the ghetto. They had instructed the ghetto police to remain at their posts while they themselves sought out predetermined addresses that each had been assigned.

They woke people quietly and politely and ordered them to take warm clothing with them, and waited as they dressed and packed their things.

The people only realised their situation when they reached the ghetto gate where they were to be loaded into trucks ...

It turned out that Murer had ordered new victims from Gens. Gens therefore prepared a list of members of the so-called underworld – people who he saw as misfits or who had annoyed the ghetto police – and gave their addresses to the executioners.[33]

Samuel Esterowicz, Perella's father, working for his Polish acquaintance in the vehicle repair workshop, witnessed a body of ghetto inhabitants being marched away for execution:

In front of the windows of our workshop the Lithuanian police were driving down the street to the Lukiškės Prison a multitude of Jews from the second [small] ghetto – men, women and children. In the passing crowd I recognised some of my acquaintances. The scene of these innocent people, my fellow Jews, being driven to their deaths shocked me to the depth of my soul – this became even more poignant when I realised that the Polish workers in the workshop looked at this horrible injustice not with sorrow but with yells of joy and satisfaction. 'Look,' they were jumping with joy, 'the Jews are taken to be killed.'

The exhibition of anti-Semitism was no great surprise for me. But what horrified me while I watched the delighted Polish workers was the depth of their hatred for us – it united all the surrounding nationalities and members of social classes. The Polish partisans, members of the AK ['Armia Krajowa', the Polish resistance army supported by the Western Powers] acted in accordance with this mood of the surrounding population. Though organized for the underground struggle against the Germans, mostly the AK was hunting the Jews who were hiding in the forest. Since they consisted mostly of local people, the Polish partisans were excellently oriented in the localities in which they operated and thus represented a greater peril for the Jews who tried to find refuge in the dense forest than did the Germans who did not dare to penetrate deep into the forest. The Lithuanians were exceptionally active in the matter of our annihilation.[34]

The implication that the AK was involved in killing Jews is a controversial one. The resistance army fought against all it regarded as occupiers of Poland, including on occasion pro-Soviet partisans. Given that many of the pro-Soviet partisans were Jewish, it is likely that some Jews were killed by the AK, though it is equally likely that this was a result of activity that was not anti-Semitic *per se*. Esterowicz commented that anti-Semitism, while widespread amongst the local population, was by no means universal, and many locals quietly helped the Jews by providing food whenever they could. Nor were all Germans anti-Semitic:

> One ... was a German soldier named Berger who had been assigned to our automobile repair worshop and with whom I became friendly. Berger exclaimed while watching the Jews being driven to their deaths: 'What this scum perpetrate here in the name of the German nation – centuries will not suffice for us to cleanse ourselves!' Upon returning from home leave Berger related an occurrence which demonstrated that the Nazi government hid the truth from the broad masses of their population. Hearing about the horrors committed by her fellow Germans in Lithuania, Berger's wife at first decided that he must have lost his mind – the tales seemed so monstrous and improbable.[35]

Those that remained in the ghettos after each 'action' struggled to find enough food to survive. Rolnikaite's family was lucky. Her mother and elder sister worked as seamstresses, earning a pittance but enough to augment their hopelessly inadequate rations, and Hendrikas Jonaitis continued to risk his own life to give them food whenever he could, either through the barbed wire or if he encountered family members being marched to or from their place of work.

Many of the shootings of Jews from Vilnius occurred in the town of Paneriai, about six miles south-west of the centre of the city. Following their strategy in Poland, the Germans moved first to decapitate Jewish society, not least because it was believed that these leading individuals might form the centre of any resistance movement. Accordingly, on 9 July, *Einsatzkommando 9* instructed its subordinate Lithuanian police units to draw up a list of the most prominent Jews in Vilnius, particularly the intelligentsia, those involved in politics, and the wealthy.[36] Three days later, Kazimierz Sakowicz, a Pole who recorded many of the events at Paneriai, saw about 300 well-dressed male Jews brought to the killing ground, and recognised some of them as prominent Jewish commercial figures.[37] At first, the killings were mainly Jewish men. It was only in August that the range of victims was extended to include women and children.

A German soldier who worked in a transport column witnessed some of the killings:

> I positioned myself about 6–8 metres from the entrance to the pit. An armed civilian stood on either side of the entrance. The watch detail brought the people in small groups to the gravel pit. At the edge of the pit was a grave, where the Jews had to go. The grave was in the shape of a cross … as it was a dry sandy area, the grave was reinforced with planks. In groups, the Jews were brought to the pit. We could clearly see members of the watch detail who were at the edges of the pit striking down with whips … a firing squad of 10 men stood about 6–8 metres from the pit … the shots were fired in salvos, so that the people fell into the grave behind them together.[38]

One of those taken to Paneriai for execution was the 19-year-old Ita Straż. She was dragged to a pit that was already full of bodies, and when a salvo of shots rang out, she fell forward onto the dead, even though she had not been hit by any bullets. More bodies fell on her as further executions followed, and shots were then fired into the pit to kill any who had survived. One such shot passed through her hand, but she managed to remain silent. She waited until dark, and then escaped, walking barefoot over what seemed like an endless sea of dead.[39]

Lithuanians involved in the shootings at Paneriai were mainly from the *Ypatingasis būrys* ('special squads'), recruited from local volunteers. They were commanded by Hauptscharführer (equivalent to an army rank of *Oberfeldwebel* or staff sergeant) Martin Weiss, an officer in the German security police. He had a reputation for cruelty; when he supervised the executions at Paneriai, he frequently made victims lie for hours – in some cases, for more than a day – on the bodies of those executed before them, before they were shot themselves. He often beat Jews at the ghetto gate if they were not displaying their six-pointed stars in the approved fashion, and personally conducted beatings of anyone caught trying to smuggle extra food into the ghetto. On one occasion, he shot a would-be food smuggler – the man had a few potatoes and a small piece of fish – on the spot. Even by the standards of the SS, he had a bad reputation. There was an incident in which a Jew had been imprisoned in the Lukiškės Prison in Vilnius, and was due to be released back to the ghetto; his jailors waited until Weiss was on leave before they released the man, knowing that Weiss would have simply shot the prisoner instead. The jailors also warned the man to make sure that he didn't run into Weiss again.[40]

The personnel of *Einsatzkommando 3* reported in January 1942 that the shootings had been conducted in such a manner that they had barely been noticed, and that the general population, including the remaining Jews, believed that those taken to Paneriai had been resettled.[41] The testimony of locals, particularly from Paneriai, suggests that they were all too aware of the killings, but were careful not to speak out. Within the Vilnius ghetto, Jews only became aware of the true nature of Paneriai towards the end of 1941, due to the activities of the local resistance movement. In the Vilnius ghetto, the resistance group used a cellar under the so-called hospital. The *Judenrat* played no part in the resistance – its members believed that by cooperating with the Germans and providing labour, they would be able to save at least some of those in the ghetto. Active resistance came mainly from younger members of the Jewish community, particularly those who were Zionists before the arrival of the Germans. Some of these had succeeded in avoiding internment in the ghetto by having documentation that disguised their Jewish background, and, at first in isolation, they began to develop networks. A Jewish girl, Tamara Katz, survived the shootings at Paneriai and, after digging her way out of a mass grave, reached Vilnius where she was sheltered by the underground. She told them about the events at Paneriai, and not long after, the group was able to get a message into the ghetto:

> All of the Gestapo's roads lead to Paneriai. And Paneriai is death. You doubters, shed your illusions! Your children, husbands and wives are no longer living. Paneriai is not a camp. 15,000 have been shot to death there ... It is true, we are weak and helpless, but the only answer to the enemy is: Resistance! Brothers! Better to fall as free fighters than live by the grace of murderers! Resist! Resist to your last breath![42]

The Germans did all they could to crush any attempt at resistance. If a member of a work detail ran away and escaped, the other workers in the detail were held as hostages, and if the escapee did not return, they were executed. Nevertheless, there was a steady trickle of young Jews from the ghetto to the nearby forests, where they joined the burgeoning groups of partisans.

On October 1941, a limited number of 'yellow certificates' was distributed to Jews in the Vilnius ghetto. Only those most capable of physical work received the certificates, and all those without certificates were rounded up and taken to Paneriai for execution. Esterowicz was able to obtain a precious certificate from his Polish employer, but many of his family were not so lucky. Perella Esterowicz left the ghetto with her parents during the 'action', and was taken in by a non-Jewish family. Her parents returned to the ghetto without her, consoling themselves that at least she was now comparatively safe. They must have had very mixed feelings when Perella decided that she wished to stay with her family, and returned to the ghetto a few days later by tagging onto a work party marching back for the night.[43]

Sometimes, resistance and help came from the most surprising individuals. Anton Schmid was an Austrian who had already helped a small number of Jewish neighbours escape in 1938. He was conscripted in 1939, but aged 39 was assigned to a rear area unit. In Vilnius, Feldwebel Schmid was tasked with helping troops who had become separated from their units to return to their parent formations. He was a man who kept very much to himself, as a friend later described:

> He was a simple, true-hearted man, in thoughts and deeds an awkward man of few words, not religious, he wasn't philosophical, read no newspaper, nor any books, he was not a great thinker, his outstanding characteristic was his humanity.[44]

Schmid discovered that his military role allowed him to issue work permits to Jews in the Vilnius ghetto, and he started to do so. The Jews regarded work permits as 'death holiday passes', as the bearer of such a permit was far less likely to fall victim to an 'action'. As a result, many people were saved from execution. But Schmid did not stop there. He regularly provided food for Jews in the ghetto, and he arranged for a birth certificate to be produced for a Jewish girl, stating that she was actually an Aryan; in other cases he arranged documents that allowed a small number of Jews to travel across Lithuania. Most of these took the opportunity to disappear. On some occasions, when Jews to whom he had issued work permits were arrested, he went to the Lukiškės Prison and had them released. Perhaps his most important contribution was a fairly regular journey that he made from Vilnius to Belarus with his truck, usually carrying timber. On most journeys, he took between 20 and 30 Jews, concealed behind the timber, with him. At the time, the repression of Jews in Belarus was far less severe than in Lithuania, and consequently he saved perhaps 300 people from imminent death. Some took advantage of the less strict regime in Belarus to run off to join the partisans.

Partly as a result of these journeys, and partly due to other clandestine movements of Jews, the notion of armed Jewish resistance – something that originated in Vilnius – spread to other centres, such as Warsaw, Białystok and Grodno. Members of the underground movement frequently stayed in Schmid's accommodation during their travels, and on occasion he made journeys specifically to help them reach their destinations.

Schmid was a solitary figure, and for obvious reasons he could not confide in his fellow Germans about his activities. It is therefore a matter of speculation as to why he acted as he did. It seems that this devout Christian acted purely on the dictates of his conscience. In late January 1942, he was arrested when a ghetto was established in Lida, in Belarus. Some of the Jews in the new ghetto were originally from Vilnius, and a few told the Gestapo how they had travelled to Lida. At his court martial, his defence lawyer stated that Schmid had tried to save Jews so that they would be available as labour for the Wehrmacht, but Schmid himself rejected this line of argument, stating clearly that he had transported Jews away from Vilnius to save their lives. He was convicted and executed by firing squad on 13 April 1942. Shortly before his death, he wrote a final letter to his wife and daughter, which he handed to the Catholic priest who attended him on his last day. The letter gives the best insight available into his motives:

Today I can tell you everything about the fate that has overtaken me … unfortunately, I have been condemned to death by a military court in Vilnius … they aren't able to secure me a pardon, and think that it [the request for a pardon] will be rejected, as all have been rejected so far. Therefore, my dears, hold your heads high. I have resigned myself to my fate … our God on high has decided that it cannot be altered. I am at peace today … our dear Lord has willed this and made me strong. I hope that he will make you as strong as me.

I want to tell you how this all came about. There were a lot of Jews here, who had been gathered together by the Lithuanian military and were shot in a field outside the city, as many as two or three thousand people. They smashed the children against the trees along the way. Can you imagine. I had to take over the 'stragglers' office', which I didn't want to do, and 140 Jews worked there. They asked me if I could take them away from here. I let myself be persuaded. You know how I am, with my soft heart. I couldn't think, and helped them, which was bad according to the court.

My dear Steffi and Gerta, you think this is a heavy blow for us, but please, please forgive me. I have only acted as a human being and didn't want to hurt anyone.

When you have this letter in your hands, my dears, I will no longer be in this world. You will not be able to write to me, but be sure that we will see each other again in a better world with our dear Lord.[45]

When word of his conviction and execution spread through his family's neighbourhood, many people openly referred to Schmid in conversations with his family as a 'traitor to the nation'. On one occasion, the family home was attacked, and windows were broken.

Of about 40,000 Jews in Kaunas in June 1941, only a small number managed to escape before the arrival of the Germans. After the initial wave of killings immediately after the arrival of the Wehrmacht, most of the shootings took place at Fort VII, one of a ring of 19th-century fortifications around the city. From mid-August, the surviving Jews were confined to the ghetto in Vilijampolė, an area of poor housing where previously about 15,000 had crowded together. Joheved Inčiūrienė was 17 when the Germans arrived; she had attempted to flee with her family, but they had travelled only 30 miles before they were overtaken by the Wehrmacht and forced to turn back.

I found it unbelievable that only a day after the assault [the arrival of German troops in Kaunas] the attitude of our Lithuanian neighbours to the Jews had changed.

... Our family was almost the first to be resettled in the ghetto. The Jews themselves had to encircle the ghetto with barbed wire. This took from 15 July to 15 August ... On 15 August, they set up armed watch posts at the ghetto gates, and free movement to and from the ghetto was stopped.

... On 17 August, the third day after the ghetto gate was closed, the Gestapo ordered that 500 men were to be gathered in preparation for archival work. On 18 August, these selected men were taken away from the ghetto gate in trucks; they were never seen again.[46]

It seems that this was the first move to eradicate the better educated members of the ghetto.

As in Vilnius, there was at first a large ghetto and a small ghetto, though on this occasion they were connected by a wooden bridge. There was the same arrangement with a *Judenrat* and ghetto police, overseen by Hauptsturmführer Fritz Jordan. Rations were completely inadequate, and every attempt was made by the ghetto dwellers to grow whatever vegetables they could. There were repeated 'actions' to reduce the population; on 26 September 1941, perhaps 1,500 elderly, women and children – those without work – were taken to Fort IV on the outskirts of the city and shot. On 4 October, the small ghetto was cleared. Those with work permits and their families were separated into one location, while the rest were driven away for execution. There was a small hospital in the ghetto – there were no medical supplies, and it served merely as a place where the sick could be gathered together – and this was simply burned down with its inhabitants still inside.[47]

On 28 October, the inhabitants of the large ghetto were sorted in a similar manner. Those deemed as 'unneeded' were transferred to the small ghetto, and from there were taken to Fort IX and shot the day after.[48] Many families that had survived together were now forcibly separated with individuals being sent to either side of the party responsible for sorting them, though in a few cases there were reprieves:

> It took almost all day before our group stood before Rauca [Hauptscharführer Helmut Rauca] ... Lena clung to my arm, her sister Rachel on the other side. It had been clear for a long time that the right side was bad. Most of our group were sent to the right. When we got there, Rauca merely waved his stick to the right. Our death sentence. I wanted to cry out that it was a mistake, that we were young and could work. But actually I only cried out in my thoughts. Then Rauca saw Lena. He stopped our row, called her out and ordered her to go to the left. 'You are far too beautiful to die,' he said. But Lena just shook her head proudly and replied that she wanted to share the fate of her family.[49]

Those who survived – it is estimated that there were now about 17,000 people left in the ghetto – faced constant danger. Many were required to work at the new Luftwaffe airfield on the edge of the city, and Luftwaffe personnel repeatedly came to the ghetto to round up people for work. Many were beaten if they showed reluctance, others were killed on the spot. Joheved Inčiūrienė took advantage of an opportunity to escape while returning to the ghetto from the airfield, and sought refuge with a schoolfriend who had already run considerable risks in bringing food to the ghetto. It was impossible for her to be sheltered indefinitely, so she tagged onto another work party returning to the ghetto, but continued to escape overnight from time to time, and then return with precious food. On one occasion, she was challenged by a Lithuanian guard, but to her great good fortune, discovered that she had attended school with his sister. The guard helped her, and his family sheltered her for a few nights. On another occasion, a Lithuanian woman betrayed her to a guard, and she was badly beaten. Eventually, she made a permanent escape, living in the countryside for several years before the arrival of the Red Army. Her family was less fortunate. Her mother and sister were transferred to a camp in Estonia, where they died, and her father perished in the Kaunas ghetto.[50]

Although the 'actions' ceased in the Kaunas ghetto during 1942, Jews continued to be shot at Fort IX. These were from within the Reich, and had originally been intended for internment in the ghetto established in Riga. However, as the Riga ghetto was full, they were diverted to Kaunas, and executed there. By the end of the year, about 6,000 Jews from Vienna, Frankfurt am Main, and Munich had been killed in the fort.[51]

The ghettos continued to function through 1942 into 1943, with a steadily falling population – despite the diminishing threat of 'actions', disease and malnutrition took a toll. In mid-1943, many of those in the Vilnius ghetto who were deemed to be the fittest for work were transferred to the Vaivara concentration camp in Estonia. At the end of 1943, the Vilnius ghetto was 'liquidated'. Mascha Rolnikaite, whose eldest sister had already left the ghetto, was present when an announcement was made that the ghetto would be evacuated, with its remaining inhabitants transferred either to Vaivara or to a work camp near Šiauliai. The latter did not exist, and the people in this group were actually destined for an extermination camp. A day later, the family joined a column of Jews who were marched to a hall, where the few remaining men were separated and taken away. The women and children remained there overnight. The following morning, they were marched out, and suddenly, a soldier separated Rolnikaite from her family:

The soldiers had formed a chain across the entire width of the road. Behind this chain – and beyond another one on the other side – was a large crowd. Mama was there. I ran to the soldier and asked him to let me through. I explained that I had been separated from my mother by mistake. She was standing over there. It was my family, and I had to go to her.

I spoke to him, beseeched him, but the soldier took no notice of me whatsoever. He looked at the women who were coming through the gate. From time to time, he pulled another over to our side. The rest were pushed into the crowd where Mama stood.

Suddenly, I heard Mama's voice. She cried that I shouldn't come to her. And she asked the soldiers not to let me through, as I was still young and could work hard …

'Mama!' I cried, as loud as I could, 'Come to me!' She merely shook her head and called to me with an oddly hoarse voice, 'Live my child! At least you should live! Take revenge for the little ones!' She drew them close to her, said something, and lifted them laboriously up one at a time, so that I could see them. Ruwele looked at me strangely … he waved with his little hand …

They were pushed to one side. I never saw them again.[52]

Perella Esterowicz recalled that many of the guards during the liquidation of the Vilnius ghetto were Estonians. She and her parents were able to survive the deportations and executions that attended the end of the ghetto through the actions of a remarkable man.

Karl Plagge was an army major in charge of a vehicle repair facility near Vilnius. Although he was a member of the National Socialist Party, believing that it was the only political party capable of restoring Germany to its rightful place, he was heavily criticised before the war for refusing to accept National Socialist racial theories. He was deeply shocked by the plight of Jews in Vilnius, and decided to take whatever steps he could to prevent killings. Like Schmid, he had given dozens of work permits to Jews since the formation of the ghetto, and he now took about 1,300 Jews from the ghetto, including the Esterowicz family, to a special labour camp that he had created next to his repair facility.

Plagge had gone to great lengths to establish the 'slave labour' camp, housed in buildings built before the war by a Jewish entrepreneur. He ensured that the workers received rations that, whilst still minimal, were at least sufficient to sustain them. He forbade his staff from mistreating the Jews, but was unable to prevent all attacks on the inmates of the camp. Taking advantage of Plagge's absence, the SS visited the camp in late 1943 to demonstrate to the inmates that their continued existence was never to be taken for granted, as Perella Esterowicz recalled:

I do not remember the exact date ... After all the workers had been mustered out on the yard where the Jewish police had built a gallows (on the command of the Germans) [as was the case in the ghettos, several Jews had been selected to form a police force to enforce 'order' in the camp], the gate suddenly opened and three Gestapo men, led by Bruno Kittel, the liquidator of the ghetto, drove in an open car. They brought with them two fugitives from our camp they had caught – a woman who belonged to a family of society's dregs nicknamed 'Pozhar' ['Fire'] and her unofficial husband. The deathly silence which had begun to reign as the Gestapo men moved towards the gallows with the condemned was broken by the piercing cry of 'Mama!' which suddenly sounded from a window on the upper floor of one of the buildings in which we saw a child's head. Before the passing of even one minute a little girl, maybe eight or ten years old, ran out from the building and rushed with a joyous cry of 'Mama!' to embrace her mother. We witnessed here a horrible, heartrending scene – the joy of the child who thought that she had found the mother she was longing for, and the face of the mother, distorted by suffering, passionately embracing her child, knowing that she was walking to her death. When the whole group arrived at the place of execution, Kittel motioned to Grisha Schneider, the camp's blacksmith ... to step forward from our lines and ordered him to be the executioner. However, when the man (whom they were hanging first) fell twice when the noose tore, Kittel ordered him to kneel down and killed him by a shot in the back of his head. Afterwards, while he was killing the woman, one of the other Gestapo men killed the child. The Gestapo was not satisfied with this, however. Having decided to shoot 36 women the next morning after the men had gone to work as a punishment, to forestall any more flights from the camp, the Gestapo ordered the Jewish police to chase all the women and children out of the rooms onto the huge yard adjacent to the buildings.

When the policeman Miganz, a man my parents knew, chased us down onto the yard, we were immediately surrounded by rifle-wielding Lithuanian police. Kittel mustered us out into rows and stood before us with his arms crossed. My mother and I were in the first row, Kittel was standing just in front of us ... Then Kittel smiled and, I guess on a sign from him, the Lithuanian police started to club us, herding us around the side of the building, toward where they were grabbing and dragging women into the black van standing in between the two buildings.[53]

Fortunately for Perella and her mother, her father managed to extract them from the women and children being herded into the van. The following March, again when Plagge was away from Vilnius, the SS returned:

In the early morning, after the men had left for their work places, the gates of the camp were opened suddenly and into the yard of our camp drove in trucks carrying a large contingent of officials of the Gestapo and of the Lithuanian police, led by Martin Weiss ...

The new arrivals scattered swiftly over the dwellings from which they began dragging out children and teenagers up to the age of 15, as well as even those few elderly who had managed to get to our camp. They took the captured to the trucks into which they pushed their prey. Heartrending scenes took place in our camp when the sobbing children vainly looked to their parents for protection. Mrs Zhukowski ... was killed by Martin Weiss with a shot from his revolver, after Mrs Zhukowski had called him 'murderer'. ... In some cases the mothers, not wanting to abandon their children in this terrible moment, shared their children's fate voluntarily. The fate of the seized children was more than terrible. As we learned later after the cessation of hostilities ... since the 'gas chambers' could not keep up with their task, the transports with the children were sent straight to the ovens. I avoided this horrible fate by hiding ...

The 'children's action' shook the camp to its very foundations. The air was filled with moans of disconsolate mothers, people moved around the camp like shadows.[54]

Eventually, in 1944, as the Red Army approached, the remaining inmates realised that the SS would in all likelihood kill them. They prepared hiding places, but had to wait for the last moment before trying to escape or hide. They waited for a sign that the moment had come, and Plagge did not let them down:

> On Saturday, 1 July 1944, Major Plagge … came to talk to us. We clustered around him, eager to hear what he would tell us about what lay before us. Major Plagge warned us that the German army was leaving Vilnius and our camp would be evacuated westward in connection with the nearing of the Russians. To emphasize his warning Major Plagge informed us in his speech that we would stop being a HKP [*Heeres Kraftfahr Park* or 'Army Freight Vehicle Pool'] work camp and would be entirely in the hands of the SS – he then carefully commented: 'And you all know full well how well the SS takes care of their Jewish prisoners.'[55]

Acting on this clear warning, many of the camp inmates took to their hiding places, and endured several days in cramped conditions, exacerbated by inadequate ventilation. Some of the Jews became deranged, even attacking other inmates; a group of young men took it upon themselves to maintain order, and killed several of the more violent deranged individuals rather than risk discovery by the Germans. Those who did not attempt to hide were shipped off to Paneriai, where they were shot. A search of the buildings by the SS revealed about 200 more inmates, and they were executed within the camp. After the Germans had abandoned the camp, the remaining 250 Jews cautiously emerged from their hiding places. Perella Esterowicz and her parents were given shelter by a Lithuanian, and thus survived the final battle for Vilnius before the Red Army took control.[56]

Plagge survived the war, and was saved from prosecution by the testimony of some of those he had saved. He personally made little attempt to defend himself, but when some of the Jews he had saved heard of his trial, they sent a representative to the proceedings. He died in 1957, still wracked by guilt that he had not saved more Jews.[57]

The ghetto in Kaunas, too, came to an end in 1944. The previous year, it was taken over by the SS and turned into a concentration camp, and in September 1943 nearly 3,000 people were removed – the fittest were sent to Vaivara, the rest to extermination camps. In late March 1944, there occurred a particularly grim 'action', in which all of the children in the ghetto were taken away. As with other ghettos, pregnancy was forbidden, but during the lifetime of the ghetto, a few babies were smuggled out, and cared for by sympathetic Lithuanian women. Like the inhabitants of the Vilnius ghetto, many Jews took part in an active resistance movement, some of them armed, and over the years about 300 escaped to join the partisans. The Germans were aware that the *Judenrat* and ghetto police were at least sympathetic to the resistance movement, and executed 34 members of the police for failing to reveal the hiding places of the resistance fighters. In July, three weeks before the arrival of the Red Army, the camp was closed, with the remaining inmates being sent either to Dachau, near Munich, or Stutthof, near Danzig. The buildings were set ablaze, and many Jews died trying to escape the flames. About 500 survived by hiding in a well-constructed bunker or by escaping to the nearby countryside.[58]

When the Wehrmacht crossed the border into Latvia, Stahlecker and his *Einsatzgruppe* were close behind. In Riga, Stahlecker once more found it surprisingly difficult to initiate a 'self-cleansing' anti-Jewish pogrom. He blamed this on the effectiveness of Soviet attempts to exterminate the non-communist Latvian leadership, but nevertheless stated in his report:

> It was possible though through similar influences on the Latvian auxiliary to set in motion a pogrom against Jews also in Riga. During this pogrom all synagogues were destroyed and about 400 Jews were killed. As the population of Riga quieted down quickly, further pogroms were not convenient.
>
> So far as possible, both in Kowno and in Riga evidence by film and photo was established that the first spontaneous executions of Jews and Communists were carried out by Lithuanians and Latvians.[59]

Other German reports also spoke of large-scale killings of Jews by locals, for example in the town of Jelgava, where 1,550 Jews were allegedly killed by Latvians; the truth was that on this occasion, the killings were carried out by *Einsatzgruppe A*.[60] The port of Liepāja had a significant pro-communist community, and partly as a result of this the town put up fierce resistance to the Wehrmacht. It proved difficult to establish a pro-German local police force, or even a suitable militia that could help with executions; consequently, the shootings of Jews and communists in the town on 29 June and 3 July were carried out by *Einsatzkommando 2*.[61]

Stahlecker states in his report that it was anticipated that even where it was possible to instigate local actions, these initial pogroms would not of themselves be sufficient to eliminate all Jews from the Baltic States. His report details the events of autumn 1941 in chilling detail:

> In accordance with the basic orders received, however, the cleansing activities of the Security Police had to aim at a complete annihilation of the Jews. Special detachments reinforced by selected units – in Lithuania partisan detachments, in

Latvia units of the Latvian auxiliary police – therefore performed extensive executions both in the towns and in rural areas.

The actions of the execution detachments were performed smoothly. When attaching Lithuanian and Latvian detachments to the execution squads, men were chosen whose relatives had been murdered or removed by the Russians.

Especially severe and extensive measures became necessary in Lithuania. In some places – especially in Kaunas – the Jews had armed themselves and participated actively in *franc-tireur* war and committed arson. Besides these activities the Jews in Lithuania had collaborated most actively hand in glove with the Soviets.

The sum total of the Jews liquidated in Lithuania amounts to 71,105.

During the pogroms in Kaunas 3,800 Jews were eliminated, in the smaller towns about 1,200 Jews.

In Latvia as well the Jews participated in acts of sabotage and arson after the invasion of the German Armed Forces. In Daugavpils so many fires were lighted by the Jews that a large part of the town was lost. The electric power station burnt down to a mere shell. The streets which were mainly inhabited by Jews remained unscathed.

In Latvia up to now 30,000 Jews were executed in all. 500 were made harmless by pogroms in Riga.

Most of the 4,500 Jews living in Estonia at the beginning of the Eastern Campaign fled with the retreating Red Army. About 200 stayed behind. In Tallinn alone there lived about 1,000 Jews. The arrest of all male Jews of over 16 years of age has been nearly finished. With the exception of the doctors and the Elders of the Jews who were appointed by the Special Commandos, they were executed by the Self-Protection Units under the control of the Special Detachment 1a. Jewesses in Pärnu and Tallinn of the age groups from 16 to 60 who are fit for work were arrested and put to peat-cutting or other labour.

At present a camp is being constructed in Harku, in which all Estonian Jews are to be assembled, so that Estonia will be free of Jews within a short while.

After the carrying out of the first larger executions in Lithuania and Latvia it became soon apparent that an annihilation of the Jews without leaving any traces could not be carried out, at least not at the present moment. Since a large part of the trades in Lithuania and Latvia are in Jewish hands and others carried on nearly exclusively by Jews (especially those of glaziers, plumbers, stovemakers, cobblers) many Jewish partisans are indispensable at present for repairing installations of vital importance for the reconstruction of towns destroyed and for work of military importance. Although the employers aim at replacing Jewish labour with Lithuanian or Latvian labour, it is not yet possible to displace all employed Jews especially not in the larger towns. In co-operation with the labour exchange offices, however, all Jews who are no longer fit for work are being arrested and shall be executed in small batches.

In this connection it may be mentioned that some authorities at the Civil Administration offered resistance, at times even a strong one, against the carrying out of larger executions. This resistance was answered by calling attention to the fact that it was a matter of carrying out basic orders.

Apart from organising and carrying out measures of execution, the creation of ghettos was begun in the larger towns at once during the first days of operations. This was especially urgent in Kaunas because there were 30,000 Jews in a total population of 152,400.

... In Riga the so-called 'Moscow suburb' was designated as a ghetto. This is the worst dwelling district of Riga, already now mostly inhabited by Jews. The transfer of the Jews into the ghetto-district proved rather difficult because the Latvians dwelling in that district had to be evacuated and residential space in Riga is very crowded, 24,000 of the 28,000 Jews living in Riga have been transferred into the ghetto so far. In creating the ghetto, the Security Police restricted themselves to mere policing duties, while the establishment and administration of the ghetto as well as the regulation of the food supply for the inmates of the ghetto were left to Civil Administration; the Labour Offices were left in charge of Jewish labour.

In the other towns with a larger Jewish population ghettos shall be established likewise.[62]

In November 1941, Hitler issued orders that the Jews in ghettos and camps in Germany and west and central Europe should be removed to the east. At first, they were taken to Minsk, but when the city reached an unacceptable level of crowding, trains were diverted to Riga. It was partially in response to this requirement that there was an escalation in killings in Riga, but as has been discussed, some of those brought to the Baltic States from elsewhere were simply shot on arrival, as there was nowhere for them to go. 30,000 of the inhabitants of the Riga ghetto were killed on 30 November and 8 December 1941, mainly in the Rumbula Forest near Riga.[63] A small proportion of those killed in these shootings were German Jews, newly arrived from the west. The small number of surviving Latvian Jews was confined to a part of the ghetto that became known as the 'small ghetto', while the rest of the area was filled with Jews from elsewhere in Europe, and was called the 'German ghetto'.

Unterscharführer Eduard Roschmann, a native of Vienna, was a member of the SD team in Riga from the start of the German occupation, and was heavily involved in the killings in and near the town. In March 1942, he was one of those who selected about 3,700 ghetto inmates for transfer to a work camp at the Daugava estuary, outside Riga. There was no such work camp, and all of those selected were shot in nearby woodland. In January 1943, he replaced Kurt Krause as commandant of the Riga ghetto. Krause had established a reputation for unpredictable sadism, switching from polite conversation to sudden violence without warning. He shot many inmates himself for small or imagined infringements, including on occasion executing children in front of their parents.[64] Krause was moved to take command of the concentration camp at Salaspils, about 12 miles from Riga. Roschmann proved to be less unpredictable, and though he was involved in several killings, many of the inmates felt a sense of relief at his appointment.

In summer 1943, a new concentration camp was established at Mežaparks on the edge of Riga, known as Kaiserwald to the Germans. Most of the Riga inmates who were fit for work were transferred here, while the ghetto itself was gradually run down. Most of those left were transferred to Auschwitz, where they perished. The inmates of Kaiserwald were used as forced labour, and were either executed or transferred to Stutthof before the arrival of the Red Army.

Compared to Lithuania and Latvia, Estonia had only a small Jewish population, of less than 4,000. These people also had the advantage that it took the Germans far longer to reach Estonia than the other two Baltic States, and consequently about 75 per cent were able to escape to the Soviet Union prior to the arrival of the Wehrmacht. Shootings of those who remained began immediately after the arrival of *Einsatzkommando 1A*. Those who survived arrest were mostly taken to a newly established concentration camp near Tartu, where they were executed. It is estimated that fewer than a dozen Estonian Jews survived the war. The Vaivara concentration camp was the largest of a complex of 22 camps created in Estonia, and was used mainly to process Jews from other countries, particularly Latvia and Lithuania, after the 'liquidation' of the ghettos established earlier in the war. One of the main workplaces for inmates of the sites was the IG-Farben oil shale works. It is estimated that only about 15 of the camp personnel were Germans; the rest were either Estonians or Russian volunteers.

The attempt to exterminate the Baltic Jews was Germany's first real experience of a 'final solution', based on mass killing, to what the National Socialists called the

'Jewish Problem'. Whilst Jews in Germany and elsewhere had faced persecution, even random killings, there had been no attempts at mass executions. Indeed, in Poland, many Germans had behaved less severely towards the Jews than towards Poles. The experience of mass shootings gave added impetus to discussions that had already started in Germany about a permanent solution to the Jewish Problem. Even in purely financial terms, shooting all of Europe's Jews was unaffordable, particularly as large parts of the Soviet Union were now under German control, adding greatly to the number of Jews in German hands. Whilst SS personnel appeared to show little reticence when it came to killing East European Jews, many officers within the SS expressed concern that they would be far more reluctant to execute German Jews in the same way.[65] The previous three solutions to the Jewish Question – the establishment of some sort of East European 'reservation' for Jews, the creation of a distant Jewish colony on an island like Madagascar, or the transfer of Europe's Jewish population to the Soviet Union – had all failed to materialise. The search for a definitive answer resulted in the Wannsee Conference of January 1942, where the use of extermination camps using poison gas was adopted. Rudolf Lange, head of the SD and security police in Latvia, attended the conference. The German experience with the Baltic Jews can be seen as part of the process that led to this decision.

The Germans were keen to ensure that the natives of the conquered lands in the east – Latvians, Lithuanians, Belarusians and Ukrainians – played a substantial role in the execution of National Socialist racial policies. There were several reasons for this. Firstly, the risk of unrest in the conquered lands was greatly reduced if the initial pogroms could be portrayed as local actions. Secondly, as has been described, the instigation of ghettos could then be camouflaged as a measure to protect Jews from further attacks. Put together, these two steps established a firm picture of Jews being in some way deserving of the attacks upon them, and thus made further punishment in the form of forced labour or even execution more justifiable. Every opportunity to portray the Jews as the enemies of the citizens of Lithuania and Latvia was exploited; for example, a report from *Einsatzgruppe A* stating that a Soviet *Istrebitelnye Batalony* ('annihilation battalion', often used to carry out a 'scorched earth' policy as the Red Army retreated) contained 'characteristically large numbers of Jews' was made public in Latvia.[66] But there was another factor in the German policy of involving local people in the killings. Explaining this factor, Hitler stated in early 1942: 'We will then have people who have sinned so much that they will stick with us through thick and thin.'[67]

This policy was extended throughout the machinery of extermination. Officers ensured that all of their men were involved in the killings, in order to reduce the risk of any individual being prepared to testify against others. Similar patterns of behaviour have been seen elsewhere, for example in the Soviet Union, in the Yugoslav civil wars of the 1990s, and in the activities of criminal organisations throughout the world.

The historiography of this period sheds a considerable light on the attitudes of different countries to the events of the German occupation. It has been argued that one of the difficulties faced by Lithuania and Latvia is that their long suppression by their eastern neighbour, from the Czars to the Stalin era, left many with a sense of being victims. Consequently, many Lithuanian and Latvian historians have struggled to come to terms with the role of their fellow citizens as oppressors rather than the oppressed.[68] For decades after the war, Lithuanian communities in the west maintained that the Lithuanian Jewish community had betrayed Lithuania by cooperating with the Soviet occupation, and that almost no Jews had been affected by Stalin's deportations. Although it was accepted that some Jews had been killed by Lithuanians immediately after the arrival of the Wehrmacht, it was maintained that this was a very small number, and the mass extermination of Jews in 1941 did not involve Lithuanians. Photographs showing Lithuanian police shooting Jews were either dismissed as forgeries, or explained by claiming that the gunmen were actually Germans, or possibly Poles and Russians, dressed in Lithuanian uniforms. In any event, it was argued, many Lithuanians had risked their own lives to save Jews, thus redeeming any crimes against the Jewish population. Finally, the communities claimed that attempts to prosecute Lithuanians in the west were inspired by the politics of the Cold War, and the influence of Jews in the western press and media ensured that Lithuanians would not get a fair hearing.

It was only in 1975 that this dogmatic view began to change. Tomas Venclova, a Lithuanian dissident, was the first to write that Lithuanian involvement in the killings was substantial, and that the prevailing view of events was misleading. Although most of the previous beliefs about the events of 1941 have since shifted, there remains a body of opinion within Lithuania that the crimes of the Jews against Lithuania were at least as great as the crimes committed against the Jews.

In the case of Latvia, historical accounts of 1941 began to move towards a more 'balanced' view earlier. This was partly due to the fact that, as will be seen, Latvians played a much larger role in providing manpower for the German war effort than Lithuanians, and consequently the Latvian role in the war came under closer examination at an earlier stage. For the first few decades after the war, Latvian historians – under the scrutiny of the Soviet Union – concentrated on placing blame for all the crimes of 1941 upon the Germans, and the Latvian nationalist politicians. This latter group was a convenient scapegoat for the post-war Soviet regime, as it was composed of individuals who were strongly anti-Soviet. Whilst Latvian historians in Latvia itself condemned those who had served in the SS, Latvian exiles attempted to portray these men as patriots who had fought primarily for their country rather than for the Germans. As with Lithuania, the fall of the Soviet Union and restoration of Baltic independence has provided an opportunity for a reappraisal of the 'German times', as the period of German occupation is known in Latvia, and there is now a widespread acceptance that whilst the Germans were the instigators of the mass killings of Jews, and the use of Latvians in the SS, the Latvians who were involved have to share in the blame.

For Estonia, matters were rather different. With only a small Jewish population, most of whom had sided with the Soviet occupation and many of whom fled before the arrival of the Germans, there was less scope for local involvement in massacres. But many Estonians worked in the labour camps set up by the Germans, and as in the other Baltic States, acceptance of their culpability for what happened in those camps has been reluctant, not least because many of the same personalities played a large role in the anti-Soviet resistance after 1945.

Chapter 5

RELUCTANT ALLIES

After the Soviet occupation, all three Baltic States regarded the arrival of the Germans as an opportunity to re-establish their lost independence. However, there were widespread rumours that, under the terms of the Molotov–Ribbentrop Pact, Hitler had quietly acquiesced to the Soviet takeover, and the refusal of the Germans to prevent the Soviet occupation – indeed, in many cases, Germany actively blocked attempts by the Baltic States to maintain their independence – should have alerted the politicians of the three nations to the fact that Germany would not necessarily support their return to independent status. Nevertheless, all three countries made an attempt to restore self-government.

From the perspective of the Germans, the plans for the administration of the new territories were remarkably incomplete. Several factors worked against the creation of a coherent and detailed plan. Firstly, unlike Stalin prior to his takeover of the Baltic States, Hitler did not have access to significant groups of expatriate Lithuanians, Latvians and Estonians who supported his regime, and who could be prepared as a future government. In addition to communist exiles in the Soviet Union, Stalin had the support of a significant minority of the native population, thus ensuring that he had a reliable source of Baltic citizens, fluent both in Russian and in their own language; the Germans had no such resource. Secondly, the chaotic infighting between different sections of the National Socialist power structure ensured that, unlike planning for the repression and killing of Jews and communists, where cooperation was widespread, each agency pursued its own agenda. Finally, even within individual German organisations, such as Rosenberg's 'Chaos-Ministerium', there were multiple factions, many of which clearly flouted the wishes and instructions of their nominal leader.[1]

Lithuania, the first country to see the Red Army expelled in 1941, wasted no time in trying to reassert its independence. When the Wehrmacht entered Kaunas, the

Lithuanian Provisional Government was in clear control of the city, and was actively trying to recreate all of its previous posts and offices. The government had intended for Colonel Kazys Škirpa, the founder of the Lithuanian Activist Front and a former envoy to Berlin, to be its new head, but the Germans prevented him from travelling to Lithuania. He remained in Germany, and in 1944 was sent to a concentration camp near Bad Godesberg. It was his good fortune that the area was ceded to the advancing Western Allies almost without a fight, but he never saw his homeland again. He died in the United States in 1979, and his remains were finally returned to Lithuania in 1995.

In the absence of Škirpa, the Transitional Government appointed Juozas Ambrazevičius as acting prime minister. At first, his relationship with the German commandant of Kaunas, General Robert von Pohl, was cordial. However, whilst not overtly hostile to the Ambrazevičius administration, the Germans did all they could to obstruct its development into a proper government. Access to the radio station and the Kaunas press was obstructed; consequently, although the Provisional Government passed over 100 laws, it had great difficulty in implementing them, or even making anyone aware of the changes. There remained in existence a courier system that had been set up during the Soviet occupation, and using this, Ambrazevičius and his ministers were able to have some proclamations published in provincial newspapers.

The Germans rapidly established their own authorities in Lithuania. The country was given the name *Generalbezirk Litauen* ('General District Lithuania'), one of four parts of *Reichskommissariat Ostland*, and was under the control of Adrian von Renteln. Like General von Pohl, he was outwardly cordial to the Provincial Government, but worked actively to undermine it. The Gestapo worked in collaboration with him to try to destabilise Ambrazevičius' government, by encouraging a group of right-wing extremists to leave the Lithuanian Activist Front and therefore split the government. Although the attempt was unsuccessful, it further fuelled divisions within the Lithuanian leadership about how far they should collaborate with the Germans, with some favouring complete cooperation, while others wished to take a more overtly independent line. The reality was that with its army in firm control of the country, Germany could impose its will in a way that was beyond the ability of the Lithuanians to resist. Finally, after only six weeks of existence, the Provisional Government was disbanded.

In Latvia, nationalists tried to emulate the events in Kaunas, and briefly secured control of the radio station in Riga on 28 June, declaring the creation of a new Latvian government. Soviet forces arrived the following day and restored control, but the capture of Riga by the Wehrmacht three days later once more provided an opportunity for Latvian nationalists. A Latvian doctor named Malmanis called for volunteers to help form a new Latvian police force. Several thousand men responded, but any attempt to create a Latvian force answerable to a Latvian administration was blocked by the Germans.

During the preparation of *Barbarossa*, the *Abwehr* (German intelligence service) established a group in East Prussia called *Latviju Kareivju Nacionālā Savienība* ('National Federation of Latvian Fighters', or LKNS), composed of former soldiers and others thought to be of potential military help. This group, and others like it created by various competing German agencies, included in its ranks members of the Latvian *Pērkonkrusts* ('Thunder Cross') movement, a group variously described as extreme nationalists or fascists. Of all the Latvian groups active in Riga and Germany before and during the German takeover, *Pērkonkrusts* was the one that had the most coherent ideology, and therefore was the most unified. At first glance, the movement might have seemed to be the ideal partner for the National Socialists, much like fascist organisations elsewhere in Europe. However, from its foundation, *Pērkonkrusts* was as strongly anti-German as it was anti-Russian. Despite this, many members of the movement sought refuge in Germany during the Soviet occupation, and established strong links with the RSHA. Once the German invasion began, these links continued, with a close relationship between *Pērkonkrusts* and Stahlecker and his subordinates in *Einsatzgruppe A*. It had been a clear policy of *Pērkonkrusts* that Jews had no place in a future Latvia, and although the degree of involvement of *Pērkonkrusts* in the killings of Jews and 'communists' in Latvia remains unclear, these killings were certainly in keeping with *Pērkonkrusts* ideology. Certainly, within days of the arrival of *Einsatzgruppe A* in Riga, members of *Pērkonkrusts* helped create *Sonderkommando A*, under the command of Viktors Arājs. His unit, often referred to as the *Arājs Kommando*, was rapidly put to work by the Germans, as will be seen below.

Although members of LKNS were allowed to accompany the Wehrmacht into Latvia, their activities were strictly curtailed. The *Pērkonkrusts* leader, Gustavs Celmiņš, was with the German forces that seized Liepāja, operating immediately behind the front line; he was wounded when his vehicle ran over a landmine, and did not reach Riga until 10 July. Despite the obstacles placed in the way of all the returning Latvians, there was clearly a strong domestic movement for self-governance and independence, as Stahlecker reported:

Different Latvian groups are trying to establish central organisations. So far, the following have appeared: 1) the Central Organisation Committee for Liberated Latvia (leader: Colonel Kreišmanis); 2) the Interim Board of Direction of Latvia (leader: former trade minister Winbergs). As with the Wehrmacht, establishment of official contacts has been refused.[2]

As several bodies vied for authority in Riga, the competing German bodies – the Wehrmacht, the *Abwehr*, Goering's *Wirtschaftsinspektion Ostland*, which was created as part of the *Reichsmarschall's* economic post as supervisor of the Four Year Plan for industrial development, and the SD – all attempted to promote their own protégés. Briefly, an advisory council of former economics minister Alfred Valdmanis, Aleksandrs Plensners, General Oskars Dankers, and Gustavs Celmiņš formed in mid-July, but fragmented within days. In an attempt to cut through the mounting chaos, Rosenberg made a personal intervention in July, wishing to appoint Oskars Dankers as the leader of the future Latvian administration. On 20 August, Dankers was finally installed in Riga.

Meanwhile, the members of *Pērkonkrusts* were discovering the limitations of the new arrangements. The organisation had helped the Germans primarily in order to gain influence, with a view to forming the core of a future government. Instead, it found that the creation of units such as the *Arājs Kommando* and recruitment of large numbers of *Pērkonkrusts* personnel into sections of the *Einsatzkommando* diminished, rather than increased, the power of the *Pērkonkrusts* leadership: the new armed formations were entirely under the control of the Germans, rather than *Pērkonkrusts*. Nevertheless, Celmiņš continued with some success to promote the organisation in public, resulting in considerable support from Latvians across the country – some 200,000 signed a *Pērkonkrusts*-inspired petition calling on the Latvian community in the United States to acknowledge the crimes committed in the country by the communists, and to show solidarity.[3] *Pērkonkrusts* was easily the most visible Latvian political movement in Riga, and was also active across the country, opening branch offices in several small towns. In many of these rural areas, *Pērkonkrusts* leaders took control of local partisan units, and on occasion used their close relationship with the German authorities to place political opponents under arrest.[4]

Whilst it is difficult to establish a clear link between *Pērkonkrusts* and the massacres of Jews, the rise of the movement certainly coincided with an increase in anti-Semitic propaganda. The movement controlled several newspapers, and other newspapers were sympathetic to its cause. These were all used to promote the movement's strongly nationalist, anti-Semitic and anti-communist message. *Pērkonkrusts* even set up a series of schools, in which its ideology was heavily promoted; perhaps with an eye on securing a future for itself and Latvia in Hitler's New Order, the schools taught that Latvians were part of the Aryan races.[5]

Celmiņš was also keen to create two Latvian divisions within the Wehrmacht, and had talks with General von Roques about this. He even travelled to Berlin in pursuit of this idea, but further progress was obstructed, particularly by Himmler. By the time he returned to Latvia in October 1941, he found that the Germans had banned *Pērkonkrusts*. The ban was first announced on 25 August, taking advantage of the absence of Celmiņš in Berlin, and appears to have been precipitated by several factors. It was increasingly clear to the Germans that *Pērkonkrusts* would continue to press for an independent – if allied – Latvia, and this was contrary to *Generalplan Ost* and the German vision of a Baltic colony. The suggestion that Latvians were Aryans seems to have been particularly irritating from a German point of view, given their plans for mass deportations of the population. It also seems that the various factions of the German administration were keen to subdue the group, which was seen as being closely related to the SD and RSHA. But the clinching factor was that the hard-line nationalist ideology of *Pērkonkrusts* was directed as much against Germans as against Russians, and the various Latvian protégés of the *Ostministerium* and the Wehrmacht worked hard to make their German friends aware of this.[6] However, it is characteristic of the sometimes chaotic consequences of the competition between different bodies within Germany that the SD continued to protect and foster its *Pērkonkrusts* members. Celmiņš remained active in encouraging Latvians to enrol in aid of the German war effort, and was appointed head of the *Latviešu Brīvprātīgo Organizācijas Komiteja* ('Committee for Organising Latvian Volunteers'), which helped raise several Latvian police battalions. When these failed to transform into proper military formations, as he had intended, Celmiņš was removed from his post. Eventually, as he adopted an increasingly anti-German line, he was arrested in 1944 and placed in the Flossenbürg concentration camp in Bavaria.

In 1941 and 1942, with the prospect of a swift victory over the Soviet Union still a strong one, the Germans were not interested in allowing any form of nationalism in the Baltic States. As the tide of war turned against them, their attitude to the Baltic nations shifted to allow for the possibility of allied states, but by then it was too late. The failure of *Generalplan Ost* to allow any degree of self-government in the Baltic States (and also in Belarus and the Ukraine) resulted in a failure to take significant advantage of the strongly anti-Soviet attitude of most of the population of these countries. It can be argued that this failure, particularly in the larger context of Belarus and the Ukraine as well as the Baltic States, was a large – possibly decisive – factor in determining the outcome of the war on the Eastern Front, and therefore the entire world war.

The Estonian *Omakaitse*, whose members had helped disrupt Red Army movements during the brief German campaign to seize Estonia, were in most cases disarmed by the Germans. Nevertheless, their numbers continued to swell, and by the end of the year, about 40,000 Estonians had volunteered for service.[7] Many of those who came forward were men who had previously been in the pre-war Estonian Army, and whose units had been absorbed into the Red Army after Stalin's annexation of Estonia – one estimate suggests that two thirds of the 15,000-strong Estonian component of the Red Army deserted, and subsequently volunteered for service in the *Omakaitse* or police.[8] A minority of these men – fewer than 2,000 – were involved in mass killings, mainly of Jews and Roma, in both Estonia and occupied Russia. A larger number was probably involved in shootings of suspected communists, including members of so-called 'destruction battalions' – units organised by the retreating Soviets to carry out a 'scorched earth' policy across Estonia. The German authorities established a labour camp at Jägala, commanded by an Estonian, Aleksander Laak; when trainloads of Jews arrived at the camp, those deemed not healthy enough for work were shot. In 1943, the camp was 'liquidated', and the remaining inmates were killed. Many of the Estonian volunteers were incorporated into police battalions, some of which served in occupied Russia and Belarus. The first such formation was given the title *Estnische Sicherungsabteilung 181* ('Estonian Security Detachment 181') when it was created in Tartu at the end of August 1941. These battalions were involved in the killing of Jews in the Belarusian town of Navahrudak. They also took part in guard duties at labour, prison and concentration camps across Estonia and other occupied territories. One section of the police, headed by Ain-Ervin Mere and Julius Ennok, was later deemed to have rounded up individuals who for a variety of reasons were thought to be potentially hostile to German interests. Many of these were then executed, as a result of death warrants issued by Estonian officials.[9]

Jüri Uluots had been the last prime minister of Estonia prior to the Soviet occupation, and he created a national council, but was careful to avoid calling it a new government; he had watched the reaction of the Germans to the Lithuanian Transitional Government, and wished to avoid following the same path. Uluots attempted to persuade the Germans to allow him to establish a new independent Estonia, but his efforts were brushed aside. Struggling to find any well-known Estonian who could be appointed to run a puppet administration, the Germans turned to Hjalmar Mäe, who had been imprisoned before the war for attempts at pro-fascist plotting. He would now run a directorate, responsible for implementing German decisions and policies. Oskars Dankers and Petras Kubiliūnas were appointed to similar roles in Latvia and Lithuania respectively.

The contributions of the three Baltic States to the German war effort were very different. In an attempt to harness the widespread anti-Soviet sentiment in the western parts of the Soviet empire, Gruppenführer Gottlob Berger, chief of the SS Head Office, suggested in October 1941:

> Perhaps – using the expression 'Legion', which will not give any new uplift to the nationalistic aspirations of these countries – we can create Latvian, Lithuanian and Ukrainian *Hilfspolizei* ['assistant police' or 'auxiliary police'] battalions.[10]

The Estonians were the first to be included in the German military, not least because they were perceived to be the most 'Aryan' of the three nations. Many Estonians had joined paramilitary police battalions after the German invasion, though it proved difficult to maintain these battalions at full strength, owing to a mixture of casualties and the fact that the original volunteers had signed up for only one year's service. In August 1942, Estonians were invited to enrol in the newly created Estonian Legion. About 500 individuals came forward and in October, were sent to the former Polish cavalry barracks in Dębica to commence training. This was intended to be the first combat formation made up of Baltic citizens, and care was taken to ensure that as many men as possible were fluent in German as well as Estonian.

By November 1942, the contingent in Dębica was sufficiently large to form six rifle companies, a heavy weapons company and an anti-tank company. Hauptsturmführer Georg Eberhardt was appointed as commander of the new battalion, and Obersturmführer Franz Augsberger became commander of the Estonian Legion. Like many others assigned to non-German formations within the SS, Augsberger was an Austrian, with experience of service in the multi-national armies of the Austro-Hungarian Empire; in the eyes of the Germans, such officers were more likely to be suitable to command units from other cultures.

This first group of individuals slowly grew in number, until there were sufficient to create three battalions. These were given the collective name *1. Estnischen SS-Freiwilligen-Grenadier Regiment* ('1st Estonian SS Volunteer Grenadier Regiment'), and in March 1943, personnel from the regiment were used to form *Battailon Narwa*. This battalion was sent to the Eastern Front, forming part of *SS Panzergrenadier Division Wiking*, replacing a Finnish battalion that had been recalled by its government.

SS-Wiking was originally designated *SS-Nordische Division 5*, then *SS-Division (Mot.) Germania* before becoming *SS-Division (Mot.) Wiking* in early 1941, and was made up largely of one regiment of ethnic Germans, one of Dutch and Flemish volunteers, and one of Scandinavians. Late in 1942, it became a panzergrenadier division, and served with distinction in the southern sector of the Eastern Front. The division had a reputation for adopting a remarkably independent attitude; its first commander, Felix Steiner, rejected the order requiring that all Soviet prisoners suspected of being commissars should be shot out of hand, with the words 'No rational unit commander could comply with such an order.'[11] Nevertheless, many Finnish soldiers in the battalion described in letters to their families how Soviet prisoners were frequently executed summarily. Herbert Otto Gille, who replaced Steiner as division commander, confronted a political indoctrination officer in the division's artillery regiment and demanded that the man remove his Nazi brown shirt; when the officer refused, Gille threatened to have him forcibly undressed in public.

When *Battailon Narwa* arrived in April 1943, the new unit was designated as division reserve and held some distance to the rear. After the abandonment of the German assault on the Kursk salient, *SS-Wiking* was dispatched to shore up the front line near Izium, about 40 miles south-east of Kharkhov, where the German 46th Infantry Division was in danger of being overrun. The Estonians were deployed in the front line for the first time late on 16 July, and the following morning, were subjected to a heavy artillery bombardment. The shelling was followed by a Soviet armoured attack, and though the Estonian infantrymen fell back at first, the success of their anti-tank company in stopping the Soviet tanks restored their confidence, and they mounted an energetic counter-attack, destroying several tanks in close-quarter fighting. Fighting continued the following day, and again the battalion managed to hold its ground, but by the third day, it began to disintegrate. The individual companies were reduced to isolated strongpoints, and determined counter-attacks by the last battalion reserves were needed to maintain a coherent line; Eberhardt, the battalion commander, was killed leading one such counter-attack. The fighting resulted in about two thirds of the battalion being killed or wounded; its personnel claimed to have destroyed 74 Soviet tanks, 27 at close quarters, and to have killed several thousand Soviet troops.[12]

By mid-August, the arrival of reinforcements from Dębica had restored the battalion's fighting strength, and it was once more in the front line. After several days of intense combat, *Battailon Narwa* had only 157 combat personnel left unhurt; unlike Eberhardt, the new battalion commander appears not to have won the confidence of his men, and some of his criticisms about his men – he apparently expressed unhappiness that one of the rifle companies allowed Soviet tanks to bypass their positions – were particularly badly received.[13]

The Estonian battalion continued to be involved in heavy fighting in the Ukraine. During early 1944, *SS-Wiking* was one of six German divisions encircled to the west of Cherkassy by the Red Army as a result of the Korsun-Shevchenkovsky Operation. The Estonians helped defend the southern flank of the resultant pocket, blocking the advance of the Soviet 5th Guards Cavalry Corps. The battalion earned the grudging respect of its Soviet opponents, though it lost many of its personnel and almost all of its equipment when *SS-Wiking* succeeded in breaking out of the pocket.[14] The remnants of the battalion returned to Estonia in March 1944, where they were formed into a new battalion as part of the new 20th SS Waffen-Grenadier Division (1st Estonian).

When the Wehrmacht reached Latvia, it found anti-Soviet guerrilla bands operating in many areas. Some of these were small and ineffective, while others, particularly those swelled by deserters from the Red Army, were substantial. One of the largest and most effective groups, commanded by Karlis Aperats, included the bulk of the signal battalion of the Soviet 24th Rifle Corps, which had been a primarily Latvian formation. It operated in and around Alūksne, in north-east Latvia, and made repeated attacks on retreating Red Army units, though much of its activity concentrated on protecting the local population. Some guerrilla bands took advantage of the chaos to attack those deemed to be pro-Soviet sympathisers, but Aperats appears to have maintained a high level of discipline in his band.

As was the case in Lithuania, the Germans sought to use Latvian units in their policy of exterminating Jews. Perhaps the most infamous Latvian formation involved was *Sonderkommando Arājs*, often referred to as the Arājs Kommando. On arrival in Riga, the SD sought out an experienced leader who would be prepared to organise and lead a Latvian unit that could be used in attacks against Jews and communists. The first person they approached was Leonīds Brombergs, but he declined the invitation; in his place, Viktors Arājs was appointed. Arājs was the son of a Latvian blacksmith and the daughter of a Baltic German family; after partly completing a law degree in Riga, he had joined the Latvian police. Composed entirely of volunteers, Arājs' new unit was active from the first days of the arrival of German forces in Latvia. After Stahlecker's initial failure to incite a 'spontaneous' local anti-Jewish pogrom, the *Pērkonkrusts*-dominated Arājs Kommando initiated attacks on Jewish shops and homes in Riga. On 4 July, the Arājs Kommando attacked the Great Choral Synagogue in Riga, setting fire to the building and throwing in hand grenades; it is estimated that 300 Jews died in the fire. Other synagogues were also attacked, with substantial loss of life. Herberts Cukurs, who had achieved fame as an aviator before the war, was a notable participant in the killings: 'Eyewitnesses heard the people who were locked inside screaming for help and saw them breaking the synagogue's windows from inside and trying, like living torches, to get outside. Cukurs shot them with his revolver.'[15]

Worse was to come. The Arājs Kommando was extensively involved in mass shootings of Jews in the months that followed, particularly whenever Jews were taken from the Riga ghetto for execution. Arājs and his men were also involved in the killings of several thousand German Jews at Rumbula on 30 November and 8 December. It is estimated that the Kommando, which never numbered more than 500 men, killed at least 26,000 Jews, Gypsies and others deemed 'undesirable'.

Within the ranks of the former Latvian army, the general Latvian dislike of Germany was perhaps less pronounced than in other parts of Latvian society. The conduct of the Red Army, both during Latvia's war of independence after the First World War and during the recent occupation, had left almost the entire nation with a deep dislike of Bolshevism, and many Latvian officers regarded military cooperation with Germany as a stepping stone towards establishing independence. As the *Pērkonkrusts* leader Gustavs Celmiņš discovered during his visit to Berlin, however, Himmler was not inclined to support the establishment of a large Latvian force. Nevertheless, using the formula suggested by Berger regarding the creation of police battalions within 'legions', several of the units created in the wake of the Red Army's withdrawal were designated *Hilfspolizei*, *Schutzmannschaft* ('defence') and eventually police battalions. One of the first was the 16th Battalion, which was dispatched from Riga to Staraya Russa on 22 October 1941. The 21st Battalion was sent to the Leningrad theatre in April 1942, where it saw extensive front-line service, as is described below. Perhaps as a consequence of the Soviet occupation, the personnel of these battalions proved enthusiastic participants in shootings of suspected communists in the occupied areas of Russia. It should be noted that many of the inhabitants of these rural parts of north Russia, where anti-Semitic sentiments had existed for generations, willingly helped the Latvians in these killings.[16] Other battalions were implicated in the Holocaust, guarding the Warsaw ghetto or escorting trains carrying Jews to the extermination camp at Treblinka.[17]

One of the strangest episodes of Baltic cooperation with German operations, indeed of the entire war, relates to Ilya Galperin, who was a child of five in the Belarusian village of Dzerzhinsk. The Kurzeme Battalion of Latvian police, led by Kārlis Lobe, was sent to the area in late 1941, and on 21 October a Lithuanian unit led by Antanas Gecevicius entered the village and killed the largely Jewish population. Galperin had been told by his mother to flee the previous evening, and wandered in the nearby forests until he ran into Lobe's battalion. When he was about to be executed, he suddenly demanded that he be given something to eat. The soldiers had a remarkable change of heart, and adopted him as a sort of mascot. Only a very small number knew of his Jewish identity, and ensured that he kept it secret. Galperin appeared in German propaganda photos, wearing a miniature Wehrmacht uniform, and was adopted by a Latvian family. His name was changed, and he spent his adult life living as Alex Kurzem, before his son discovered his true story many years after the end of the war.[18]

There was considerable friction between the Latvians and Germans, for several reasons. Firstly, the Germans assigned liaison officers to all Latvian battalions. Although these officers were intended to act purely as advisers and to help with communications, many regarded themselves as being in a supervisory role, and acted accordingly. Inevitably, this was interpreted by the Latvians as unwelcome interference. Secondly, there was a serious disagreement between Obergruppenführer Friedrich Jeckeln, the German officer with overall authority for police units throughout the Baltic States, and Captain Gustavs Praudiņš, commander of one of the battalions. Jeckeln had Praudiņš arrested and charged with treason, allegedly for showing hostility towards Germany. Although he was convicted and sentenced to death, the Latvian civil administration succeeded in preventing his execution. Praudiņš was reduced to the rank of private, though he later rose to *Sturmbannführer* and earned several medals; the main consequence of the affair was a further deterioration between the Latvians and the Germans. A third cause of friction and suspicion was the sudden death of the Latvian Colonel Rudolfs Kandis in Krasnoye Selo in May 1942. The official German report stated that Kandis committed suicide after an argument with a German officer, but many Latvians suspected that the German officer shot him during the argument.[19]

The first Latvian police battalion to enter the front line on the Eastern Front was deployed near Krasnoye Selo in June 1942. It found itself involved in heavy fighting the following month, and despite being equipped with a variety of weapons captured from the Czech, Soviet and French armies, it acquitted itself well. Unfortunately, this did little to improve relations. Towards the end of the year, when it became known that Germany was creating an Estonian Legion, the Latvians became further disenchanted, feeling that they were being treated as inferiors. The Latvians remained determined to try to create combat formations that would be under their own control, so that they could defend Latvia if and when the Red Army returned. To this end, Alfreds Valdmanis, the Director of Justice in the civil administration, submitted a memorandum in November 1942. He described the historical relationship between Latvia and Germany, Latvia's success in achieving independence, and the dashing of Latvian hopes that the Germans would help restore independence after they had expelled the Soviets. He went on to argue that Latvia needed to have a political goal if it was to join the Germans wholeheartedly in the war against the Soviet Union, and that the only way that this could be achieved was by granting Latvia independence, even if this was of a limited nature. The precedent for such an act was the status of

Slovakia. In return, Latvia would raise an army of 100,000, though these troops would only be used in the defence of Latvia. The memorandum was returned by the local German authorities within days. They advised Valdmanis that they did not feel able to submit the memorandum to higher authorities in its current form; the Latvian duly amended and resubmitted it.

The memorandum was then passed to Obergruppenführer Gottlob Berger, the head of the *SS-Führungshauptamt*, the Berlin-based headquarters of the non-combat elements of the SS. Berger advised Himmler that the memorandum represented political manoeuvring by the Latvians, but Himmler decided to visit the Leningrad front personally to assess the anti-Bolshevik fighting spirit of the Latvians who were already in the front line. He found that the Latvian battalions had continued to be involved in heavy fighting, earning repeated commendations in official reports, and in January 1943 – with Hitler's approval – announced the creation of a Latvian Legion, thus removing the resentment that Latvians were being treated less favourably than Estonians. He also held discussions with Rosenberg about the possibility of granting at least some degree of autonomy to the Baltic States, but although they collaborated to produce a document recommending such an arrangement, it was rejected by Hitler.[20]

The Germans had actually drawn up plans for conscription of Latvians in December 1942, outlining a requirement for 90,000 men, who would serve variously as helpers for the Wehrmacht, soldiers in the Latvian Legion, further reinforcements for police battalions, and labourers for the war effort. Such conscription of the nationals of an occupied country was illegal, and as a consequence, attempts were made to show that the men were actually volunteers. The civil administration protested strongly about anything that looked like compulsory service, and demanded that the commander of the Latvian Legion should be a Latvian. The Legion was to be trained in Latvia, and deployed exclusively in the northern part of the Eastern Front. Food, pay and all other conditions for members of the Legion were to be the same as for Germans in the Wehrmacht. Hinrich Lohse, Reichskommissar for Ostland, rejected these demands, but faced with the threat of complete Latvian non-cooperation with the creation of a legion, he had to accede. The main sticking point remained the issue of command. At first, the Germans appeared to agree that the Legion would be commanded by General Rūdolfs Bangerskis, but later announced that this had been a misunderstanding. The commander of the new Latvian division within the Legion would be a German, but his second-in-command would be Latvian. Bangerskis would instead become Inspector General of the Latvian Legion. The exact nature of his duties was never specified, something that he was able to use to his own advantage.[21]

The two Latvian police battalions near Leningrad were serving as part of the 2nd Motorised SS Infantry Brigade, alongside Dutch and Flemish soldiers. The brigade served with distinction both during the Soviet Operation *Iskra* ('Spark'), which succeeded in establishing a land corridor into Leningrad, and the attacks to draw away the Germans from critical parts of the front. The Latvians were particularly heavily involved in the fighting around Siniavino. With the intention of converting the brigade into an entirely Latvian formation, Himmler ordered the Dutch and Flemish battalions transferred elsewhere, and eventually in May 1943, the unit was renamed the *2. Lettische SS-Freiwilligen Brigade* ('2nd Latvian SS Volunteer Brigade'). Earlier, the two Latvian police battalions were pulled out of the front line at the same time as the Dutch and Flemish troops were transferred out, and in conjunction with a third battalion commenced training as the first formal units of the Latvian Legion, under the overall command of Brigadeführer Fritz von Scholtz. They were in action in March 1943 to the south-west of Leningrad, near Verkneye-Koirovo, their first battle as part of the Legion, though shortly afterwards they were once more pulled out of the front line and given new uniforms and ranks, to reflect their new designation as a regiment of the SS. A large draft of reinforcements arrived from Latvia to bring them up to strength; contrary to the agreement between Lohse and the Latvian civil administration, these men had received only a minimal amount of training before being sent to the front, and when the brigade returned to the front line along the River Volkhov in May, it was barely ready for combat. Fortunately – perhaps as a result of the trackless marshes, which earned this sector the nickname 'The End of the World', there was little fighting in the sector through the summer. In September, the brigade went into action to contest a hill on the southern end of its sector, and finally prevailed, after suffering heavy casualties.[22]

Voldemars Veiss, who had been a Latvian army officer between the wars, was the Latvian officer who was effectively second-in-command of the brigade. He was awarded the Iron Cross during the fighting in September 1943, and in January 1944 became the first Latvian to earn the Knight's Cross, after successfully defending Nekokhovo from repeated Soviet attacks. He was killed in April 1944 after suffering wounds from a grenade explosion.

There continued to be friction between the Germans and Latvians. In addition to the 2nd SS Brigade, efforts were made to convert the Latvian Legion into a new formation, 15th SS Waffen-Grenadier Division (1st Latvian), in March 1943. The Latvians complained that there were insufficient NCOs and officers for this new division, and that attempts to bring it up to strength were constantly undermined by the transfer of troops to the 2nd SS Brigade. The division was also hampered by shortages of equipment; in some cases, men were issued with weapons that were different from those that they had used in their often inadequate training. In November 1943, even though the division was, in the opinion of its officers, not ready for combat, it was committed to the front line near Leningrad, and performed well in defensive fighting. Some battalions of the division were assigned to *ad hoc* battlegroups, as was normal practice in the Wehrmacht, and on many occasions, the German units in the battlegroups seized the new machine guns and other equipment of the Latvians, further adding to the tension between the two sides.

Towards the end of 1943, it was decided to upgrade the 2nd SS Brigade into a division. Designated the 19th SS Waffen-Grenadier Division (2nd Latvian), it was created in January 1944. As will be discussed later, it soon found itself in the thick of the fighting to the south of Leningrad.

Of the three countries, Lithuania provided the smallest military contingent to the German cause. Initially, the country's classification as being the least 'worthy' of the three countries – its population was largely Catholic, and was perceived by the National Socialist leadership as heavily tainted with Polish and Slav blood – meant that there was little question of Lithuanians being asked to serve in the Reich's armed forces. It was only as the war situation began to deteriorate, and Germany was desperate for manpower, that the issue was revisited. By then, there was even less enthusiasm than ever amongst Lithuanians to fight for Germany.

During the German occupation, the Lithuanian police formed a total of 25 battalions. These units should be distinguished from regular police units in towns and cities; they existed specifically for internal security purposes, such as protecting military installations and combating insurgents and partisans. The first battalions were formed from the Lithuanian Activist Front volunteers who fought the retreating Red Army in Kaunas, and from Lithuanians who deserted from the Red Army; these men came primarily from the Soviet 29th Corps, and were based in and around Varėna. At first, it had been the intention of the Lithuanians to organise these men into a fledgling army, but the Germans refused to allow this to happen, and on 9 July 1941, most of the units that had been given provisional army names were renamed *Selbstschutzeinheiten* ('self defence units'). Over the next few years, the battalions went through a variety of name changes before they were finally given the title 'police battalions'.

One of the first units to be formed was the *Tautos Darbo Apsauga* ('National Labour Service Battalion' or TDA) in Kaunas. Colonel Jurgis Bobelis, who had been appointed by the self-proclaimed Lithuanian interim government, called for volunteers to come forward on 28 June 1941, and by 4 July he had over 700 men at his disposal. Two companies were immediately assigned to *Einsatzkommando 3A* at Fort VII. One company was tasked with guarding the Jews who were brought there in a steady stream, while the other company carried out the executions, under German supervision. As the killings continued, both in Kaunas and through the activities of Hammann's *Rollkommando*, almost all of the personnel of the TDA were directly involved.[23]

The reaction of the Lithuanian soldiers to their gruesome tasks was varied. One of the junior officers of the battalion was Lieutenant Juozas Barzda, who had been a member of the Lithuanian Army prior to the Soviet occupation. He commanded 3 Company of the TDA, and was involved in several of the major massacres of Jews during 1941. He also took part in killings of Jews and Soviet prisoners in Belarus, but by 1944, he had joined the *Lietuvos Laisvės Armija* ('Lithuanian Freedom Army' or LLA), fighting against the returning Red Army. He was killed in December 1944 when, while taking part in a parachute drop, he drowned in a lake. Bronius Norkius, a former air force officer, was also a lieutenant in the TDA. He achieved fame for raising the Lithuanian flag over Kaunas Cathedral on 23 June 1941, but like Barzda he was implicated in many of the killings in that year. He died in an accident in the Soviet Union in 1943. A third lieutenant, Anatolijus Dagys, was also a member of 3 Company, and like the other two was noted to perform with distinction during the mass executions of Jews.[24] It is characteristic of the ambiguity with which many in Lithuania regard their past that in view of Norkius' act of defiance of the Soviet authorities in June 1941, his grave has been proposed as a national monument, despite his involvement in the killings later that year.

Other members of the TDA were shocked and demoralised by what they were required to do. Many requested permission to leave the battalion, and by 11 July 1941, less than two weeks after the establishment of the TDA, 117 men had been discharged. Captain Bronius Kirkila, commander of 1 Company, committed suicide on 12 July, and a steady stream of men simply deserted. Four of the battalion's lieutenants submitted their resignations and were dismissed.[25] None of these events had the slightest effect on the pace of the killings.

The 2nd Lithuanian Police Battalion, confusingly later renamed as the 12th Battalion, was formed on 7 August 1941 under the command of Major Antanas Impelivičius, using a cadre of men from the TDA. At first, the battalion was stationed at the Šančiai Barracks in Kaunas, and was responsible for guard duties, but in October, under the supervision of the German Major Lechthaler, it moved to Minsk. Here, working in cooperation with 707th Infantry Division, it was responsible for pacification. The commander of 707th Infantry Division, Generalmajor Gustav

Freiherr von Bechtolsheim, later reported that the Lithuanians helped his men execute 630 'suspicious elements' in the second week of October – mainly those deemed to be communists or Jews – and were also involved in the killing of about 1,300 people in the nearby towns of Kliniki and Smilovichi.[26] By the end of the month, with help from elements of *Einsatzkommando 3* and the German personnel that had accompanied its deployment from Kaunas, the Lithuanian 2nd Police Battalion had killed over 14,000 people.[27]

The killings of Jews in the town of Sluck shocked even the local German military. The local commandant wrote to Minsk in protest:

> Referring to the ways of performing the operation, I had to regret that it equalled to sadism. The town itself looked horrible during the operation. Indescribably cruel German police officers, and particularly the Lithuanian partisans, forced the Jews, including Belarusians, out of their homes and pushed them into one place. Firing was heard throughout the town, and in certain streets piles of the Jewish victims appeared … protect me from this police battalion in future![28]

The pace of killing continued. On 9 and 10 November, the battalion killed 8,000 people, mainly Jews, in Borissov. Three days later, another 3,000 were killed in Kleck. By the end of the year, when the battalion returned to guard duties, it had either killed or aided in the killing of 46,000 people, the great majority of them Jews.[29]

Several Lithuanian battalions spent periods of time in the Ukraine, where they were frequently involved in mass killings. The 4th Police Battalion, created in Kaunas on 25 August 1941, later renamed the 7th Battalion, was sent to the Ukraine in mid-1942. Here, the battalion's personnel were involved in the slaughter of Jews in Vinica and Nemirovo. Several of the battalions in the Ukraine found themselves sent to the front line as an increasingly desperate Wehrmacht attempted to shore up its defences, and suffered heavy casualties in combat.

It is estimated that ten of the 25 Lithuanian police battalions were involved in large-scale killings of Jews. Their personnel are thought to have killed some 78,000 individuals.[30]

In February 1943, partly to offset the losses suffered by Germany at Stalingrad, the *SS-Führungshauptamt* called for the creation of new SS divisions to help address the widespread manpower shortage. It was proposed that both Lithuania and Latvia would contribute a division. Brigadeführer Wysocki, who was the *Höhere SS- und Polizeiführer* ('senior SS and police commander' or HSSPf) for Lithuania, was instructed to raise a body of volunteers to form the new unit. He approached two former Lithuanian colonels, Anatanas Reklaitis and Oskaras Urbonas, and invited them to become commanders of two of the new division's regiments. They declined to take part, and the number of volunteers coming forward remained woefully inadequate, numbering barely 200, not least because the Lithuanian administration successfully hindered the process. Wysocki lost his post and was replaced by Brigadeführer Harm, but he had just as little success, and the planned division was never created. Humiliated by their failure, the Germans declared that Lithuanians were not fit to wear SS uniforms, and threatened to force all able-bodied male Lithuanians to work in labour camps, but the Lithuanians continued to refuse to cooperate; they did not object to the creation of a Lithuanian division, but insisted that it should remain entirely under the control of Lithuanians. Furthermore, they insisted, the division should not serve outside Lithuania.

Negotiations dragged on into early 1944, when the demands on German manpower were even more severe. In February, the Germans agreed to the Lithuanian demands, and a further call for volunteers was made. Somewhat to the surprise of everyone, both Lithuanian and German, some 19,000 came forward. Immediately, the Germans decided to use the men – far in excess of their expectations – as replacement drafts for existing Wehrmacht units, in direct contravention of what had been agreed with the Lithuanian administration, but after further negotiations, the volunteers were all organised into 13 police battalions and a reserve unit.

In late March 1944, Generalfeldmarschall Walter Model, commander of Army Group North, announced a requirement for 15 Lithuanian units to act as guards at airfields across Lithuania. There was consternation amongst the Lithuanians, who feared that these units would not be under Lithuanian command. In May, the Germans announced a general mobilisation of manpower, explicitly stating that the new units would be under German command. There was widespread unrest amongst the units created in February, and to avoid the possibility of such a large number of armed men breaking free of German control, the German authorities disbanded all 14 units. Of their manpower, about 3,000 agreed to remain in service, and were assigned to flak formations.

In late summer 1944, as the Red Army reached the eastern parts of Lithuania, there was a final attempt to raise troops to fight for the ailing German cause. Generalmajor Helmuth Mäder was commander of Army Group North's *Waffenschule* (weapons school), a training establishment created to remedy inadequate training amongst new recruits, and used the personnel of the school in the defence of Šiauliai. With two Lithuanian captains, Izidorius Jatulis and Jonas Cesna, he attempted to organise two infantry regiments and an artillery regiment from the remnants of police battalions and elements of the newly created *Tevynes Apsaugas Rinktine* ('Fatherland Defence Force' or TAR, akin to the German Home Guard or *Volkssturm*). Poorly trained and equipped, the battalions of the new formation fought in the last battles on Lithuanian soil.

The initial euphoria throughout the Baltic States after the arrival of the Wehrmacht evaporated in a matter of weeks, as it became abundantly clear to everyone that the Germans came as occupiers, not liberators. Under the control of the occupation authorities, the newspapers produced a steady stream of articles encouraging everyone to show more gratitude to Germany for the expulsion of the hated Bolsheviks, to little avail. Underground newspapers in all three countries highlighted German connivance in Stalin's seizure of the region in 1939 and 1940, and a Dutch visitor to the area in June 1942 found almost nobody who could be regarded as a genuine Germanophile.[31] One of the Lithuanian underground newspapers, *Nepriklausoma Lietuva*, compared the Nazis directly with the Bolsheviks, speculating on which were responsible for the murders of the most innocents.[32]

As cynical resignation replaced the euphoria of the expulsion of the Red Army, people began to consider how to resist the German occupation. Armed resistance seemed out of the question – there was little desire to assist the Red Army in overcoming the Wehrmacht and restoring Soviet rule. However, there were small groups of pro-Soviet partisans who were active from the outset. Antanas Sniečkus had been First Secretary of the Communist Party of Lithuania during the Soviet occupation, and was also head of the Department of National Security. He played a leading role in the organisation of the mass deportations of 1941, even having his own brother and his brother's family deported. In November 1942, the *Lietuvos Partizaninio Judėjimo Štabas* ('Lithuanian Partisan Movement') was created in Moscow to coordinate activity in Lithuania, with Sniečkus at its head. In practice, this proved to be largely a figurehead organisation, formed in an attempt to show that there was a large number of Lithuanians who wished to fight for the return of Soviet rule. In reality, although a few thousand Lithuanians did take part in partisan attacks against German targets, many of the partisans were members of the Red Army who had been left behind during the chaotic retreat, or Soviet personnel who infiltrated into the area during the war. In addition, there were small but significant Jewish partisan cells active in the forests around Vilnius, including one led by Abba Kovner, who attempted to organise an armed rising in the Vilnius ghetto. His *Fareynikte Partizaner Organizatsye* ('United Partisans Organisation' or FPO), which adopted the slogan 'We will not let them take us like cattle to the slaughter', was opposed by the *Judenrat*, which was under constant pressure from the Germans – Jacob Gens, the leader of the

Judenrat, was told that unless he brought the organisation to an end, the entire ghetto would be liquidated. Under pressure from the rest of the ghetto population, the FPO disarmed. Some of its members were arrested, while others fled to the forests. Yitzhak Wittenberg, who had been arrested and then rescued by the FPO, handed himself over to the Gestapo, but was found dead in his cell. It is believed that he was poisoned, possibly using poison that Gens gave him before he was handed over to the Germans.[33]

The Lithuanian Activist Front, which had organised the Lithuanian Provisional Government at the beginning of the German invasion, continued to press for at least a degree of autonomy, if not complete independence. The Germans rejected all such suggestions, and in September 1941, Leonas Prapuolenis, the leader of the LAF, was sent to Dachau. Two groups of those opposed to German rule were then formed in Lithuania, the *Lietuvių Frontas* ('Lithuanian Front') and the *Laisvės Kovotojų Sajunga* ('Union of Freedom Fighters'). These came together towards the end of 1943 to form the *Vyriausiasis Lietuvos Išlaisvinimo Komitetas* ('Supreme Committee for the Liberation of Lithuania'), which managed to maintain contact with Sweden and the west. The intention of the committee was to await a suitable moment to reassert Lithuanian independence; there was a hope that, as had been the case in 1918, the end of the war might provide a moment of opportunity. Unfortunately for the committee, the Gestapo was aware of similar moves in Estonia, and in 1944 moved to intercept a suspected Estonian courier. The person arrested was Colonel Kazimieras Amraziejus, a member of the Lithuanian group, and eight members of the committee were then identified and rounded up.[34]

In Latvia, anti-German partisan activity was at first limited almost exclusively to the eastern parts of the country, which had a large ethnic Russian population. Many of these partisans were initially trained in the Soviet Union, and then infiltrated into Latvia. The Soviet occupation had left most of Latvia with a strongly anti-Soviet sentiment, and the small number of Latvian communists had in the main left with the Red Army; most of those who stayed behind were denounced and handed over to the Germans, and shot. Some of those infiltrated back into Latvia were Latvian soldiers who had been conscripted into the Red Army, and had retreated with their parent regiments into the Soviet Union. Many now volunteered to return to Latvia as partisans, and whilst some may have been motivated by a desire to fight the Germans, most simply used it as a means of returning home, and disappeared within days of being parachuted into Latvia. A 250-strong unit of Latvian partisans attempted to work their way through the front line south of Lake Ilmen and then to move across country to Latvia, but was intercepted and easily destroyed by the Germans, who commented:

Apparently most of the Latvians merely wished to return to their homeland in this manner, or the leadership was so bad that it completely lost its head and let its troops get out of hand.[35]

As was so often the case in the occupied territories, it was German activity that proved to be the trigger for increased partisan activity. The population of the eastern Latvian province of Latgale, with its high percentage of ethnic Russians, was the subject of a major German drive in 1942 to collect men for forced labour inside the Reich. One such action, codenamed *Winterzauber* ('Winter Magic'), saw 99 villages in Latgale burned to the ground and over 6,000 inhabitants shipped off for forced labour in early 1943; an additional 3,600 people were shot for allegedly supporting partisans.[36] In addition to killing suspected partisans and their supporters, and gaining a supply of labourers, these operations were designed to create a desolate landscape where partisans would find it much harder to survive. For the local population, it was often an almost impossible situation. If they helped the partisans, they risked death at the hands of the Germans; if they refused to help the partisans, they risked death from the partisans, who regarded a failure to support them as treason. Indeed, until autumn 1943, almost all partisan activity in Latvia was directed against the civilian population, to extract food, clothing and shelter, with almost no attacks on German military targets.[37] On occasion, locals were forced to join the partisans, while others were executed as suspected German spies. Some of the activities of the partisans were irritating enough to lead to German reprisals. After one attack, German security police burned 119 peasants to death in the village of Pirčiupis in June 1944.[38] But like their German enemies, the partisans also carried out arbitrary revenge attacks. In 1944, a group of partisans commanded by Vasili Kononov, a Latvian of Russian ethnicity, came under fire near the village of Mazie Bati. Two days later, they returned to the area, and shot nine of the inhabitants of the village.[39]

Partisans in Latvia reported the tensions between the Germans and Latvians to their commanders in the Soviet Union, and in an attempt to increase recruitment, the Soviet Union began a propaganda campaign that tried to portray German rule as a continuation of the old domination of the area by the Baltic German aristocracy, and claimed that the partisan movement was composed of Latvian patriots. Nevertheless, the majority of Latvian partisans were either from within the Soviet Union, or ethnic Russians from Latgale – for example, the 235-strong partisan brigade *Sarkanā Bulta* ('Red Arrow'), which was active in north Courland in 1944, had only 68 Latvians in its ranks.[40]

It was only towards the end of the war, as the certainty of German defeat became ever clearer, that there was a significant increase in the number of Latvians joining the partisans. Even at this stage, there were tensions between the largely ethnic Russian communists amongst the partisans and their more nationalist Latvian comrades, whenever former members of the German-controlled police or the Latvian SS attempted to desert. The communists were inclined to treat them as enemy Fascists, while the Latvians were more welcoming. Some found that they could not escape their past. Arvīds Štrauss went into hiding in 1944 to escape enforced service in the German cause; when he heard of attempts to raise a national army towards the end of the year, he reappeared, but then deserted when it became clear that this new formation had no future. He then joined the 'Red Arrow' partisan brigade, but was captured by a German patrol in the last days of the war, and imprisoned in Talsen. A few weeks later, the Red Army arrived. He was promptly shipped off to a Gulag in the Soviet Far East.[41]

Many partisan units made exaggerated claims of their efficacy, and given the importance of the partisan war to Soviet ideology, their claims were often accepted with little attempt to validate them. One unit, commanded by Vilis Samsons, later claimed to have destroyed some 130 German trains, but there is no corroborating evidence of train losses in German records, and the claim is probably an exaggeration, if not a complete fabrication. Soviet accounts claim that there were 24 major partisan units, organised in March 1944 into four brigades, each with between 500 and 3,000 men. After the war, Soviet accounts of Lithuanian partisan activity described the destruction of 364 German trains, over 2,000 cars and trucks, and 18 local German garrisons; these claims do not correlate with German reports of losses.[42] Activity increased as the war continued, not least due to the continuing exploitation of Latvia as an occupied territory, and in January 1945, an SS officer recorded with glum resignation: 'It is clear to the Latvians that the German civil authority is the greatest enemy of their people. It has never done anything good for them, and it never will.'[43]

The first anti-German leaflets appeared in Riga in October 1941, as German attitudes to the 'racially inferior' Latvians became widely known. A heavy-handed renaming of roads in Riga, with the creation of 'Adolf-Hitler-Strasse', 'Goering Ring', and 'Rüdiger von der Goltz Ring', together with Germanisation of the education system, reminded many Latvians of the days when they were dominated by the Baltic German aristocracy, and the acquisitive behaviour of senior German officials further alienated local people; *Reichskommissar* Lohse seized a large mansion on the Baltic shore near Riga, and had several nearby houses torn down to improve the view from his new residence. Rations for Latvians were about half those for civilians in Germany, or for those Baltic Germans who returned to the territory, having left as part of the *Heim ins Reich* policy. Oskars Dankers protested about the inadequate rations on several occasions, to little avail. Enforced recruitment of

Latvians for work in Germany further alienated people who had greeted the German soldiers with flowers and gifts.

Most of the public displays of resistance in Latvia met with disapproval and repression. On 15 May 1942, the anniversary of Karlis Ulmanis' seizure of power, several young nationalists gathered at the Freedom Memorial in Riga, and were promptly arrested. There were plans for a march by students on Latvian National Day in November 1942, culminating in a declaration of independence, but the Germans became aware of the plans and prevented the demonstrations from taking place.

Meanwhile, Latvian officials continued to press for some degree of independence. Some Germans, like Otto Drechsler, favoured a degree of home rule, perhaps along the lines of the governments in Moravia or Slovakia, but others remained adamantly opposed. In January 1943, Alfred Rosenberg submitted a multi-part proposal to Hitler, calling for the restoration of all private property, creation of autonomous governments, and the mobilisation of national troops which would then serve alongside the Wehrmacht. Adhering to his policy that the Baltic States were subject nations, not allies, Hitler rejected the proposals, though he allowed some restoration of private property. Full restoration was not possible; when the Germans took over from the Soviets, they had seized many of the former private firms for their own use, and were therefore not willing to hand them back to Latvians.

In parallel with the development of underground movements in Lithuania, the Latvians created the *Latvijas Centrālā Padome* ('Latvian Central Council' or LCP) in August 1943, seeking like the Lithuanians to create a body that might take advantage of conditions at the end of the war to declare independence. The body met with like-minded Lithuanians in Riga in January 1944, and meetings with representatives of all three nations met in the Latvian capital four months later. The Germans succeeded in identifying members of the LCP towards the end of 1944, and arrested most of its leadership; its head, Konstantins Čakste, died in captivity shortly after.

The soldiers of the Latvian Legion had little doubts about the way that their nation had been left isolated. One wrote: 'We have no friends either in the east or the west. They all only want to rule and be overlords, which is why we now want – and perhaps even more so at a later time – to fight for independence.'[44]

Unlike in Latvia and Lithuania, Estonians were able to make use of neighbouring countries to escape from German rule. Many Estonians fled to Finland, where they formed an Estonian regiment in the Finnish army, allowing them to fight the hated Soviets without coming under German command. There were only small numbers of pro-Soviet partisans active in the country, almost all of them Soviet soldiers who had been left behind or parachuted into the area. Their activity was further curtailed after the Germans captured one of their members, Karl Sära, who revealed the names and locations of many of the other partisans under interrogation.

The Estonian Directorate led by Hjalmar Mäe was more passive than Baltic politicians in Latvia and Lithuania in demanding independence, though the question arose repeatedly in a variety of forms. Generalkommissar Karl Litzmann felt that a lack of any autonomy was markedly destroying Estonian enthusiasm for supporting the German cause, but Hitler continued to overrule any such suggestion. Eventually, Estonian politicians came together to form the *Eesti Vabariigi Rahvuskomitee* ('Estonian Republic National Committee' or EVR) in early 1944. The Gestapo swiftly attempted to suppress the committee, though as will be seen it played a small part in events in September 1944 as the Red Army advanced across Estonia.

The Germans were not alone in raising formations of Baltic citizens. In May 1942, the Red Army created the 16th Latvian Rifle Division, which was assigned to the Soviet 48th Army, part of the Bryansk Front, in early 1943. At about the same time, the 8th Estonian Rifle Corps was created, and was deployed in the northern sector. Although both formations contained large numbers of Baltic citizens, largely those who had fled with the Red Army during the German conquest in 1941, most of their senior officers and large numbers of their lower ranks had little or no connection with the Baltic States. Some were descendants of former Baltic citizens who had moved to the Soviet Union, but many were simply Soviet conscripts who were assigned to the new formations. Nevertheless, the propaganda value of these formations, particularly after the war, when they were portrayed as showing how Baltic citizens had fought to help the Red Army drive the Germans out of the Baltic region, was substantial.

As the tide of war turned against the Germans, the front line once more approached the Baltic States. Disillusioned with German rule, yet fearful of the return of Soviet control, the people of the three countries could do little more than watch helplessly while their destiny was decided by their powerful neighbours.

Chapter 6
NARVA, JANUARY TO APRIL 1944

Apart from sporadic air raids and a few partisan attacks, the Baltic States spent all of 1942 and 1943 free of fighting between the armies of their giant neighbours. When the battlefront moved back to their territory in 1944, a great deal had changed from 1941.

Army Group North, which had surged across Lithuania, Latvia and Estonia in its imperious drive towards Leningrad, still had its 16th and 18th Armies. 4th Panzer Group, renamed 4th Panzer Army, departed in the winter of 1941 to take part in the great battle for Moscow, and thereafter moved to the Ukraine. Without its armour, Army Group North besieged Leningrad for months, isolating the city from the south, with only the roads across the ice of Lake Ladoga during the winter providing any supply route for the population and garrison. Casualties amongst the Soviet people and troops in the city were terrible, with over a million soldiers killed and nearly 2.5 million wounded, sick or missing. The civilian population fell by over a million – about 400,000 were evacuated, and the rest succumbed to the German bombardment or died of sickness or starvation.

The details of the long siege, which was finally broken in January 1944, have been covered in several books.[1] The significance of the siege was that for the Germans, it was regarded as a lesser theatre than the Ukraine, and consequently had lower priority for supplies and reinforcements. During this time, the repeated attempts by the Red Army to lift the siege, and – in the early stages – the attacks by the Wehrmacht, aimed at completing their encirclement, resulted in huge casualties for both sides. The steady stream of reinforcements reaching the Soviet forces ensured that the balance of power steadily tipped in their favour. The Luftwaffe had lost control of the skies over the entire Eastern Front, and Soviet armaments production totally dwarfed German output. The increasing partisan war also disrupted German supply lines and tied down resources behind the front line. German figures of their strength on the Eastern Front in late 1943 showed about 2.5 million men, with an additional 500,000 Finns, Rumanians and Hungarians. The Soviet forces, according to German estimates, numbered over 6 million.[2]

Whilst Army Group North retained its two infantry armies, its leadership had changed. 18th Army had originally been commanded by Georg von Küchler; he was now commander of Army Group North itself, and had been replaced as commander of 18th Army by Generaloberst Georg Lindemann. Lindemann had commanded an infantry division in France in 1940, before leading L Corps during the early phase of *Barbarossa*. The army consisted of five Wehrmacht infantry corps and III SS Panzer Corps. These formations were deployed from the Gulf of Finland to Lake Ilmen, a front line of nearly 200 miles.

Alongside Lindemann's army was 16th Army. Its former commander, Ernst Busch, now commanded Army Group Centre, and had been replaced by General Christian Hansen. He was a veteran of Army Group North, having led X Corps from the first day of the German invasion. In addition to his old X Corps, he had an additional three corps at his disposal.

On paper, these were still formidable armies. For example, I Corps, which was transferred from one army to the other during the winter of 1943–44, listed no fewer than 16 infantry and security divisions in its ranks; the army group as a whole included 44 infantry divisions and a panzergrenadier division. However, none of these was remotely at full strength, and the true strength of I Corps, for example, was probably closer to three or four divisions. Another huge weakness was the lack of armour. The only armoured assets available to Küchler's entire group amounted to a battlegroup from the *SS Panzergrenadier Division Polizei* and the *SS Panzergrenadier Division Nordland*, both part of III SS Panzer Corps. To make matters worse, many of III SS Panzer Corps' tanks consisted of some Panthers that were from an early production run, and had mechanical problems, rendering many of them immobile despite the best efforts of the repair companies. In addition, there were understrength battalions of assault guns and Tiger tanks, but not in sufficient numbers to make a radical difference; the entire tank strength of Army Group North amounted to only 146 tanks, while German estimates put Soviet strength at 650 tanks.[3] Whilst the terrain between the Estonian border and Leningrad favoured defensive warfare, any significant Soviet armoured breakthrough was likely to be decisive, as there were no mobile forces available with which to intercept any such breakthrough. Indeed, the entire army group had little by way of reserves.

The organisation and equipment of German formations had changed, though much remained the same. The infantry divisions at the start of the war were weak in terms of mobility and anti-tank firepower, and there had been little improvement. By contrast, the increasing mechanisation of the Red Army – at least partly as a result of the steady supply of equipment from the United States and Britain – meant that the German infantry would fight at a significant disadvantage. Panzer divisions, though initially absent from Army Group North in 1944, had changed significantly. They now had a single regiment of tanks, organised as two battalions. One of these battalions was meant to be equipped with the Pz.IV tank, and the other with the newer, harder-hitting Panther, but in early 1944, many divisions had not received these vehicles, and still operated a variety of older tanks. The *Sturmgeschütz* brigades were still equipped with the tried and trusted StuG III, based on the old Pz.III chassis, but most now had vehicles armed with the longer, more penetrative 75mm gun. Alongside these brigades were the Tiger tanks of the *Schwere Panzer Abteilung*. These 57-ton vehicles, armed with the famous KwK-36 88mm gun, first saw action near Leningrad in 1942, and were capable of dealing with any enemy threat they might encounter. However, their limited numbers – only 1,347 Tiger Is were built in the entire war, compared with over 36,000 T34s – meant that their availability and therefore their impact was limited.

Facing Küchler's depleted formations were several Soviet fronts. Opposite 18th Army were the Leningrad and Volkhov Fronts, commanded by Leonid Alexandrovich Govorov and Kirill Afanasevich Meretskov respectively. Govorov, an artilleryman by background, had taken command of the Leningrad Front in April 1942. Later that year, he launched spoiling attacks that prevented Manstein from mounting a possibly decisive assault on Leningrad, and masterminded Operation *Iskra*, which finally established a tenuous land corridor between the besieged city and the outside world. His Leningrad Front consisted of four armies. Romanovsky's 2nd Shock Army, with two rifle corps, was in the isolated pocket around Oranienbaum, which had survived every attempt by the Germans to reduce it in the previous two years. Cherepanov's 23rd Army faced the Finns north of Leningrad, and south of the city were Nikolaev's 42nd Army with three rifle corps, and Sviridov's 67th Army with two rifle corps. In addition, the front had substantial reserves, including two full rifle corps.

The Volkhov Front faced the Germans from Siniavino to Lake Ilmen, consisting of Starikov's 8th Army with a single rifle corps, Roginsky's 54th Army with two rifle corps, and Korovnikov's 59th Army with three rifle corps. It was these two powerful fronts that would launch the decisive Soviet drive to break Army Group North. Although the initial fighting took place to the east of the Estonian border, the battles that took place in Estonia were a direct continuation of the earlier campaign closer to Leningrad, and the details of these earlier operations are therefore of importance to what followed.

Although there was little prospect of a renewed German drive to take Leningrad, the city remained within bombardment range of German artillery. The narrow land corridor, too, was easily interdicted by the Germans. Consequently, an operation to drive back Army Group North had a high priority for the Red Army. The Germans were aware of a likely attack, and had made good use of the terrain behind their front line to build an extensive series of defences in depth. In order to improve his defensive positions, Küchler wanted to withdraw to a shorter line further west, freeing troops that could then act as reserves; without such reserves, Küchler argued, it was inevitable that any Soviet attack would eventually succeed in penetrating his lines. As was almost always the case, Hitler refused to accept any withdrawal.

Closer to the Estonian border lay the Panther Line, a defensive position that – in conjunction with the Wotan Line – was intended to run across the entire Eastern Front. Plans for the fortifications had first been drawn up the preceding summer, with the intention of creating a line against which the Red Army would bleed itself dry. Although many of the fortified positions were built as planned, there were also substantial gaps in the line, and Küchler had little confidence in it. He went so far as to avoid mentioning it by name; like others on his staff, he was concerned that the existence of a defensive line to the rear of the troops at the front might encourage them to retreat to its presumed safety rather than fighting in their current positions. In any event, the line had been widely breached further south, with the result that even if Küchler were to be given permission to withdraw to the line, he would find his southern flank exposed, creating the possibility of encirclement.

German assessments of any coming attack were that the Red Army lacked the resources for a sustained effort. Although Küchler was aware of the increased strength of 2nd Shock Army in the Oranienbaum area, he believed that these reinforcements had come from Leningrad itself. With ongoing Soviet attacks near Vitebsk, it seemed unlikely that a major attack would come in the north. This led Küchler to conclude that despite his lack of reserves, his men would be able to hold their positions.[4]

Govorov had a completely different view. In late 1943, he proposed a major attack by his forces to join the Oranienbaum bridgehead with the front line south of Leningrad, by attacks towards Krasnoye Selo. Once this had been achieved, he would commit 67th Army to the attack and capture Krasnogvardeisk, while the forces that had seized Krasnoye Selo pushed on towards Kingisepp. Meretskov, too, was optimistic that a new offensive could be carried out, and suggested that he attack towards Luga from near Novgorod in order to prevent the German 18th Army from retreating to the west. *STAVKA* modified these proposals, adding attacks by the 2nd Baltic Front, to the south of Meretskov's armies; this would tie down the southern flank of the German 16th Army, preventing any transfer of forces to the north.

The main force of the Soviet attack would be delivered by 2nd Shock Army from Oranienbaum and 42nd Army, immediately south of Leningrad. Additional fire support would come from the guns of the Soviet Red Banner Fleet. The attack would be supported by over 650 aircraft – by contrast, it was estimated that Lindemann's 18th Army had fewer than 150 planes available. In addition, Meretskov's Front fielded nearly 600 aircraft, opposed by only about 100 protecting the German 16th Army. To make matters worse for the Germans, the passivity of the German defences allowed the Red Army to concentrate its assault formations at key points. Govorov was able to place over 70 per cent of all his infantry, all of his tanks, and nearly 70 per cent of his artillery with his two main assault formations, 2nd Shock Army and 42nd Army.

Although there had been extensive partisan activity between the front line and the Estonian border, often tying up the minimal reserves available to the Germans, there had been no attempt to coordinate this with planned Soviet attacks. On this occasion, the Leningrad Headquarters of the Partisan Movement issued specific instructions, calling for risings in specific areas. The partisans in the region were organised into four brigades, and the tasks they were assigned varied from reconnaissance, through interdiction of rail and road routes, to uprisings with a view to establishing partisan-controlled areas where civilians could be protected.[5]

At the southern end of Army Group North's sector, the Soviet 2nd Baltic Front drove 16th Army back from Nevel in December 1943, and on 12 January launched a new attack on the German lines. Bitter fighting resulted in only modest gains for the Red Army, but 16th Army was effectively tied to its positions. 18th Army, further north, could not expect any reinforcements from the south. Indeed, Küchler was forced to send some of his meagre reserves to shore up 16th Army, and the loss of a section of the Leningrad–Nevel railway line to the Red Army significantly hindered lateral movement by German forces.

The troops on the front line near Leningrad on the night of 13–14 January 1944 reported heavy snowfall. Despite this, Soviet bombers carried out extensive nocturnal attacks, and at first light, Govorov's forces unleashed an artillery bombardment that lasted a little over an hour. One estimate suggests that over half a million shells and rockets were fired.[6] Fog had replaced the falling snow, making observation of the effects of the barrage difficult, but the Soviet infantry launched its initial attack on schedule at 1000hrs. Three rifle divisions, backed by a tank brigade and two tank regiments, battered their way into the lines of III SS Panzer Corps, where 9th and 10th Luftwaffe Field Divisions held the front. These units were first formed in late 1942 when Hitler ordered surplus Luftwaffe personnel to be reassigned to the army, but rather than release the men, Goering created entirely new divisions, which proved to be almost complete failures when they were deployed that winter. With few personnel experienced in the hardships of ground warfare on the Eastern Front, the divisions were no match for the resurgent Red Army, and though they improved in the following months, they remained inferior to regular infantry divisions. They had only two infantry regiments, but were often assigned to sections of the front line that a full-strength infantry division would have been stretched to hold. In autumn 1943, the Luftwaffe divisions became part of the army, improving their command structures and integration, but they remained weak.

The initial Soviet advance made only modest progress. By the end of the first day, 2nd Shock Army's leading elements had penetrated less than two miles into the German lines. There was particularly heavy fighting at the village of Gostilitsy, at the centre of the front line around the Oranienbaum bridgehead but, given the terrain and the strength of the German positions, there were grounds for cautious optimism. Intelligence reports suggested that although the German lines were strong, the fortifications facing 2nd Shock Army were not as deep as elsewhere. If the Soviet forces could break through, the frozen ground would hinder the Germans in establishing new positions.

The night brought no respite for III SS Panzer Corps. The Soviet assault forces continued their advance, and the following morning, 42nd Army also began to attack. 10th Luftwaffe Field Division was rapidly approaching the end of its strength, and in an attempt to shore up the front line, the Germans committed their local reserves, which amounted to four battalions. Despite this, 2nd Shock Army continued to make steady progress. Further east, 42nd Army's assault penetrated nearly three miles in the centre:

Mortar and artillery impacts could not be distinguished from the explosions of bombs, the noise of Stalin Organs, and the guns from the ships at Kronstadt. At 0820, the fire jumped to the rear, and the Russian companies and battalions marched through the trenches, which were flattened by the fire. From 391st Infantry Regiment [part of 170th Infantry Division, deployed east of Ropsha], which was now led by Oberst Arndt, the battalion commanders Hauptmann Moeller and Hauptmann Meyer fell in the battle ... the few combat capable

soldiers remaining in the main battle line did their best. They held their positions
... as the new waves came in upon them, even though the fire of friendly heavy
weapons were landing on the friendly main battle line and in the anti-tank ditches
behind it.[7]

Although 170th Infantry Division's centre was driven back, the flanks of the Soviet
assault were held up in bitter fighting with German troops in their dense fortifications.

To the south, the Volkhov Front opened its attack to recapture Novgorod. After a
heavy artillery bombardment, 59th Army, commanded by Ivan Terentevich
Korovnikov, began to work its way through the defences on the right flank of the
German 18th Army. The Germans had prepared their defences well, and the difficult
terrain made it hard for the Red Army to make maximum use of its numerical
advantage. Progress on the first day was slow, but steady, with some of the best gains
coming in the south, where an operational group commanded by Major General
Teodor-Verner Andreevich Sviklin crossed the frozen Lake Ilmen and took the
defenders by surprise. About 12 miles north of Novgorod, Soviet troops advanced and
seized an important road junction at the village of Nekhokovo and isolated two
German regiments. The Latvian brigade dispatched a battlegroup to restore the
situation, and recaptured Nekhokovo on 16 January. Fierce fighting continued in the
area through the following day, before the Latvians pulled back a short distance after
covering the withdrawal of the two trapped German regiments. For his leadership in
the fighting, Standartenführer Voldemars Veiss, who had commanded the Latvian
battlegroup, was awarded the Knight's Cross.[8]

It was a familiar pattern of fighting that was repeated over and again on the
Eastern Front. The initial German positions held up well to the Soviet assault, but
with only minimal reserves available, any major Soviet penetration through the
defences rapidly became unstoppable. On 16 January, 2nd Shock Army succeeded
in penetrating the entire German defensive line along its front, though 42nd Army
continued to make slow progress. Although the German defenders continued to
counter-attack wherever they could, and inflicted heavy casualties on the Soviet
forces, the two pincers of the Red Army's advance inched ever closer. By the end
of 17 January, they were less than 12 miles apart. In the south, the German
XXXVIII Corps rushed to shore up the line with its only reserves, a single regiment
from 290th Infantry Division and another regiment from SS Division *Nord*,
whereas Korovnikov was able to add another two rifle divisions, an armoured car
battalion, two tank brigades and a self-propelled artillery regiment. The German
28th Jäger Division put up the best resistance it could, but was steadily driven

back, and by the end of 16 January, the Red Army had opened a 12-mile breach in the German defences.

Despite the threat of encirclement that hung over the German units caught between the attacks in the north, Lindemann remained confident. He had deployed 61st Infantry Division to help shore up 10th Luftwaffe Field Division, and had almost no other reserves available, but reported that the Red Army, too, had committed all its reserves. The following day, Lindemann's estimate was proven to be hopelessly optimistic. 2nd Shock Army deployed its reserves, immediately penetrating the German lines. When elements of its 168th Rifle Division made contact with the spearheads of 42nd Army, several German formations were surrounded in a small pocket immediately outside Leningrad. On 19 January, Krasnoye Selo fell to the advancing Soviet forces, and the encircled German troops decided to attempt an escape before it was too late:

> At 2000, it was observed from Kotselovo that the battle had flared up along the Krasnoye Selo–Kipen road. Several tanks rolled to the west, droning loudly and firing heavily. Tracer rounds lit up their way from the east … and made it clear they had closed the ring … Oberst Fischer (commander of 126th Infantry Division) decided to regroup his division quickly and break out of the encirclement … all who were to break out to Telesi stood ready south of Kotselovo at midnight. 42nd Infantry Regiment was now at the head of the division. On both sides, assault guns supported the attack wedge … tracer rounds and the flames of Telesi illuminated the battlefield. Nobody who experienced this would ever forget it.[9]

About a thousand men were left behind, together with almost all the heavy weapons of the units that had been encircled.

In the south, Korovnikov widened his assault, preventing both XXVII and XXVIII Corps from freeing any forces to be dispatched to the crisis in the north. His attacks converged on Novgorod, and Lindemann belatedly requested permission for a withdrawal. Although Küchler agreed, Hitler did not. Lindemann ordered his men to abandon Novgorod anyway, even as the city was encircled:

> On the night of 19 January, those troops of 28 Jäger Division encircled in Novgorod received the order to break out. The seriously wounded had to be abandoned in the ruins, the medical staff volunteering to remain behind with them, and all who could carry weapons, including the walking wounded, tried to withdraw under cover of darkness … German formations and units became mixed and confused …

All suffered from the wet and lack of sleep and food, and unless supply column commanders took most energetic action to maintain contact, replenishment failed. Luftwaffe divisions disintegrated, and in some of the infantry divisions nearly all of the regimental and battalion commanders were killed or wounded. Divisional infantry strengths fell to only 500 men.[10]

Although the initial breakout succeeded, elements of 28th Jäger Division, 1st Luftwaffe Field Division, and *SS-Nord* fell victim to a second encirclement immediately to the west of Novgorod when the Soviet 6th Rifle Corps and 372nd Rifle Division met in a second pincer movement. Few escaped. The city of Novgorod, in German hands since August 1941, was recaptured, though little of it remained. Nearly all its buildings were in ruins, and only 50 of its inhabitants had survived the occupation. The rest had been shipped to Germany as forced labour.

The enforced evacuation of civilians for labour duties caused considerable anger, and undoubtedly stimulated many to join the partisan movement. Küchler was determined to evacuate as much of the population to the east of the Panther Line as possible, but as an intelligence report from 18th Army stated during the autumn of 1943, the policy faced considerable difficulties:

Many people are saying that they would prefer to be clubbed to death on the spot rather than take part in this evacuation. Even members of the population who are still pro-German rightly suspect that such a march will cause incredible misery and cause the loss of countless lives. Considering the state of people's clothing, the lack of food or proper transport and the expected weather, the participants – particularly women and children – will soon be in an indescribable state.[11]

Outside Leningrad, the German troops still clinging to their defences closest to the city were in desperate danger. Hitler finally relented early on 20 January and authorised their withdrawal. In some cases, the withdrawal threatened to become a rout. The Soviet offensive continued on 21 January with major attacks towards Krasnogvardeisk and Luga. Küchler desperately demanded that he be allowed to pull back to the Panther Line, but Hitler insisted on a fighting withdrawal – otherwise, he argued, the Red Army would arrive at the defensive line with sufficient strength to force its way through.[12] In vain, Küchler pointed out that his army, too, would suffer heavy losses in such an attritional withdrawal, and would then lack the strength to hold the Panther Line. Although Army Group North received some welcome armoured reinforcements, in the shape of 12th Panzer Division from Army Group

Centre and the 70 Tiger tanks of *Schwere Panzer Abteilung 502*, it remained in a perilous position.

Under heavy pressure in the north, 9th Luftwaffe Field Division lost its commander, Oberst Ernst Michael, on 22 January, and he was replaced by Oberst Heinrich Geerkens, who had commanded the division's *Jäger Regiment 17*. Two days later, he too was killed in action. Both men were posthumously promoted to *Generalmajor*. Meanwhile, with his forces driven out of their dense defensive positions, Lindemann informed *Oberkommando des Heeres* (the German Army High Command or OKH) that he intended to retreat further. OKH could either accept his decision, he wrote, or send someone to replace him.[13] Although Soviet spearheads continued to reach positions before the retreating Germans, the bulk of the German line fell back intact. The rearguard was made up primarily of infantry commanded by Oberst Paul Wengler of 227th Infantry Division, reinforced by several tanks from *Schwere Panzer Abteilung 502*. On several occasions, fast-moving Soviet forces cut the road behind them, but the Tiger tanks were practically immune to any light weapons these units could carry, and were able to reopen the line of retreat. Otto Carius, a Tiger tank commander and one of the greatest German tank 'aces' of the war, recalled defending a village during a long, cold night:

> Soon the village was under extremely heavy fire. The Russians had noticed that it was occupied and wanted to 'clean up' the affair before they advanced further to the west. Their methods showed, however, that they certainly didn't suspect an entire 'Tiger' company in the village.
>
> I saw muzzle fire in the woodline. It moved farther to the right from flash to flash. Those had to be tanks moving along the woodline. They wanted to reach the road at the opposite end of the village. Obefeldwebel Zwetti was in position there.
>
> Behind him was von Schiller's tank. I radioed to Zwetti. With the help of a flare, I could determine that a T34 was moving no more than 50 metres away from Zwetti. Due to the firing, we couldn't hear any motor noises. Because of that, the enemy had already made his way to the village. Zwetti shot his neighbour into flames, but we saw in astonishment a second T34 in the middle of the village street, right next to von Schiller.
>
> It often proved fatal to the Russians that they kept completely buttoned up. Because of that, they could scarcely see anything, especially at night. They also had infantrymen riding on the tank, but even they didn't recognise the situation until too late.

Von Schiller wanted to turn his turret but in the process hit the Russian tank with his cannon. He had to back up first in order to be able to knock it out. I didn't feel confident enough to shoot. One of the craziest situations I ever experienced!

After Zwetti had finished off another three tanks, the Russians pulled back. Apparently, the losses they suffered were enough. We stayed in radio contact for the rest of the night and could hear the Russians quite well on one channel. That meant they couldn't be too far from us.

At the break of day, our infantrymen approached the T34 somewhat carelessly. It still stood directly next to von Schiller. Except for a hole in the hull, it was undamaged. Surprisingly, as they went to open the turret hatch completely, it was closed. Immediately thereafter, a hand grenade flew out of the tank and severely wounded three soldiers.

Von Schiller once again took the enemy under fire. Not until the third shot, however, did the Russian tank commander leave his tank. He then collapsed, severely wounded. The other Russians were dead. We took the Soviet lieutenant to division, but he couldn't be interrogated any more. He succumbed to his injuries along the way.

… I remember how we cursed the stubbornness of this Soviet lieutenant at the time. Nowadays, I have another opinion.[14]

Carius' opinions of Soviet tanks and their commanders shed some light on how the numerically inferior German forces succeeded in holding their own for so long during the war:

Our guidelines were: 'Shoot *first*, but if you can't do that, at least hit first.' The prerequisite for that, of course, is fully functioning communications from tank to tank and also among the crew. Furthermore, quick and accurate gun-laying systems need to be present. In most instances, the Russians lacked both of these prerequisites. Because of that, they often came out on the short end of the stick, even though they frequently didn't lag behind us in armour, weapons, and manoeuvrability.

… The personal aggressiveness of the commander while observing was decisive for success against numerically vastly superior enemy formations. The lack of good observation by the Russians often resulted in the defeat of large units. Tank commanders who slam their hatches shut at the beginning of an attack and don't open them again until the objective has been reached are useless, or at least second rate. There are, of course, six to eight vision blocks mounted in a circle in every cupola that allow observation. But they are only good for a certain sector of the terrain, limited by the size of the individual vision block …

Unfortunately, impacting rounds are felt before the sound of the enemy's gun report ... Therefore, a tank commander's eyes are more important than his ears. As a result of rounds exploding in the vicinity, one doesn't hear the gun report at all in the tank. It is quite different whenever the tank commander raises his head occasionally in an open hatch to survey the terrain. If he happens to look halfway to the left while an enemy anti-tank gun opens fire halfway to the right, his eye will subconsciously catch the shimmer of the yellow muzzle flash.

... No one can deny that the many casualties among the officers and other tank commanders were due to exposing their heads. But these men didn't die in vain. If they had moved with closed hatches, then many more men would have found their deaths or been severely wounded inside the tanks. The large Russian tank losses are proof of the correctness of this assertion.[15]

Govorov harried his army commanders forward, ordering 2nd Shock Army to push forward to Kingisepp and the Estonian frontier, while 67th Army advanced south to Luga. At the same time, Meretskov would ensure that Korovnikov's 59th Army advanced on Luga from the east, in an attempt to catch the German forces in a pincer. Lindemann's forces, which had withdrawn from the north towards Estonia, succeeded in holding off 2nd Shock Army, not least because Fediuninsky showed little imagination in attacking the German rearguards, often squandering the lives of his men in costly frontal attacks on prepared positions. On 23 January, Govorov's impatience with his subordinate began to show:

You have not fulfilled your mission of the day ... In spite of my orders, the army's formations continue to mark time in front of the severely damaged enemy forces, neither suffering casualties nor achieving decisive success. As has been the case before, the corps commanders are displaying slowness, are directing combat weakly, and not directing the corps to employ manoeuvre and decisive movement forward. Exploiting our slowness, the enemy, who is conducting cover force operations in small groups, is withdrawing his main forces south and south-west from Krasnogvardeisk and Elizavetino.[16]

Heavy fighting flared around Krasnogvardeisk, held by General Wilhelm Wegener's L Corps. In addition to 11th and 170th Infantry Divisions, he had what remained of four other divisions, together with 215th Infantry Division and parts of 24th Infantry Division at Pushkin and Slutsk. The Soviet 123rd and 117th Rifle Corps assaulted Krasnogvardeisk, while 110th Rifle Corps attempted to outflank the

German forces still clinging to Pushkin. By 23 January, the town was encircled from three sides, but Krasnogvardeisk continued to hold out. Nevertheless, the situation deteriorated steadily for Lindemann, and by the end of 24 January, he had lost contact with 16th Army to the south. Fediuninsky's 2nd Shock Army continued to grind forward, cutting the railway between Krasnogvardeisk and Kingisepp on 26 January, but despite repeated requests, Hitler continued to refuse permission for a withdrawal of the hard-pressed formations. The reconnaissance battalion of III SS Panzer Corps, *SS-Panzer-Aufklärungs-Abteilung 11* – shortly thereafter given the honorific title 'Hermann von Salza' – used its mobility and firepower to try to hold off the Soviet forces:

> In the pale light of morning, Russian armour broke through the morning grey on a broad front and rattled toward Gubanitsy over the open terrain. At first there were seven. Then, behind them, a whole mass of them. In addition to the T34s, there were all possible types, even old models. The gunners of *5/SS-Panzer-Aufklärungs-Abteilung 11* brought the enemy tanks into their telescopic sights. Six out of the seven Soviet tanks in the first wave were knocked out. Then it was the second wave's turn. It turned into a tank engagement, the likes of which I had never seen. The bark of the cannon filled the air. Round after round was fired from the barrels of the heavy anti-tank guns. The crews worked feverishly behind the gun shields. I had counted 61 tanks, many of which were right in front of us at that point. And the battle raged on. SS-Rottenführer Spork headed for the Soviets at top speed in his *Kanonenwagen* [a half-track with a 75mm short-barrelled gun mounted on the back] and knocked out one tank after another over open sights at short range. I could not even hope to guess how long the fighting had gone on, having lost all sense of time. The surviving Russian tanks turned away. The breakthrough attempt was a failure.[17]

The battle at Gubanitsy cost the Red Army 48 tanks, 11 of them destroyed by Casper Spork. A little to the south, Wengler's battlegroup from 227th Infantry Division – with support from a small number of Tiger tanks – held onto the town of Volosovo for several days while stragglers from the shattered front streamed back. In honour of their commander, Wengler's men nicknamed the town 'Wenglerovo'.

On 27 January, Küchler was ordered to attend a National Socialist conference in Königsberg, in East Prussia, where he had to endure speeches by Hitler calling for his followers to remain faithful to the belief in final victory. Küchler told the conference that the winter fighting had cost 18th Army 40,000 casualties, and that his men were fighting as hard as could be expected. Hitler publicly disagreed, suggesting that he believed that the army could show more determination.

With Hitler's admonitions loud in his ears, Küchler returned to the front, calling on his men to show more resolve. Despite this, Generalleutnant Eberhard Kinzel, his chief of staff, took it upon himself to advise Lindemann to begin a withdrawal. Late on 27 January, 18th Army's forces began to pull back, destroying bridges as they went. The fighting around Krasnogvardeisk came to a head on 25 January, with the Soviet 108th Rifle Corps, reinforced by a tank brigade, pushing into the town from the west. At the same time, 117th Rifle Corps battled forward from the north, and the town fell on 26 January. The German 11th Infantry Division suffered heavy casualties in the fighting, but contrary to the claims of the Soviets, was not destroyed and managed to withdraw. Nevertheless, the pursuit of the retreating Germans posed a constant threat. The mobile elements of III SS Panzer Corps had to fight repeated actions to keep the main line of retreat open. Converging along several roads, the German forces made for Kingisepp and the crossings over the River Luga. It was the intention of the German High Command to attempt to hold the line of the Luga, but Soviet forces were already across the river south of Kingisepp. Any defence of the Luga around the city would be short-lived.

Further to the south-east, Soviet forces advancing from the east showed a lack of urgency in pressing the Germans, allowing Lindemann to complete an orderly withdrawal. Attempts by Sviridov's 67th Army to envelop the German XXVII and XXVIII Corps from the north were frustrated by 12th Panzer Division, but nevertheless, Govorov continued to edge closer to Luga from the north. Unfortunately for the Red Army, the Volkhov Front, which should have been pushing forward from the east towards Luga, and tying down the two German corps, made painfully slow progress. Küchler had rushed whatever minimal forces he could scrape together to try to maintain the link between his two armies, and created a thin, fragile line of several units. *Kampfgruppe Schuldt*, comprised of elements of 2nd SS Brigade, the remnants of 28th Jäger Division, and elements of three other divisions, lined up alongside *Kampfgruppe Speth* with 1st Luftwaffe Field Division and elements of *SS-Nord*, and *Kampfgruppe Feurguth* with 290th Infantry Division and the rest of *SS-Nord* in the path of Korovnikov's 59th Army. Despite the weakness of this line, the Soviet 6th Rifle Corps, supported by a tank brigade, almost came to a halt on 24 January, at least partly because the Soviet units had suffered heavy losses in driving the Germans out of their dense fortifications over the previous fortnight; the tank brigade had been reduced to only eight tanks.[18] Korovnikov had an additional rifle corps at his disposal, but instead of throwing it at the weak German line, he dispatched it further south, where it ran into difficult terrain and also made little headway. 12th Panzer Division's battlegroups continued to shuffle back and forth across the front, and although the southern flank of the Soviet Volkhov Front made good progress, 59th Army inched forward, despite receiving substantial reinforcements. Further to the south, the 2nd Baltic Front also showed an inability to prevent an orderly German withdrawal. Consequently, 16th Army was able to pull back to new positions, and released substantial forces – 8th Jäger Division, elements of 21st Luftwaffe Field Division, parts of 32nd and 132nd Infantry Divisions, *Sturmgeschütz-Abteilung 303*, and 58th Infantry Division – to the aid of Lindemann's 18th Army.[19]

Despite these reinforcements, pressure continued in the north. 10th Luftwaffe Field Division's commander, Generalleutnant Hermann von Wedel, was badly wounded on 29 January. He was evacuated to a military hospital in Estonia, where he died a week later. His division, now lacking any cohesion, was disbanded, and its survivors added to the ranks of 170th Infantry Division. By the end of the month, 18th Army was in a perilous state. Its infantry strength, already weak at the beginning of the year, had shrunk by over two thirds, and Hitler's insistence on it continuing to hold its ground, with deep Soviet salients driven into its lines, resulted inevitably in gaps in the front line, in addition to the gap to 16th Army in the south. On 30 January, Küchler managed to secure permission to retreat to the River Luga, but only if he was then able to restore continuity along the front. Soviet forces were already over the Luga, between Luga and Kingisepp, and Küchler's staff protested that the orders were unworkable. The result was the sacking of Küchler, and his replacement by Generalfeldmarschall Walter Model.

Highly decorated in the First World War, Model had served in the Reichswehr between the wars, when he was strongly influenced by the defensive theories of Generalleutnant Fritz von Lossberg. He was a staff officer in the early campaigns of 1939 and 1940, accompanying 16th Army across Luxembourg and northern France, and commanded 3rd Panzer Division at the onset of *Barbarossa*. He led XLI Panzer Corps during the battle of Moscow, and thereafter showed great defensive skill in command of 9th Army during 1942 and 1943. He was now dispatched to restore the situation in the north.

Model became a field marshal at the age of 53 (he was promoted two months after taking command of Army Group North), the youngest man to hold this rank in the Wehrmacht. Heinz Guderian once described him thus: 'A bold inexhaustible soldier … the best possible man to perform the fantastically difficult task of reconstructing a line in the centre of the Eastern Front.'[20] He was by all accounts a man who was outspoken to the point of tactlessness, and many of the army's conservative officers regarded him as suspiciously pro-Nazi. His hard-driving attitude earned him the respect of his men, but in most of his posts, his staff officers found it hard to cope with him – when he took over XLI Panzer Corps, the entire staff requested transfers.[21] His outspoken attitude even extended to Hitler; when the Führer challenged his deployment of part of 9th Army in 1942, he stared down the German leader with the words, 'Who commands the 9th Army, my Führer, you or I?'[22]

The prickly, energetic Model rapidly asserted his personality on the staff at Army Group North. It was clear to him that regardless of Hitler's orders, it would be suicidal for 18th Army to attempt to hold its current positions. Aware of Hitler's aversion to withdrawals, he articulated the concept of a 'shield and sword' defence, in which the army group would allow a withdrawal from the north into a salient around Luga – the shield – and would then use the forces freed up to mount a sword-like counter-thrust further west against Soviet forces approaching the Estonian border. But even these measures would require time to be executed. Fediuninsky's 2nd Shock Army, which had broken through the German defences around the Oranienbaum bridgehead, was now ordered to force the line of the Luga, and to reach and cross the River Narva. 42nd Army would advance on Fediuninsky's southern flank, driving to Lake Peipus, while 67th Army and the entire Volkhov Front attempted to capture Luga itself.

The first phase of the Soviet reconquest of the Baltic States was therefore a direct continuation of the rolling offensive that had driven the Germans back from the gates of Leningrad. 43rd and 122nd Rifle Corps from 2nd Shock Army launched determined attacks on Kingisepp throughout 30 and 31 January, inflicting heavy losses on *SS-Panzergrenadier-Regiment 23 Norge* and *SS-Panzergrenadier- Regiment 24 Danmark*, composed mainly of Norwegian and Danish volunteers respectively. With Soviet forces bypassing the town and crossing the frozen river to north and south, the SS abandoned Kingisepp, blowing the bridges as they left. Elements of III SS Panzer Corps and LIV Corps fought a determined rearguard action to the frozen River Narva, about ten miles to the east, and used explosives to disrupt the ice, in an attempt to prevent the Red Army from achieving early crossings. Nevertheless, the day after the fall of Kingisepp, the Soviet 4th Rifle Regiment, part of 43rd Rifle Corps, managed to establish a small bridgehead north of the city of Narva, while 122nd Rifle Corps crossed the river about six miles further south in the frozen Krivasoo swamps.

In Estonia, the approach of the front line led to a significant change of heart in the leadership installed by the German occupiers. Until now, the Directorate had opposed attempts to mobilise the population for war, but with the Red Army coming ever closer, the acting prime minister, Jüri Uluots, announced a different policy. In a radio broadcast on 7 February, he supported mobilisation, hinting that armed Estonian forces might do more than merely fight the Red Army, and – aware that the Germans would monitor his words – added that their creation could have 'a significance much wider than what I could and would be able to disclose here'.[23] With the end of the war coming closer, Uluots – like other Baltic politicians – hoped that there would be an opportunity, as there had been in 1918, for Estonia to make a bid for independence. Meanwhile, the civilian population of Narva was evacuated, and the town prepared for a major battle.

Model, meanwhile, attempted to reshuffle his meagre resources. Lindemann was ordered to adopt a defensive line closer to Luga, reducing the length of front line substantially. 12th Panzer Division would attack to restore contact with 16th Army to the south, and thereafter – in conjunction with 58th Infantry Division – would drive down the Luga valley to link up with the forces facing Fediuninsky on the Narva. Such an operation was probably beyond the strength of the forces deployed, given the unfavourable ratios of strength between the opposing sides, but the most pressing concern was to shore up the defences on the Narva. If these were to give way, the consequences could be catastrophic for 18th Army, Army Group North, and indeed the entire German position on the Eastern Front. The capture of Narva would open the way for the Red Army to advance along the Estonian coast to Tallinn, allowing the Red Banner Fleet to venture out further into the Baltic. The oil shale plant on the Estonian coast, one of the few remaining oil resources that the Reich still controlled, would be lost, and a rapid advance by Soviet troops across Estonia, to the west of Lake Peipus, would threaten to roll up the entire German front line. Politically, the consequences could also be serious. Hitler was aware that the Finns were attempting to negotiate a ceasefire with the Soviet Union, and keeping control of the Estonian coast was vital if this was to be prevented.

Narva now became the focus of the fighting. The city first developed as an established settlement in the 13th century when the Danes built the imposing Hermannsburg fortress on the west bank of the Narva. Downstream of the city, the east bank of the Narva climbs rapidly, compared with the relatively flat land to the west; consequently, Soviet forces approaching from the east had a good view of the German positions, and were able to observe troop movements and call down artillery fire whenever targets presented themselves.

On 2 February, Model visited the Narva positions. Otto Sponheimer, commander of LIV Corps, was given command of all the forces along the river, directly subordinate to Army Group North, first as *Gruppe Sponheimer*, then as Army Detachment Narva after Sponheimer was replaced by General Johannes Friessner on 23 February.

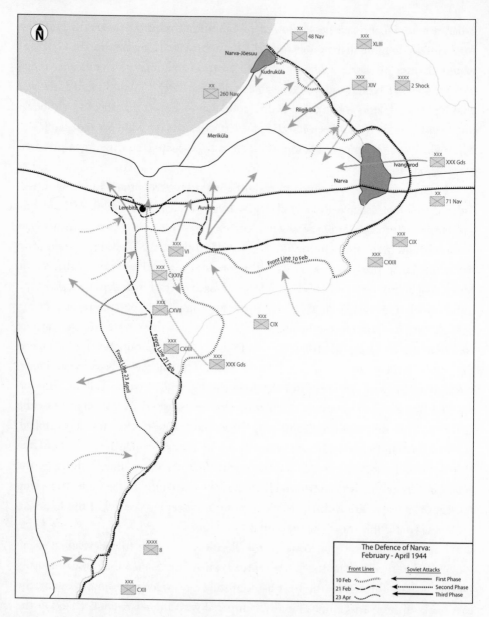

The Defence of Narva:
February - April 1944

A steady stream of reinforcements arrived to shore up the line, so that by the last week of February, Army Detachment Narva had an impressive array of forces at its disposal. One of the new units to be sent to the area was the Panzergrenadier Division *Feldherrnhalle*, dispatched from Army Group Centre. Originally built around the remnants of the 60th Motorised Infantry Division, which was destroyed in Stalingrad, this division contained large numbers of former members of the *Sturmabteilungen* or SA, the pre-war paramilitary wing of the National Socialist Party; it was therefore named in honour of Hitler's failed attempt to seize power in 1923. It now provided much-needed armoured support for the hard-pressed forces on the Narva.

The Red Army, too, was reinforcing the area. 43rd Rifle Corps sent more troops across the Narva, and managed to push forward a little over a mile, but failed to make further progress in the face of resistance from 227th Infantry Division and the *SS Panzergrenadier Brigade Nederland*. A German counter-attack followed, driving the exhausted Soviet infantry back across the river at Kudruküla in early February. The following day, the Germans had a welcome surprise: the 30 survivors of a company from *SS-Norge*, cut off during the retreat, managed to reach German lines after a 14-day march. Sadly for them, their Norwegian *Untersturmführer* was killed by German fire when they crossed the frozen Narva.[24]

In an attempt to outflank the German defences, the Red Banner Fleet attempted to land two naval infantry brigades on the coast late on 13 February in a flotilla of 26 vessels of varying sizes.[25] The intention was to achieve a landing near the town of Meriküla, but Estonian military planners had considered such a landing as a possibility at least since 1939. Consequently, the artillery positions constructed as part of the German Panther Line allowed for such a landing, and the first wave of Soviet troops found themselves faced by tough defences. Nevertheless, they succeeded in reaching Meriküla, where they surrounded the headquarters of *Kampfgruppe Berlin*, a mixed force responsible for defending this section of coast. As it began to grow light the following day, a German counter-attack restored contact with the Germans trapped in Meriküla. Backed by the German coastal artillery and a small group of Tiger tanks from *Schwere Panzer Abteilung 502*, a mixed force of Estonian and German troops crushed the landing attempt, despite a Stuka raid that erroneously bombed the Tiger tanks. The Soviet forces lost about 750 dead or captured.[26]

The Krivasoo bridgehead had also received reinforcements, with 109th Rifle Corps joining 122nd Rifle Corps. The combined force struggled forward about seven miles to the north-west in a futile attempt to envelop Narva from the south, suffering heavy casualties at the hands of *SS-Panzergrenadier Division Nordland*, 170th Infantry Division, and the fresh troops of *Feldherrnhalle*. However, 30th Guards Rifle Corps, deployed a little to the south-west, made better progress. The railway station at Auvere changed hands several times before the Soviet troops were able to secure it on 17 February, but a counter-attack by *Feldherrnhalle* brought the advance to an abrupt halt. Like the attempted naval operation on the Baltic coast, there was an attempt to bypass the German defences to the south with an attack across Lake Peipus. The 90th Rifle Division seized the island of Piirissaar on 12 February and went on to establish a small bridgehead on the western shore two days later near Jõepera. An immediate counter-attack by two regiments, one Estonian and one German, eliminated both the bridgehead and the troops on Piirissaar.

There was a palpable sense of frustration in the Soviet command. The terrain – the relatively narrow corridor of land, much of it swampy, between the northern shore of Lake Peipus and the Baltic coast – left limited room for manoeuvre, and the Red Army was reduced to trying to batter its way through the German defences. Govorov complained that Fediuninsky's 2nd Shock Army made poor use of reconnaissance and failed to plan properly, particularly for artillery support after the onset of an attack. Coordination between infantry, armour and other arms was also weak.[27] Aware of the effect of the fighting on the ceasefire negotiations with Finland, Stalin ordered STAVKA to issue a blunt instruction on 14 February:

> It is mandatory that our forces seize Narva no later than 17 February 1944. This is required both for military as well as political reasons. It is the most important thing right now.
>
> I demand that you undertake all necessary measures to liberate Narva no later than the period indicated.[28]

Fediuninsky had received additional reinforcements, in the shape of 124th Rifle Corps as well as small units of tanks, and these were added to the southern bridgehead. In conjunction with 122nd Rifle Corps, these forces attacked again, though to little avail. 30th Guards Rifle Corps suffered further heavy casualties, and was almost wiped out as a functional combat unit. In combination with 61st Infantry Division and *Schwere Panzer Abteilung 502*, Panzergrenadier Division *Feldherrnhalle* succeeded in driving 124th Rifle Corps back to its start line. Although the Red Army continued to hold a dangerous salient projecting north towards the rear of the Narva position, its divisions were unable to press home their advantage and envelop the German defenders. Perhaps the only crumb of comfort was that a brigade of Estonian troops disintegrated on its march to the front and withdrew in confusion, with many of its men taking the opportunity to disappear back to their homes.[29]

It had been Model's intention to fight the main battle to the east of the Narva valley, but his 'sword and shield' plan proved to be impossible to implement. Soviet forces continued to bear down towards Luga from the north, and the mobile forces deployed for Model's sword – 126th Infantry Division, 12th Panzer Division, and 12th Luftwaffe Field Division – ran headlong into the attacking 42nd Army in the area east of Lake Peipus. In confused, heavy fighting, the Germans could make no headway, and with the line under pressure elsewhere, Model had to abandon his plans.

Luga was abandoned on 12 February, and Lindemann's 18th Army fell back towards what had once been known as the Panther Line. 12th Panzer Division, which had been in almost continuous action since it arrived in the area, fought a series of actions to hold off the Soviet 42nd Army, which constantly threatened to cut the line of retreat of the troops pulling back from Luga. Further south, the Soviet 8th Army advanced faster than its northern neighbour, 59th Army, and ran into trouble as it approached Luga from the south-east. A surprise German counter-attack resulted in its temporary envelopment, requiring the Volkhov Front to redirect elements of 59th Army south to rescue 8th Army. This gave the retreating soldiers of Lindemann's army some precious time to recover, and despite repeated attempts, the German units that had encircled much of 8th Army were unable to wear down and destroy the trapped Soviet formations.

There were further difficulties for the Germans south of Lake Ilmen. Here, the Soviet 1st Shock Army attacked immediately south of Staraya Russa at the beginning of February. It was badly understrength, with only four rifle divisions on a front that extended 60 miles, and its forces – which, unlike in other Soviet offensives, scarcely attempted to concentrate their numbers at one location – made little headway. The 2nd Baltic Front's 22nd Army and 10th Guards Army attacked further south against the German 16th Army, but tough German resistance and deteriorating weather resulted in minimal progress. Nevertheless, with 18th Army withdrawing in the north, 16th Army faced the possibility of its northern flank being exposed, and there was a further threat at the southern end of 16th Army, where it appeared that the Red Army was receiving substantial reinforcements. Here, much of the winter had been spent in a futile attempt by the Soviet forces to capture the city of Vitebsk from Army Group Centre's 3rd Panzer Army, and discontinuation of these attacks freed up resources to be deployed against 16th Army. Model ordered Hansen's 16th Army to withdraw to the west. Soviet units failed to detect the German withdrawal in time to hinder it, and a combination of poor weather, skilful German defence, lengthening Soviet supply lines, and the inability of the Soviet Air Force to keep up with the advance, allowed 16th Army to withdraw safely.

Back on the Narva line, the newly formed 20th SS Waffen-Grenadier Division (1st Estonian) had arrived at the front. The division was created from the 3rd Estonian SS Brigade, which had been serving with 16th Army, and the remnants of *Bataillon Narwa*. The new division was deployed to replace the shattered 9th and 10th Luftwaffe Field Divisions against the Soviet bridgehead north of Narva. For many of the Estonians, this was familiar terrain; in the years before the war, the Estonian Army had often trained in the area in anticipation of a possible attack by the Soviet

Union. On 20 February, the division's two regiments attacked and broke the Red Army's bridgehead into two parts. The following day, an attempt to reduce the section of the Soviet bridgehead around Riigiküla made little headway, in the face of near-continuous Soviet artillery fire from the east bank. After extensive preparations, a further attack against the small Soviet pocket was launched on 24 February, which had been celebrated as Estonian Independence Day before the war. While a battalion of the Estonian division made elaborate preparations for a frontal assault, a smaller group of soldiers infiltrated into the Soviet trenches. It now became impossible for the Soviet artillery to provide close support without hitting their own men, and by the end of the day, the pocket had been reduced.

The other half of the Soviet bridgehead north of Narva was a little larger, and was defended by 378th Rifle Division, supported by perhaps 20 assault guns. On 29 February, the two regiments of the Estonian division attacked the heavily fortified positions. Within hours, one battalion of *SS-Waffen-Grenadier Regiment 46* had lost almost all its officers, but under the resourceful leadership of Unterscharführer Harald Nugiseks, the attack continued. However, determined resistance continued until 6 March, when the bridgehead was finally eliminated. Nugiseks, who was wounded in the fighting, was awarded the Knight's Cross.

Despite the impatient orders from Moscow, Govorov found that his front was in danger of losing the initiative on the Narva line. In addition to Fediuninsky's exhausted 2nd Shock Army, he had Korovnikov's 59th Army and Starikov's 8th Army available, and on 22 February, he issued new instructions. The main effort would be to expand the bridgehead south of Narva, with 2nd Shock Army striking north-east towards Narva while 59th Army attempted to advance west. 8th Army, still in the process of arriving from its earlier operations towards Pskov, would be available to exploit 59th Army's advance, by operating on its southern flank in a drive into the heart of Estonia.[30] On 1 March, while the Germans were busy with operations against the remnants of the northern bridgehead, Govorov's forces began their assault. Despite a few days' rest, Fediuninsky's divisions made little headway. To their left, 43rd and 109th Rifle Corps from 59th Army attacked the German 214th Infantry Division after a heavy, though apparently ineffective artillery bombardment. The German division had spent most of the war on garrison duty in Norway, and was not yet 'acclimatised' to conditions on the Eastern Front. In three days of heavy fighting, it was driven back, and several elements were surrounded. As more German forces – elements of 11th and 58th Infantry Divisions – arrived, the Soviet advance slowed and halted. Fighting continued for several days before an attack by 11th Infantry Division succeeded in breaking through the Soviet lines and reaching some of the units that had been encircled.

On 18 March, Fediuninsky's army tried again with 109th Rifle Corps and the remnants of 30th Guards Rifle Corps. Otto Carius was in a bunker near his vehicle, and witnessed the heavy artillery preparation with which the Red Army attempted to batter the stubborn German defences into submission:

Out of the blue, they laid down a barrage that left nothing to the imagination. It covered the entire front of our bridgehead. Only Ivan could lay down a barrage like that.

Even the Americans, whom I got to know later on in the west, couldn't compete with them. The Russians shot with every available weapon, from light mortars all the way up to heavy artillery …

The entire 61st Infantry Division sector was covered with such a barrage that we thought all hell had broken loose. We were right in the middle of it, and it was completely impossible for us to get to our tanks from the bunker.[31]

At first, the attack appeared to make progress, and succeeded in cutting the Tallinn–Narva railway line. Carius and two other Tiger commanders managed to hold their sector of the line, despite their accompanying infantry being driven off. It took most of the day for Carius to persuade his supporting artillery to open fire – the gunners had remained under the misapprehension that German infantry were still occupying their positions, and would thus be hit by the barrage that Carius requested. As a third Soviet attack seemed imminent, and Carius despaired of beating it off, the artillery fire finally began, badly disrupting Soviet preparations. Not long after, there was a final attack in battalion strength, which Carius defeated again, shooting up another three T34s.

The following morning, Carius led three Tigers and a few dozen infantry in a dawn counter-attack to recapture two ruined houses that had formed the German front line. Although the infantry succeeded in occupying the western house, they discovered that the eastern ruin was more strongly held, with several anti-tank guns and heavy machine guns:

It should be noted that that was typical of the Russians. If they sat anywhere for just a few hours – especially at night – they hauled up materiel like ants and dug into the ground like gophers. Even though we had constantly experienced that, we never could figure out how they actually did it. Despite all our efforts, we were not successful in regaining the second strongpoint. During our firefight, Ivan started a counterattack with two T34s and a small infantry unit.

We were able to beat them back and their tanks were knocked out in the process. Shortly thereafter, heavy mortar and artillery fire of extremely heavy calibre began to arrive. We had two killed and two wounded. It was not possible for the remaining four to take the strongpoint, let alone hold it.[32]

A final Soviet counter-attack was beaten off, and fighting died down. Throughout the battle, Carius and his comrades were frustrated and angered by the refusal of their company commander, Oberleutnant von Schiller, to come to the front line. It was therefore particularly irritating to them when the Wehrmacht daily report mentioned that the company, led by Schiller, had fought with distinction.[33]

The Germans held a narrow salient projecting into the Soviet lines, with the village of Lembitu at the base. The Soviet forces made further attempts to reduce the salient, with the village changing hands several times. The German infantry were reduced to just a handful of men, but backed by Carius' Tigers, they continued to cling on. When the fighting died down on 22 March, the front line had barely moved from before the Soviet attacks began. Carius calculated that his small group of tanks had destroyed 38 tanks, four assault guns, and 17 artillery pieces. Although the infantry supporting him had suffered heavy losses, Carius' platoon had only one man wounded when a heavy mortar round struck a tank and penetrated a hatch; a young soldier, new to the battalion, lost a foot as a result. Soviet infantry losses are unknown, but were far heavier than those of the Germans.[34]

The final phase of the campaign came with a determined German attempt to destroy the Soviet bridgehead. The German salient that Carius had defended with such determination – known to the Germans as the 'boot' on account of its shape – divided the Soviet bridgehead into two bulges, known as the 'east sack' and 'west sack'.

On 26 March, an attack was mounted using 11th and 227th Infantry Divisions, the former supported by an *ad hoc* tank formation commanded by Oberst Graf Hyazinth von Strachwitz. Strachwitz was a colourful figure, who had commanded a tank battalion during the Battle of France and *Barbarossa*, and was wounded during the fighting in Stalingrad in 1942. Injured in October, he was one of the few men to escape the encirclement, being flown out in a transport plane. The following year, he was given command of the panzer regiment of Panzergrenadier Division *Grossdeutschland*, and as in his earlier commands, his energetic leadership from the front line earned him the adulation of his men and the praise of his contemporaries. But despite his decorations – he was the first man other than a division commander to be awarded the Oak Leaves to the Knight's Cross – and membership of the National Socialist Party, he appears to have been a member of a group of officers opposed to Hitler. After the war, he claimed that it was the fate of the 6th Army in Stalingrad, and in particular the sacking of his corps commander, General Gustav von Wietersheim, for alleged incompetence and defeatism, that convinced him that Hitler had to be stopped. There was a plot during early 1943, involving Strachwitz, Rittmeister Georg *Freiherr* von Boeselager, and Fabian von Schlabrendorff, either to arrest Hitler on a visit to the Eastern Front, or to kill him with a time-bomb placed on his plane. In the event, Hitler landed at a different location from that expected by the conspirators, and the bomb malfunctioned due to the cold.[35] None of the conspirators were arrested. Now, in early 1944, the *Panzer Graf* ('Panzer Count'), as his men called him, found himself once more in the front line, commanding a mixed force of tanks, including Tigers from *Schwere Panzer Abteilung 502*.

Strachwitz made his first attempt to reduce the Soviet bridgehead with an attack against the 'west sack'. Carius and his Tigers were to hold their positions in and near the 'boot', while the main attack was delivered from the west. The road designated for the attack was too narrow for the Tigers, and Strachwitz personally led the attack, riding in the leading Pz.IV. Despite difficulties caused more by the terrain than the Red Army – the swampy ground to either side of the narrow road softened during the day, effectively preventing any off-road movement by the armoured vehicles – the attack was a success, and the 'west sack' was eliminated.

The next operation on 6 April was against the 'east sack', and on this occasion, Carius and his Tigers would be in the forefront of the attack. The road east ran past the two ruined houses where Carius had fought so hard to hold back the Soviet attack turned south and crossed the main railway line between Narva and the west, and a short distance beyond the line entered an area of woodland. After a preliminary bombardment, Carius and three other Tiger tanks surged forward across the railway line, apparently catching the Soviet defenders by surprise. As the Red Army belatedly brought artillery fire to bear, the Tigers and accompanying infantry penetrated further to the south. Although they succeeded in holding their positions through a long night of Soviet counter-attacks, further penetration to the south proved impossible. Nevertheless, a substantial portion of a division from the Soviet 109th Rifle Corps was destroyed, and large numbers of tanks belonging to a tank brigade were either destroyed or found abandoned. It seemed that the Soviet forces had assumed, after the successful German reduction of the 'west sack', that Strachwitz's tanks would attempt a similar operation against the base of the 'east sack' and had positioned their defences accordingly, and were taken completely by surprise by an attack from the north.[36]

The *Oberkommando der Wehrmacht* (Wehrmacht High Command, or OKW) report for 31 March made the most of the German success, somewhat exaggerating the gains:

> The bulk of several Russian divisions were encircled and destroyed in several days of offensive operations in the trackless forests and marshes southwest of Narva, with effective support from artillery, rocket launchers, tanks and fighter-bombers. Repeated enemy relief attacks failed. In this attack, the enemy lost over 6,000 dead, several hundred prisoners, and 59 guns, as well as numerous other weapons and war materiel of all kinds.[37]

On 19 April, with the spring thaw making all movement difficult, the Germans attempted to reduce the rest of the Soviet bridgehead, using the Tiger *Abteilung*, Strachwitz's tanks, and elements of 61st, 122nd, 170th and *Feldherrnhalle* Divisions. Confused fighting lasted several days, with both sides suffering short-term encirclements for periods of time. The attack was finally called off on 24 April, having made limited headway. Strachwitz received the Diamonds to the Knight's Cross for his efforts before being assigned to a new command. Carius was awarded the Knight's Cross.

The Soviet version of events was completely different from the earlier OKW report:

> The Hitlerite command decided to restore the rail line and, to that end, launched a counterattack on 26 March. During the course of two weeks, the enemy launched attack after attack. At a cost of heavy losses, the enemy managed to drive a wedge into the Soviet defences, but part of their forces were encircled and destroyed, and the remainder withdrew to their jumping-off positions.[38]

It was the end of the winter fighting in the area. Govorov's armies, attacking almost continuously for three months, had driven the Germans back from Leningrad into Estonia in less than a month, but despite repeated efforts, and substantial reinforcements, had failed to break through the Narva line. For the Germans, the satisfaction of stopping the Soviet advance was tempered by the heavy losses they had suffered. A resumption of fighting would have to wait until the dramatic events of the summer.

Further south, the Latvians had been involved in heavy fighting against Soviet forces attempting to advance directly towards Latvia, to the south of Lake Peipus. The 2nd Latvian SS Brigade had now been upgraded to form the new 19th SS

Waffen-Grenadier Division (2nd Latvian), and in order to create a new field command that would allow the two Latvian divisions to fight alongside each other, the SS established VI SS Corps in October 1943. This new corps, consisting of the two divisions, was tasked with occupying part of the Panther Line along the River Velikaya. The first commander of the corps was Obergruppenführer Karl von Pfeffer-Wildenbruch, a man held in high regard by senior Latvian officers.

In this sector, the line had been poorly positioned. The east bank of the Velikaya consisted of a line of hills, giving the Soviet troops the advantage of overseeing the Latvian positions. Attempts by Standartenführer Veiss to push the front line forward, in order to secure the hills and improve the position, were only moderately successful; the Latvians had been in constant retreat for days, often engaged in exhausting and costly combat with the pursuing Red Army, and the men were unwilling to abandon the shelter of the bunkers of the Panther Line.

On 1 March, units of the Red Army attacked across the frozen Velikaya, the beginning of a series of battles that continued through most of the month. On 16 March, the Latvians were driven from Hill 93.4 near Sapronovo, one of the few pieces of high ground on the west bank, and after a series of bloody reversals the following day, they succeeded in recovering their positions on 18 March. A week later, after a heavy bombardment, the Red Army tried again, forcing 15th SS Waffen-Grenadier Division – the southerly of the two Latvian divisions – to concede ground. Determined counter-attacks failed to destroy the Soviet bridgehead, and in early April, the battered Latvian division was pulled out of the front line.

Heavy fighting continued in the sector held by 19th SS Waffen-Grenadier Division into April. Standartenführer Veiss was wounded by a grenade on 7 April, and died of his wounds several days later. Soviet attempts to break through continued until the middle of the month before the spring thaw intervened. The Latvians estimated that they had held off at least 11 Soviet rifle divisions, though the cost to themselves was considerable. To mark the day of the heaviest fighting, the Latvians proclaimed 16 March as Latvian Legion Day. It was the only occasion that the two Latvian divisions would fight side by side under a Latvian commander.[39]

Chapter 7
BREAKING THE DEADLOCK: SUMMER 1944

Relative calm descended upon Army Group North and the Soviet Fronts that faced it, as the fighting along the Narva died down with the spring thaw. Whilst the Red Army had much to celebrate, there was nevertheless a sense of missed opportunity. Leningrad was now completely safe from German attack, and the front line had approached – and in the case of the Narva bridgeheads, crossed – the old 1939 frontier of the Soviet Union. But despite being badly battered, Army Group North had survived. Its defence along the Narva had demonstrated that the Wehrmacht remained more than capable of tough resistance, resulting in heavy Soviet casualties.

A similar pattern was seen elsewhere along the Eastern Front. In the central sector, there was particularly heavy fighting during the winter to the north of Vitebsk, where 1st Baltic Front succeeded in taking Nevel and Gorodok, but then spent several weeks battering in vain at Vitebsk itself. The city was left in a dangerous salient, with Soviet forces to the west, north and east. Despite its being an obvious target for a Soviet assault, Hitler refused to allow its evacuation; instead, it was declared a fortress, to be defended to the last man. Further south, Soviet forces pursued the Germans after their failure to break through during the battle of Kursk and forced German positions along the Dnepr. The 1st and 2nd Ukrainian Fronts succeeded in encircling a substantial German force near the city of Cherkassy, and even though the Germans succeeded in breaking out and at least some of the troops in the encirclement escaped, it seemed as if further successes were imminent. With this in mind, Stalin urged his commanders to maintain pressure along the entire Eastern Front, in the belief that such relentless attacks would eventually create a collapse on part of the front, which could then be exploited to break up the entire German line. But as was the case in the north, the immobilising spring thaw, combined with exhaustion of the attacking Soviet formations, prevented a decisive breakthrough.

As the weather grew warmer, the Germans anxiously prepared for a resumption of the Soviet onslaught. Hitler and OKH concluded that the Red Army's main effort would fall in the Ukraine, a belief fed by elaborate Soviet deception measures. Empty goods trains were repeatedly spotted leaving the area during the day, and were believed to have transported men and equipment into the front near the city of Kovel. The trains did indeed enter the region during the night, but unknown to the Germans, they were as empty as when they were spotted by German reconnaissance during the day. The real Soviet build-up was opposite Army Group Centre.

The three armies of Army Group Centre could not fail to detect the Soviet forces massing against them. Although they may have underestimated the total Soviet strength, it was clear to the officers and men of 3rd Panzer Army, 4th Army and 9th Army that they faced a major assault. Despite the incontrovertible evidence, OKH remained convinced that the main effort would come further south. By 10 June, this steadfast opinion was beginning to shift:

> When it is still considered that the attack against Army Group Centre will be a secondary operation in the framework of overall Soviet offensive operations, it must be taken into account that the enemy will also be capable of building concentrations in front of Army Group Centre, whose penetrative power cannot be underestimated in view of the ratio of forces between the two sides.[1]

Refused permission to pull back, the exposed German troops of Army Group Centre could only watch and wait, listening anxiously to reports of the invasion of Normandy by the Western Allies. On 22 June, the third anniversary of the German invasion, the blow fell, as the huge Soviet forces massed for Operation *Bagration* were unleashed. In three days, Vitebsk was encircled, and fell on 27 June, with the loss of the German LIII Corps. Further envelopments followed at Mogilev and Bobruisk, followed by another encirclement at Minsk. By this stage, the Germans were in total retreat, with only isolated resistance by a small number of panzer divisions, fighting desperately in the face of the unstoppable tide.

The disintegration of Army Group Centre created two immediate problems. Firstly, there was an urgent need to transfer forces to fill the huge gaps left by the loss of up to half a million men. With a pressing requirement for troops in France to face the Western Allies in Normandy, the only sources of reinforcements for Army Group Centre were either a few divisions on garrison duty in places like Norway, or the army groups in the northern and southern sectors of the Eastern Front. Such transfers of troops would weaken their former sectors, making them in turn vulnerable to further Soviet assaults.

The second problem was that the rapid Soviet advance across Belarus to the Polish frontier in the wake of *Bagration* exposed the flanks of the army groups immediately to the north and south. In the case of Army Group North, this provided an opportunity to bypass the stubborn German defences that had held up the Soviet advance in the last weeks of the winter offensive. As troops were sent from Army Group North to try to re-establish a line in the centre, the weakened German 16th and 18th Armies began to look increasingly vulnerable.

The catastrophic plight of Army Group Centre forced the German High Command to consider radical options. OKH proposed the abandonment of Estonia and parts of Latvia, with a withdrawal of forces to the line of the River Daugava. Johannes Friessner, who had replaced Lindemann as commander of Army Group North, presented this proposal to Hitler on 12 July. The response can have come as little surprise to anyone: Hitler ordered Army Group North to stand firm on the Narva, or die in the attempt.[2]

The following weeks saw rapid and dramatic developments across the entire Eastern Front. These battles often occurred at the same time, but in an attempt to provide a coherent account, they will be described first in the south, where the Soviet armies on the northern flank of *Bagration* pushed into Lithuania and Latvia, and then in the north, where the traditional invasion route between Estonia and Russia, along the Baltic coast, remained the scene of bitter fighting and enormous bloodshed.

The first crisis for the German forces in the Baltic States came towards the end of *Bagration*, as General Ivan Khristorovich Bagramian's 1st Baltic Front and General Ivan Danilovich Cherniakhovsky's 3rd Belarusian Front advanced on the northern flank of the great Soviet advance. Despite suffering heavy losses in the initial phase of *Bagration*, 1st Baltic Front remained a powerful force, and as he advanced, Bagramian repeatedly raised concerns about the German Army Group North hanging over his right flank. The German forces there, he felt, represented a potential threat, but also an opportunity: a drive against them could result in the isolation and eventual destruction of Army Group North. In other words, in keeping with Stalin's philosophy during the winter offensives, he wished to exploit the collapse of German forces in front of him and to induce a similar collapse elsewhere.

Bagramian was the son of an Armenian railwayman, and the first non-Slavic Soviet officer to be given command of a front. He had been a member of an Armenian nationalist group during the Civil War that followed the Russian

Revolution, and was briefly expelled from the Frunze Military Academy in 1934 when this was discovered; fortunately for him, his arrest was successfully challenged by Anastas Mikoyan, an Armenian member of the Politburo.[3] At the beginning of *Barbarossa*, he was deputy chief of staff of the South-western Front, and was one of the few officers to survive the front's collapse in the Western Ukraine. After taking part in the planning of the Soviet counter-attack in the battle of Moscow, he was involved in Timoshenko's disastrous Kharkov counter-offensive of 1942, and was demoted in the aftermath, even though he had attempted to persuade both Timoshenko and Stalin that the operation was going badly awry.[4] Partially rehabilitated, he commanded first 16th Army, then 11th Army, and further impressed Stalin during the preparations for the battle of Kursk. After his appointment to command of 1st Baltic Front, he headed up the assault on Vitebsk during the winter of 1943–44, before leading his front during *Bagration*.

Cherniakhovsky was also the son of a railwayman, this time from the Ukraine. He was younger than many of his contemporary generals, and his early experience of the Second World War was when he led his 28th Tank Division in a doomed counter-attack against Hoepner's 4th Panzer Group during the early fighting in Lithuania. In early 1943, he achieved fame while commanding 60th Army when he liberated Kursk, creating the salient that was the centre of the following summer's fighting. He was the youngest man to be appointed to command of a front, and showed great flair in shifting his front's axis of attack during *Bagration*, something that he repeated during the closing months of the war in East Prussia.

Bagramian's forces reached Lake Narach in north-west Belarus on 4 July, and were now ordered to press on towards Kaunas and Vilnius. As well as the symbolic importance of these cities, securing either of these objectives would open the way for a push to the Baltic coast, which would isolate Army Group North. The German line facing Bagramian's 1st Baltic Front was composed of General Gerhard Matzky's XXVI Corps, part of the remnants of 3rd Panzer Army. Matzky, who had served as military attaché in Tokyo until 1940, took command of 21st Infantry Division in 1943 and XXVIII Corps in early 1944. During the defensive fighting south of Pskov he earned the Knight's Cross, before taking command of XXVI Corps.

One of the few formations available to 3rd Panzer Army that was in good shape was 7th Panzer Division, newly arrived from Army Group North Ukraine. It detrained north of the town of Lida, in north-west Belarus, and as they arrived on 5 July, its troops were dispatched to the north, in order to set up a protective front some 30 miles south-east of Vilnius. Many of the division's personnel would have remembered their passage through this area three years ago, when they led the triumphant

Wehrmacht in its apparently unstoppable drive into the Soviet Union. The current state of affairs in their new theatre of operations came as a shock to the panzer troops:

> There was great turmoil at the front, with some units retreating in complete disarray as individual soldiers. The command staff received no reports from the 'front' and could give no information about the enemy, still less which formations they had earlier fought, and there was a complete lack of cohesion.[5]

In a series of running battles, 7th Panzer Division fell back steadily towards the west. Like all motorised German formations, it was hamstrung by fuel shortages, and on 10 July, Generalmajor Karl Mauss, the division commander, was forced to order the destruction of disabled tanks that were being towed. Crossing into Lithuania on 10 July, Bagramian's spearheads passed 7th Panzer Division's northern flank, reaching the outskirts of Alytus, over 40 miles west of the German front line. Whilst the bulk of the panzer division continued to face east, defending the river crossing at Varėna, just inside Lithuania, a battlegroup fought its way towards Alytus in the face of strong Soviet anti-tank defences. Under constant pressure, 7th Panzer Division fell back to the south-west, crossing the River Niemen at Merkinė late on 13 July. In response to urgent requests for help from the garrison commander of Alytus, who had almost no troops at his disposal, Mauss dispatched a battlegroup to the town, where despite assurances to the contrary, it was promptly dispersed in small detachments. In any event, the town couldn't be held. Strong Soviet attacks on 15 July forced the Germans back, leaving some elements of the 7th Panzer Division battlegroup to the north-west of Alytus, while the rest fell back to the west. Here, it proved possible to halt the Soviet advance on high ground:

> The day brought the division a defensive success through the deployment of all available forces against a continuously attacking enemy. On this day, enemy forces of between 10 and 12 regiments in strength attempted to break through with the use of the heaviest artillery, anti-tank, mortar and air support, particularly west of Alytus. Nevertheless, the main point of effort was clearly disrupted, particularly through the use of artillery.[6]

One of 7th Panzer Division's panzer battalions had been in France, re-equipping with new Panther tanks, and its return to the division provided a most welcome boost in strength. Heavy fighting continued, and late on 27 July, the division was ordered north to Kaunas, to deal with a dangerous development that threatened to open up the entire German front.

On Bagramian's southern flank was Cherniakhovsky's 3rd Belarusian Front, opposed by a mixture of units, with the most prominent being 5th Panzer Division. The division had been heavily involved in a fighting withdrawal from Mogilev to Minsk and from there to the Lithuanian and East Prussian borders, and despite its losses remained a powerful force. The bitter fighting made a big impression on the soldiers involved, as the commander of one of 5th Panzer Division's panzergrenadier regiments recorded:

> These battles were the toughest that I had ever experienced, and in the main fitted the motto: Let the enemy come forward, give him a punch on the nose, disengage, attack ourselves, and disappear again. This meant the most strenuous efforts by everyone from the commanders to the youngest grenadiers. There was absolutely no more thought of sleep. Words cannot describe what was required during these days in terms of heroism, operations, and endurance. It would be wrong to single out a few individuals or units, as all gave their best.[7]

Together with a scattering of *ad hoc* units, it now formed the newly reconstituted XXXIX Panzer Corps – the previous formation of this name had been effectively destroyed east of the Beresina, losing two corps commanders in two days – commanded by General Dietrich von Saucken. The son of Prussian landowners, Saucken had a long and illustrious career behind him, having commanded 4th Panzer Division with distinction from December 1941. Badly wounded shortly after winning the Knight's Cross in early 1942, he served as commandant of *Panzertruppenschule* ('School for Armoured Troops') in Krampnitz. He then returned to 4th Panzer Division, earning the Oak Leaves to the Knight's Cross in August 1943 and the Swords to the Knight's Cross during the following winter.

Several panzer divisions – notably 4th, 5th and 7th – fought as 'firefighters' during the aftermath of *Bagration*, attempting to intercept the advancing Soviet spearheads. In this role, they were generally very effective wherever they ran into the Red Army, but the combination of their small number and the disruptive effect of constant fuel shortages, ensured that the Soviet advance continued, even though many Soviet units, too, were now getting towards the end of their supply lines and were weakened as much by mechanical attrition as by German resistance. Shuffled back and forth, none of the panzer divisions were able to intercept Cherniakhovsky's exploitation forces closing in with Vilnius. Nevertheless, 5th Panzer Division succeeded in drawing off a significant part of Cherniakhovsky's Front.

In any event, fighting had already begun in the 'historic capital' of Lithuania. The German garrison consisted of the remnants of 14th and 299th Infantry Divisions, an infantry battalion and artillery battalion of 170th Infantry Division, and an assortment of other small units. Even though none of the panzer divisions on the front could reach the area, reinforcements were en route, in the form of a battalion of the 16th *Fallschirmjäger* (parachute) Regiment. Even as the paratroopers arrived at the city airport in a stream of Ju52 transports, the tangled web of relationships between Poles, Germans, Lithuanians and pro-Soviet partisans erupted.

General Aleksander Krzyżanowski, who had been an artillery officer in 1939, was commander of the local elements of the Polish Home Army. He was a devoted Polish nationalist, and at first attempted to build a broad anti-German coalition, though negotiations with Lithuanian, Belarusian and pro-Soviet resistance groups proved fruitless. At the end of 1943, partly in response to a request from Panteleimon Ponomarenko, First Secretary of the Communist Party of Belarus, Stalin approved orders to pro-Soviet partisans to disarm elements of the Home Army – in the words of the order: 'Should there be any resistance on the part of the Polish partisans, they must be shot on the spot.' This effectively brought to an end any possibility of cooperation between pro-Soviet partisans and the Polish Home Army. Consequently, like other Home Army leaders, Krzyżanowski responded to Soviet attacks on his forces by coming to regard the Soviet Union as an enemy in the same way that he viewed Germany.[8] As hostilities with pro-Soviet partisans grew more problematic, Krzyżanowski held negotiations with German officials, including Seidler von Rosenfeld, a local SD officer, and Julian Christiansen, the head of the local branch of the *Abwehr* (German military intelligence) in January and February 1944 respectively. Christiansen suggested a detailed protocol, in which Germany offered to arm Krzyżanowski's men, including with light artillery, in exchange for a cessation of hostilities between the Home Army and German forces, and Polish cooperation with the occupying authorities in terms of economic production. Although Krzyżanowski refused to accept the protocol, he came to an arrangement with Christiansen whereby the Germans would ensure that weapons and supplies were left in weakly guarded areas, where they could easily be captured by the Home Army and used against pro-Soviet partisans.[9]

In May 1944, there were armed clashes in and around Vilnius between the Polish Home Army and Lithuanian forces commanded by Povilas Plechavičius, culminating in a pitched battle near the town of Murowana Oszmianka. The outcome was a clear Polish victory, and a series of reprisals followed, first with Lithuanian units attacking Polish civilians, then with Polish attacks on Lithuanians.

As Soviet forces approached Vilnius, the German authorities contacted Colonel Lubosław Krzeszowski, one of Krzyżanowski's subordinates, and suggested that the Germans and the Home Army combine forces against the Red Army. In return, civilian control of Vilnius would be handed over to Poland, and a number of Polish prisoners held by the Germans would be released. Krzeszowski rejected the offer, not least because the Poles had plans of their own. The Home Army intended to use the arrival of the Red Army as an opportunity to seize control of parts of Poland from the Germans, with coordinated uprisings in several cities under the codename *Burza* ('Tempest' or 'Storm'). In Vilnius, the operation was codenamed *Ostra Brama* ('Gate of Dawn'), after a famous landmark on the south-east edge of the old heart of the city. Late on 6 July, the Home Army tried to seize Vilnius in an attempt to gain control of the city before the arrival of the Red Army. In the preceding days, the Home Army had effectively secured much of the countryside around the city, but the unexpectedly fast advance of the Soviet forces – about a day ahead of Polish expectations – resulted in Krzyżanowski moving his own timetable forward. Consequently, Krzeszowski had fewer troops at his disposal than he might have wished, and his men were left in possession of only the north-east part of the city. Much of the Polish 77th Infantry Regiment found itself held at arm's length to the east of Vilnius, its movements further hampered by a German armoured train. Elements of the Polish 85th Infantry Regiment took up positions to the west, beyond the River Vilnia, threatening the German lines of retreat. It is striking that despite years of Soviet and German occupation and tens of thousands of arrests, the AK continued to organise itself into formations that drew their ancestry from the pre-war Polish Army.

Soviet forces arrived outside Vilnius at about the same time that the Poles launched their attack. 35th Guards Tank Brigade, part of General Rotmistrov's 5th Guards Tank Army, was involved in heavy fighting with the German paratroopers at the airport, from where fighting gradually spread into the city. On 8 July, Krylov's 5th Army reached the city outskirts, while the Soviet armour gradually encircled the garrison.

It had been Krzyżanowski's intention to secure the city for Poland before the arrival of the Red Army, but the planners of *Burza* had always intended that the Poles would cooperate at a tactical level with the Soviets, though they would attempt to set up their own Polish civil authorities before the Red Army could establish pro-Soviet administrations. Unlike in many of the other 'fortresses' that Hitler insisted were defended to the last man, the Vilnius garrison put up a stiff fight, inflicting heavy losses on their opponents. Rotmistrov's tanks had suffered considerable losses in Minsk, and now found themselves engaged in close-range combat against a determined enemy, equipped with weapons such as the *Panzerfaust*, that were at their most effective in this environment. Nevertheless, there could be no question of the Germans holding on for long.

Relief was on the way. The rest of 16th *Fallschirmjäger* Regiment arrived by train near Vilnius early on 9 July, and almost immediately it was assigned to an *ad hoc* battlegroup, *Kampfgruppe Tolsdorff*, which went into action outside the western outskirts. Another formation dispatched to try to stem the Soviet flood was 6th Panzer Division, which had been recuperating in Soltau in Germany after suffering heavy casualties earlier in the year. As the men of the panzer division arrived, they were hastily organised into two battlegroups. *Gruppe Pössl* consisted of a battalion of tanks from the *Grossdeutschland* division, a battalion of 6th Panzer Division's panzergrenadiers, and artillery support; it was ordered to advance to make contact with Tolsdorff's group on the outskirts of Vilnius, and thence to link up with the garrison. *Gruppe Stahl*, with two panzergrenadier battalions and artillery support, would attempt to hold open the line of retreat.

The attack began on 13 July, with Generalleutnant Waldenfels, the commander of 6th Panzer Division, and Generaloberst Georg-Hans Reinhardt, commander of 3rd Panzer Army, accompanying Pössl's group. The thin screen of Soviet and Polish forces to the west of Vilnius was unable to stop the thrust, which reached Rikantai, about eight miles outside the city. Here, contact was established with *Gruppe Tolsdorff*, which in turn had a tenuous connection with the Vilnius garrison. During the afternoon, German wounded were evacuated from Vilnius and along the road to the west.

The Soviet response to the German breakout was slow. Late on 13 July, uncoordinated attacks along the narrow escape route were repulsed, but the following day there were several crises as increasingly strong Soviet pincer attacks cut the road repeatedly. Finally, as darkness fell on 14 July, the Germans withdrew to the west. About 5,000 men from the garrison were able to escape, but over 10,000 were lost.

The Soviet authorities proclaimed the liberation of Vilnius on 13 July, but there was still the question of what to do with the Polish Home Army forces that had fought both against the garrison and against *Gruppe Tolsdorff* to the west of the city. Krzyżanowski and his fellow officers wished to use their men to recreate the pre-war Polish 19th Infantry Division, itself a controversial unit in that it was raised by Poland in the Vilnius region after that area was seized by Poland. On 16 July, Krzyżanowski and his officers were invited to a conference with the leadership of the 3rd Belarusian Front, as a report by the NKVD recorded:

Yesterday [i.e. on 17 July] at 0800 hours, under the pretext of an inspection by the commandant of the Front, commandants of brigades and regiments [of the Home Army] were gathered around the village Bogusze. Altogether, 26 officers, including

9 commandants of brigades, 12 unit commanders, and 5 staff officers of the Polish Army were gathered.

When directed by us to turn in their weapons, they refused, and only after the threat of force were they disarmed.

… Today, at dawn, we began combing operations through the forests, in which, according to our estimates, the Poles were present. … It was ascertained that during the night they marched away to the south. Because of the steps taken, we caught up with them, and disarmed them.

According to the situational reports for 1600 hours, 3,500 men were disarmed, among them, 200 officers and NCOs.

During the disarming, 3,000 guns, 300 machine guns, 50 heavy machine guns, 15 mortars, seven light artillery pieces, 12 vehicles, and large number of grenades and ammunition were confiscated.[10]

Lubosław Krzyżanowski was imprisoned until October 1947. A year after his release by the Soviet authorities, the Polish security service arrested him, and he died of tuberculosis in 1951.[11]

Another Polish officer involved in the fighting in and around Vilnius was Maciej Kalenkiewicz. He served as a combat engineer during the German invasion of Poland in 1939, and escaped to France during the first winter of the war. From there, he moved to England, and returned to Poland in a parachute drop in December 1941. Although his unit was captured by the Germans, Kalenkiewicz and his men managed to recover their weapons and fought their way to freedom, killing all their captors, though Kalenkiewicz himself was injured during the brief firefight. He was one of the main authors of the plan to seize Vilnius, and in June 1944, he was once more wounded. He developed gangrene, necessitating the amputation of his hand, and consequently was unable to take part in the fighting for Vilnius; when the Soviets began to arrest Home Army personnel, he led his men – a battalion of the Polish 77th Infantry Regiment – into the Rudnicka Forest, where they regrouped with other Polish fighters, until perhaps 2,000 men had gathered. Aware that they were being monitored by Soviet aircraft, the Poles decided to disperse, with Kalenkiewicz taking command of a contingent of about 100. Conscious that the Soviets were harassing the local population, arresting any suspected of being supporters of the Home Army or in any other respect hostile to the Soviet Union, Kalenkiewicz sent a signal to his superiors, warning them that he and his men were 'as good as dead', and all would be lost unless the Western Allies could intervene, perhaps by establishing air bases in eastern Poland. On 19 August, a unit of Soviet soldiers from the NKVD moved against Kalenkiewicz and his small band, near the village of Surmonty near the border with Belarus. The Poles beat off the first attack, but after receiving reinforcements, the NKVD detachment attacked again, swiftly overrunning the Home Army men. Kalenkiewicz and 36 of his men were killed.

The ruthless elimination of the AK throughout Poland, but particularly in the Vilnius region, was an essential prerequisite to Stalin's preferred solution of reassigning the area to Lithuania. The Poles were far better armed and organised than the Lithuanian nationalist partisans, and far more numerous; they would have opposed the imposition of Lithuanian sovereignty, and the compulsory resettlement of Poles in the region to territories further west. Given their close links with the Western Allies and the pre-war Polish administration, the fighters of the AK were never going to be tolerated by the Soviets after they had seized control of Poland.

For a few days after the fall of Vilnius, the front line appeared to stabilise to the west of the city. Despite his success in capturing Vilnius, Cherniakhovsky was disappointed with the performance of his subordinates. Pavel Alexeyevish Rosmistrov, commander of 5th Guards Tank Army, was heavily criticised for allowing his armour to become embroiled in costly urban combat in both Minsk and Vilnius, and was removed from command. Both Cherniakhovsky and Bagramian were forced to pause while supplies were brought up to the front, and the shattered remnants of German divisions that had almost been destroyed during *Bagration* had a brief respite. But on 28 July, Cherniakhovsky renewed his offensive, pushing forward towards Kaunas. The Red Army was only 30 miles from Kaunas, and on the second day of the new assault, the Soviet troops had already covered nearly half this distance in some locations. On 30 July, Soviet spearheads from 33rd Army penetrated the threadbare German line and reached the Niemen valley to the south-east of Kaunas. Immediately, the Soviet armoured reserve for the operation, 2nd Guards Tank Corps, was committed to the sector; bypassing the German forces pulling back towards Kaunas, the Soviet tanks raced on to Vilkaviškis, far to the south-west of the city. From here, the tank corps was close to the East Prussian frontier, but also had the option to swing to the north and isolate Kaunas. The city was given up almost without a fight on 1 August, the German forces pulling back to the west.

On Cherniakhovsky's northern flank, Bagramian pushed on from Lake Narach into Lithuania towards Švenčionys. Initially, STAVKA assigned him the objectives of Panevezys, Kaunas and Šiauliai. Although Bagramian received reinforcements in the form of 2nd Guards Army and 51st Army, neither of these formations would be available until mid-July, and at first, he was left to push on with 6th Guards Army and 43rd Army, both weakened substantially by the fighting during *Bagration*, reinforced by the similarly understrength 1st Tank Corps. Fortunately for Bagramian, the German forces in front of him were in an even worse state.

At first, Bagramian made good progress, but the arrival of Strachwitz and his small group of tanks shored up the defence. The armies of Bagramian's front were covering such a large sector of front – estimated at about 120 miles – that he struggled to make adequate progress. Accordingly, the objective of Kaunas was transferred to Cherniakhovsky's front, allowing Bagramian to concentrate on driving west towards Šiauliai. 2nd Guards Army and 51st Army now arrived and immediately made better headway, capturing Panevėžys on 22 July and thus completely outflanking the German defences at Daugavpils. Bagramian assigned 3rd Guards Mechanised Corps to 51st Army, and powerful motorised formations pushed forward rapidly to Šiauliai, reaching the eastern outskirts on 25 July. Oberst Hellmuth Mäder, who had taken command of Army Group North's *Waffenschule* (weapons school) after being badly wounded on the Narva front, deployed his men – a mixture of instructors and trainees from the weapons school, and other *ad hoc* companies made up of rear area units and stragglers – in the town, and succeeded in holding Šiauliai for two days, inflicting significant losses on the Soviet forces and buying invaluable time for other German units to pull back to the west.

For Bagramian, there was now finally an opportunity to deal with Army Group North, something that he had wished to do ever since the early successes of *Bagration*. 51st Army was ordered to strike north from Šiauliai and, over the next three days, pushed forward against weakening opposition. Elements of 3rd Guards Mechanised Corps, supported by 279th and 347th Rifle Divisions, pushed a mixture of German units from I Corps out of Jelgava on 31 July, on the same day that 35th Guards Mechanised Brigade, also from 3rd Guards Mechanised Corps, took Dobele. Tukums fell the same day, and shortly after, Soviet soldiers from 347th and 416th Rifle Divisions reached the Gulf of Riga a few miles away. Army Group North was cut off from the Reich.

On Bagramian's northern flank was General Andrei Ivanovich Yeremenko's 2nd Baltic Front, which had not been involved in *Bagration*. Nevertheless, Yeremenko's armies maintained considerable pressure on the German lines to prevent redeployment of forces to other sectors. VI SS Corps came under repeated attack from 22 June, and as the catastrophic collapse of Army Group Centre developed, orders were issued to pull back the entire front line to prevent it being outflanked from the south.

On 9 July, supply units and ammunition were evacuated to the rear in preparation for a general withdrawal the following day, but early on 10 July Yeremenko's armies unleashed a surprise attack. The shortage of ammunition brought about by the previous day's withdrawals greatly hampered the defensive capabilities of the Latvian divisions, and instead of an orderly withdrawal, the line was pulled back in almost constant contact with the Red Army. As a consequence, many of the new defensive positions were overrun by the pursuing Soviets before they could be manned properly. The fighting reached the city of Opochka on 13 July, but the line of the Velikaya could not be held, and the retreat continued. 15th SS Waffen-Grenadier Division's 32nd Grenadier Regiment found itself isolated on the southern flank of the division, and attempted to retreat to the west, fighting its way through a group of Soviet partisans in dense woodland. On 16 July, after a gruelling march of two days, the survivors reached the River Isa, not far from the Latvian border. From here, they turned north, encountering and destroying a small Soviet force. Mounted in the vehicles they had captured from the Soviets, the remaining men, led by Obersturmbannführer Aperats, attempted to seize a bridge over the River Zilupe. Although they secured a small bridgehead, they then came under heavy attack by Soviet forces, including a substantial number of tanks, and the Latvian regiment was completely destroyed. Aperats chose suicide rather than surrender after he was seriously wounded. Sturmbannführer Hazners, accompanied by only four men, managed to reach the lines of the German 93rd Infantry Division.[12]

The Latvian divisions regrouped near Kārsava, within the borders of Latvia. The combat strength of both divisions was greatly reduced by their casualties, and as it was the weaker of the two formations, 15th SS Waffen-Grenadier Division handed over its artillery and much of its manpower to 19th SS Waffen-Grenadier Division. It was perhaps typical of the manner in which the people of the Baltic States were exploited by both the Soviet Union and Germany that, now the war was once more returning to Baltic territories, a proportion of those who had taken up arms specifically to defend those territories should be moved elsewhere, to suit the needs of their powerful occupiers; 15th SS Waffen-Grenadier Division was pulled out of the front line and sent to the rear for reorganisation and replenishment, eventually being transferred to West Prussia in August.

The Soviet 10th Guards Army crossed the border into Latvia, seizing Zilupe on 17 July, pushing on to Ludza on 23 July. Further south, 22nd Army and 3rd Shock Army advanced towards the vital river crossings at Daugavpils, and when the German 290th Infantry Division, protecting the road that ran north-east from Daugavpils towards Rezekne, came under pressure, the Germans were forced to react. Otto Carius and his fellow Tiger tank crewmen of *Schwere Panzer Abteilung 502* had been employed in a number of minor actions since their battles near Narva, and on 20 July were ordered to move up to the front to prevent a Soviet breakthrough that might threaten both Daugavpils and Rezekne. As he led his company forward along the road from Daugavpils towards Rezekne, Carius came across German units fleeing the Soviet advance:

> What transpired in front of our eyes is barely capable of description. It wasn't a withdrawal any more, but a panic-stricken, headlong flight.
>
> Everything and everybody was heading toward Dünaburg [Daugavpils] – trucks, wheeled vehicles, motorcycles. Everything was completely loaded down. No one could be persuaded to stop. It was like a river that swells whenever its tributaries flow into it after a rainstorm.[13]

Just short of the village of Malinovka, Carius encountered a junior officer who told him that the village had been occupied by Soviet tanks. A brief reconnaissance suggested that Soviet infantry was not present in any significant numbers, and swiftly Carius made a plan to retake Malinovka: he and another tank commander would drive into the village at full speed and engage any enemy tanks there, while the other six tanks in the company took up positions on high ground to the south and engaged any Soviet tanks that attempted to retreat.

The attack lasted less than 15 minutes, resulting in the swift recapture of the village. Some of the tanks appeared to have been left with only one or two crewmembers aboard – the rest were apparently busy collecting loot. Without losing any tanks, Carius and his company claimed to have destroyed 17 JS-2 tanks and five T34s. From Malinovka, they moved on to ambush the rest of the Soviet tank brigade, inflicting further heavy casualties.[14] However, the Soviet forces in the area at the time, 5th Tank Corps, gave different losses for 41st Tank Brigade (ten T34s) and 48th Guards Heavy Tank Regiment (five JS-2s), as the heavy tank regiment reported:

> At 1200 the enemy opened coordinated fire of tanks and SP-guns from the region of Malinovo [Malinovka]. Taking cover in folds in the terrain, the regiment started a firefight with the enemy. Enemy aircraft actively operated overhead. As a result of bombing and enemy artillery fire the regiment suffered losses – five tanks were set ablaze. The regiment was withdrawn from combat and laid an ambush in the forest south-east of Malinovo.[15]

To confuse matters even further, the official after-action report of *Schwere Panzer Abteilung 502* records that Carius and his company destroyed 17 tanks in Malinovka on 22 July, and makes no mention of the ambush that Carius describes after the initial combat.[16] Given that Carius was writing several years after the events he described, it is likely that the other more contemporary accounts are more accurate.

During the operation, Carius claimed, he recovered a Soviet officer's map, which suggested that the Red Army intended to bypass Daugavpils to the north and then attack the city from the north and north-west. The commander of 290th Infantry Division, *Generalmajor* Rudolf Goltzsch, rejected the map as misinformation and insisted on positioning his heavy weapons to the east of Daugavpils. Whatever the truth of this account, Soviet forces from 6th Guards Army and 4th Shock Army closed in from both the east and north, and on 24 July, Carius was dispatched with four Tigers to protect the north-west approaches of Daugavpils. As he reconnoitred a village on a motorcycle-sidecar combination, Carius found himself under heavy fire:

We jumped from the motorcycle. Lokey [the driver of the motorcycle] reached the ditch intact, but a shot shattered my left thigh. Crawling, we attempted to get back to the village, but my strength soon left me. I ordered Lokey to scram and alert Leutnant Eichhorn, but the loyal man didn't want to leave me in the lurch …

In the meantime, the Russians had crossed over the road and into our ditch. Every time we moved, they fired. The bullets whizzing past me didn't hit Lokey either, because he was covered by me. In the end, he got away with a flesh wound. I intercepted the other rounds. I received a shot that penetrated through my upper left arm and another four hits in the back. Because the many wounds, especially those in the back, were bleeding heavily, I was soon completely exhausted and didn't get any farther … Suddenly, my rapidly dwindling will to live was revived. The engine noise of my tanks could be heard clearly – the sound of salvation to my ears! Eichhorn and Göring had heard the shooting and moved out to see what was going on. In addition to my elation, my hopes were revived that I would get out of that fix alive.

But then death suddenly stood in front of me! Three Russians had approached our rear and suddenly surfaced three metres behind me. I will never forget that sight for the rest of my life. I was bleeding from my many wounds, had no more strength, and heard the engines of my Tigers, which were probably coming too late after all.

… A Soviet officer stood in the middle. He called out, 'Ruki werch!' – 'Hands up!' The soldiers to his right and left held machine pistols aimed at us.

… My tanks came racing up then. With machine guns firing wildly into the area while on the move, they didn't hit anything. The sudden appearance of the Tigers naturally gave the Russians a shock. Both soldiers ran off immediately, but the Soviet officer raised his pistol to finish me off. In my condition I didn't desire to look death in the eye. I turned towards my approaching tanks. That was my good fortune and my salvation!

The Russian pulled the trigger three times, but he was so excited that two shots went wide and only one hit. The round went extremely close to the spinal cord in my neck, but miraculously not one tendon or artery was hit … if I hadn't turned toward my Tigers, the shot would have gone through the larynx and these lines here would never have been written![17]

Badly wounded, Carius was hauled onto the back of a tank and evacuated. He made a full recovery, and was awarded the Oak Leaves to the Knight's Cross, the medal being presented personally by Himmler while Carius was convalescing.

Meanwhile, in an attempt to restore the situation north of Daugavpils, 290th Infantry Division was ordered to attack to the north, while elements of I Corps further north tried to attack south. Unfortunately, retreating German combat engineers had destroyed many of the culverts along the road the attack followed, greatly hindering the movements of the remaining Tigers of *Schwere Panzer Abteilung 502*. Malinovka, where Carius destroyed a disputed number of tanks, was recaptured. To the north-west of Daugavpils, Leutnant Eichhorn, who had helped in Carius' rescue, achieved considerable success against advancing Soviet tanks, claiming to have shot up 16 heavy tanks on 25 July. The following day, as he attempted to continue his advance to the north and north-west, accompanied by an infantry regiment from 290th Infantry Division, he ran into the Soviet 239th and 311th Rifle Divisions, supported by tanks and anti-tank guns. Two Tigers were lost in quick succession, and the German force pulled back towards the Daugava. The infantry regiment was ferried across to the left bank, and Eichhorn drove back into Daugavpils. The road he had used the previous day was now in enemy hands, and the two remaining Tigers came under heavy fire; although both managed to reach the town, they suffered heavy damage that rendered them incapable of combat.[18]

A further three Soviet rifle divisions pressed into Daugavpils from the north-east, with two more advancing west on the left bank of the Daugava. Ivan Ivanovich Chinnov, commander of 360th Rifle Division, was with the leading elements of his division as it advanced, and was killed instantly when a sniper opened fire on his group. His *aide de camp* was wounded in the same attack, and died later; the division pressed on with renewed urgency. Nevertheless, the German forces in Daugavpils were able to withdraw across the river on 27 July with relatively little interference from the Red Army. Further north, the Soviet 10th Guards Army reached and secured

Kārsava and Rezekne on the same day. Heavy fighting erupted around Varakļāni, where the German 263rd Infantry Division held off 7th Guards Rifle Corps for several days, but exploiting successes a little further south, the Soviet 4th Shock Army reached the River Daugava at Līvāni on 1 August. The Latvians of 19th SS Waffen-Grenadier Division continued to put up tough resistance a little further north, but were steadily levered back; nevertheless, their delaying action at Cesvaine in conjunction with 83rd Infantry Division helped buy sufficient time for other German units to withdraw. Thereafter, Yeremenko's northern armies were forced to pause while supplies were brought forward; the grateful Latvians took advantage of this to reinforce 19th SS Waffen-Grenadier Division with new drafts.[19] A little to the south, Jēkabpils came under attack on 7 August, and was given up three days later as the Soviet 22nd Army applied relentless pressure. 10th Guards Army attempted to outflank the stubborn resistance of VI SS Corps by pushing forward to Madona on 12 August, but here, too, the lengthening Soviet supply lines forced a brief pause in operations.

On the Narva front, Friessner's response to Hitler's orders to hold the existing line at all costs was to build a series of positions some nine miles west of Narva, making use of some modest high ground. On 21 July, he asked for permission to withdraw to these positions, now known as the Tannenberg Line; only a few miles from the coast, and with boggy terrain to the south, it constituted a strong defensive position. It was clear that the Leningrad Front was about to resume offensive operations, and with no significant reserves available, Friessner regarded a prolonged battle along the Narva as potentially disastrous.

The German success in halting the first Soviet attempts to take Narva had helped to bring to an end the tentative ceasefire talks between Finland and the Soviet Union in April 1944. In an attempt to force the Finns to the negotiating table during the winter, Stalin ordered air attacks on Helsinki, but despite three major raids during February, few bombs hit their targets in the face of well-organised air defences. Although a Soviet offensive in June expelled the Finns from most of the territory they had seized in 1941, German supplies and troops persuaded the Finnish government to hold firm. Nevertheless, the war had almost exhausted Finland, and the nation continued to look for ways out of the conflict. General Mannerheim, the Finnish president, had warned the Germans that if Estonia were to fall back into Soviet hands, it would be impossible for Finland to remain in the war, as possession of the Estonian coast would give Soviet forces the ability to operate almost with impunity along the Finnish coastline. In these circumstances, his nation would have to accept whatever terms were imposed by Stalin.[20] Consequently, Hitler was extremely nervous of agreeing to any measure that might weaken Finnish resolve. However, Mannerheim assured him that a small withdrawal to the Tannenberg Line would not pose any problems for Finland, and Hitler gave a relieved Friessner permission to withdraw from the Narva.

Govorov's Leningrad Front had been preparing for a resumption of its earlier offensives, and had steadily built up the strength of the units in the bridgehead to the south of Narva. Two rifle corps from 8th Army would attack north from the bridgehead tip to seize the railway station at Auvere, and from there would push on towards the Baltic coast, with the support of two further rifle corps as a second echelon. At the same time, 2nd Shock Army would attack north of Narva, attempting to break through the lines of III SS Panzer Corps. Once it had done so, it would link up with 8th Army, encircling whatever remained of the German forces in and around Narva.

In addition to its previous formations, 2nd Shock Army now also included 8th Estonian Rifle Corps. Originally created from Estonians conscripted into the Red Army in 1941, this corps rarely had more than a 50 per cent complement of Estonians. Large numbers of Soviet soldiers who were descended from Estonians were included in its ranks, and some formations within the corps, such as 19th Guards Rifle Division, were wholly Russian in character. It would now go into combat along the River Narva, attacking Estonian troops fighting for Germany.

Artillery preparation for the Soviet attack began a day before Friessner requested permission to withdraw to the Tannenberg Line, the existence of which was still unknown to the Red Army. After four days of sporadic bombardment, a major barrage on 24 July fell on the German lines for two hours. Then, with ongoing artillery support, the Soviet 122nd Rifle Corps, supported by a tank brigade, attacked and penetrated the main German defences held by 11th Infantry Division. The neighbouring 117th Rifle Corps also attacked, encircling the Estonian 45th Infantry Regiment.

Almost immediately, German forces counter-attacked. A tank battalion from *SS-Nordland*, with infantry and artillery support, moved forward to face 117th Rifle Corps, and a confused battle followed. At one point, the commander of the German battlegroup, Obersturmbannführer Paul-Albert Kausch, found himself isolated with a small body of men. They fought off repeated Soviet attacks, and finally resorted to calling down artillery fire on their own position. Elsewhere, too, the Soviet attack was repulsed, with little gain. Soviet losses were estimated at about 3,000, compared with German casualties of 800. For his determined defence, Kausch was awarded the Knight's Cross a month later.

Meanwhile, in accordance with the plan to withdraw to the Tannenberg Line, German troops began to pull back from Ivangorod, at the tip of the small bridgehead held by the Wehrmacht to the east of Narva. As the men slipped quietly back across the Narva, the Soviets spotted their withdrawal, and attempted to rush the bridge. Although demolition charges had been placed on the bridge, they failed to detonate, and the bridge fell into Soviet hands. However, the Red Army's success was only temporary. A determined counter-attack by combat engineers from *SS-Nordland*, led by Hauptsturmführer Wanhöfer, recaptured the bridge, allowing it to be destroyed.

On 25 July, 2nd Shock Army launched its attack along the Narva, after another ferocious artillery bombardment. The Soviet 131st and 191st Rifle Divisions carried out an assault across the river, in the face of fierce resistance from the Estonian troops on the west bank. As the day wore on and ammunition stocks fell low, the defensive fire weakened, allowing the Soviet forces to secure bridgeheads. 191st Rifle Division immediately turned south towards Narva, while 131st Rifle Division began to push west. On the outskirts of Narva, 191st Rifle Division ran into a battalion from the Estonian 3rd Regiment, led by Obersturmbannführer Alfons Rebane. Rebane had a reputation for tactical skill, and demonstrated this by pulling his men out of their front line positions immediately before the Soviet bombardment, into a second line of trenches. From here, they defended themselves with determination, and as other

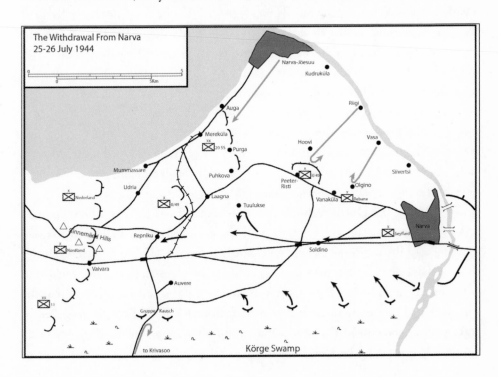

The Withdrawal From Narva
25-26 July 1944

German and Estonian forces began to retreat towards the Tannenberg Line, he skilfully moved his men to the west to try to retain contact. Regrouping in the country estate in Olgino, his battalion continued to inflict heavy losses on the pursuing Soviet troops.

With Soviet forces now across the lower Narva in strength, the evacuation of the German troops within the city itself gained pace. The rearguard was made up of *SS-Panzergrenadier-Regiment General Seyffard*, a regiment of Dutch SS soldiers from the *SS-Nederland* brigade, reinforced by a battalion from the brigade's *SS-Panzergrenadier-Regiment De Ruyter* and a pair of assault guns, with Rebane's Estonians covering their northern flank and a battalion of *SS-Panzergrenadier-Regiment Norge* to the south. Obersturmbannführer Benner, the commander of *Seyffard*, was new to his command, relatively unfamiliar with the area, and matters were made worse when contact with higher commands was disrupted by Soviet artillery fire during the afternoon of 25 July. At 2130hrs, an Estonian messenger arrived in Benner's headquarters in Narva, with the unwelcome news that Soviet forces had succeeded in cutting the road at Olgino. Benner immediately dispatched the battalion from *De Ruyter* and the two assault guns to help Rebane's Estonian battalion reopen the road, and a night attack succeeded in driving back the Soviet forces. A further Soviet penetration a mile further west at Peeterristi was also cleared.

With Soviet troops still pressing the German defences to the south-west of Narva, a withdrawal was now urgent, but Benner signalled that he could not leave Narva at the designated time. Unsure about the safety of the road running through Olgino and Peeterristi, Benner ordered his men to withdraw along the railway line, to the south of the road. Rebane's Estonians and the *De Ruyter* battalion safely withdrew along the road, while *Seyffard* slowly retreated along the railway line, leaving Narva at midnight and reaching Soldino, barely three miles to the west, at 0500hrs on 26 July. Further to the west, the railway ran through woodland, and rather than continue along this course, Benner decided to strike north-west to try to reach the road route. Moving slowly across marshy terrain, *Seyffard* was spotted by Soviet aircraft and came under near-continuous artillery and aerial attack.

By 0800hrs, the Dutch regiment was only a mile from Laagna, where German assault guns tried in vain to break through to the encircled rearguard. Unable to make any headway, Benner turned south, and shortly before he ordered his radio vehicles destroyed, learned that Repniku was still occupied by German forces, and decided to try to break through. At 1730hrs, *Seyffard* launched its last attack, unaware that the Germans had in any event been driven back from Repniku. Benner was killed in the opening moments of the attack, and within 30 minutes the regiment had been completely scattered. Many were killed, others taken prisoner. Only a small group of men led by Untersturmführer Nieuwendijk-Hoek escaped, reaching the Tannenberg Line a week later.[21]

On 26 July, Soviet troops moved into the deserted city of Narva, which had been reduced to ruins, mainly as a result of Soviet aerial and artillery bombardment, partly through deliberate demolitions by the retreating Germans. It is estimated that only 2 per cent of the city's buildings were still standing.[22] Although the Red Army was now across the Narva and firmly established in Estonia, and despite the destruction of *Seyffard*, the operation had not been a major success from the Soviet perspective. Most of Army Detachment Narva had succeeded in pulling back to the Tannenberg Line, and casualties had been heavy – German losses totalled about 2,500, compared with over 23,000 Soviet casualties.[23]

SS-General Felix Steiner's III SS Panzer Corps began to dig in along the Tannenberg Line with *SS-Nederland* on the northern flank, SS Waffen-Grenadier Division (1st Estonian) in the centre, and *SS-Nordland* to the south. 11th Infantry Division lay to the south of Steiner's corps, still blocking the Soviet 8th Army. The main Tannenberg positions were amongst the three Sinnemäed Hills, which formed a rough east-to-west line, and gave the defenders a good field of vision across the plain to the Narva; Fediuninsky's 2nd Shock Army's line of approach was therefore clearly visible to the Germans. Govorov shifted reinforcements to Fediuninsky's army in an attempt to make good the losses it had suffered forcing the Narva, and to allow it to continue its advance. Fediuninsky now had 109th Rifle Corps, 122nd Rifle Corps, and 124th Rifle Corps, as well as two independent rifle divisions. To his south, Starikov's 8th Army had 112th and 117th Rifle Corps and two independent rifle divisions, as well as a force of brand-new 'Josef Stalin' II tanks. These heavyweight vehicles had first seen action in the fighting near Kursk the previous year, and at 46 tons were substantially heavier than the ubiquitous T34s. However, their 122mm gun was hampered by a relatively low muzzle velocity, reducing its penetrative power. The ammunition for the gun came in separate parts, with the shell and propellant being loaded separately, giving it a low rate of fire, and in any case, with only 28 rounds of ammunition in the tank, its ability to engage in sustained warfare was limited. In total, the two Soviet armies had over 54,000 men, compared to barely 22,000 Germans. Obergruppenführer Anton Grasser, commander of Army Detachment Narva, advised higher commands that without reinforcements, he was unlikely to be able to hold on for long.

Meanwhile, there had been a further change of personnel at Army Group North. Friessner and his chief of staff, Generalleutnant Eberhard Kinzel, had both been replaced. The new commander was General Ferdinand Schörner. As a junior officer in the First World War, Schörner was highly decorated for repeated bravery. He continued to serve as an officer in the inter-war Reichswehr, and commanded an infantry regiment in Poland and France in the opening campaigns of the war. He led a division on the Finnish front during the opening of *Barbarossa*, rising to command XIX Mountain Corps before taking command of XL Panzer Corps in the Ukraine in 1943. Here, he established a reputation as a hard, determined commander, who imposed iron discipline on his men. Nevertheless, his corps fought effectively around Nikopol, and in early 1944 he commanded 17th Army in the Crimea, before rising rapidly to take control first of Army Group South Ukraine and now Army Group North.

Schörner was popular with Hitler, as a man who could be trusted to hold a position with the sort of iron resolution that Hitler often complained was missing from many of his generals. A physically intimidating man, he sometimes showed considerable imagination in how to get the best from his troops. During the fighting in Sevastopol in 1944, he issued an order that any soldier of 17th Army who succeeded in destroying a Soviet tank at close quarters would receive a leave pass. Given the parlous plight of the German forces in the Crimea, this represented one of the few ways of getting out alive, and it is likely that it inspired many infantrymen to engage Soviet tanks at considerable risk to themselves. Later in the war, his ruthless use of field courts martial to arrest, try and execute anyone regarded as a deserter often resulted in completely innocent men being needlessly killed. On one occasion, a senior NCO was ordered by his commander to go back from the front line to the division's repair workshops, and then to return to the front with repaired fighting vehicles. Unfortunately for the NCO, his instructions were verbal, and despite his protestations, he was summarily convicted and executed.[24]

Like Model, Schörner was able to use the trust placed in him by Hitler to carry out withdrawals that would have attracted the anger of the Führer if any other commander had attempted them. He endorsed Grasser's opinion that Army Detachment Narva was in a perilous position, but was unable to provide any reinforcements – Hitler had ordered him to assemble forces with which Army Group North could counter-attack towards the south, in an attempt to restore Army Group Centre's lines. For the moment, Grasser would have to do the best he could.

The Soviet commanders intended to give the Germans as little time as possible to prepare their new positions. They hurried their men forward, trying to take advantage of any weakness in the German line after the destruction of *Seyffard*, and with considerable aerial and artillery support, the lead formations attacked on 26 July. The newly arrived Flemish 6th SS Volunteer Assault Brigade *Langemarck* took the brunt of the onslaught, losing many of its officers on its first day in the area. Elements of the Soviet 8th Army's 117th Rifle Corps pressed home their advantage, attacking into the exposed flank of *SS-Nordland*. By the end of the day, the east side of the most easterly of the Sinnemäed Hills was in Soviet hands.

During the night, the Germans mounted a counter-attack, led by the anti-tank company of *SS-Panzergrenadier-Regiment 24 Danmark*. Several tanks belonging to the Soviet 98th Tank Regiment were destroyed, and almost all the German positions were recovered. The following morning, there was a fresh artillery bombardment, and the positions held by *Danmark* and *Langemarck* once more came under pressure. The survivors of *Langemarck* were driven back from their positions to the middle hill of the three hills, though one of their number, Unterscharführer Remi Schrijnen, remained behind at the controls of a 75mm anti-tank gun. Despite being wounded, he continued to beat off Soviet tanks, and together with the infantrymen of *Danmark*, he accounted for the destruction or immobilisation of about 20 Soviet tanks. Nevertheless, despite a counter-attack by several assault guns from *Nordland*, led by the division commander, Gruppenführer Fritz von Scholtz, most of the eastern hill was in Soviet hands by midnight.

Late on 27 July, General Schörner arrived at Army Detachment Narva's headquarters. He stressed the importance of holding the current positions. The eastern hill was to be recaptured immediately, and the position was then to be held. As he set off to inform his men of their orders, Scholtz was severely wounded by a Soviet artillery bombardment. Although he was evacuated to the west, he died before he reached the military hospital at Rakvere. During the night, the reconnaissance battalion from *Nordland*, supported by a battalion of Estonian infantry, launched the counter-attack. Fighting continued into the next day, with most of the Estonian battalion being wiped out. The attack failed to make headway, and the Germans fell back to the central hill.

On 28 July, Fediuninsky deployed substantial artillery reinforcements and launched an assault on the northern part of the German defences. Unterscharführer Schrijnen continued to knock out tanks from his lone position in the front line, and the Soviet assault was beaten off. During the afternoon, there was a further savage bombardment of German positions, but in anticipation of this, the survivors of *Langemarck* had edged forward from their positions, so the bulk of the bombardment fell on empty trenches. When 2nd Shock Army attacked, it was once more beaten off, though *Langemarck* was almost at the end of its strength. Towards evening, German troops attempted once more to recover the eastern hill, but withdrew after suffering heavy losses. Steiner ordered his corps to abandon its foothold on the eastern hill and pull back to the central hill during the night.

Despite their heavy losses, the German lines were still intact. They were aware that Soviet losses were far greater, but in the context of Soviet numerical superiority, this seemed to make little difference. On 29 July, there was a further heavy artillery and aerial assault against the central hill, followed by an attack by infantry, supported by several JS-2 tanks. While 8th Army's two corps moved forward against 11th Infantry Division, attacking from the south and the east, 2nd Shock Army's 109th Rifle Corps attacked *Nederland* and 3rd Estonian Regiment on the northern side of the German defences. Despite the order to withdraw the previous evening, there were still scattered Danish defenders on the eastern hill, and the Soviet infantry of 117th Rifle Corps suffered heavy losses before the Danes were driven back. Nevertheless, the Red Army made steady progress. The central hill was pressed from three sides, though a cluster of anti-tank and anti-aircraft guns near the crest prevented Soviet armour from overrunning the positions completely. In the north, 2nd Shock Army was able to bypass the weakening German defences and reach the western hill, with a small force pushing forward to enter Vaivara. But just as it seemed as if the German defences might be about to give way, Steiner released his last reserve, a small group of tanks that had been held back for the critical moment. Led by Obersturmbannführer Kausch, the tanks advanced in three troops, driving back the Soviet forces either side of the hills. The limitations of the JS-2 tanks suddenly became critical – with many out of ammunition, they were forced to retreat, and without their support the Soviet infantry too fell back. By the end of the German counter-attack, only a single Panther tank was left operational, but for the moment, a Soviet breakthrough had been prevented. The Estonian Sturmbannführer Paul Maitla scraped together the remnants of several units, with several wounded volunteers from the field dressing stations volunteering to join him, and accompanied the remaining Panther in a further counter-attack with his battalion of 45th Infantry Regiment. By nightfall, the central hill was secure in German hands, despite further Soviet attacks. For his actions, Maitla was later awarded the Knight's Cross.

There was further heavy fighting the following day. 8th Army succeeded in making some headway south of the German positions, but although Soviet forces managed to penetrate into the German lines, last-minute counter-attacks once more threw them back. On 31 July, the Estonians defending the central hill found themselves almost out of ammunition in the face of yet another massed Soviet assault, and were rescued at the last moment by the arrival of reinforcements from *Danmark*.

The signing of the Molotov-Ribbentrop Pact in Moscow on 28 September 1939. Ribbentrop is signing the document; Molotov is standing behind him, next to Stalin.

Georg von Küchler, the commander of 18th Army, at the beginning of *Barbarossa* (second from right), with Army Group North commander Leeb (left), photographed in September 1941.

Rosenberg helped formulate German policy for the occupied territories on the Eastern Front. The failure to implement his policies was partly due to their impracticability, and partly due to internal Nazi Party rivalries.

Ernst Busch, the commander of 16th Army during Operation *Barbarossa*, photographed here in the summer of 1944.

Leeb (centre) in discussions with the commander of his army group's armoured forces, Erich Hoepner (second from right), photographed shortly after the beginning of *Barbarossa*.

XLI Panzer Corps' commander (second from left) being briefed by Walter Krüger (second from right) in July 1941, shortly after the latter had assumed command of 1st Panzer Division.

Two leading personalities of LVI Panzer Corps: Erich Brandenburger (left foreground) briefing his corps commander, Erich von Manstein (right foreground) in July 1941.

The *Panzergraf* photographed in early 1944.

One of the leading Tiger 'aces', Carius became a pharmacist after the war.

A former Latvian Army officer, Veiss was an early enthusiast for using the German occupation as an opportunity to drive pro-Soviet supporters from Latvia.

After commanding Army Group Narva earlier in 1944, Friessner took command of Army Group North in the summer.

The commander of III SS Panzer Corps awarding the Knight's Cross to the Estonian Obersturmbannführer Harald Riipalu, in August 1944.

Two Latvian SS soldiers in a trench with a *Panzerschrek* anti-tank weapon in Courland, winter 1944–45.

Trapped in the Courland pocket, German troops resisted repeated Soviet attempts to overrun them to the end of the war.

Central Latvia was the scene of bitter fighting as the Red Army tried to isolate Army Group North in 1944.

With no real prospect of victory, a German soldier awaits the next Soviet assault in the autumn of 1944.

Although the Germans did not attempt to hold Riga to the bitter end, Soviet artillery and air strikes, combined with deliberate German destruction as they withdrew, left the city in ruins.

As pressure on Army Group North increased, all means of transport available were put to use to withdraw remaining units through Riga into Courland.

The Courland Bridgehead was entirely dependent on seaborne supplies, which were brought ashore by any means possible through the winter of 1944–45.

Soviet infantry advance in the face of determined resistance in Latvia, 1944.

TOI AUSSI /
ES CAMARADES T'ATTENDEN
ANS LA DIVISION FRANÇAISE DE L
WAFFEN·SS

IGA TÕSINE EESTLANE
EESTI LEEGIONI!

Whilst many were coerced into serving in the foreign divisions of the SS, others volunteered, often in response to recruitment campaigns in occupied territories from France in the west to Estonia in the east.

Unterscharführer Scholles, a clerk in the *Danmark* regiment, carried ammunition forward to the front line:

At the northern slope of Hill 69.9 [the most westerly hill], we dashed to the west slope of Grenadier Hill [the central hill] and paused for a bit. I looked for a suitable way to Grenadier Hill. The communications trenches had been ploughed up. Dead were everywhere. A gruesome picture and a fearful stench under the burning heat of the midday sun. At the north-east slope of Hill 69.9 there were dead Russians and Germans on the communications road across the position. All of the bunkers on the north slope of Hill 69.9 had been shot to pieces and burned out, in spite of their unique position on the slope. The stink of decomposing corpses flowed from the collapsed bunkers. An artillery barrage forced us to take full cover.

After the enemy fire let up, we made it at a dead run across the 250m of open, flat terrain to the west slope of Grenadier Hill. We made our way up the slope with difficulty. I headed for Bachmeier's command post, which was in a crater-shaped defile. We found Hauptsturmführer Bachmeier [commander of the disparate SS units on the central hill] in a tunnel. He maintained a positive view of the situation.

Suddenly Soviet artillery opened fire. After 20 minutes it shifted to infantry fire. A breathless messenger ran up and reported an enemy penetration to Bachmeier. Without delay, Bachmeier set out at the front of a strong reserve squad with an immediate counterattack and cleaned up the penetration.[25]

An exhausted lull descended on both armies. Soviet losses had been shocking, especially given the minimal progress that had been made. Nevertheless, III SS Panzer Corps was also badly weakened, with battalions reduced to barely company strength. On 1 August, Fediuninsky brought forward two divisions to raise the strength of his battered army, and resumed his attacks on 2 August. Once more, each assault was preceded by a powerful artillery bombardment, but although the Soviet troops repeatedly advanced up the slopes of the central hill, they were unable to hold it in the face of German counter-attacks. Finally, on 10 August, Govorov ordered Fediuninsky to stop his attacks.

Soviet casualties had been terrible. Divisions were reduced to a few hundred men, and the Germans claimed to have destroyed over 160 tanks. It is estimated that the Red Army lost perhaps 35,000 dead and 135,000 wounded, compared with total German losses of about 10,000. Fediuninsky and Starikov had little space in which to manoeuvre, with only a narrow strip of open ground between the hills and the coast, and almost impassable swamps to the south; consequently, they were forced to launch a series of costly frontal assaults. Even in these circumstances, their failure to break through the German lines – it is estimated that the balance of power in terms of manpower alone gave the Red Army an advantage of greater than 11 to 1 – is remarkable. One reason for the success of the Germans was their very effective use of artillery. Several batteries that had originally been used to bombard Leningrad had been brought back to Estonia, and Steiner devised intelligent fireplans that allowed the collective weight of all the artillery at his disposal to be brought to bear in a single strike. In addition to Germans, the SS troops who defended the Tannenberg Line included men from Estonia, Denmark, Belgium, the Netherlands and Norway, and the fighting has sometimes been described as the 'Battle of the European SS'. It should be remembered, though, that many of the troops, and particularly most of the officers, were still Germans.[26]

Army Group North was now isolated in Estonia and northern Latvia, with most of Lithuania in Soviet hands. The following weeks would see a determined attempt by the Wehrmacht to restore contact, and further Soviet offensive operations in the Baltic States.

Chapter 8

FROM *DOPPELKOPF* TO *CÄSAR*

When the tanks of Bagramian's 1st Baltic Front reached the Gulf of Riga, they effectively represented the high tide mark of the great Soviet offensive that tore the Eastern Front apart during the summer of 1944. For a few days, the German authorities in Latvia, both military and civilian, waited for further blows. The German line to either side of the corridor established by the Soviet 51st Army consisted of the thinnest of screens – for large parts of the front line to the west, the only defenders consisted of Latvian farmers and local landowners, hastily grouped together into some form of home guard. In northern Courland, close to the coast, was a small group of SS units, assigned the name *SS Panzer Brigade Gross*; it amounted to perhaps ten tanks and two companies of infantry, created from SS training units in Ventspils. About 25 miles to the south was *Gruppe Hierthes*, consisting of two battalions of Latvians reinforced by anti-aircraft units, and a similar distance south of Sturmführer Hierthes' battalions were the remnants of *Gruppe Mäder*, with two infantry battalions, an artillery battalion, a small group of paratroopers, and a number of Latvian police and paramilitary units, again with anti-aircraft guns in support.[1] Between these units, and between Oberst Mäder's southern flank and 3rd Panzer Army's IX Corps, there were large stretches of open territory.

The presence of just two or three relatively fresh rifle corps would have resulted in major gains for the Red Army. Much of Courland could have been overrun, and there was also the possibility of a thrust towards Riga from the west. But the lunge to the coast represented the last effort of a force that, despite its huge successes, was approaching exhaustion. The front line had moved over 350 miles since 22 June, and supply lines had been stretched far beyond what was sustainable. Casualties on the German side were severe, with nearly half a million men killed, wounded or taken prisoner – probably sufficient to ensure the eventual defeat of Germany – but Soviet losses, as was almost invariably the case in the great battles of the Eastern Front, were even heavier, at over 770,000. Bagramian's front alone had lost over 41,000 men killed.[2] Soviet armour losses, too, had been enormous, with over 2,900 tanks and assault guns knocked out.[3] Many of these would be returned to service in a relatively short time, but the task facing the repair teams, and the logistics units that attempted to keep up with them and bring forward supplies at the same time, was enormous.

There were similar problems elsewhere along the Soviet front line. The Red Army reached the eastern outskirts of Warsaw, triggering the uprising in the city by Polish resistance fighters, and although it was most convenient for Stalin to sit and wait for the Germans to destroy the anti-communist Home Army, the reality was that the armies outside Warsaw were as exhausted as Bagramian's troops. In addition to their losses and overstretched supply lines, they had suffered a setback at the hands of the German XXXIX Panzer Corps, whose main strike power was provided by 4th Panzer Division. Acting with their old speed and flexibility, the German forces took advantage of the increasing lack of coordination of the Soviet spearheads and launched a counter-attack east of Warsaw, smashing 3rd Tank Corps and greatly reducing the strength of 8th Guards Tank Corps.[4]

Coming at the end of a summer of unprecedented disasters for the Wehrmacht, the isolation of Army Group North was a huge setback. Armies had been isolated before – most notably when 6th Army was surrounded and eventually destroyed in Stalingrad – but this was the first time that an entire army group was separated from the Reich. Restoration of contact was given a high priority, and the Wehrmacht began to scrape together a strike force capable of breaking through to Schörner's army group.

Slowly, the German front was stabilising again. Following the fall of Kaunas, Cherniakhovsky's 3rd Belarusian Front continued to push on towards the East Prussian frontier. An armoured force reached the German town of Schirwindt before being driven back by elements of Panzergrenadier Division *Grossdeutschland* on 5 and 6 August. Nevertheless, for the next three days, Cherniakhovsky urged forward his 33rd Army to attack again towards Schirwindt, and a little further north elements of 39th Army and 5th Guards Tank Army attempted to force their way towards Tilsit along the northern bank of the River Niemen. However, German counter-attacks made good progress. *Grossdeutschland* beat off all attacks towards the East Prussian border, while 7th Panzer Division, which had fallen back into south-west Lithuania, was extracted from the front line and replaced by 252nd Infantry Division. Bitter fighting raged between the infantry division and the two tank corps of 5th Guards Tank Army, leaving the town of Raseiniai, the scene of the momentous tank battle of

1941, in ruins. The mobile forces of 7th Panzer Division were thus freed up to probe towards the north, establishing firmer contact with *Gruppe Mäder*. It was even possible to start pulling *Grossdeutschland* out of the front line.

Meanwhile, at the northern point of the front line, Standartenführer Gross started to probe forwards. His armour reached within two miles of Tukums, though an attack on the town itself was abandoned. Reconnaissance units were able to filter forwards and establish the most tenuous of contacts with Army Group North to the east of Tukums. 4th Panzer Division began to move north from Poland on 11 August. The trains carrying the division crossed East Prussia; for many of the soldiers of the division, it was their first sight of their homeland for several years, and it roused mixed feelings. On the one hand, there was joy at seeing Germany again, but on the other hand, their journey highlighted the proximity of the front line to East Prussia.

As had been the case since the end of 1941, Army Group North consisted of 16th and 18th Armies. In order to facilitate better coordination of all German forces north of the German frontier, Raus' 3rd Panzer Army was temporarily assigned to Army Group North. Plans were rapidly drawn up for establishment of a strong link between 16th Army and 3rd Panzer Army, and were presented to Hitler on 8 August. The proposal was to move *Grossdeutschland* to the front opposite Raseiniai, to give the appearance of a threatened push to retake both Raseiniai and Šiauliai. Further north, there would be two thrusts, one with one or two panzer divisions and an infantry division towards Šiauliai, and another with three or four panzer divisions towards Jelgava. The following evening, the proposal was assigned the codename *Doppelkopf*, the name of a card game that was popular with German soldiers at the time. Perhaps as a result of Hitler's influence, the plan had developed somewhat more grandiose aspects. After restoring contact with 16th Army, the attacking panzer divisions would then turn south towards Kaunas, with the intention of thrusting into the rear of the Soviet forces facing 3rd Panzer Army. It seems that this additional aspect of the plan was ignored from the outset by the division and corps commanders involved as entirely unrealistic.[5]

Prior to its move north, *Grossdeutschland* launched a further assault in its current sector on 9 August, recapturing the town of Vilkaviškis in a surprise attack. The advance began before first light, and taking advantage of misty conditions, the assault group bypassed the Soviet defences south of the town before turning north; they had effectively surrounded Vilkaviškis to the west, south and east before they were even spotted. Heavy fighting erupted as German units penetrated into the town, but by nightfall, only a few isolated pockets of Soviet troops remained, and they slipped away during the darkness.[6]

Intelligence reports reaching 3rd Panzer Army suggested that the Red Army was indeed exhausted after its long offensive, perhaps even overextended; prisoner interrogations revealed that 5th Guards Tank Army had only 40 operational tanks left, out of an establishment strength of over 500.[7] It therefore seemed an ideal moment to launch the counter-attack towards Šiauliai, and the planning for *Doppelkopf* gained pace. XXXIX Panzer Corps would launch the main assault, with 4th, 5th and 12th Panzer Divisions forming *Gruppe Libau* and attacking in two thrusts from the area north-east of Telšiai, with the intention of pushing through to Jelgava. Meanwhile, the 101st Panzer Brigade, created from what remained of 18th Panzergrenadier Division, was placed under the command of Oberst von Lauchert and dispatched by sea to reinforce *Gruppe Gross* in northern Courland. From here, the combined force, under the energetic command of Hyazinth von Strachwitz, would drive through Tukums to reach Riga. Further south, XL Panzer Corps, with *Grossdeutschland* and 14th Panzer Division, would advance on Šiauliai from the south-west. 7th Panzer Division would reinforce the attack at a later date.

From the outset, there were tensions between the various German commands. 3rd Panzer Army was of the opinion that the assault should start on 17 August, as it would take at least that long for all elements to assemble. By contrast, due to the perilous plight of 16th and 18th Armies, trapped north of the Soviet breakthrough to the coast, Army Group North pressed for an earlier start to the attack. There would have to be an unhappy compromise between waiting until sufficient forces had been gathered to have maximum effect, and the pressing need to break through to the trapped armies.

Meanwhile, the Red Army reshuffled its forces. 1st Guards Rifle Corps, part of 51st Army, was the main force in the Soviet-held corridor that ran from Jelgava to the Gulf of Riga. To the south, 5th Guards Tank Army received badly needed reinforcements in the shape of 100 new T34 tanks, and was ordered to prepare to drive north-west from its current positions around Kelmė to the area west of Šiauliai, while 4th Shock Army was transferred to 1st Baltic Front. Its 3rd Guards Mechanised Corps was deployed south of Jelgava, while 1st Tank Corps, weakened by the summer fighting, remained in reserve in the area east of Šiauliai. The German counter-attack would face formidable resistance.

The Red Army also detected the northward movement of German armour. Its assessment of the power of the Wehrmacht, though, was somewhat wide of the mark; the overall strength of Army Group North was reported to be 700,000 personnel, more than 1,200 tanks and assault guns, about 7,000 artillery and mortars, and 400 combat aircraft. The Leningrad Front and the three Baltic Fronts, by contrast, had

900,000 troops, over 3,000 tanks and assault guns, about 17,500 artillery and mortars, and about 2,650 combat aircraft, under the collective command of Marshal Vassilevsky, the Deputy People's Commissar for Defence.[8] Even if the Soviet assessment of German strength had been accurate, the Wehrmacht would have faced a formidable struggle.

On 13 August, Vassilevsky reported to Stalin that 'it is possible that the enemy intends to cut off the salient that we have pushed to the Gulf of Riga from both sides'. In order to hinder this, orders were issued to 1st Baltic Front to attack towards Riga with 4th Shock Army and 6th Guards Army, to tie down forces of the German 16th Army. 43rd Army would hold its positions to the south of Jelgava, facing towards Riga, but would join the attack as it developed. In the corridor to the Baltic, 51st Army would establish strong defensive positions, with 2nd Guards Army to its south.

Bagramian took the German preparations seriously:

The greatest worry for us was the tip of the salient that we had pushed forward to the west of Riga ... it was 40 to 60km wide. The front was held by four rifle divisions from 1st Rifle Corps and 63rd Rifle Corps. It was clear to us that we could not hold the front with four battle-weakened divisions. But we had no more forces at our disposal. It was certain to us that the enemy would try to cut off this salient at its base, and this would be made all the easier for the enemy as we transferred more forces to the Gulf of Riga. In short, there was no doubt that the Fascists would attack. But unfortunately, until just before the beginning of the attack, we did not know from which direction, and with what forces.[9]

During their advance, Bagramian's forces encountered the modest bands of pro-Soviet Latvian partisans, who provided intelligence on German troop dispositions. These reports suggested that German troops on the southern and western approaches to Riga were massing for a breakout; the reality was that 16th Army lacked sufficient armour to make any such attempt. In order to prevent such a breakout, Bagramian decided that, while 51st Army would take up a defensive posture in the face of the anticipated German attack from the west, 4th Shock Army and 43rd Army would prepare to launch an attack towards Riga. At the very least, this would disrupt German plans for a breakout.

On 14 August, the German IX Corps launched an attack with 252nd Infantry Division, reinforced by elements of 7th Panzer Division, immediately north of Raseiniai. The operation, codenamed *Greif*, was seen as a preparatory attack for *Doppelkopf*, and succeeded in taking most of the town. Over 60 Soviet tanks were reported knocked out, and 7th Panzer Division was extracted from the front line in preparation for the main operation. Late on 15 August, the divisions earmarked for the main thrust began to move from their forming up areas to the front line. As the troops wound their way along narrow roads, grim news from the west spread from man to man: the Western Allies had made an almost unopposed landing on the French Mediterranean coast. The difficulty of the task before them also became clear even before they reached the front line:

> Everything was small, tiny copses, little hills, narrow roads, small bridges, drainage ditches and streams everywhere. In short, it was no country for armoured warfare, we could see that already after a few kilometres. Above all, the curvy, small roads and the bridges, which were too weak for our 'heavy bears', made things difficult for us. For sure, the combat engineers worked constantly and gave almost superhuman service, but still, here a ford proved unreliable, there a bridge collapsed under a heavy tank. Detours had to be reconnoitred, the columns constantly stopped before new obstacles. Where the tanks could still operate, it wasn't possible for the fuel trucks to follow – and we desperately needed fuel with this constant driving. In the end, the 100km journey to our start line was achieved. But how many small acts of heroism had to occur during the dark of this night that would never be counted.[10]

Doppelkopf began on 16 August, a day earlier than 3rd Panzer Army had originally wanted. Despite the presence of five panzer divisions and a panzergrenadier division, the number of German tanks was disappointingly small – only 133 in XXXIX Panzer Corps, and only 148 in XL Panzer Corps. The weather, dry and sunny, was perfect for armoured operations. In the north, *Gruppe Gross*, which had pulled back from the outskirts of Tukums, made little progress in the face of determined resistance. With the allocation of 101st Panzer Brigade, still en route by sea, and assorted staff and communications elements, the group was somewhat grandiosely named *Panzer Division Strachwitz*. Further south, XXXIX Panzer Corps crossed its start line at 0800hrs. 4th and 5th Panzer Divisions were able to field substantial forces, and made good progress, but 12th Panzer Division still awaited the arrival of all its elements. 5th Panzer Division attacked in two battlegroups, and the southern one had to conduct an assault across the River Venta at Papilė, where it encountered heavy resistance and was forced to shift its point of attack, attempting to bypass the town to the south, as Alfred Jaedtke, commander of a panzergrenadier battalion, recalled:

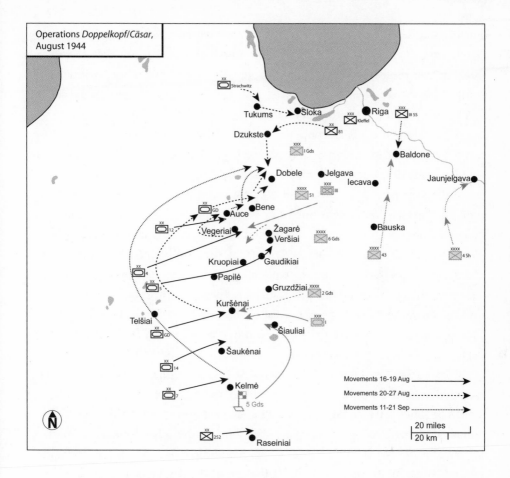

Operations *Doppelkopf/Cäsar*, August 1944

The armoured group had only just overcome the most forward Russian elements in battle and had not yet penetrated the enemy's lines adequately deeply, so the shift to the south meant that when marching past the town, it came under substantial anti-tank fire both from there [the Soviet forward positions facing west] and also in the left flank. This was the result of excellent directed fire from the Russian artillery …

There were still a few irritations from Russian anti-tank guns that were well-positioned in woodland about 6km north-east of Papilė. But the resistance was swiftly overcome. In the adjoining woodland (about 8km deep), we surprised a battalion of Russian artillery, a swift capture for our tanks. Weak enemy resistance in Mažūnaičiai was quickly crushed. On it went towards Kruopiai. Everywhere teemed with Russians, but there was never any meaningful resistance. It seemed they were from scattered units or rear area formations. The morale of our men was outstanding. After the numerous fighting retreats, we were at last advancing again, as in the old days.[11]

Further south, XL Panzer Corps thrust forward with *Grossdeutschland*. Held up by poor roads, the division struggled towards Kuršėnai, where it was able to secure a crossing over the River Venta when it captured an intact rail bridge. A little to the south, 14th Panzer Division also seized a bridge over the Venta near Šaukėnai, but 7th Panzer Division ran into heavy resistance north-east of Kelmė.

With its armoured forces concentrated in a relatively small area, 3rd Panzer Army left other parts of the German front exposed to enemy attack. XXVI Corps on the southern wing of the army defended a substantial part of its line with the weak 549th and 561st Grenadier Divisions; relatively newly raised, these formations had a large proportion of men previously deemed unfit for front line service through age or infirmity, and lacked both a core of veterans and any combat experience. Even as *Doppelkopf* began, elements of the Soviet 11th Guards Army, 33rd Army and 5th Army attacked in this sector. 6th Panzer Division was able to put up good resistance, but was driven back, and the attacks achieved significant penetrations in the sectors held by the two grenadier divisions on the flanks of the panzer division. These advances were a direct threat to East Prussia, and had to be countered. Consequently, the 1st Infantry Division, en route for deployment in *Doppelkopf*, was diverted to help reinforce XXVI Corps.

Bagramian received reports of varying seriousness. On the one hand, the defences facing XL Panzer Corps seemed to have held up well, though they claimed to be facing attacks by about 250 German tanks, i.e. a number almost as great as the entire German armoured strength along all axes of attack, but on the other hand, the reports of armoured attacks by XXXIX Panzer Corps gave little indication of their strength or which German units were involved. By the end of the day, he had confirmation that 126th Rifle Division had been forced back by elements of *Grossdeutschland* and 7th Panzer Division. Vassilevsky advised the move of 5th Guards Tank Army to the Šiauliai area be accelerated, and Bagramian harangued the commanders of 51st Army and 2nd Guards Army to make greater efforts to identify the units that were attacking them, and to move all artillery assets to the front line to provide maximum support.[12]

At dawn on 17 August, 4th Panzer Division assaulted Soviet defences around the village of Vegeriai, which had brought the previous day's advance to an end. The village was taken swiftly, but attempts to push east made slow progress, due to a mixture of difficult terrain and determined resistance from well-positioned anti-tank guns. By the end of the day, the division had pushed forward barely three miles, though 12th Panzer Division made somewhat better progress to the north. 5th Panzer Division's southern battlegroup succeeded in reaching Gaudikiai, but like 4th Panzer Division to the north, was held up by tough anti-tank defences. Two days of fighting had moved the front line forward perhaps nine miles.

Grossdeutschland attacked and took the town of Kuršėnai, but 14th Panzer Division made little headway after its bridge over the Venta was damaged by artillery fire. Here, Bagramian's order to deploy artillery in the front line had a marked effect, as he described in a style in keeping with most Soviet accounts of the era:

Colonel Pavlenkov's 1187th Artillery Regiment had the hardest time. The gunners defended themselves to the last round. The crew of an anti-tank gun led by the communist Kustov alone sent five tanks, including two Tigers, up in flames. As German infantry with machine pistols approached the gun, they were engaged with hand grenades. Finally, only the gun-aimer Podgorny was left alive of the crew. Despite being wounded, he fired the last shell and then with the driver of the supply vehicle moved the gun to a safe location. Kostov and Podgorny were awarded the title Heroes of the Soviet Union by the Praesidium of the Supreme Soviet of the USSR on 24 March 1945.[13]

7th Panzer Division suffered a major setback as it attempted to attack from Kelmė, as one of its officers recorded in his diary:

The attack was already in full flow. The battlegroup gathered in a large dip in the land during the afternoon. It was generally quiet. The armoured unit officers had just started a discussion in the commander's half-track when an apparently stray sighting round exploded in the dip. Immediately after there was a second shot. By chance, this round detonated in the regimental commander's half-track. All the men in the vehicle were killed (the commander, adjutant, signals officer, driver and radio operator). Consequently, the entire command of the division's groundbreaking battlegroup was knocked out.[14]

Oberstleutnant Weitzel, commander of the division's 6th Panzergrenadier Regiment, was killed, as well as his adjutant and the adjutant of the division's Panther battalion. Whilst open-backed half-tracks allowed panzergrenadiers to deploy easily, they were very vulnerable to plunging artillery fire, as 7th Panzer Division discovered at its cost.

In the midst of the ongoing fighting, there was another round of changes in the German command. Model was dispatched to take command of the Western Front, and was replaced as commander of Army Group Centre by Georg-Hans Reinhardt. Raus took command of 3rd Panzer Army.

From the Soviet perspective, the attack by XL Panzer Corps appeared to pose the greatest threat, though 51st Army reported that the forces attacking it – mainly 4th and 5th Panzer Divisions, though the Soviet forces had not yet identified them – consisted of 'about 200 tanks and strong infantry formations'.[15] 1st Tank Corps and 103rd Rifle Corps were dispatched to Šiauliai from 1st Baltic Front's reserves. Although 5th Guards Tank Army was moving to the area, Bagramian was frustrated to learn that it had only 17 tanks ready for combat, in place of the 500 tanks he had expected. General Konsantin Skorniakov, commander of 1st Baltic Front's tank and mechanised forces, responded by presenting the report of Major General Petr Kalinichenko, 5th Guards Tank Army's chief of staff:

> We have been in action for almost two months, taking part in operations at Vitebsk and Kaunas and have suffered losses. For sure, not just from the enemy, but also through wear and tear, and a shortage of spare parts. The army lost many tanks on the roads around Šiauliai. Moscow has dispatched a really substantial amount of equipment to us. We hope that we will be given time to restore our units and restore order to their ranks. The trains carrying [replacement] tanks are already underway.[16]

Meanwhile, after receiving further reports of a build-up of German forces near Riga, Bagramian dispatched two infantry divisions and a mechanised division to the front closest to Riga, while holding a further tank formation in reserve. An anti-tank brigade was transferred to Bagramian's front from Cherniakhovsky's 3rd Belarusian Front, and an additional three such brigades made available from strategic reserves. Given the nature of the terrain, with limited line of sight and relatively poor roads, these anti-tank guns were precisely the weapons needed to hold up the German advance.[17]

The painfully slow advance of XXXIX Panzer Corps continued on 18 August. 12th Panzer Division seized high ground immediately south of Auce, and after reorganising its forces overnight, 4th Panzer Division attacked with two battlegroups, pushing forward perhaps two or three miles before running into a Soviet counter-attack by about 40 tanks; prisoner interrogations identified these as being part of 3rd Guards Mechanised Corps. The pace of the attack gave the Soviet forces ample time to prepare their defences, as 5th Panzer Division's Jaedtke found:

> Setting off the following morning towards Veršiai, we were surprised to encounter a *Pakfront* [a coordinated line of anti-tank guns] only 3km north-east of Gaudikiai, which brought heavy fire down upon us. The individual anti-tank guns were well-camouflaged on the edge of a wood either side of the road, which we had to capture through about 6km of woodland. After our artillery had brought heavy fire to bear

on the edge of the wood – at our request, there were a few smoke rounds in the last salvo – we attacked. We broke into the wood under cover of the smoke. The Russians fled and left 10–12 anti-tank guns behind.

Advancing further, we discovered that the woodland road was more of a clear lane, about 60–80m wide, with a few young saplings. The Russians had positioned even more anti-tank guns in key positions, which were hard to spot and were protected by infantry. We therefore had no choice but to advance with dismounted panzergrenadiers either side of the road and to try to clear the anti-tank guns from our path, while our tanks leapfrogged forward. This was a time-consuming enterprise and we only advanced slowly, as the woodland either side of the road was full of Russian infantry, who we had to guard against, to prevent them from making things unpleasant for our tanks and the half-tracks, which were amongst them and only manned by drivers and co-drivers. The road was also unpleasantly mined. They were only freshly planted and could be found relatively quickly by Hauptmann Pilch's combat engineers and removed. After about two or three hours we reached the end of the woodland. The first tanks and half-tracks advanced into Veršiai, another kilometre ahead, and reported it free of enemy. We aligned ourselves along the wood edge and the company commanders reorganised their units, which had been disrupted in the woodland. We could see Žagarė about 5km to the north. Oberstleutnant Herzog appeared and ordered further reconnaissance to the north, and for both main roads to be guarded to the north and south until II/14 [2nd Battalion, 14th Panzergrenadier Regiment] arrived. At that moment, there was an unholy burst of 'fire magic' – apparently from numerous Katyushas – simultaneously on the wood edge and the dip beyond. As we were right by there, driving to the designated blocking positions, a radio message arrived from Regiment HQ: 'Immediate withdrawal to Gaudikiai!' That could not be right. I used Oberstleutnant's radio to contact the regiment's signals section. 'The radio message is correct. There's trouble on the right flank. Hurry!'

So, back along that stupid woodland road. A panzergrenadier company led, then three platoons of tanks, then the bulk of the battalion, and at the rear a tank platoon with panzergrenadiers. This tank platoon with panzergrenadiers was to hold the edge of the wood near Verniai until it was certain that we had once more reached the western edge of the wood. Even as we drove back, I heard the sounds of fighting from Gaudikiai. Hauptmann Elmers, commander of the 2nd Panzergrenadier Company, who had driven ahead, reported by radio: 'Enemy tanks in combat against our artillery.' A battalion of our artillery was positioned on the high ground north of Gaudikiai and was now in close-quarter combat with 15–20 Sherman tanks. A few guns fired over open sights. For my two tank platoons at the wood edge, the Sherman tanks were most handily positioned, as most had their rears to us. It did not take long before Hauptmann Eysser, who had proved himself in many battles and had been awarded the Knight's Cross, shot up almost all the enemy tanks with his tanks. Two or three enemy tanks reached the wood, but were later found abandoned by their crews and were blown up.[18]

The Soviet tanks were from one of several groups deployed to disrupt the German advance. Taking advantage of the terrain and the gaps between the advancing German units, they attempted to isolate and destroy the German spearheads, as Hauptmann Nökel, another member of 5th Panzer Division, recorded:

> During the course of the night [of 17/18 August], the enemy had driven past the right flank of the advancing division with three tank formations, each with 25 to 30 tanks, mostly Shermans and Josef Stalin Is, and attacked our deep right flank during the morning with strong artillery support between Gaudikiai and Kruopiai. Their aim was to destroy our spearheads, stopping our thrust. This attack was defeated with heavy enemy losses. East of Gaudikiai, the rearguard tanks of II/31 [2nd Battalion, 31st Panzer Regiment] shot up nine enemy tanks, near Gaudikiai the artillery with direct fire and Eysser's tank company (3/31) together shot up 25 enemy tanks. At Kruopiai, *Panzerjägerabteilung von Ramin* [the division's anti-tank battalion] knocked out 25 enemy tanks marching up. The division was mentioned in the Wehrmacht report for shooting up 56 tanks. The enemy tanks that attacked at Gaudikiai without infantry totally surprised us. Firing from all barrels, they overran my headquarters and that of Oberstleutnant Herzog in the edge of a wood east of Gaudikiai. They drove directly towards a battery of 116th Panzer Artillery Regiment's 2nd Battalion, deployed in an open plain. Here they drove to their destruction in the cross-hairs of the artillery; the battery suffered heavy losses.[19]

Further to the south, *Grossdeutschland* continued to edge towards Šiauliai, supported by 14th Panzer Division. Opposing the German divisions was the Soviet 1st Tank Corps, and a division of 'Latvian' soldiers. Like the Red Army's Estonian divisions, this division probably contained only a minority of native Latvians, with the rest of its strength made up of a mixture of ethnic Latvians from within the Soviet Union and Russians who had no Latvian ancestry whatever. Nevertheless, Bagramian recorded the deeds of father and son team Dauetas, who fearlessly engaged German tanks with anti-tank rifles and grenades, destroying a tank and a 'Ferdinand' assault gun. Given that there were no Ferdinands deployed in the battle, this was at best a case of mistaken identity, though far from unique. It was commonplace for all German assault guns and tank destroyers to be identified as Ferdinands, which at 65 tons were regarded by the soldiers of the Red Army as particularly formidable foes; similarly, soldiers on all fronts frequently claimed that the German tanks they had encountered were Tigers. Other members of the Latvian division were also singled out for high praise, and it seems clear that they were involved in heavy fighting, and generally acquitted themselves well. Indeed, the slow advance of the German troops is itself testimony to the determination of the Latvian division to hold its ground.[20]

General von Saucken, commander of XXXIX Panzer Corps, had a meeting with 3rd Panzer Army's chief of staff, where he expressed his concerns that the attacking divisions were too far apart to achieve maximum effect. For the moment, though, the operation continued as envisaged. Once XL Panzer Corps had taken Šiauliai, he was assured, the two corps would move closer to each other and the threat to the flanks of XXXIX Panzer Corps would be greatly reduced.[21] On the other side of the battlefield, Bagramian received reassuring reports that his front line was holding firm. Indeed, he felt sufficiently confident about his defences to order 3rd Guards Mechanised Corps to be pulled out of the front line and held in reserve.

It took until early on 19 August for *Gruppe Strachwitz* to assemble sufficient forces to launch a major attack. Attacking with about 60 tanks, the *Panzergraf* made good progress, forcing the Red Army into a defensive ring around Tukums, held by two rifle divisions of 1st Guards Rifle Corps. 4th Panzer Division intended to attack to take Žagarė, but spent most of the day fending off repeated Soviet attacks. For a while, the two battlegroups of the division were in danger of being isolated, but determined local counter-attacks steadily restored the situation.

The counter-attacks in 4th Panzer Division's sector had an impact on 5th Panzer Division to the south. After waiting in vain for 4th Panzer Division, which was a little to the north-west, to catch up, 5th Panzer Division's *Gruppe Friedrich* and *Gruppe Herzog* were ordered to resume their own advance. They made good progress and reached Žagarė, but their previous tenuous contact with 4th Panzer Division disappeared as a Soviet force counter-attacked deep into the seam between the two divisions, and they came under repeated attack by Soviet units. With the aid of a Stuka squadron, they succeeded in beating off the attacks, but were left feeling increasingly isolated. Similarly, *Grossdeutschland* pushed closer to Šiauliai, but had to abandon plans for further attacks, as both its flanks were exposed. 2nd Guards Army, the main force opposing it, was now reinforced by further elements of 1st

Tank Corps and 5th Guards Tank Army. As Bagramian described, the intense fighting was often at the closest of quarters:

On this day, the divisions of 11th Guards Rifle Corps, covering the south-west approaches to Šiauliai, were particularly valuable to us. For sure, the corps commander, General Rozhdestvensky, was wounded, but my old friend, Major General Aruschanian, had the command structure firmly in hand. He thus blocked the enemy's intention to achieve a breakthrough with two infantry regiments and several dozen tanks in the sector of 85th Rifle Regiment from Major General Sakurenkov's 32nd Guards Rifle Division. Although the artillery destroyed many tanks, many more penetrated into the regiment's positions. There, they were attacked by the riflemen with anti-tank grenades and Molotov cocktails. Sergeant Gribeniuk from 4th Rifle Company threw himself under the tracks of a tank with an anti-tank grenade, which he then detonated. The sergeant was posthumously awarded the title Hero of the Soviet Union.[22]

For the men of the panzer divisions, it was a different experience from previous battles, as Hans Schäufler, a signals officer in 4th Panzer Division, recorded:

For us this was an entirely new type of war, these tough struggles in the tightest of spaces, the bitterly conducted fighting for every metre of ground. We had to break up the enemy's positions step by step. It was no impulsive surge forward, rather a painstakingly led fight in a restricted space. Coming out of the spaces of Russia, we only got used to this new war slowly.

Soon, the first Josef Stalins were positioned against us. After eight of them were blown into the air by our fire in a short time, this spell too was broken. They were huge structures with outrageous turrets and a gun like a tree-trunk.

… At night we always withdrew a little, and pushed on in the morning. One defensive system behind another. The breakthrough simply wouldn't come.[23]

14th Panzer Division, which had started the assault in relatively good shape, had been additionally reinforced by 20 Tiger tanks belonging to *Schwere Panzer Abteilung 510*, but three days of fighting had made a substantial dent in its capabilities. On 19 August, it was involved in a fierce clash with Soviet armour along the line of the Ventos canal, and although it claimed to have destroyed 15 Soviet tanks, the division took significant casualties too. The division's 106th Panzergrenadier Regiment suffered the loss of its commander, his adjutant, a battalion commander, and the battalion commander's replacement in just a few hours. Engineering teams reported that in addition to enemy-inflicted losses, the division had suffered a substantial number of Panthers breaking down with engine and gearbox problems, while the Pz.IVs and assault guns suffered steering gear and brake failures. Spare parts were hard to find, and on many occasions, vehicles had to be cannibalised to keep others running.[24]

There was a further discussion at higher levels of the German command about the future course of the operation. The chiefs of staff of Army Group Centre and 3rd Panzer Army concluded that the chances of successfully driving on to Jelgava looked poor, and that there was far greater likelihood of success for *Panzer Division Strachwitz*, as the northern force was now known, in reaching 16th Army. Bagramian and his army commanders, too, discussed the situation, concluding that they had prevented all German efforts to break through so far, and remained confident that they would continue to block the two German panzer corps. However, with his reserves increasingly depleted, Bagramian was relieved to receive further intelligence refuting earlier reports that German armour was concentrating near Riga for a breakout by 16th Army. This allowed him to release further troops to face the threat from the west. In particular, he was able to withdraw Colonel-General Ivan Mikhailovich Chistiakov's 6th Guards Army from its current position south-east of Riga, with the intention of inserting it between 51st Army and 2nd Guards Army.

On 20 August, *Grossdeutschland* was ordered to shift its attacks somewhat to the north, towards Gruzdžiai. This would allow it to achieve contact with XXXIX Panzer Corps' divisions, held up before Žagarė, and would eliminate some of the threats to the flanks of the German thrusts. Aware that the German point of effort was slowly shifting north, Bagramian ordered 3rd Guards Mechanised Corps to deploy around Žagarė, and ordered 43rd Army to release 19th Tank Corps in order to create an operational reserve. But the most important development of the day came in the north, where Strachwitz had finally assembled his forces. He attacked and took Dzukste, then pressed on to Tukums. There was a substantial force of Soviet tanks in the town, but help for Strachwitz came in the form of the arrival of the heavy cruiser *Prinz Eugen* off the coast. The warship fired over 250 rounds into Tukums with its 8-inch guns, destroying about 40 Soviet tanks, after which Strachwitz swiftly overran the Soviet defences. From here, the *ad hoc* division turned east, pushing through weak Soviet resistance to Sloka, where contact was established with elements of 16th Army. But despite relatively limited losses from Soviet action, Strachwitz finished the day with only nine Panther tanks; most of the rest had broken down en route, and were now subject to counter-attacks as the Red Army tried to close the narrow corridor that Strachwitz had established.

Perhaps in an attempt to justify their own failure to stop Strachwitz, units of the Soviet 51st Army reported that Tukums had come under attack from at least 300 German tanks.[25] Bagramian dispatched 19th Tank Corps and 60th Rifle Corps to reinforce 51st Army, and to restore the Soviet corridor to the Baltic. There was an even more alarming development later in the day, when General Iakov Kreizer, commander of 51st Army, reported that German forces had landed along the coast in an amphibious operation involving 35 ships. Furthermore, Kreizer continued, powerful infantry and armoured forces were threatening Tukums from the east. Neither of these reports was actually true; the suggestion of amphibious landings was probably the result of the intervention of *Prinz Eugen* and a small number of accompanying destroyers in the fighting at Tukums, and although a small force had been prepared by 16th Army to cooperate with Strachwitz, it did not amount to a serious threat. Nevertheless, the reports persuaded Bagramian that 1st Guards Rifle Corps, still clinging to the line near Tukums, was in danger of being outflanked and overwhelmed. Consequently, he ordered the corps to pull back both of its divisions about 15 miles to the south.

The previous day's discussions between German staff officers were renewed, with suggestions that some of the armoured forces struggling towards Žagarė and Šiauliai might be moved to the north, so that they could exploit Strachwitz's success. Saucken pressed for a resumption of the attack towards Jelgava, on the grounds that even if a decisive breakthrough was unlikely, his corps was tying down substantial Soviet forces. If one or more of his divisions were to be redeployed to the north, he argued, such a move would take at least two days, by which time it was highly likely that sufficient Soviet forces would also have been moved north to force the redeployed German forces to fight their way through to Tukums and on to 16th Army. For the moment, it was agreed that the attacks would continue, though planning began for the withdrawal of *Grossdeutschland* from its current position, with a view to redeployment further north in support of Strachwitz. In the meantime, 7th and 14th Panzer Divisions, attacking south of *Grossdeutschland*, were ordered to close the gap between their spearheads.[26]

4th and 5th Panzer Divisions continued to struggle forward. 4th Panzer Division was ordered to deploy its southern battlegroup in support of 5th Panzer Division, which allowed the latter to reach the outskirts of Žagarė, but at the cost of slowing down 4th Panzer Division's own advance. As darkness brought a pause in the fighting, there were yet more discussions between higher commands. Generaloberst Heinz Guderian, chief of staff at OKH, remained confident that there would soon be a major breakthrough towards Jelgava. By contrast, the local commanders were far gloomier. *Grossdeutschland* remained bogged down in heavy Soviet counter-attacks, and Saucken estimated that it would take his corps at least five more days to reach Jelgava. New orders were therefore issued overnight: *Grossdeutschlamd* was to be pulled out of line as previously planned, and would move to the north of 4th and 5th Panzer Divisions, which would continue their attack towards Jelgava.

Confusion remained in the far north of the battle, with a battlegroup from the German 52nd Security Division in Tukums, and some Soviet units withdrawing towards the south, while others continued to try to hold their positions. On 21 August, whilst the rest of 52nd Security Division attempted to establish a stronger connection between Army Group Centre and Army Group North, 4th Panzer Division resumed its attacks, pushing forward north of Žagarė in conjunction with elements of 12th Panzer Division, under almost constant attack from the air. Near the village of Bagaci, about five miles north-west of Žagarė, 4th Panzer Division had its first encounter with heavyweight Josef Stalin tanks. A unit of about 15 such tanks attempted to halt the German advance, and in a brisk action, seven Stalins were knocked out.[27]

By the end of the day, Saucken felt that there was the possibility of turning south with at least part of 4th Panzer Division to attack towards Žagarė, in order to allow 5th Panzer Division to resume its advance. However, it became clear by mid-morning on 22 August that the Soviet defences were far too strong. Numerous Soviet attacks forced 4th Panzer Division onto the defensive, with little ground being gained by either side. Towards the end of the day, Raus had a radio conversation with Saucken, and they agreed to shift the emphasis of the attack to the north: rather than continue along the original axis of advance towards the still-distant Jelgava, 4th Panzer Division would join *Grossdeutschland* and attack through Auce. Raus then discussed this with Reinhardt, commander of Army Group Centre, with much of the conversation centred on the issue of timing. Finally, they agreed that Saucken would attack Auce as soon as possible, rather than waiting for the full weight of *Grossdeutschland* and 4th Panzer Division to assemble.

Soviet reconnaissance flights spotted the redeployment of *Grossdeutschland* and 4th Panzer Division, and advised Bagramian that two panzer divisions were moving from the Žagarė area towards Auce. He decided therefore to attack from Žagarė with 51st Army, and from Šiauliai with 2nd Guards Army. 19th Tank Corps supported 51st Army in driving back elements of 12th Panzer Division, but was then pulled out of line and sent north to counter the German build-up at Auce. As *Grossdeutschland* pulled out of its positions, 2nd Guards Army reported that it had advanced perhaps seven miles; the reality was that the Germans had intentionally pulled back to a stronger defensive position.

The corridor that Strachwitz had established to Army Group North was slowly being consolidated, helped considerably by Bagramian's decision to withdraw 1st Guards Rifle Corps to the south. The German units cautiously probed south, with 81st Infantry Division from 16th Army occupying Dzukste, about 16 miles south of Tukums, early on 23 August. At midday – far earlier than Saucken had anticipated when he opposed the redeployment of divisions to the north – the first redeployed elements of *Grossdeutschland* and 4th Panzer Division attacked towards Auce under the aegis of XXXIX Panzer Corps, and although 4th Panzer Division's battlegroup was held up by tough resistance at the western edge of the town, *Grossdeutschland* made better progress a little to the north, penetrating the second line of Soviet defences in the early evening. Plans to replace 5th Panzer Division in the sector to the south of Žagarė with 201st Security Division were delayed by a Soviet attack on Kruopiai by 1st Tank Corps and 103rd Rifle Corps, which took the town in heavy fighting. A German counter-attack was launched, using the elements of 5th Panzer Division that had been extracted from the front line as part of the plan to withdraw the entire division, and fighting continued in the area for several days, effectively tying down the German forces and preventing their redeployment elsewhere, though the price for the Red Army was high, with over 50 tanks being destroyed by 5th Panzer Division in and around Kruopiai.[28]

After regrouping overnight, 4th Panzer Division attacked Auce at first light on 24 August, taking the town by 0800hrs. From here, the division attempted to push on to Bene, in order to protect *Grossdeutschland's* exposed southern flank, but progress was slow along narrow, heavily mined roads. *Grossdeutschland* made better headway, penetrating the Soviet defences to the north-east of Bene, but Saucken was increasingly worried that a gap was opening up between his two assault divisions. Raus urged him to continue to bypass Soviet defences by edging ever further to the north, and orders were sent to XXXIX Panzer Corps to this effect in the afternoon – Raus was determined that the tough defences facing 4th Panzer Division should be outflanked and then destroyed by envelopment from the north, rather than by further frontal assaults.

Both sides had suffered heavy losses in the fighting. In previous battles on the Eastern Front, the advantage in such combat had usually been with the side that controlled that battlefield at the end of the day – it had the opportunity to recover damaged vehicles and restore them to service, something that the Wehrmacht in particular had done to good effect. For example, despite heavy fighting, 4th Panzer Division's operational tank strength at the end of 25 August was 41, compared to only 21 two days earlier.[29] During *Doppelkopf*, though, the balance of power remained relatively unchanged. Although the Red Army continued to lose tanks at a steady rate, and German possession of the battlefield prevented their recovery, a constant stream of reinforcements kept the front-line units – particularly 3rd Guards Mechanised Corps and 19th Tank Corps – from having to be withdrawn; on 14 August alone, trains brought 60 new tanks to the Šiauliai area.[30] Nevertheless, *Grossdeutschland* continued to advance, reaching a point about five miles to the south-west of Dobele on 25 August. On its southern flank, 4th Panzer Division laboured towards Bene, and as a further development in the steady northward drift of the German point of effort, Raus ordered that 14th Panzer Division be extracted from the front line south of Auce and transferred to the northern flank of XXXIX Panzer Corps.

During the night, 4th Panzer Division once more reorganised its forces, and early on 26 August attacked south from its positions to the north-west of Bene. As before, progress was minimal, and a simultaneous attack towards Bene from the south-west by 12th Panzer Division also foundered in the face of strong resistance. *Grossdeutschland* continued its advance, making contact with elements of 81st Infantry Division advancing south from Dzukste, immediately to the north of Dobele. Saucken described the situation of his corps in a report to Raus:

> So far, we have destroyed over 800 enemy anti-armour guns [i.e. tanks, assault guns and anti-tank guns] and have thus ensured that the enemy has had to deplete his other front lines almost completely ... artillery ammunition is short. We have had to pull our heavy field howitzers out of the firing line, as they only have a few rounds left for self-defence.[31]

A further attempt was made by 4th and 12th Panzer Divisions to take Bene on 27 August, but, as before, the attacks faltered in the face of the Soviet defences. Towards the end of the day, Generalleutnant Clemens Betzel, the commander of 4th Panzer Division, reported to Saucken, his corps commander (and a former commander of the division):

> The tough, constant and extremely costly fighting of the last few days against a determined enemy, who in terms of weapons and men has a relatively large superiority, has left the troops so exhausted that a pause of one or two days is urgently needed before a resumption of attacks.[32]

The divisions of Army Group North were weak in armour, and there had been recurrent discussions about the transfer of some of 3rd Panzer Army's panzer divisions to 16th Army once contact between Army Group Centre and Army Group North had been re-established. With little prospect of *Doppelkopf* achieving its original objective, i.e. establishing such contact via the capture of Jelgava, and in any case with clear contact having been established along the coast, 3rd Panzer Army sent a new order to XXXIX Panzer Corps late on 27 August, bringing *Doppelkopf* to an end:

> 14th Panzer Division [which had now been extracted from the front line] is to be dispatched for use by Army Group North at Jelgava. As the attack by the corps' left flank is not to be continued, as part of the increased defensive preparation on the entire corps front against expected enemy armoured attacks, the attack on the inner wings of 12th and 4th Panzer Divisions is to be resumed, with the intention of throwing the enemy out of the salient to the south and west of Bene, and thus release forces from the front. Contact by the left flank with 81st Infantry Division is to be strengthened.[33]

The operation had lasted 12 days, and the German divisions had advanced perhaps 30 miles. They had been stopped about 20 miles short of Jelgava, but despite failing to achieve this, the operation had restored contact with Army Group North. The divisions of XXXIX and XL Panzer Corps could claim with some justification that their assaults tied down sufficient Soviet forces to allow Strachwitz and his diminutive division adequate freedom of manoeuvre to reach Army Group North. Nevertheless, *Doppelkopf* represented a rare concentration of German armour in any part of the front in this stage of the war, and in almost any other period of the conflict, success for the attackers would have been almost guaranteed. On this occasion, despite the overstretched Soviet supply lines and the casualties suffered by Bagramian's armies during their long advance, the Red Army retained its numerical superiority throughout the operation, and made particularly good use of defence-friendly terrain to hold up the German attacks. Another factor identified by the Germans was the failure of the panzergrenadiers in the assault formations to attack with the same vigour as in previous years. As Gerd Niepold, the chief of staff of 12th Panzer Division during the operation, concluded several years later, over three years of fighting on the Eastern Front had lowered the quality of the personnel of the panzergrenadier regiments, whose replacement drafts were far inferior in terms of training to the men who had led the Wehrmacht's advance into the Soviet Union in 1941. Whilst this may seem like a harsh judgement on the men who fought so hard to reach Jelgava, the after-action reports of every division showed that the loss of key veteran officers often resulted in attacks faltering in a manner that would not have occurred in earlier years. NCOs were meant to take over in such circumstances, but by late 1944, few had the experience or training to cope with the demands of *Auftragstaktik*.[34]

Bagramian later claimed that his front accounted for over 15,000 German casualties during the operation, and knocked out 380 tanks and assault guns.[35] German records show that at the beginning of the operation, the German divisions had a total of only 281 operational tanks and assault guns between them, and though replacement vehicles arrived during the course of the operation, the Soviet figures seem unrealistically high; inevitably, both sides were prone to exaggerate the losses of their enemies. The true number of casualties on both sides during this operation will never be known with any degree of accuracy.

During this entire period, there was more heavy fighting further north. In 1941, when the Wehrmacht had advanced apparently irresistibly towards Leningrad, there had been no significant fighting around Narva, unlike the Soviet efforts in 1944. There were two reasons for this. Firstly, the Red Army in 1941 was in complete retreat, and simply lacked the forces to contest the Narva region. Secondly, even if an attempt had been made, it would have been rendered irrelevant by the swift advance of German forces to the east of Lake Peipus. In 1944, the Red Army had tried in vain to batter its way into Estonia via the Narva positions, but now that the entire Eastern Front was hugely weakened, there was a possibility of outflanking the German defences, by invading Estonia from south of Lake Peipus, much as the Wehrmacht had used this route to bypass the Narva in 1941.

In the area south of Lake Peipus, Maslennikov's 3rd Baltic Front enjoyed a substantial advantage over the German defences, and as a result of German transfers of forces to the stricken Army Group Centre outnumbered them over 4:1 in terms of men and armour, and over 14:1 in terms of artillery. To make matters worse, these ratios included large numbers of poorly equipped and poorly trained Estonian militia amongst the ranks of the German forces.

The Soviet forces launched their attack on 10 August. Hans Gollnick's XXVIII Corps immediately came under pressure, and by the end of the day, the Soviet 67th Army had broken through the German lines. Pechory, the last major town on the Soviet side of the old border, fell to 67th Army the following day, while the neighbouring 1st Guards Army pushed on towards Voru, reaching and capturing the town on 13 August. It was clear that the weakened southern flank of the German 18th Army could not continue to hold the front line. Schörner therefore ordered that the sector from Lake Võrtsjärv to Lake Peipus was to be covered by Army Detachment Narva, allowing 18th Army to concentrate its limited forces between Lake Võrtsjärv and the Latvian border. Hastily, a defensive line was established to prevent a swift Soviet advance to the Baltic coast.

After a brief pause, Maslennikov's armies had resumed their advance on 16 August, forcing back the weak 207th Security Division. There was a clear threat to the city of Tartu, and Army Detachment Narva now hurried to restore the front. Brigadeführer Jürgen Wagner was dispatched from III SS Panzer Corps with the last tanks and assault guns from the *Nordland* division and the *Nederland* brigade, a battalion of 5th SS Volunteer Assault Brigade *Wallonien*, artillery support, and an infantry regiment from 11th Infantry Division. The units began to arrive at the front late on 16 August, and swiftly incorporated local Estonian *Omakaitse* into their ranks. It remained to be seen how well this new defensive line would withstand the Soviet forces.

Earlier in the summer, Govorov's Leningrad Front had laid plans for an amphibious assault across Lake Peipus to outflank the stubborn defences of Army Detachment Narva. Now, the flotilla that had been designated for the operation, commanded by Captain Arzhavkin, was assigned to Maslennikov, with a view to carrying out a crossing of the lake in conjunction with 3rd Baltic Front's attack into southern Estonia. The flotilla consisted of about 40 small vessels, many of them armed, and in order to improve the chances of success of any amphibious operation, Soviet aircraft carried out repeated attacks against the port of Mustvee, on the north-west shore of Lake Peipus, from which the Germans operated a number of gunboats, and by the beginning of August, most of the German vessels had been sunk or damaged. Lieutenant General Alexei Aleksandrovich Grechkin, deputy commander of the 3rd Baltic Front, was given command of a mixed force, comprised mainly of 128th and 191st Rifle Divisions, and on 16 August, elements of 191st Rifle Division, covered by artillery on the east bank, crossed the narrow strait that divided Lake Peipus from Lake Pskov and landed at Mehikoorma, rapidly establishing a substantial bridgehead.

The local defences consisted merely of poorly armed Estonian *Omakaitse* fighters, who could do little to stop the Soviet landings. However, several squadrons of Stuka dive-bombers from Hans-Ulrich Rudel's *Schlacht-Geschwader 2* attacked in the late morning, just as the second wave of Soviet troops was being ferried across the strait, inflicting heavy casualties. A third wave of troops was also bombed later in the day. It appears that Soviet planners had not anticipated any significant threat from the air, and it was not until 17 August that Soviet fighters put up serious resistance to German attacks. Despite the dive-bomber attacks, some 7,000 men were landed at Mehikoorma, where they gradually enlarged their foothold, linking up with 67th Army's 86th Rifle Division late on 17 August.[36]

Pressure on the German line was unremitting. A mixed force of Estonians and a battalion from 11th Infantry Division came under heavy assault on 20 August on the approaches to Tartu, and despite powerful artillery support, the German troops pulled back to Melliste, barely five miles from the city outskirts. Further west, the battalion from *Wallonien* drove Soviet spearheads from Kambja, but on 23 August, elements of 1st Guards Army resumed their drive towards Tartu. There were heavy losses on both sides before the Walloons gave up Kambja, pulling back to the west of Tartu. A little further west, a battalion from the 45th SS Grenadier Regiment (1st Estonian) was in the village of Nöo. The main defences stopped the Soviet drive, but the 282nd Rifle Division discovered a thinly manned stretch of front line west of the village. Accompanied by a tank brigade, the division bypassed the Estonian defences and pushed north five miles to Kärevere, seizing the vital bridge over the River Emajõgi.

With a serious threat developing to Tartu from the south-east, south and now the west, Army Group North attempted to restore the situation with an armoured counter-attack. Hyazinth von Strachwitz's armoured group, fresh from its triumph in *Doppelkopf*, was hurried north to launch an attack from near the southern point of Lake Võrtsjärv, marching north-east to strike the 1st Guards Army in its flank. The

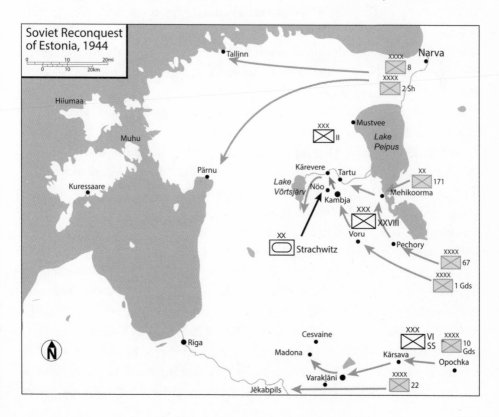

intention was to thrust through Elva to Nöo, but the operation suffered a disaster on 23 August. Whilst driving to his headquarters, Strachwitz was involved in a serious car crash; the small *Kubelwagen* (amphibious vehicle, the German equivalent of a jeep) he was travelling in left the road and rolled over several times, killing both the driver and Strachwitz's orderly officer. The *Panzergraf* himself suffered a fractured skull, fractured ribs, and injuries to arms and legs. He was fortunate to survive, and there was no question of him continuing in command of his tanks.

The following day, the assault group, consisting of 101st Panzer Brigade and SS Panzer Brigade Gross, attacked alongside *SS-Panzer-Aufklärungs-Abteilung 11*. Although the SS reconnaissance battalion managed to penetrate to Tamsa, a few miles south-west of Nöo, Soviet defences proved too strong for the main armoured group to achieve a significant penetration. In any event, elements of 1st Guards Army bypassed the northern flank of the armoured counter-thrust, and reached the lower tip of Lake Võrtsjärv. The Soviet spearheads were now barely 40 miles from the Baltic, threatening to isolate Army Detachment Narva in Estonia. The armoured counter-thrust was abandoned, and its forces fell back to defend against a further Soviet drive to the west.

The Soviet 67th Army was concentrating against Tartu, and launched a determined attack with four rifle divisions to take the city on 25 August. Bitter street-fighting reduced much of the city to rubble, but by the end of the day, the exhausted German defenders were forced to abandon Tartu and retreat north-east over the River Emajõgi. On either side of Tartu, Soviet infantry succeeded in crossing the river and securing small bridgeheads, and Wagner tried desperately to salvage his shattered units. *SS-Panzer-Aufklärungs-Abteilung 11* was now assigned to his command, and with its mobility and firepower, it succeeded in stopping several Soviet penetrations. Sturmbannführer Leon Degrelle, commander of the *Wallonien* assault brigade, succeeded in establishing a defensive line around the Soviet bridgehead north of Tartu, and overall command of the German front between Lakes Võrtsjärv and Peipus was assigned to General Wilhelm Hasse's II Corps.

With the German lines in disarray and Soviet forces across the Emajõgi at several points, there was a danger of multiple Soviet advances, either west to the Baltic, north into the rear of the Tannenberg positions, or north-west to Tallinn. Estonian soldiers who had been serving as part of the Finnish *Jalaväerügement 200* ('Infantry Regiment 200') or *JR 200*, and had returned to Estonia as part of the amnesty declared at the beginning of August, had been formed into the 3rd Battalion, 1st Estonian Regiment, and were hurried south to the front. On 30 August, reinforced by an Estonian police battalion and a small force of German tanks, they attacked the Soviet bridgehead at Kärevere, which was defended by two rifle divisions. After a stiff fight, the Soviet forces fell back, and the Estonians not only eliminated the bridgehead, but also captured the bridge intact. Further attacks followed, reducing the Soviet bridgeheads closer to Tartu. By 6 September, elements of II Corps had reached the northern edge of the city, but could make no further progress.

To the south-west, 16th Army also came under heavy pressure as the Soviet 2nd Baltic Front attempted to force its way through to the coast. Most of the line was defended by the German *Korpsgruppe Risse* and *Korpsgruppe Wagner*, created from the remnants of burnt-out infantry divisions and whatever other men were available. General Paul Laux, commander of 16th Army, was killed when his reconnaissance plane was shot down by a Soviet fighter, and he was replaced by General Carl Hilpert. As much through Soviet exhaustion as their own efforts, the defenders were able to bring the Soviet attack to a standstill.

Slowly, stability returned to the front, mainly because the Soviet forces paused to regroup before launching what they intended would be lethal assaults to destroy Army Group North. On 10 September, Felix Steiner, commander of III SS Panzer Corps, was summoned to a meeting at Hitler's headquarters in Rastenburg for a conference. Here, Hitler informed him that Estonia was to be abandoned. Finland had resumed negotiations with the Soviet Union in August, and on 4–5 September a ceasefire came into force between the two nations. One of the main rationales for holding Estonia – to prevent the Soviet forces from gaining bases that they could use to attack Finland – was therefore eliminated. The other two reasons to stay in Estonia were to make use of the oil shales on the Baltic coast, and to continue to recruit troops in Estonia. Neither of these was sufficient to justify a continued German presence, especially given that at three different points – in southern Estonia, to the west of Riga, and between Šiauliai and Klaipėda – the Red Army was in a good position to sever all contact between the armies in the Baltic States and the German Reich.

However, it was perhaps typical of Hitler's thinking that the abandonment of Estonia would not be complete. Iron ore from Sweden, he insisted, would remain vital to the German war effort, and in order to ensure that this continued, a German bridgehead was to be established around Tallinn. This would continue to be held indefinitely.

Steiner objected to the proposal, knowing that his own corps would probably be required to hold the Tallinn bridgehead. Hitler dispatched him back to Estonia, assuring him that further details and a final decision would follow, but Steiner had no intention of allowing his men to be sacrificed in what he regarded as a lost cause. On his return, he ordered rear area units to dispatch non-essential personnel to Germany, and his staff requisitioned as many motor vehicles as possible. These were then distributed primarily to 11th Infantry Division and 20th SS Waffen-Grenadier

Division (1st Estonian), to ensure that they were as mobile as possible. He also discussed Hitler's intentions with Schörner, who agreed that the proposal for a Tallinn bridgehead was absurd. He promised to take this up with Hitler directly.

None of Steiner's actions to date were particularly controversial, but he crossed a distinct line when he contacted Major General Sodla and Colonel Sinka, officers in the Estonian military, and told them of German intentions. Quietly, arrangements were made for seaborne evacuation of a limited number of Estonians by sea.[37] Meanwhile, Schörner decided to order Army Detachment Narva to make preparations for an organised withdrawal. He had no intention of having to organise such a complex undertaking under pressure of a Soviet attack.

In Latvia, both 3rd Panzer Army and Bagramian's front were tidying up the aftermath of *Doppelkopf*. Since the termination of the operation, they had enjoyed relative peace, but the German armoured forces had largely remained in place, in anticipation of a Soviet thrust towards the west. On 11 September, three days before the great Soviet assault on Army Group North, Reinhardt asked 3rd Panzer Army whether it might be possible – if a Soviet attack towards the west did not materialise – to launch a German attack, in order to tie down Soviet forces that might otherwise be unleashed against 16th Army. Raus replied that he had a total of 420 tanks and assault guns available, and recommended a limited attack north of Bene. OKH wanted the attack to begin immediately, if necessary with whatever forces were already in the relevant sector, but Raus strongly advised against this; given the resistance that the panzer divisions had encountered during *Doppelkopf*, he argued, it was best to concentrate forces before an attack.

There was considerable discussion about the relative merits of attacking north of Bene, or even further north at Dobele. Šiauliai was also considered as an option, but on 14 September, it was decided that an attack through Bene was the best choice. Orders were accordingly issued for a commencement of an attack on 16 September, codenamed *Cäsar*. It was expected that this operation would relieve the pressure that was building up on Riga.[38] Raus was not greatly optimistic about the prospects of the operation. He advised OKH that fuel was limited for his divisions, and that he did not regard it as likely that he would gain a great deal of territory. However, he was confident that the attack would tie down and destroy substantial Soviet forces.

Despite German fears of a Soviet attack towards the west, this was not yet part of Bagramian's planning. For the moment, he turned his attention to a small group of about 900 men from 346th Rifle Division, who had been cut off close to the coast of the Gulf of Riga by the restoration of the link between Army Group Centre and Army Group North. On 2 September, this group radioed that it planned to attempt a breakout. Three days later, led by Major Bubli, commander of 1164th Rifle Regiment, some 700 men succeeded in reaching Soviet lines.[39] Meanwhile, he submitted his plans for his front's participation in the coming offensive against Army Group North. He felt that whilst he could contribute to the capture of Riga, his main contribution would be to restore his corridor to the Gulf of Riga, and ordered 51st Army, supported by 5th Guards Tank Army and the independent 1st and 19th Tank Corps, to prepare for such an operation on 20 September. However, plans were also made for the assault towards Riga.

Amongst the obstacles facing Bagramian's front were the Rivers Mēmele and Lielupe. Crossing these in the face of resistance would be hard enough; maintaining supply lines across them for a rapid advance would be still harder. Bagramian was therefore relieved when General Vasili Kosarev, the front's Chief of Engineers, offered a solution. It would be possible to dam the Mēmele and the Muša – a tributary of the Lielupe – and thus lower the river to a more manageable level.[40] Preparations were also made at a political level:

> The political work was very effective, as there were strong Party organisations amongst the companies. The total of Communists amongst the troops was about 173,000 … in 4th Shock Army and 43rd Army, the Communists and Komsomol members formed 27 to 40% of the personnel. In every division, there were permanent representatives of the political organisation of the Front and individual armies, who exhorted their comrades to raise their efforts using various means and methods. Before the attack, 43rd Army's council called a special assembly. Its declaration stated that the attack would be supported by over a thousand guns, about a thousand planes, as well as many tanks and self-propelled guns. When I saw this declaration, I was worried whether we were handing the enemy information that he might be able to use. But then I accepted the text, as I told myself that nothing could save the Fascists, and the morale effect of this document on the soldiers would be enormous. This declaration was at the heart of the meetings of the troop formations and played an important role in increasing their combat spirit.[41]

Malyschev's 4th Shock Army launched its preparatory attacks on 11 September, attempting to take the Germans by surprise. A decoy smokescreen was used to distract German attention away from the main assault, which was launched by 22nd Guards Rifle Corps. The Soviet forces swiftly secured a bridgehead over the Mēmele.

On 14 September, Beloborodov's 43rd Army was due to begin its assault, but the original attack was delayed by bad weather. As planned, 1st Baltic Front's engineers had completed their damming work, lowering the level of the critical rivers by about 20 inches, and as the weather improved through the day, the assault was launched at 1300hrs. Crossings over the Mēmele and Lielupe were swiftly seized, and Beloborodov's 1st and 84th Rifle Corps made good progress. By the end of the day, Soviet forces had reached Iecava, their objective for the first day, but to the disappointment of Bagramian and other senior officers, the delays brought by the morning's bad weather prevented the seizure of the town. Lauchert's 101st Panzer Brigade, which had been part of Strachwitz's improvised division, was committed to block the Soviet advance near Bauska, and with German resistance rapidly increasing, Bagramian ordered Beloborodov to bypass Iecava. On 15 September, 3rd Guards Mechanised Corps – considerably replenished since its battles during *Doppelkopf* – advanced to the east of the town, followed by 1st Rifle Corps. Bagramian was aware from aerial reconnaissance reports that German forces were being fed into the defensive line south of the Latvian capital, and urged 3rd Guards Mechanised Corps and 43rd Army to advance as fast as they could. The following day, Beloborodov reported that his leading units had reached Baldone, only 12 miles from Riga.

Early on 14 September, 2nd and 3rd Baltic Fronts also launched attacks along the entire front of Army Group North. 14th Panzer Division was dispatched to shore up the front to the east of Riga at Ērgļi. On 16 September, even as Beloborodov's 43rd Army advanced almost within touching range of Riga, Schörner flew to Rastenburg and gave Hitler a detailed and pessimistic report of his army group's situation. He had no significant reserves left, and the collapse of his front was only a matter of time. There were insufficient men to hold off the Red Army whilst simultaneously preparing 'fortress' positions as Hitler wished, and only a withdrawal would prevent the annihilation of the entire army group. After only 15 minutes' discussion, Hitler agreed to an immediate withdrawal, codenamed *Aster*.

Detailed orders for such an operation had been in preparation for several days, and now slipped into action. III SS Panzer Corps was to pull back on 18 September to Pärnu on the Baltic coast, with II Corps forming a rearguard that would withdraw a day later. Generalmajor Gerok was given command of a mixed group that would fall back to Tallinn, from where it would be evacuated by sea.

Meanwhile, using whatever forces he could scrape together, Generaloberst Hilpert, commander of 16th Army, attempted to mount counter-attacks south of Riga. Although these achieved little, General Chistiakov, commander of 6th Guards Army, advised Bagramian that a substantial force of perhaps 300 German tanks and assault guns was preparing to attack towards Dobele: Soviet reconnaissance had spotted the

German build-up for *Cäsar*. Reluctantly, Bagramian was forced to concentrate on defending against renewed activity by 3rd Panzer Army.[42]

Cäsar, 3rd Panzer Army's spoiling attack to relieve pressure on Army Group North, began on schedule on 16 September, with *Grossdeutschland* and 4th Panzer Division attacking north of Bene. At first, despite 6th Guards Army apparently detecting the German build-up the previous day, the two German divisions appeared to have surprised the Red Army, and *Grossdeutschland* in particular made good progress, advancing some five miles before encountering strong resistance. The terrain was dotted with small woods and, as had been the case with *Doppelkopf*, the Soviets made excellent use of the available cover to deploy powerful anti-tank forces. 4th Panzer Division encountered increasingly tough resistance, forcing the initial attack to grind to a halt after minimal gains. General von Saucken, the commander of XXXIX Panzer Corps, and Reinhardt visited the headquarters of 4th Panzer Division's 33rd Panzer Regiment to discuss matters with General Betzel, the division commander. A renewed attack was agreed, but again made minimal progress despite sustaining heavy losses. At the end of the day, Saucken recommended shifting 4th Panzer Division's units further north, in order to take advantage of *Grossdeutschland*'s success. 7th Panzer Division, the third component of the German operation, began to form up on the northern flank of *Grossdeutschland*, and towards the end of the day made its initial attack, gaining a little territory before nightfall, apparently through a hitherto-undetected gap in the Soviet defences. Consequently, it was decided to extract 4th Panzer Division's main battlegroup from its current position and deploy it in support of *Grossdeutschland* and 7th Panzer Division.

The commanders of the 51st Army and 6th Guards Army advised their front commander that their men had destroyed about 60 German tanks, but had still been driven back, though only a short distance. Whilst it seems that – as was often the case with such claims by either side – this estimate of enemy losses was an exaggeration, there was no doubt that the German assault formations had taken punishing losses. The commander of 4th Panzer Division's 33rd Panzergrenadier Regiment wrote that it had been 'a black day' for his regiment, with over 100 killed or wounded, including two company commanders killed and five other officers wounded.[43] Chistiakov also sent Bagramian news of a document that his men had captured: a proclamation from Schörner to his troops, ordering them to resist at all costs, and warning that any man found behind the front without orders was liable to be shot.[44] With both 2nd and 3rd Baltic Fronts reporting increased German resistance, Bagramian was urged to continue his advance on Riga. In bitter fighting, 43rd Army took two days to consolidate its hold on Baldone, while further east, 4th Shock Army battered its way to Jaunjelgava. Beloborodov also reported repeated German counter-attacks, and Bagramian later claimed that the Germans had massed two panzer divisions and four infantry divisions in the area. The reality was that Army Group North had very limited armoured assets at its disposal, and even if four infantry divisions were present, they probably amounted to less than a division in terms of numbers.

Overnight, *Gruppe Betzel*, a large part of 4th Panzer Division, moved from its positions on the southern wing of *Grossdeutschland* to 7th Panzer Division's sector in the north. Attacking in mid-morning on 17 September, the armoured battlegroup, with some 120 tanks and self-propelled guns, made good progress at first. Slightly to the south, 7th Panzer Division attacked with about 70 tanks, assault guns and self-propelled guns, with *Grossdeutschland* at the southern end of the attack, fielding another 137 tanks, assault guns and self-propelled guns. These substantial force concentrations were achieved in part by reinforcing the attack formations with other units – 4th Panzer Division included a tank battalion from 12th Panzer Division, and *Grossdeutschland* was reinforced by a battlegroup from 5th Panzer Division. Unfortunately for the German divisions, the territory they were contesting, with woodland stretching almost as far as Dobele, was singularly unsuitable for the operation of massed armour. Gefreiter Riesche, from 5th Panzer Division, recalled the day:

At first light, he [the enemy] made a grand racket with his artillery; quite the full load. We were guarding the main road to Semkino south-east of Dobele. 8 Coy was to our left. There were constant air attacks, all hell was loose overhead. There was a constant noise, clattering and crashing, and nobody could leave the vehicle.

Our machine guns in front of us were firing, answering Ivan. The Katyushas fired, then anti-tank guns and artillery from Ivan, followed in turn by our mortars and artillery. Amongst this, repeated enemy aircraft, with no sign of our own. This tale of battle raged on the entire day. I stayed in my gun-aimer's seat. We mounted a reconnaissance raid to Semkino, fire struck our vehicle, one wounded. Back to Battalion HQ, to take the wounded to the battalion doctor. Then back to our old position. Ivan's air attacks were ever grimmer. Bombs blasted our wood, Ivan blazed away with fixed weapons. For us it was just a case of 'Hatches open', incoming fire, 'Hatches closed!' We had infantry with us, mainly lying under the vehicle.[45]

Hauptmann Nökel, commander of a battalion of 31st Panzer Regiment and part of the 5th Panzer Division battlegroup attached to *Grossdeutschland*, was singularly unimpressed by the terrain over which he was meant to advance:

It came to the most absurd situations. These included tank attacks through dense, tall trees. Escorted by a few infantry patrols, our tanks broke unto the trackless woodland on a broad front and wove through the trees. To do this, the guns had to be turned to 6 o'clock (to the rear), to avoid damaging them. If the infantry or tank commanders saw the enemy, the tanks had to drive back to an open area, the guns turned to 12 o'clock (to the front), and then drive forward again, engage the enemy with machine guns and main armament, then turn the turret to the rear again and weave further through the wood. Although the battalion achieved considerable defensive successes and earned the approbation of the division commander [of *Grossdeutschland*], we were delighted when we were able to return to the ranks of our own division and get a few days' rest.[46]

By the end of the day both 4th and 7th Panzer Divisions ran into tough resistance on the northern side of the advance. *Grossdeutschland* struggled to make headway through the dense woodland, and finally reached its objective, the high ground immediately to the south of Dobele. The battle returns from the divisions reflected the terrain over which they had advanced; they claimed the destruction of only a dozen Soviet tanks and assault guns, and eight anti-tank guns.[47]

18 September once more brought heavy air attacks against the German forces. Nevertheless, a coordinated attack by 4th and 7th Panzer Divisions reached the high ground a little over two miles west of Dobele. Both Raus and Reinhardt travelled to Saucken's headquarters to discuss the situation during the afternoon. Reinhardt advised his subordinates that in addition to tying down a substantial portion of the Soviet armoured forces, XXXIX Panzer Corps had forced the Soviet leadership to abandon their plans for a renewed drive to the Gulf of Riga. The objectives of *Cäsar*, he concluded, had been achieved, and *Grossdeutschland* should prepare for a defensive tank battle, as a Soviet tank corps was expected to launch a counter-attack the following day. 4th and 7th Panzer Divisions were to continue their attack, but only in order to establish firm contact with Army Group North's 81st Infantry Division, to the north of Dobele.

For the next three days, the two panzer divisions battered their way forward. As ever, the terrain proved as much a hindrance as the Soviet defenders, who were primarily from 204th Rifle Division and 71st Guards Rifle Division. For 4th Panzer Division, the battle for Hill 92.0 to the west of Dobele turned into a bitter and costly struggle. After bitter fighting that lasted for most of 18 September, Betzel pulled his division back a short distance and launched a new assault after dusk. At first, the attack went well, but when a small farmhouse went up in flames, it provided enough illumination for the Soviet anti-tank guns to bring that attack to a halt. The commander of the division's Panther battalion was badly wounded by almost the last shot of the night, but the following morning, after a furious bombardment of the hill, the German attack finally succeeded in securing the hilltop.[48] Late on 21 September, 4th Panzer Division reached the railway line to the north-west of Dobele, and linked up with 81st Infantry Division. The operation was at an end.

Rudolf Meckl, a *Leutnant* in 4th Panzer Division's 35th Panzer Regiment, was badly wounded by Soviet artillery fire while attempting to repair broken tracks on his tank. He was evacuated to the naval hospital in Liepāja, where he found himself in a partitioned ward, with about 40 other badly wounded men. They were mainly soldiers for whom the surgeons could do little, and most died of their wounds. One of the wounded was a fellow *Leutnant*, whose injuries were less severe than those of his comrades, and had been acquired in a singularly unfortunate manner:

[Leutnant] Hänsgen was the commander of a *Panzerjäger* staff company, and his wounding was a direct consequence. Anyone who remembers the small Courland roads, which were flanked closely by deep ditches, knows that possibilities of escaping a sudden air attack were limited, and often the only hope was the poor training of the Russian pilots.

But Hänsgen hadn't thought of that. When he was driving along such a road in the command vehicle and suddenly saw the shadow of an aircraft overhead, he dived headlong out of the vehicle into the ditch. He had forgotten beforehand to switch off the engine and apply the handbrake properly. His vehicle ... then promptly followed the gentleman into the ditch. The result was a complex lower leg fracture and transfer to the naval hospital in Liepāja.[49]

Despite being adorned by a large red cross, the building housing the naval hospital was hit in several Soviet air attacks; whilst such conduct in the west would have been regarded as unacceptable, neither the Germans nor the Soviets regarded themselves bound by the Hague Convention when it came to conduct on the Eastern Front. Meckl later recalled the nightmare of the attacks:

With every explosion, huge lumps of mortar and plaster fell on the beds. But we were captive, secured to our beds by our wounds, and experienced the fearful suffering of the helpless. Panic lurked in the shadows. But it didn't break out, not even when a shock wave smashed the windows in the ward, raining glass splinters over the beds ...

There were three nurses who prevented blind self-destruction breaking out as a result of the fear of the immobilised.

One would have expected the strict, uncompromising East Prussian Alla capable of looking fear boldly in the face without mucking about, but it was remarkable to see the same thing in the other two nurses: young things, recently arrived from the homeland ...

They stood between the rows of beds like guardian angels, their calm and watchful gaze moving searchingly from face to face, and where one of the helpless souls buckled under the unbearable strain and anxiety, they laid a cool, gentle hand on the snow-white face; thus it remained calm in death's waiting room.

I learned thus of the silent courage of these young women, who voluntarily abandoned the safety of the shelters to help the wounded through the hell of fear, that a man's heedless bravery is nothing compared to the warm-hearted love of a woman.[50]

In many respects, *Cäsar* would have been a more effective operation if it had been conducted with strong infantry formations rather than armour. The problem for the Germans was that such infantry divisions were simply not available; Raus felt that of his infantry formations, only 1st Infantry Division had anything approaching the level of effectiveness required for prolonged combat on the Eastern Front. Despite gaining only about seven miles, the operation forced the diversion of Soviet forces from both the Riga front and a renewed push to the Gulf of Riga.

Far to the north, the withdrawal of Army Detachment Narva went relatively smoothly, except for the *ad hoc Division zbV 300* (*Division zur besondere Verfügung* or 'Special Purpose Division'). Formed from the remnants of 13th Luftwaffe Field Division and four Estonian border guard regiments, the division was deployed as two brigades on a broad front immediately north of Lake Peipus. Its withdrawal route was along a single corduroy road through the marshes that had protected the southern flank of the Tannenberg positions earlier in the year, and an initially orderly withdrawal rapidly degenerated late on 18 September, as one of its officers reported:

I had to leave my command post at 2100 in order to perform traffic control duties with my staff. Chaos ruled where the corduroy roads from the northern and southern brigades came together. No one had told us that half of the southern brigade was to march back with us on the same corduroy road. There was no rest for us from 2200 to 0200 during the night of 19 September. All of the units had to be funnelled in on a single road. The Estonians did not understand any German. Everything had to be accomplished by pushing and poking. The small Baltic horses got stuck in the mud holes again and again.[51]

Soviet forces had meanwhile crossed the Emajõgi and threatened to cut off the German line of retreat. *SS-Panzer-Aufklärungs-Abteilung 11*, the reconnaissance battalion of III SS Panzer Corps, repeatedly functioned as an armoured battlegroup, attempting to fight a series of delaying actions across a broad front. Reduced to less than 2,000 men, *Division zbV 300* broke into three groups, each led by a German colonel, which then attempted to make their way back through the wilderness. The 7th Estonian Rifle Corps, fighting in the Red Army, overran the area, and few of the men in the three German groups escaped. Some of the wounded Estonians from the German division took shelter in a church in the village of Avinurme. When the Estonians from 8th Rifle Corps arrived, they massacred the wounded and other prisoners.[52]

Gerok's force, consisting of a mixture of Estonian *Omakaitse*, artillery batteries, and elements of both 11th Infantry Division and 20th SS Waffen-Grenadier Division, fell back to Tallinn. The Soviet pursuit was close behind, and fighting around the perimeter erupted briefly on 21 September. There was no intention of a prolonged resistance, and troops and other personnel embarked aboard the waiting ships in a steady stream. The first convoy of five steamers left at first light on 22 September. Finally, two German torpedo boats took off the last defenders, and the city was in Soviet hands by the end of the day. During the brief operation, Admiral Theodor Buchardi's ships had lifted a total of 80,000 people from Tallinn. Soviet aircraft repeatedly attacked the ships, sinking several, including the hospital ship *Moero*, which went down with the loss of over 600 people, but losses amounted to less than 1 per cent of those embarked from Tallinn. For the soldiers of Govorov's Leningrad Front, who had spilt so much blood attempting to force the Tannenberg Line, there must have been a sense of unreality about the swiftness with which they overran Estonia.

The Estonians had been preparing for a German departure for months. The *Eesti Vabariigi Rahvuskomitee* ('National Committee of the Estonian Republic') declared the return of independence on 18 September, and there were isolated clashes between Estonians and retreating German units. Jüri Uluots, the last prime minister before the Soviet occupation in 1939, was terminally ill with cancer, and appointed Otto Tief as prime minister. Although the committee appealed to the Soviet authorities for recognition, they must have known that there was little prospect of this occurring, and had laid plans for the government to flee into exile. Estonian soldiers under the leadership of Admiral Johan Pitka seized Toompea Castle in Tallinn even as the Germans were leaving, and then attempted to fight off the Soviet troops of the Leningrad Front. The uneven battle was quickly over, with Pitka disappearing in the fighting, presumed killed.

Uluots escaped to Sweden, where he died in early 1945. Tief was arrested and sent to Siberia; he survived a long spell of imprisonment, and returned to Estonia long after the war, dying there in 1976. The attempt to re-establish the Estonian Republic was over almost before it began.

The swift advance of 2nd Shock Army across the Emajõgi, scattering the German 87th Infantry Division and 207th Security Division, was unable to intercept the retreating German forces, which hurried to reach the area west of Lake Võrtsjärv before they could be encircled. The last German unit in Estonia was the *Nederland* brigade, and after destroying the port facilities in Pärnu, the rearguard fell back towards Latvia. The last fighting took place on the line of the River Lemme, immediately north of the border. Late on 24 September, after a final action against advancing Soviet tanks, the Dutch SS soldiers retreated into Latvia.

There was no rest for the retreating elements of III SS Panzer Corps. The crisis on the southern approaches to Riga demanded urgent attention, and on 22 September, *SS-Panzergrenadier-Regiment 24 Danmark* was attached to 14th Panzer Division, with orders to attack towards Baldone from the north, with *SS-Panzergrenadier-Regiment 23 Norge* on its eastern flank. The few remaining tanks and assault guns of *Nordland* were also committed in support of the attack, which began on 23 September. The tanks of 14th Panzer Division were delayed, and the SS panzergrenadiers launched their attacks with only the support of the vehicles from *Nordland*. As 14th Panzer Division's tanks finally arrived, a Soviet counter-attack began, and bitter fighting raged all day. By dusk, the Germans had gained perhaps three miles, though at a terrible cost – *Danmark* alone lost nearly 300 men.[53]

On the eastern flank of the attack, *Norge* pushed forward towards Baldone, reaching the outskirts of the town on 25 September. By this stage, the regiment's losses left it in no state to continue its advance. Indeed, Bagramian's forces rallied and counter-attacked, with minimal ground changing hands. Obukhov's 3rd Guards Mechanised Corps was in the thick of the fighting, as Bagramian later described:

> It was almost impossible to determine who was attacking and who was defending. When the Fascists had to defend in one sector, our troops were cut off by other counterattacks. But we wanted to retain the initiative at any cost.
>
> During these tense days, Obukhov reported that as the rifle divisions had lagged behind, his brigade had to fight in a situation in which enemy units lay to his rear. But he refused to fall back to the main forces of 43rd Army. Obukhov never feared being encircled. He was a master of the art of manoeuvre and kept a clear head when he was isolated from the main force.[54]

The front line south of Riga stabilised on 27 September. Almost all of 16th Army was now in or around the Latvian capital, with 18th Army defending to the east. Soviet intelligence also suggested that the bulk of 3rd Panzer Army's strike power lay in the north, as a result of *Doppelkopf* and *Cäsar*; consequently, the front line between Šiauliai and Klaipėda was weakly defended. Furthermore, the panzer divisions that had struggled to make any headway in the two operations had suffered substantial losses, and there was therefore still a chance of pushing through to the Gulf of Riga. On 23 September, Bagramian planned to visit the front line around Jelgava to investigate options, only to receive orders from Moscow: he was to stop all operations to reach the Gulf of Riga. Further orders followed, and it became clear that the axis of attack was to shift to the south and west, with a drive to the Baltic coast at Klaipėda.

In Estonia, after taking Tallinn, the Soviet 8th Army moved on to attack the Estonian islands. Just as in 1941, control of these islands was critical for freedom of movement by naval vessels in the northern Baltic. The three islands of the archipelago – Saaremaa, Hiiumaa and Muhu – were defended by 23rd Infantry Division, supported by a naval anti-aircraft battalion, two naval artillery battalions, and a battalion of assault guns. 218th Infantry Division was also designated to help hold the islands, but would not arrive until 1 October. There were a few skirmishes between Estonian nationalists and the German garrison, but these were swiftly suppressed.

The Soviet forces designated to take the islands, from 8th Army, were the 8th Estonian Rifle Corps and 109th Rifle Corps. The shallow waters around the islands were generally unsuitable for large vessels, and in order to attempt a landing, the assault formations were equipped with DUKW amphibious vehicles, acquired from the United States.

On 29 September, Soviet aircraft made repeated attacks on the German positions on the islands. The first Soviet troops came ashore in Muhu towards the end of the day. Only a small portion of the German force committed to hold the islands was on Muhu, and it withdrew across a causeway to Saaremaa without putting up any significant resistance, destroying the causeway behind it. Next, there were landings on Hiiumaa, on 2 October. This time, the Germans put up strong resistance, but were forced to evacuate the island. An attempt to follow up this success with a landing on Saaremaa two days later, ended in disaster, however, when German naval artillery subjected the beachhead to heavy fire, and an infantry attack then wiped out the landing party.

The following day, the Red Army tried again, sending a strong force from General Pärn's 8th Estonian Rifle Corps ashore. This time, the landings were successful, and Soviet armour followed. On 6 October, the Soviet forces began to advance, and to the west of Kuressaare, two battalions from 23rd Infantry Division found themselves isolated. Elements of the Soviet 249th Rifle Division, many of them Estonians, had partially bypassed the German group when they encountered one of the German battalions late on 8 October. The Germans were attempting to withdraw to the south, and for a brief moment, managed to pass themselves off as a Soviet unit as they marched alongside the Soviet force, but fighting erupted after light cast by flares allowed the Germans to be identified. One battalion of Soviet troops was swiftly overwhelmed, but a second Soviet formation – an anti-tank battalion – had sufficient time to set up a defensive line. In confused, bloody fighting, the German force broke through the Soviet line and managed to withdraw to the south; the other German battalion, retreating south on a parallel route, took advantage of the confused fighting to get through without having to fight. Both sides lost about 300 men, and all who were unfortunate enough to be taken prisoner were shot out of hand.

The Germans were aware that they had little chance of holding the entire island, and had always intended to withdraw to the Sõrve peninsula at the southern tip. They made good use of the defensive positions built by the Red Army prior to 1941, and fought a slow retreat to the peninsula, inflicting heavy losses on 8th Rifle Corps. By 10 October, however, the Germans were confined to the small peninsula. In an attempt to outflank the defensive line across the isthmus at the northern end of the peninsula, the Soviet forces attempted an amphibious landing on 11 October near Löu, midway down the western coast; the operation was spotted in good time by the defenders, and crushed by a combination of artillery fire and an infantry attack against the few men and vehicles who managed to get ashore. A second attempt to land on the peninsula on 12 October was similarly defeated. Nevertheless, 8th Rifle Corps was able to push the Germans perhaps a third of the way south along the peninsula before grinding to a halt.

German naval units started to operate in support of the ground troops on 10 October. The heavy cruiser *Prinz Eugen*, with occasional support from the cruisers *Lützow* and *Admiral Scheer*, repeatedly bombarded targets ashore, their heavy guns striking with great accuracy. On 15 October, when returning through dense fog to her home station of Gotenhafen, the German name for the Polish city of Gdynia, Oberwachtmeister Dammert recalled:

When it was returning from engaging land targets, the *Prinz Eugen* was shaken by a mighty blow in the thick fog.

On the bridge, the initial perception was that the ship had run into a mine. The order to 'Batten down all compartments!' was given by signal bell. The doors and hatches of all the compartments were closed to prevent the damaged cruiser from taking water and sinking.

It soon turned out, however, that the *Prinz Eugen* had rammed the light cruiser *Leipzig* amidships in the vicinity of Hela, close to Gotenhafen.

On that 15 October the crew of *T20* performed beyond the call of duty. The torpedo boat, commanded by Kapitänleutnant Lampe, came upon the site of the collision and was the first to find the damaged ships. The *T20* came up on the *Leipzig* and secured to her undamaged starboard side. The torpedo boat then took part in the towing operation in which the *Leipzig* was towed from the stern to Gotenhafen.

… The following morning I determined from the forecastle that I could see the Baltic Sea *through* the hole in the flank of the *Leipzig*. It was not until afternoon that the *Leipzig* was freed with the help of several tugs and torpedo boats. In the process, the tugs attached several long wire cables to the *Prinz Eugen* …

After our ship had been freed from the *Leipzig* we entered Gotenhafen under our own power. The *Leipzig* had to be towed in. In the harbour we could then examine the damaged bow of the *Prinz Eugen*. Repair of the ship began soon afterward.[55]

Prinz Eugen was unable to operate at sea for several weeks. *Leipzig* was lucky to survive the collision, being sliced open down to her keel by the heavy cruiser's bows.

With such a small area of Saaremaa left in their control, the Germans began to withdraw forces from the island. 218th Infantry Division was evacuated on 13 October, by which time events had progressed elsewhere in the region.

Forced to improvise as a consequence of the collapse of Army Group Centre in the summer, the German High Command demonstrated that it was still capable of mounting complex operations at short notice. Both *Doppelkopf* and *Cäsar* were handicapped by difficult terrain, where strong infantry formations might have been more effective, but in the aftermath of *Bagration*, such forces were very scarce, and were desperately needed to shore up the front elsewhere; 1st Infantry Division, the only infantry formation in 3rd Panzer Army that Raus regarded as being up to standard, had been intended for use in *Doppelkopf*, but had to be deployed further south to protect the East Prussian frontier. *Aster*, the evacuation of Estonia, was planned and executed at very short notice, and surprised both the Soviet and German High Commands in how well it was carried out. Without the rapid redeployment of III SS Panzer Corps to the Riga area, it seems likely that Bagramian would at least have been able to reach Riga, if not take the city, which would have resulted in the probable destruction of 16th and 18th Armies. For the moment, the front line had been salvaged, but the balance of power had shifted irrevocably in favour of the Red Army. The Wehrmacht could only wait to see where the next blow would fall.

Chapter 9

THE ISOLATION OF ARMY GROUP NORTH

The city known to the Germans as Memel and to the Lithuanians as Klaipėda originated after the Teutonic Knights built a castle in the territory of the Curonians, in order to provide a base from which they could subjugate the pagan tribes of the area. Shortly after its creation in 1252, the name of the castle and the town that had grown up around it was reduced from Memelburg to Memel, and this name persisted until 1923, though it was known to the Lithuanians as Caloypede, Klawppeda, or Cleupeda. The name is thought to be related to the terrain around the city, either derived from the words *klaidyti* (obstruct) and *pėda* (foot), referring to the boggy landscape, which was difficult to cross, or perhaps the Curonian *klais* (flat, open, free) and *ped* (ground), referring to the relatively flat area where the original castle was built. Even in the days of the Teutonic Knights, the nature of the terrain probably played a major part in military operations in the area, as well as giving places their names.

The city, and therefore the area around it, was always part of East Prussia, from the time when the state was controlled by the Teutonic Knights to the creation of the Kingdom of Prussia. It therefore became part of Germany in 1871, and its isolated position as the most northerly city of the new nation contributed to its slow industrialisation. The area was home to large numbers of Lithuanians, and a census in 1910 showed that 45 per cent of the nearly 150,000 people living in Memel or the surrounding territory – known as Memelland – regarded Lithuanian as their first language. However, the distribution of the German and Lithuanian populations was not uniform. Within the city itself, Germans were in a substantial majority, while Lithuanians dominated the surrounding countryside.

As has been discussed, there was considerable disagreement about Memelland at the end of the First World War. The Poles wanted the region incorporated into Poland, possibly instead of Danzig, which was to be awarded 'free city' status. Lithuania was firmly against any such arrangement, as it would deprive the country of any major seaport, and give Poland an almost encircling presence around Lithuania. Some, though at first probably only a minority, of ethnic Lithuanians living in the territory, and in the neighbouring area of East Prussia, called for union of the area they knew as 'Lithuania Minor' to be joined to the new state of Lithuania.[1] In view of the conflicting demands, the Treaty of Versailles detached Memelland from Germany and placed it in the care of the League of Nations. Britain was offered the opportunity to manage the territory, but declined, whereupon the French agreed to become administrators. A battalion of French troops arrived in February 1920, and Gabriel Petisné became the head of the new administration.

Negotiations dragged on for several years. Lithuania's claims were hamstrung by the fact that the Western Powers had not actually recognised Lithuania as an independent nation, and there were attempts to try to link together several different issues. In March 1922, the British proposed that the Lithuanians should accept Polish control of Vilnius; in return, the Western Powers would grant Memelland to Lithuania, would recognise the country as an independent state, and would provide financial assistance. Unwilling to concede on the Vilnius question, the Lithuanians rejected this proposal, after which the Western Powers leaned ever more towards a Danzig-like 'free city' status for the region. Faced with such a development, Lithuanian politicians decided to take matters into their own hands.

Although General Silvestras Žukauskas, commander of Lithuania's small army, claimed that his men would be able to disarm the French garrison in as little as a day, the Lithuanians were unwilling to enter into a potential conflict with France, still clinging to the hope that they would be able to establish lasting alliances with the Western Powers. Instead, they turned to the model of Żeligowski's Mutiny, by which Poland had seized Vilnius. At first, it seemed that the plot faced huge obstacles. Although many people within Memelland were ethnically Lithuanian, they had lived under German rule for centuries, and most had even adopted Lutheranism. They tended to regard Catholic Lithuania as a backward, rural country, and were inclined to support 'free city' status. Secret funds were established to promote pro-Lithuanian (and anti-Polish as well as anti-German) propaganda, and slowly the mood of Memellanders began to shift. In Germany, there was widespread acceptance that a return of Memelland to Germany was, at the moment, out of the question, and, concluding that at an unspecified date in the future it would be easier for Germany to recover Memelland from Lithuania than from Poland, the German government made clear to the Lithuanians that Germany would not object to a Lithuanian seizure.

In January 1923, a group calling itself the Supreme Committee for the Salvation of Lithuania Minor declared that Lithuanians in Memelland were being oppressed by foreign powers, and called on the powerful Lithuanian paramilitary organisation *Lietuvos Šaulių Sąjunga* ('Lithuanian Riflemen's Union') to come to the aid of their fellow countrymen. Some 1,000 well-armed volunteers crossed the border and seized control of most of the area, though in Klaipėda itself, Petisné refused to hand over power. There was an exchange of fire on 15 January, which resulted in the deaths of 12 insurgents, two French soldiers and a German policeman. By the time French reinforcements arrived the following day (aboard a Polish ship), the city was under Lithuanian control.

Although the Western Powers deeply disapproved of the Lithuanian action, they were faced with a *fait accompli* in a distant part of Europe, and there was no appetite to spill the blood of their soldiers for such an obscure cause. There continued to be tensions, but a final convention was agreed in 1924, handing the region to Lithuania. Although the convention guaranteed considerable autonomy to Memelland, the German population, who formed 80 per cent of those living within Klaipėda itself, continued to regard themselves as Germans, and wished for reunion with their homeland. The National Socialists first established a branch in the city in 1933, and their strongly nationalist agenda resonated with the German population; the Lithuanian authorities responded by banning the party, and imprisoning its local leadership. Inevitably, this led to protests within Germany, which were exploited by the National Socialists to show that the League of Nations was unable or unwilling to protect Germans in Memelland.

With tensions between Lithuania and Poland continuing, especially in the context of the Vilnius question, there was always a possibility of war between the two countries, and in 1938 the Germans made plans for a seaborne invasion of the territory, supported by land forces in East Prussia, should a conflict break out between Lithuania and Poland. With a resurgent Germany asserting itself aggressively elsewhere, for example in the Sudetenland, the Lithuanian government decided that it was best not to antagonise Hitler, and after Germany presented an 11-point memorandum, Lithuania lifted restrictions on the National Socialist Party, resulting in a huge increase in party membership. Ernst Neumann, the leader of the original National Socialist movement in the territory, was released from prison, and immediately resumed his energetic activities. Many people joined local *Selbstschutz* ('self defence organisation') units, organised in a similar way to the SA in Germany and wearing identical uniforms. During the December elections to the local assembly, pro-German candidates secured 25 of the 29 seats.

It was inevitable that German attention would fall upon this small enclave of 'oppressed' Germans, and in 1939, Berlin demanded the return of Memelland to Germany in an ultimatum delivered verbally by Joachim von Ribbentrop on 20 March to the Lithuanian Foreign Minister, Juozas Urbšys, who was passing through Berlin on his way home from the coronation of Pope Pius XII. Although the only records of this ultimatum to have survived are from the report that Urbšys gave to his colleagues on his return to Kaunas, it seems that Germany threatened military action unless Memelland was returned to German control.[2] The Lithuanian government felt that it had no real choice. The Memelland Assembly was expected to reconvene on 25 March, and was likely to pass a motion calling for return to Germany, and the threat of German military intervention had to be taken seriously, given German conduct in the Sudetenland. The convention that had settled matters in 1924 did not allow Lithuania to reassign sovereignty over the region without the consent of the other signatories of the convention, so the Lithuanians contacted both France and Britain to discuss the matter. Although both Western Powers expressed sympathy for the Lithuanians, neither was prepared to take any steps to support resistance to the German demands.

Hitler set sail for Klaipėda aboard the pocket battleship *Deutschland*, accompanied by the *Admiral Graf Spee*, *Nürnberg*, *Leipzig*, *Köln*, and a fleet of smaller ships. He intended to go ashore on 22 March, but negotiations between Ribbentrop and Urbšys dragged on into the night, leaving Hitler to cope with the throes of seasickness on a windy night at sea. A five-point treaty was finally signed shortly after midnight, and the following day Hitler was able to enter Klaipėda, at the same time that the German 1st Infantry Division, a formation recruited mainly in East Prussia, marched into the city from the south, led by the division mascot, a large dog.

The loss of Memelland was a major blow to Lithuania. Although it formed only 5 per cent of the country's land area, it comprised perhaps a third of Lithuania's industrial base, and over 70 per cent of Lithuania's foreign trade passed through the port. The resulting dependence upon Germany played a major part in local politics in the months that followed.

In the autumn of 1944, war threatened the area once more. Prior to the first isolation of Army Group North, Bagramian had considered a thrust to the Baltic coast at or near Klaipėda, but decided that the risk to the flanks of any such advance was too great; instead, he opted to turn north and push on to the Gulf of Riga. In late September, the western option once more came under active discussion, and

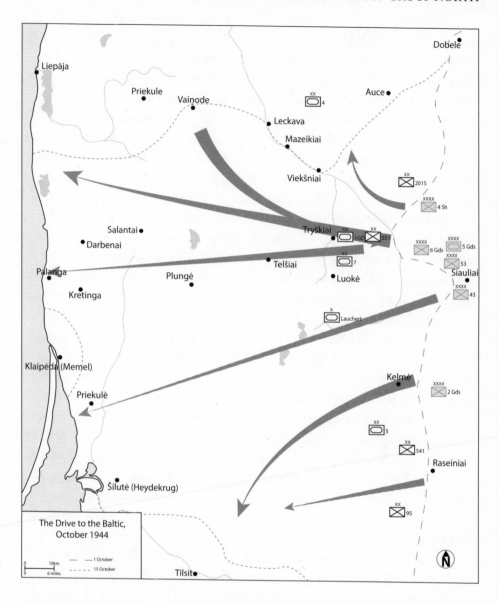

The Drive to the Baltic,
October 1944

Bagramian received new orders on 24 September, that his front was to move the bulk of its forces from the Riga axis to the Klaipėda axis, in order once more to isolate Army Group North. The entire operation was to be prepared in six days, and executed within a further 11 days. At the same time, 2nd and 3rd Baltic Fronts would renew their attacks towards Riga, to tie down as much of Army Group North as possible, far away from Bagramian's axis of advance.[3]

There were several advantages in switching the axis for Bagramian's front. Firstly, STAVKA calculated that this could be achieved faster than German forces could be redeployed; it would therefore be possible for Bagramian to operate in an area with far weaker German units facing his assault formations. Secondly, unlike the heavily contested territory immediately west of Riga, the approaches to Klaipėda had seen no fighting since 1941, and the roads and bridges were therefore in relatively good condition. Thirdly, Memelland was currently part of the Reich, and its capture would be an event of great political significance for the Red Army, particularly with Anglo-American forces approaching the Reich's western frontiers. Nevertheless, the timescale for preparing the operation was daunting, requiring the movement of about half a million men, a thousand tanks, 10,000 guns and mortars, and all their associated supplies, over a distance of up to 120 miles across roads already heavily degraded by the fighting of August and September. In order to release Bagramian's 4th Shock Army and 51st Army from the Riga axis, 2nd Baltic Front would have to move 10th Guards Army and 42nd Army south, and use them to replace 3rd Shock Army and 22nd Army; these latter two would then replace Bagramian's armies outside Riga. And, of course, this had to be achieved without the Germans becoming aware of it.

Bagramian and his army commanders began detailed planning on 25 September. It was decided to mass roughly half of the front's strength on a narrow frontage of only 12 miles, allowing for a concentration of up to 200 guns per kilometre (5/8 mile) of front. 6th Guards Army, with 2nd, 22nd and 23rd Guards Rifle Corps, 103rd Rifle Corps and 19th Tank Corps, would attack across about half the width of the selected sector, aiming to reach the Telšiai-Plungė area within five days. 43rd Army, with 1st, 19th, 90th and 92nd Rifle Corps, would attack alongside, with its axis of advance slightly to the south. 2nd Guards Army, with 11th and 13th Guards Rifle Corps, 44th and 54th Rifle Corps, and 1st Tank Corps, would attack south-west from Šiauliai. 5th Tank Army would be held back as the main exploitation force, intended to be inserted between 6th Guards Army and 43rd Army on the second day to rush on to the Baltic coast. Obukhov's 3rd Guards Mechanised Corps would be held back as front reserve, allowing it a little more time to recover from its losses in the September fighting.

Secrecy was an absolute priority for Bagramian:

As always, we did all we could to keep the attack preparations secret. This time, we laboured to use every opportunity. First, we rigorously restricted the circle of those in the know. We formally struck the word 'attack' from our vocabulary. Everything was carefully planned and executed. This also required well-organised leadership by the staff. General Kurasov [Bagramian's chief of staff] played an outstanding part in this ... in addition, the movement of troops and equipment on all roads during the day was of course forbidden.

This time, we did not rely just upon camouflage, but also sought to mislead the enemy. Generals Malyshev [commander of 4th Shock Army] and Obukhov were ordered to simulate the resumption of the attack on Riga from the south, to strengthen their reconnaissance, to regroup, and to allow trucks to be seen driving to the front. Additional preparation instructions were given via wire communication.

The same happened with General Kreiser in the Jelgava area. We simulated the building of defences at Šiauliai. Obstacles were reinforced, trenches deepened, the network of communication trenches widened.[4]

Despite the best efforts of all his staff, Bagramian had to ask Moscow for more time to prepare for the operation. He was relieved when the start of the attack was delayed to 5 October. On the eve of the attack, the Soviet commanders gathered for a final briefing. They were advised that the Germans had established three lines of defence. The main position consisted of a series of field fortifications over a three-mile depth, with a second line of much deeper positions. Finally, there was a third position, stretching from Tilsit to Klaipėda. Although the assessment of the strength of the main position was perhaps overstated, other observations made by Colonel Klebnikov, Bagramian's intelligence officer, were accurate:

When describing 3rd Panzer Army's dispositions, Colonel Klebnikov described a further peculiarity of the enemy's defences, namely the linear deployment of his forces. All five infantry divisions were in the first defensive line as if along a string. One only had to break through this string with a forceful thrust, and there would be no further cohesion, as there were no strong reserves to the rear. Actually, to the south-west of Šiauliai, in front of the left flank of 43rd Army, armoured troop formations had been detected; the same applied to the seam with 3rd Belarusian Front, where aerial reconnaissance had detected the concentration of considerable infantry forces. As was later determined, these were from *Panzergruppe Lauchert* (about the equivalent of a tank brigade) and 21st Infantry Division.

The main forces of Army Group North were positioned as before in the Riga area and 36km east of the city. General Yeremenko [commander of 2nd Baltic Front] had told me in a telephone conversation that the enemy was ensconced in the strong Riga Positions, which would cost 2nd and 3rd Baltic Fronts considerable efforts and losses to penetrate.

The main danger to us was from the armoured forces south of Riga. Tanks and infantry had been spotted in concentrations on the south-west approaches to the city. These consisted of one panzer division and two infantry divisions, which were in reserve. The breakthrough of 3rd Mechanised Corps in the area that extended 9.5 miles from the southern edge of Riga had forced Schörner to position this strong reserve on the road to the city.

We were particularly pleased to learn from the reconnaissance chief and the commander of 3rd Air Army that the panzer divisions that had given us so many headaches in August and September were as before south-west of Jelgava. It therefore seemed that the Fascists had not noticed our regrouping. If they were now to discover something, it would be too late. Nevertheless, we made some allowances. It was simply impossible to keep the regrouping of an entire Front secret. Apparently, enemy reconnaissance in the first days of October had spotted something. This was probably the reason why Schörner had slowly pulled the panzer divisions back, in order to move them further towards Memel. But this plan came too late.[5]

Raus' 3rd Panzer Army had two corps protecting the western approaches to Klaipėda. Of these, Hans Gollnick's XXVIII Corps was the one that would feel the full weight of Bagramian's attack. Between them, XXVIII Corps and XL Panzer Corps to the south had five infantry divisions, as Bagramian's intelligence had assessed, and they were indeed strung in a very thin line, covering over 120 miles. The division in the path of the main Soviet thrust was 551st Grenadier Division, commanded by Siegfried Verhein. During the course of the coming fighting, like all grenadier divisions, it would be redesignated as a Volksgrenadier division, but despite its grandiose name, it was a weak formation. Its regiments were actually up to strength in numbers, but they had been formed largely from rear area units, personnel transferred to the army from the navy and Luftwaffe, and men previously deemed unfit or too old for front-line service. The division had little experience of war, particularly under the harsh conditions of the Eastern Front, and had had no opportunity to establish the essential cohesion required to survive a Soviet assault. Furthermore, it was defending a sector of 29 miles, leaving its positions hopelessly thin.

German staff officers first considered the possibility of a Soviet attack towards Klaipėda as early as 25 September, but at this stage, it was considered merely as one possible option. There continued to be considerable concerns about a possible Soviet operation once more aimed at reaching the Gulf of Riga. Nevertheless, the arrival of more elements of III SS Panzer Corps from Estonia in the area south of Riga allowed for plans to be made for 4th and 7th Panzer Divisions and *Grossdeutschland* to be moved to protect the approaches to Klaipėda. Hitler continued to fantasise about a renewal of German offensives, and on 28 September Schörner returned from a meeting in Germany with the news that Hitler still wished to attack towards the north-east from Šiauliai, i.e. a resumption of *Doppelkopf.* The reaction of Schörner's subordinates is not known.[6]

German reconnaissance belatedly detected the Soviet preparations, spotting that 6th Guards Army had moved south-west on 29 September. The whereabouts of 5th Guards Tank Army – Bagramian's most powerful force – remained unknown. By the following day, it was clear that an attack was being prepared in the general Raseiniai–Kelmė area, and plans were made to move 7th Panzer Division to this sector. In the meantime, plans were drawn up for a German offensive, codenamed *Blitz,* which would attack north-east from the Raseiniai area, with a view to destroying or at least disrupting Soviet forces that were now known to be gathering in the Šiauliai area. It was planned that forces for this attack would begin to gather at the end of October, with a view to a start date of 3 November. *Grossdeutschland* was alerted to move to XXVIII Corps, and its first elements, a battalion of Tiger tanks and the reconnaissance battalion, set off late on 3 October. The rest of the division would follow as soon as trains could be provided. 5th Panzer Division was also on the move, assigned on 2 October to strengthen the defences of XL Panzer Corps; like *Grossdeutschland,* its redeployment was held up by a shortage of trains. Finally, *Gruppe Lauchert* was sent from its current deployment in the Riga defences to XL Panzer Corps. But, as Bagramian had already concluded, these moves were too late to prevent the Soviet attack from gaining crucial momentum.

Despite Bagramian's preparations, his forces were a long way from recovering from their losses earlier in the year, particularly in terms of infantry. The rifle divisions should have had nearly 12,000 men, but most had barely 7,000, with some as few as 3,000 men. Many of these were barely trained recruits, often forcibly conscripted from the newly liberated areas of the western Soviet Union. Nevertheless, 1st Baltic Front enjoyed a substantial superiority over the German forces it faced, particularly given its concentration on such a narrow front.

5 October dawned with widespread fog, preventing Bagramian from unleashing his considerable air power. Indeed, some of his army commanders wanted to postpone the attack, but aware that 3rd Panzer Army was belatedly moving its armour to counter his own redeployment, Bagramian felt he had to proceed as planned. In any event, by 1100hrs, the fog had lifted sufficiently to allow the Soviet artillery to open fire.

The initial Soviet bombardment was concentrated on the main German battle line over its full depth, for about 20 minutes. Then the infantry assault began. Although there were immediate gains in some sectors, 551st Grenadier Division put up considerable resistance, throwing back the first two waves of attacks in many areas.

The third wave, however, swept the remnants of the division aside. In an attempt to restore the situation, the *Grossdeutschland* reconnaissance battalion was dispatched to the front. Commanded by Rittmeister Schroedter, the battalion encountered a Soviet regiment moving westwards, and launched a swift counter-attack into its flank, throwing it back in confusion. Without pausing, Schroedter moved east to the main battle positions, where he encountered a battlegroup from 551st Grenadier Division, fighting on under the command of Hauptmann Licht. The combined force managed to hold the front line until darkness, but with no contact with friendly units on either flank, and Soviet forces swiftly pressing on to the west, Schroedter ordered a withdrawal.

The first elements of 7th Panzer Division began to go into action against the advancing Red Army. The division's panzer regiment encountered Soviet tanks from 19th Tank Corps, part of Chistiakov's 6th Guards Army, advancing towards the Shisma, a small river several miles behind the original front line. Lacking infantry support, the Germans pulled back to the river, where they were involved in a night action against Soviet tanks and infantry. Whilst the German tanks succeeded in halting the Soviet forces facing them, they found – like the *Grossdeutschland* reconnaissance battalion – that they had been bypassed on either side, and were forced to pull back early on 6 October.

Bagramian was keen to maintain momentum in his attack, and ordered Colonel-General Vasili Timofeevich Volskii's 5th Guards Tank Army, the main exploitation force of the operation, to press forward. At the same time, 4th Shock Army attacked the German line to the north of the main battle area, throwing back the weak 201st Security Division. In an attempt to shore up the security division, elements of III SS Panzer Corps – two battalions of combat engineers, a battalion of artillery and the SS reconnaissance battalion – were deployed in support under the title *Sperrgruppe Schäfer*. Although the German line was slowly forced back, the presence of this small, mobile group prevented any of the Soviet penetrations from developing into complete breakthroughs.[7]

One of the major problems faced by 1st Baltic Front's staff officers was the task of coordinating the movements of so many troops in such a confined area, especially given the relatively primitive nature of the local roads. Chistiakov's 6th Guards Army in particular struggled to bring its second echelon troops forward, and Volskii asked for a delay of a day before his tank army advanced, to prevent his units from becoming entangled with those of the first wave. The roads were choked with supply units struggling to bring ammunition, food and fuel to the infantry and supporting armour that had penetrated the German defences; the factors that had hindered the Germans so much during both *Doppelkopf* and *Cäsar* now proved equally problematic for the Red Army.

At the same time as Bagramian's main assault, 2nd Guards Army opened its attack further south. The Soviet forces included a substantial Latvian contingent:

> The reinforced battalion of 156th Rifle Regiment, from 16th Latvian Rifle Division, advanced particularly briskly. Led by the battalion commander, Captain Belan, the Communists and Komsomol members were the first into the enemy positions and tore through the entire [enemy] unit. The division commander, Colonel Urbšas, exploited this success and set his main force in motion. Lieutenant Colonel Lyssenko attacked Kelmė with his 249th Rifle Regiment. The reconnaissance battalions of the divisions of 11th and 13th Guards Rifle Corps excelled themselves. The 18 year old Komsomol member Michail Yepishkin, from 2nd Guards Rifle Division's battalion, particularly stood out. When they came under fire from high ground, he attacked from the rear with some others of a similar age. In a brief fight, they engaged the Fascists with hand grenades and raised a red flag on the high ground. They called their comrades from the 1st Guards Rifle Regiment forward.
>
> For his heroism, Yepishkin was awarded the title Hero of the Soviet Union.[8]

XL Panzer Corps, responsible for this sector of the front, initially had only a single major formation at its disposal, 548th Grenadier Division, which was as weak as all such new divisions; there was a general view in the Wehrmacht that divisions with numbers greater than 500 were of very limited use, particularly on the Eastern Front. 5th Panzer Division was en route to the area, but to date, only a small portion of its forces had arrived. Gotthard Heinrici, the corps commander, had no option but to order the deployment of these limited forces close to the front line. 5th Panzer Division's anti-aircraft battalion, whose powerful 88mm guns were of particular value as anti-tank weapons, was ordered late on 5 October to deploy to the east of Kelmė, but Hauptmann Braumüller, the battalion commander, left the bulk of his heavy weapons to the west of the town, wishing to prevent them from being overrun in the first phase of any Soviet assault.[9]

By the end of the first day of the attack, Bagramian had good reasons to be satisfied, even if he had not been able to deploy his exploitation forces as fast as he might have wished:

> We drew up the first reckoning. 6th Guards Army and 43rd Army had penetrated between 14 and 17km into the enemy's positions and had widened the breakthrough to 176km ... formations of 6th Guards Army had succeeded in reaching the Tryškiai area, right on the edge of the second defensive line ... Right at the front,

as before, was the 16th Latvian Rifle Division, whose 249th Rifle Regiment had forced the Krozenka and had secured the Šiauliai–Kelmė road.[10]

Interrogation of prisoners by the advancing Soviet units identified the presence of 5th and 7th Panzer Divisions and *Grossdeutschland*, and on 6 October, 2nd and 3rd Baltic Fronts renewed their attacks towards Riga, to prevent Schörner from moving more forces to intercept the Soviet drive to the coast. Although the German defences around the Latvian capital continued to hold firm, the bulk of 16th and 18th Armies remained tied down, unable to release forces for the major battle that was now raging to the west. Volskii's 5th Guards Tank Army was finally released to push on to the Baltic coast, and by mid-afternoon reached the town of Ubiške, where well-positioned German anti-tank guns took advantage of swampy ground to stop the Soviet advance, much as Soviet defenders had done against *Doppelkopf*. After a brief discussion with Bagramian, Volskii turned his spearheads south to bypass the German position. At Luokė, they encountered *Kampfgruppe Fabisch* from *Grossdeutschland*, freshly arrived from the north. The German force was able to repulse the Soviet forces, but these were merely the tip of the spearhead. The bulk of the Soviet armour merely bypassed the German unit and drove on towards the west.[11]

Other German formations were also being moved to deal with the new threat. On 6 October, 4th Panzer Division was ordered to move its Panther battalion, with a reconnaissance company and a battalion of combat engineers, to the village of Viekšniai, in order to counter the thrust of 4th Shock Army. XXXIX Panzer Corps dispatched whatever rear area units it could scrape together to try to build a new front line facing south, but speed was of the essence. When the battlegroup from 4th Panzer Division reached Viekšniai, it found the area already occupied by Soviet forces, mainly from 119th Rifle Division. According to 4th Panzer Division's unit history, the battlegroup swiftly retook the village.[12] Bagramian gives a different account, in which the Germans suffered substantial losses as they attempted to penetrate into 119th Rifle Division's artillery positions.[13] The outcome of both accounts was the same: the Soviet attempt to advance through Viekšniai was brought to an abrupt halt.

In the south, the Soviet forces, with 1st Tank Corps now in the lead supporting the Latvians and the 3rd Guards Rifle Division, swept past the flanks of Braumüller's anti-aircraft formations, mainly to the north, and bypassed Kelmė. As they passed to the west, they overran Braumüller's guns almost before they could go into action. Four Soviet tanks were destroyed at close range, but ten guns were lost. More elements of 5th Panzer Division had arrived overnight, but the division's panzer regiment could field only 15 Panthers and 12 Pz.IV. With this small force and the bulk of the division's 14th Panzergrenadier Regiment, Oberst Herzog, commander of the division's panzer regiment, launched a counter-attack into the southern flank of the Soviet forces streaming to the west. The German battlegroup claimed to have destroyed 26 Soviet tanks, but was unable to close the gap to *Gruppe Lauchert*, about six miles to the north. 1st Tank Corps continued to drive west, with 5th Panzer Division's reconnaissance battalion attempting to keep up with it on its southern flank. By the end of the day, the German division was strung out over about 12 miles, and Karl Decker, the division commander, gave up the unequal struggle, ordering his men to make contact with 548th Grenadier Division to the south-east. Even if he had been able to concentrate his division's fighting strength, the absence of the vital supply elements left his men desperately short of fuel and ammunition.[14]

The weather became overcast and rainy on 7 October, but this was not sufficient to prevent Bagramian's air support from operating. With more elements of *Grossdeutschland* and 7th Panzer Division arriving overnight, XXVIII Corps attempted to build on the check achieved at Ubiške, by establishing a new front line stretching to Tryškiai. The retreating remnants of 551st Grenadier Division were incorporated into the line, but the southern flank of the position had already been turned by Volskii's deviation, and the Germans were forced to pull back further. Bagramian, who was already impatient with Volskii's slow rate of advance, continued to harangue his subordinate to get his tanks moving faster, but even without the full weight of 5th Guards Tank Army, the Soviet forces continued to put huge pressure on the Germans. *Gruppe Fabisch*, consisting of a battalion of panzergrenadiers supported by a few assault guns and an artillery battalion, was joined in Luokė by a substantial part of 7th Panzer Division's panzer regiment, as well as perhaps a battalion or more of stragglers from 551st Grenadier Division. The tanks were deployed on the southern flank of the German position, and as a group of Panthers advanced in a local counter-attack, they came under heavy fire from their southern flank, suffering several losses.[15] Soviet artillery fire on Luokė steadily grew heavier, with a salvo of Katyusha rockets causing terrible casualties when the *Grossdeutschland* field dressing station was hit.

Soviet infantry began to penetrate into the village, and with Soviet armour from Malakov's 19th Tank Corps already bypassing the position to the south, the German forces were ordered to withdraw. As they withdrew, the tanks of 7th Panzer Division attempted to take as many infantry with them as they could, but suddenly found themselves under intense small-arms fire. Partially surrounded, they fought their way clear, though most of the infantry riding on the tanks were killed. As they broke out of the encirclement, one of the tanks slipped into a ditch full of German soldiers attempting to take cover. Unaware of the presence of the infantry, the tank driver continued to drive on, and the crew of the following tank could only watch in horror as the soldiers trapped in the trench were literally torn apart by the tank's tracks.[16] As they pulled back towards Klaipėda, the German tanks could do nothing to prevent the Soviet 19th Tank Corps from driving through open space on their southern flank.

The defences at Luokė were swiftly overwhelmed. A panzergrenadier battalion from *Grossdeutschland* failed to receive the order to withdraw at the same moment as the other units, and was encircled. Late on 7 October, the battalion succeeded in breaking through to the west, leaving much of its heavy equipment behind. Another battalion from the division encountered a battalion of T34s from 19th Tank Corps. After an initial probing attack, the Soviet battalion, commanded by Major Pissariev, bypassed the town to the north before turning back and attacking from the north-west. The Soviet tanks inflicted heavy losses on the German forces, but the arrival of a group of German assault guns allowed the panzergrenadiers to rally on the western outskirts, where they were able to prevent a further Soviet advance.[17] Several Tiger tanks from *Grossdeutschland* also found themselves isolated, but adopted all-round defence until dusk, when they were able to drive through the Soviet lines without incident and reach German lines.

On the southern flank of the Soviet operation, 39th Army from the neighbouring 3rd Belarusian Front joined in the attack. Facing it was 95th Infantry Division, which had almost been completely destroyed during *Bagration*. Although its ranks had been filled with replacements, many of these were of a similar calibre to the men used to create the new grenadier divisions. Survivors of 197th and 256th Infantry Divisions had also been incorporated into the division, but there had been no time for training and other exercises that would have allowed the disparate units to bed down together. The division's left flank gave way almost immediately, and 39th Army's leading elements rampaged through the division's artillery positions. The rest of the division fell back in disorder, with no contact with friendly forces on either flank. For Decker's 5th Panzer Division, this was a singularly unwelcome development, requiring the panzer division to spread its forces even more thinly in an attempt to provide some sort of screen along the southern flank of the Soviet breakthrough.

Despite these successes, Bagramian continued to fret about Volskii's apparent lack of urgency. He had further cause for concern on 8 October, when the weather turned much wetter, making many areas swampy and therefore further hindering armoured movement. Chistiakov's 6th Guards Army reported increasingly strong German counter-attacks on its right-hand formation, 22nd Guards Rifle Corps, at Mazeikiai. A little to the south, 29th Tank Corps, part of Volskii's 5th Guards Tank Army, finally joined the advance, swiftly capturing first Telšiai and then Plungė. But 3rd Guards

Tank Corps, part of the same army, continued to be held up some distance from the front by heavily congested roads, and Bagramian once more berated Volskii for not moving forward faster. Nevertheless, by the end of the day, Bagramian's leading formations were fast approaching the third line of German defences that 1st Baltic Front had identified at the outset of the operation.

These defences ran broadly along the Reich frontier, and had been given the grand title 'East Prussian Defence Position'. The line of fortifications had been created by Erich Koch, *Gauleiter* – Party chief – of East Prussia, in his role as Reich Defence Commissar. Although Koch spent a great deal of time and energy on the fortifications, whose construction was overseen by Kurt Knuth, one of his subordinates, the defence position left much to be desired. Originally, the intention had been that the positioning of fortifications would be directed by local army commanders, and that the National Socialist Party's role would be merely to provide manpower and resources, but there was a lack of engineering officers to oversee the task, with the result that the political aspect of the fortifications assumed a greater degree of importance than their military value. Many fortifications were badly positioned, and although Koch was able to announce that the first month of construction saw the completion of nearly around 14,000 miles of trenches and the excavation of over 41 million tons of earth, many of these trenches were too shallow to be of any major military value. Koch also had a bad reputation for using every opportunity to benefit his own supporters, and the construction of the East Prussian Defence Position was no exception. One of his subordinates was 'General' Fiedler, who had been a senior officer in the fire service in East Prussia. He was the owner of a cement works, and persuaded Koch to authorise the manufacture of large numbers of so-called 'Koch-pots', which consisted of a concrete tube with a hinged metal lid. These were buried upright in the ground, and were designed to be manned by a single soldier, who would hide in the pot until a Soviet tank was close enough to be engaged with a *Panzerfaust*. Soldiers regarded them with contempt, as the concrete from which they were manufactured was prone to fragmentation if hit by small-arms fire, and any soldier inside the one-man fortification felt isolated and alone. The diversion of so much concrete meant that there was much less available for use in other fortifications, which might have been of greater military value.[18]

It is not clear how much Bagramian knew about the true nature of these defences; perhaps veering on the side of caution, he decided that rupturing the line before the retreating German units could deploy along them was a high priority, hence his constant urging of his front-line units to continue the pace of their attack. Late on 8 October, he received a gratifying report from Chistiakov: 79th Tank Brigade, part of

19th Tank Corps, had captured the German airfield at Vaiṇode, only 25 miles from the Baltic coast. Further south, the spearheads of the Soviet advance were less than 12 miles from Klaipėda. Less impressive was the news from Volskii's 5th Guards Tank Army. The bulk of its forces appeared to be stopped along the line of the River Minija. An increasingly irritated Bagramian demanded that Volskii should at least attempt to bypass the German defences, and then press on to the Baltic coastline; he gave a deadline of midday on 10 October for the completion of this order.[19]

The southern axis of the Soviet advance was making good progress. 5th Panzer Division was forced to dispatch its reconnaissance battalion to deal with a deep penetration by Soviet forces in the lines of 548th Grenadier Division, and then late on 8 October, orders arrived for the division to fall back to the East Prussian Defence Position in order to prevent Soviet forces from breaking through to Tilsit. As an officer of the division recalled, this was no simple task:

> What such a move entailed, with complete enemy air superiority, enemy tanks that had already broken through, and columns of refugees on the retreat roads, can barely be described.[20]

The evacuation of the civilian population in the face of the Soviet advance was something that had been discussed repeatedly as the front line approached German territory. There were many Germans living in south-west Lithuania, even outside the boundaries of Memelland, and many of the Lithuanian residents of the region were also not enthusiastic about the return of Soviet rule; despite the bitter disappointment of German occupation, they remembered the previous Soviet occupation as being even worse. Any evacuation would fall under the remit of the local Party structure, and whilst the Party had been energetic in demanding that the Wehrmacht turned over territory to its control in the victorious years, there was huge reluctance to reverse the process as the Wehrmacht retreated. Had the military been given control of the area to their rear, they would have been in a position to order a timely evacuation, but for the moment, everything behind the immediate front line remained firmly under Party control. In any event, on 5 October, as the Soviet attack began, Schörner announced that there was no requirement for any evacuation. Raus, who was perhaps less devout in his adherence to Hitler's doctrines than his superior, disagreed with this policy, and immediately urged Party officials to organise an evacuation. At first in a trickle, then in an increasingly disorganised flood, refugees began to struggle towards East Prussia, heavily burdened with hopeless quantities of baggage. Many such columns were overrun by the advancing Red Army, while others greatly hindered the movements of the Wehrmacht. Only in Klaipėda itself – which had the highest density of German citizens in the entire zone affected by the fighting – was the evacuation conducted in a timely and relatively efficient manner.

The hasty redeployment of German formations now began to have its inevitable effect. Priority had naturally been given to the combat elements of the panzer divisions and *Grossdeutschland*, but as the fighting vehicles began to run out of fuel and ammunition, the need for their supply elements became increasingly vital. By the end of 8 October, the Tiger tank battalion of *Grossdeutschland* was forced to abandon several tanks – more than had been lost as a result of the fighting with the Red Army. Nevertheless, *Grossdeutschland* continued to be one of the few units putting up strong resistance to the Soviet advance. It reorganised into three battlegroups – *Kampfgruppe Schwarzrock*, *Kampfgruppe von Breese*, and a third built around the reconnaissance battalion – and attempted to hold positions along the Minija and around Kretinga and Salantai. *Kampfgruppe von Breese* suffered heavy losses in an encounter with advancing Soviet armour from Volskii's tank army, and then pulled back to Kretinga. Here, they found that their road crossed a bridge over the railway, where a train was burning after being hit by an air raid. Some of the wagons were laden with ammunition, and there were a few nervous moments as the battlegroup crossed the bridge, still under aerial bombardment.[21]

A combination of increasing German resistance and lengthening Soviet supply lines began to slow the advance of 1st Baltic Front. Near Vainode, 51st Guards Rifle Division, part of Chistiakov's 6th Guards Army, found itself under heavy counter-attack, which it beat off with difficulty. 43rd Army, aiming to reach the coast to the south of Klaipėda, continued to make good progress with its eight rifle divisions, as did 2nd Guards Army, with 1st Tank Corps, 3rd Guards Rifle Division and 16th Latvian Rifle Division in the lead. By the end of 9 October, its spearheads had penetrated the first positions of the East Prussian Defence Position, even before 5th Panzer Division could occupy the defences. With Soviet forces advancing freely on either flank, the German division abandoned attempts to defend an extended front line, and pulled back towards Tilsit. To the west, the town of Šilutė, known to the Germans as Heydekrug, was captured by the Red Army before many of its civilians had left. Much of the local population fled to the coast immediately to the north. Here, protected by a paper-thin screen of *ad hoc* German units, they waited in fear while German engineers ferried them across to the Kurische Nehrung, the narrow line of sand dunes about six miles off the coast. Fortunately for them, the Soviet forces made little attempt to destroy the small enclave, which was evacuated over five days. Many of the residents of Priekulė were caught by the leading Soviet elements before they could leave, and the survivors who reached the pocket on the coast brought terrifying tales of rape and murder.

Late on 9 October, Bagramian finally received word from Volskii. A shortage of fuel, he wrote, was preventing him from advancing. General Nikolai Papivin, commander of 3rd Air Army, advised that he had transport aircraft available, and fuel was immediately flown out to the armoured spearheads. Finally, Volskii confirmed that all was ready for a final push to the coast on 10 October.[22] On the northern flank of the advance, Soviet forces bypassed the German battlegroup in Viekšniai, and only a determined counter-attack by the Panther tanks, supported by a company of panzergrenadiers, salvaged the situation. A little to the west, other Soviet forces attempted to secure crossings over the River Venta, and the heavy Tiger tanks of *Schwere Panzer Abteilung 510* went into action near Mazeikiai. Reinforced by *Sperrgruppe Schäfer* from III SS Panzer Corps, the Tigers, supported by a battalion of 4th Panzer Division's panzergrenadiers, fought their way along the road from Mazeikiai to Viekšniai, eliminating three more Soviet bridgeheads. Interrogation of Soviet prisoners suggested that elements of at least three Soviet divisions had been involved. Other elements of 4th Panzer Division moved to secure Leckava; an attempt to advance onto the left bank of the Venta and push west failed in the face of Soviet anti-tank defences, but contact was established with 61st Infantry Division, which was deploying to the north-west.[23] The German line along the northern side of the Soviet breakthrough was therefore stabilising, but the westward advance of Bagramian's armies seemed unstoppable. Here, it seemed the further they advanced, the greater the impact of their success on the Germans:

The rhythm of the battle meant that the enemy was greatly demoralised on the main axis of our thrust. One particularly noticed this in the prisoners, whose numbers grew from day to day. They were dismayed, willingly gave information, and repeatedly exclaimed, '*Hitler kaput!*' How little they resembled those who I had seen in the first days of the war in the Ukraine!

The enemy's line of retreat resembled a huge cemetery. Everywhere there were tanks, guns, trucks – and bodies. Even the soldiers, who had seen and experienced so much before, found these scenes gruesome. But it was the right punishment for the crimes committed by the Fascists![24]

From the very start of the war between Germany and the Soviet Union, the brutality of the fighting exceeded that of any other European theatre. The Soviet Union was not a signatory to the Hague Conventions, and from the outset of the war, Hitler had urged his troops to show no mercy to the conquered. Millions of Soviet citizens died during the German occupation, some as a result of acts of violence and others as the inevitable consequence of starvation after German occupation authorities seized food and shipped it back to Germany. Many Soviet regiments had a policy of sharing their stories of family members who had died during the war, and the appetite for revenge was therefore strong, from the lowest infantryman to the highest general. Throughout the long campaigns, both sides showed great inconsistency in the treatment of those taken prisoner, often executing them out of hand. Soviet soldiers were also often used as slave labour or – in the early phases of the war, before worker shortages forced Germany to rethink its policies – deliberately starved. Whilst food supplies for German soldiers taken prisoner by the Red Army were also hopelessly inadequate, this reflected the general shortage of food throughout the Soviet Union; many Soviet citizens received little better.

10 October would prove to be the decisive day of the campaign. After a heavy artillery bombardment, the tanks of 5th Guards Tank Army finally surged forward. 29th Tank Corps reached and took Kretinga in a pincer attack from north and south. To the north of Kretinga, in Dimitravas and Darbėnai, there were work camps full of concentration camp prisoners. It was normal policy for the SS to evacuate such camps before the arrival of Soviet soldiers, and if such an evacuation were impossible, the inmates of the camps were often simply shot. On this occasion, the speed of the Soviet advance appears to have made any such measures impossible. The sight of so many malnourished prisoners shocked many of the battle-hardened Soviet soldiers, further feeding the implacable desire for revenge.[25]

The Soviet 3rd Guards Tank Corps found itself heavily engaged with the retreating battlegroups of *Grossdeutschland*. Fighting continued all day as the battlegroups conducted a fighting withdrawal, slowly falling back through Plikiai towards Klaipėda. Elements of 31st Tank Brigade pushed on and reached the Baltic coast near Palanga, effectively severing the link between the German 16th and 18th Armies and the rest of the Reich. In a gesture that would be repeated several times as Soviet forces pushed to the Baltic coast in the closing months of the war, the soldiers marked their arrival by filling water bottles with sea water and sending them back to higher commands.[26] Elsewhere, Beloborodov's 43rd Army approached Klaipėda from the south-east, and despite increasing German resistance, succeeded in reaching the coast south of the city. The initial aim of the Soviet operation – to separate Army Group North from the Reich, and to isolate Klaipėda – had been achieved in only six days.

The contrast between the various offensives mounted by both sides in such a short time is striking. *Doppelkopf*, the German attack to restore contact with Army

Group North, was launched after several panzer divisions – all of them weakened by losses – were assembled in western Lithuania and Latvia, and although contact along the Baltic coast was achieved, the main drive towards Jelgava was blocked. Similarly, Bagramian's attempts to batter into Riga from the south and south-west also failed in the face of determined resistance. Both operations were conducted on fairly confined battlefields, where the defenders were able to anticipate the coming attack. The terrain favoured the defenders, and the attacking formations were unable to manoeuvre around the prepared positions. By contrast, the successful drive to Klaipėda was on a much larger battlefield, and over terrain more suitable for mobile warfare. Also, unlike the two previous operations, a successful defence would have required a substantial redeployment of forces. The Germans lacked the troops to prepare strong defensive positions along their entire front, and although the area chosen for the operation was a fairly obvious one, the Red Army successfully masked its preparations until it was too late for the Germans to respond in a timely manner. The use of infantry-rich formations to achieve the initial breakthrough was also a 'luxury' that was not available to the Germans during *Doppelkopf*, after their catastrophic losses as a result of *Bagration*. In both *Doppelkopf* and *Cäsar*, the panzer divisions were required both to break the Soviet defensive line and then to exploit the resultant breaches if they appeared; by contrast, Bagramian massed sufficient forces to ensure that even though his main exploitation force – 5th Guards Army, commanded by the hapless Volskii – failed to make a significant impact until the operation was almost over, the Germans could not hold back the forces committed to the original breakthrough.

Now that Klaipėda was isolated by land, and Army Group North was trapped in western Latvia, Bagramian ordered his army commanders to prepare for what he expected would be the inevitable German counter-attacks. He anticipated an operation from Army Group North, using troops released by the steady German withdrawal through Riga, aimed at restoring contact between Army Group North and the Reich. To this end, 5th Guards Tank Army was ordered to withdraw from the front line, so that it could be held in reserve to deal with any German attacks. At the same time, there was the threat of a German attack from East Prussia, where 3rd Baltic Front's 39th Army was withdrawn in preparation for an offensive by Cherniakhovsky's front into East Prussia. On 12 October, Chanchibatse's 2nd Guards Army reported that the 16th Latvian Rifle Division had come under attack by a unit not previously identified in the battle, the *Fallschirm* (parachute) *Panzer Division Hermann Goering*. This division – nominally part of the Luftwaffe – had been sent to the area from central Poland, and to Bagramian's relief, its initial attack on the Latvian division was beaten off.[27] Bitter fighting raged for another day; German and Soviet accounts attempt to portray their own role in the fighting as a defensive success, and it seems that neither side was able to make any significant headway as the front slowly stabilised along the line of the River Niemen.

Bagramian's assessment of German intentions was correct: as early as 9 October, Schörner proposed a counter-attack from western Latvia towards Klaipėda and from there towards East Prussia. However, this attack was contingent on Hitler agreeing to the evacuation of Riga, in order to release sufficient forces for the operation. As was often the case, Hitler agreed to such a proposal from one of his favoured commanders, where he would have refused to yield an inch if another army group commander had made such a request. By this stage, much of Riga was within artillery range of the Red Army, and the only relatively safe route from the area east of the city into Courland was along the beach road. The withdrawal from Riga was codenamed *Donner* ('Thunder'), and with 227th Infantry Division forming a rearguard, Schörner's troops conducted an orderly withdrawal through the city, destroying the bridges over the Daugava as they fell back. The men of the 19th SS Waffen-Grenadier Division must have experienced particularly bitter moments as they pulled back, crossing the Daugava to the south of Riga; they had continued their hard-fought retreat across their homeland, almost constantly in contact with the Red Army. The battles a few miles to the east of Sigulda, holding what became known as the Segewold Positions while German units further north pulled back from the Estonian border, were remembered by Latvian veterans as particularly bloody.[28] By 13 October, most of the Latvian capital was under Soviet control. Shortly thereafter, the 3rd Baltic Front was disbanded.

Whilst he prepared to repulse the expected German counter-attack, Bagramian wanted to maintain pressure on the two trapped German armies:

> It seemed to me at the time that it was important in this situation that the formations of Army Group North retreating from the fortified area around Riga should be followed by 2nd and 3rd Baltic Fronts without regrouping or any pause in the attack in order to prevent their unhindered retreat. One had to inflict a defeat on them, as the Fascists would take up strong defensive positions in the woody and swampy terrain of Courland and would be able to save themselves from our blows. It was vital to make maximum use of the dry time of year for a concerted attack to destroy the enemy's forces in Courland with the combined power and resources of the Baltic Fronts and the Baltic Fleet before the wet season typical of the Baltic region arrived.[29]

The dissolution of 3rd Baltic Front, with some of its forces being withdrawn into strategic reserve, was therefore not welcome news to Bagramian. Nevertheless, he made a bid to capture the vital port of Liepāja, on the west coast of Courland. Originally developed as a base for the Czarist navy, the port – known to Germans as Libau – was vital if the forces in Courland were to survive; the port of Ventspils, further north, was too small to support the two trapped armies. Chistiakov was therefore ordered to send forces north in an attempt to secure Liepāja before the German line could solidify. In an attempt to counter this, Schörner dispatched III SS Panzer Corps to the area around Priekule. Late on 12 October, Chistiakov's army penetrated through dense woodland immediately to the north of Skuodas, and *SS Panzergrenadier Brigade Nederland* rushed two battalions to the area. Combining with elements of 11th Infantry Division, the SS mobile forces succeeded in surrounding the Soviet troops that had broken through, and over the next two days reduced the pocket. A little to the west, 4th Panzer Division had been joined by 12th Panzer Division on its western flank, and on the same day that Chistiakov attempted to push through to Liepāja, the two German divisions launched an attack to clear the woodland to the south of the River Venta. Two days of heavy fighting followed, with the divisions making slow but steady progress; the terrain was every bit as difficult as that encountered during *Doppelkopf*, but the Soviet defences were less well organised, and by the end of 13 October, with their reserves still not committed, the German divisions were confident that they would be able to build momentum in the coming day, particularly as they had cleared almost all of the woodland that so favoured the defenders.

Chistiakov had not abandoned his attempts to drive into Courland, if only to disrupt German plans, and on 13 October, his forces breached the lines of 61st Infantry Division, midway between the two German panzer divisions and III SS Panzer Corps. 4th and 12th Panzer Divisions were ordered to stop their attack. 225th Infantry Division would relieve them, allowing them to be pulled out of line in preparation for Schörner's planned counter-attack towards Klaipėda. Bagramian's estimate of the forces available was substantial: he later wrote that Schörner had no fewer than seven or eight panzer or panzergrenadier divisions at his disposal. The truth was that Army Group North had 4th, 12th, and 14th Panzer Divisions, together with the few remaining armoured formations of III SS Panzer Corps.

In Berlin, Heinz Guderian, Chief of Staff at OKH, made the first of several requests to Hitler for the evacuation of Army Group North. The divisions of 16th and 18th Armies, he argued, had been badly weakened during the fighting of 1944, but retained a solid core of experienced soldiers. These forces could be used to bolster the fragile front line that ran along the borders of East Prussia and into Poland and beyond. Bagramian and his colleagues also expected such a move, but Hitler refused. Courland was to be held at all costs, he maintained. Its evacuation would weaken the resolve of the Baltic soldiers serving in the SS, and the territory could serve as a springboard for future offensive operations against the Red Army. The professional soldiers of the Wehrmacht – and indeed of the Red Army – could not comprehend how the occupation of Courland by so many German divisions could be justified on the grounds of improving the fighting spirit of one Estonian and two Latvian divisions, and talk of future offensive operations was, in every sense of the word, incredible. However, Bagramian recorded that the Germans would have struggled to make sufficient shipping available for an evacuation, and this is probably true. Although the success of the German navy and merchant marine in rescuing hundreds of thousands of Germans from East and West Prussia in 1945 might suggest otherwise, there would have been little military advantage in evacuating the personnel of Army Group North without their equipment, and there simply was not sufficient shipping for such a massive undertaking. An evacuation would have been difficult and time-consuming, especially given Soviet air superiority, and the likelihood of substantial losses at sea. Furthermore, it is likely that Soviet forces facing the Courland 'bridgehead' would either have overwhelmed the German front as German troops were withdrawn, or would have been able to move to the Eastern Front faster than their German counterparts could be redeployed via a seaborne evacuation.

4th Panzer Division was assembling in the area immediately north of Priekule, in preparation for a major attack to restore contact between Army Group North and the rest of the Wehrmacht. The new assault would be close to the coast; this would allow German naval units to offer support, and was also the shortest possible path for such an assault. The operation, codenamed *Geier* ('Vulture'), would involve all three of the panzer divisions trapped in Courland, with 4th Panzer Division close to the coast, 14th Panzer Division operating alongside, and 12th Panzer Division as a second echelon. With support from 126th, 87th and 11th Infantry Divisions, the panzer divisions would first thrust to Klaipėda, and from there would push on to East Prussia. But even as detailed planning for the operation began, Chistiakov continued to put pressure on the German lines. On 15 October, in the sector held by VI SS Corps, 19th SS Waffen-Grenadier Division (1st Latvian) experienced a heavy artillery bombardment, followed by a determined thrust to the north of Dobele. The following day, after another heavy artillery preparation, an assault was made in III SS Panzer Corps' area against the segment of front held by *Nordland* and 30th Infantry Division, to the east of Priekule. Immediately, a deep penetration was achieved, forcing Schörner to commit 4th Panzer Division to restore the situation. Early on 17 October, the division's artillery fired in support of *Nordland* and 30th Infantry Division, but the division diary suggests that III SS Panzer Corps had restored the situation sufficiently to require minimal further assistance.[30] Fighting continued for several days, with no significant ground being gained by either side. Over a week of heavy fighting resulted in the Red Army advancing no more than a mile, on a front of about six miles, for disproportionately heavy losses.

The tardy advance of 5th Guards Tank Army was one of the few areas of concern for the Red Army High Command. Vasily Timofeevich Volskii, who had taken command of the army after Rotmistrov was demoted earlier in the year, was suffering from tuberculosis, and although he remained with his army through the winter, he was hospitalised in early 1945. He died the following year; it is not clear how much his illness affected his ability to command his formations.

To the rear of the front line, the Soviets set about restoring their control of the Baltic States. Bagramian regarded the moment as a happy one:

Lithuania, Latvia and Estonia, which had had to suffer under the yoke of the Fascist invaders for over three years, were once more free and independent, and returned to the family of Socialist Soviet Republics ... the members of the 16th Latvian Rifle Division, 130th Lithuanian Rifle Corps and 8th Estonian Rifle Corps fought on their home soil with great enthusiasm and unsurpassed courage.

The workers of the Baltics, who had fought against the Fascist invaders for three years, made a great contribution to our victory. The most active form of their fight was the deployment of partisans and the patriotic underground organisations, at whose spearheads were the national staffs of the partisan movement. The central committees of the Communist Parties of Latvia, Lithuania and Estonia and their First Secretaries A.J. Sniečkus, J.E. Kalnberzin and N.G. Karotamm led the work of these staffs. Day and night they deployed their numerous partisan battalions and brigades in combat against the enemy. The entire land knew I. Sudmalis, the courageous leader of the Riga underground movement, the fearless Latvian patriot M. Melnikaitė and E. Aartee, the commander of the Estonian partisans. Partisans and army personnel of many nations had fought in the Baltics. This showed the unity and friendship of our people, the unifying Soviet patriotism and the vitality of the socialist order.[31]

As has been discussed, partisan activities in the three Baltic States were actually fairly minimal, and in the main were carried out by Russians rather than Lithuanians, Latvians or Estonians. Imants Sudmalis had been an active member of the Latvian Communist Party before the war and was arrested several times during the 1930s; he fled his homeland in 1941, fighting with Belarusian partisans before his clandestine return to Latvia in 1942. He was captured in early 1944, and executed in May; although Soviet sources credit him with organising substantial partisan forces, there is little objective evidence for the efficacy of these units. Marytė Melnikaitė was only 17 when the Red Army first occupied Latvia, but she too left her homeland in 1941, returning in 1943; she was almost immediately wounded and captured during an encounter with German anti-partisan units, and subsequently executed. Although Aartee was an Estonian who fought as a partisan against the Germans, this was mainly to the east of the Estonian–Soviet frontier.

For many – perhaps most – Baltic citizens, reality was somewhat different from Bagramian's view. An early consequence of the arrival of the Red Army in the Baltic States was a wave of summary executions. In Lithuania, between 400 and 700 people were summarily shot in Kaunas, Zarasai and Šiauliai without any legal process.[32] Another early impact of Soviet rule that was felt in all three Baltic States was forcible mobilisation of manpower for the Red Army. Many of these recruits, particularly those who had deserted from the various SS or police formations raised by the Germans, were deployed in the first waves of attacks without weapons, in order to draw German fire.[33] Estonia saw a call-up of all men aged between 18 and 33 in August 1944, even while fighting continued on Estonian territory. Partly due to the ongoing combat, but more due to the unwillingness of Estonians to answer the call-up, it was repeated in March 1945. As with forcible recruits from Latvia and Lithuania, those who claimed to have had no involvement with the German occupiers were sent to serve in the ongoing war against German forces in Courland, while those who had performed 'non-armed' service for the Germans were instead used as forced labour. Whilst this was onerous, it was less likely to result in death, resulting in more and more men claiming 'non-armed' service for the German authorities. At the end of their forced labour, this declaration came back to haunt some of them, when they were labelled as war criminals and dispatched to Siberia.

Many Latvians, Lithuanians and Estonians had their first experiences of the return of Soviet rule at the hands of the Red Army. As was the case in the eastern provinces of Germany, rapes were frequent and widespread, especially after the better trained and better disciplined first wave of Soviet troops had moved on. It was commonplace for Soviet soldiers to treat all Baltic citizens as 'fascists', which served to accentuate a deep-seated Russian belief in their superiority over those who were from the Baltic States. This attitude even extended to children, who were labelled as 'fascist children' and treated badly as a result.[34]

The assertion of Soviet control over every aspect of the Baltic States commenced almost as soon as the territory had been cleared by the Red Army. In the eastern parts of Latvia and Lithuania, the resumption of Soviet policies from 1940 was already underway by the time that Riga was abandoned by the Wehrmacht. Soviet organisations and administrative structures were once more imposed, and were dominated by non-Baltic citizens; even by the end of 1945, ethnic Latvians made up only 35 per cent of the Latvian Communist Party.[35] Nevertheless, assertion of Soviet control was often hampered by a shortage of suitable personnel to take policies forward. In Tallinn, a visiting group of western journalists found little enthusiasm for Soviet rule in late 1944:

> The Estonians, it soon became evident, despised and feared the Russians ... I don't think a single one of us spoke to a single person during the whole trip who had a good word to say for the Russian re-occupation – except, of course, the spokesmen produced by the Russians.[36]

Deportations of elements of the population began almost immediately, and continued for eight years. By 1953, Latvia alone had lost 100,000 citizens as a result of deportations, perhaps 10 per cent of the pre-war Latvian population. To this figure should be added some 330,000 deportees from Lithuania, and about 100,000 from Estonia. In addition to those regarded as having collaborated with German rule – and this included even low-ranking officials in most parts of the civilian administration – the same categories that had been targeted in the pre-war deportations were once more selected. Those who had in some way collaborated with the Germans were labelled 'war criminals', while those who were thought to be Baltic nationalists were regarded as 'enemies of the people'. Inevitably, as will be seen later, the harshness of Soviet rule and the widespread availability of weapons resulted in a burgeoning resistance movement, and the families of those suspected of being involved in the armed resistance were also likely to be deported.[37]

There were three main motives for the deportations. Firstly, the policy allowed for the population to be 'cleansed' of those regarded as hostile to Soviet rule. Secondly, the previous Soviet occupation had shown how the largely rural populations of the three countries were opposed to collectivisation of land, and the deportations were designed to reduce or eliminate this resistance. Thirdly, the threat of deportation was regarded as a major weapon in the suppression of the anti-Soviet armed resistance; not only were the families of suspected resistance fighters deported, but also the widespread depopulation of the rural landscape – similar to the German anti-partisan policy of creating 'dead zones' – would deprive resistance fighters of support and supplies.

Even Latvian communists adopted a pro-Russian (and implicitly anti-Latvian) attitude, perhaps out of a sense of self-preservation. Many sought to portray ethnic Russians as the saviours of the Latvian nation. Whilst some Latvian communists were opposed to Stalin's clear intention to 'Russify' Latvia, it was over a decade before any felt bold enough to articulate nationalistic views without fear of immediately being branded 'anti-communist'.

With the isolation of Army Group North, almost all of the Baltic States were back in Soviet hands, with only Courland and the city of Klaipėda still being held by the Germans. The details of the fighting for Klaipėda are beyond the scope of this account. The three German divisions within the city when it was surrounded – 58th Infantry Division, 7th Panzer Division and *Grossdeutschland* – first came under serious attack on 10 October. Despite extensive artillery and aerial bombardment, the attacks, which continued for three days, were beaten off with heavy losses; the support of German warships off the coast proved to be invaluable, with their ability to respond rapidly and accurately with massive firepower proving decisive at key points in the battle.[38] After a pause of only two days, Bagramian tried again, and though the German 58th Infantry Division was forced back on the northern side of the city, the defensive line continued to hold. A final attack was made on 23 October, and this too failed to make significant headway. Thereafter, both sides slowly withdrew forces from the area, and the city was finally evacuated by the Wehrmacht in January 1945, as Soviet forces pressed into East Prussia.

As will be seen, Courland was the scene of bitter fighting for what remained of the war, every bit as intense and costly as the battles that had brought the Red Army to the Baltic coast. The status of the German forces trapped in Courland, though, was – and remains – controversial. Stalin dismissed the 'bridgehead' as little more than an open-air prison compound, where the remnants of nearly 30 German divisions were confined in an increasingly irrelevant part of Europe, while the main battlefront moved west. This view, which has been largely the opinion of Soviet and Russian writers in the post-war era, is in contrast to the German view, which was that the divisions of Army Group Courland, as it became known, played a vital role in tying down significant Soviet forces, which would otherwise have accelerated the collapse of the Eastern Front. The determined attempts by the Red Army to reduce Army Group Courland suggest that the Soviet leadership was not content merely with trapping and containing the German divisions, but to an extent, the German viewpoint may have been fuelled by the desire of the trapped German soldiers to believe that their continuing struggle was worthwhile. Hans Christern, commander of 4th Panzer Division's panzer regiment, wrote after the war:

> Who was actually tying down whom? In the Courland bridgehead, were we tying down Russian forces and thus preventing them from contributing to the overwhelming of the defences of German soil, which was carried out step by step in East Prussia? Or were the Russians tying us down? Was it their intention, by mounting major attacks, to deceive us that they regarded us as a dangerous threat to their deep eastern flank, which they had to eliminate at all costs? Or in reality did they want to prevent us from being available for the defence of 'Fortress Germany' when the final round began?
>
> The battles in Courland left us no time to think through such doubts. But the doubts were there, and they tormented us. What could we do, other than push them to the backs of our minds, as the demands of the moment required, as we heard the endless noise of battle on the Courland front?[39]

The rationale for the Soviet assaults on Courland is not clear, and is likely to be complex. Firstly, Courland now represented the last significant area of 'Soviet' territory that had not yet been liberated. However inevitable the final surrender of German forces might be, the political significance of recovering this last patch of 'Soviet' soil was considerable. Secondly, when the Red Army invaded Latvia during the Latvian war of independence in the aftermath of the First World War, parts of Courland were the only areas that were not captured, and it was from these small pockets, particularly around the port of Liepāja, that the Latvian nationalists and their German allies drove the Red Army back. Whilst there was little prospect of German and Latvian forces repeating this feat in late 1944, Stalin was aware that circumstances might change rapidly. Like Churchill, he was already looking to the future beyond the defeat of Germany. There is ample evidence that even at this late stage, he feared that the Western Allies might decide to support Germany against the Soviet Union, in which case Hitler's dream of using Courland as a base for future offensive operations might yet prove to have some basis in reality; the revival of Latvian fortunes in the Latvian war of independence was due in no small part to the presence of British warships in the Baltic and western support in the form of weapons, and Stalin knew first-hand that the British and Americans were able to supply their allies with considerable materiel. It therefore seems likely that the attempts to reduce Army Group Courland were driven by several motives.

Chapter 10

COURLAND, OCTOBER TO DECEMBER 1944

Following the disbandment of the Livonian Brothers of the Sword in 1562, the Duchy of Courland and Semigallia was created from the area of Latvia between the west bank of the River Daugava and the Baltic Sea. Its first duke was Gotthard Kettler, the last Master of the Sword Brothers. Although he was a vassal of the King of Poland, Kettler, whose family came from Westphalia, ran his duchy on strictly German lines, supported by the German nobility, and reduced most of the native population to the status of serfs.[1]

Jacob Kettler, grandson of the first Duke of Courland, came to power in 1642. He travelled widely throughout Western Europe, and became an enthusiastic proponent of western mercantilism and colonialism. A ship from the duchy had visited the West Indies in 1637, and established a colony on Tobago, which was promptly destroyed by the Spanish. In 1654, three years after Courlanders had established Fort Jacob on an island in the mouth of the Gambia River, the warship *Das Wappen der Herzogin von Kurland* ('The Arms of the Duchess of Courland') arrived off the coast of Tobago, and succeeded in establishing a new colony called Jacobsstadt. The entire island was named 'New Courland', much to the irritation of the Dutch, who established their own colony; aided by an influx of Huguenot refugees from France, this colony rapidly outgrew the Courland outpost. In 1652, Swedish troops occupied Courland, and Duke Jacob was taken prisoner. In the years that followed, his formidable fleet of armed merchantmen was destroyed, and the two colonies seized by the Dutch.

Although Tobago was briefly returned to Courland at the end of the Northern Wars in 1660, Duke Jacob lacked the power to keep the colony alive, and the foreign adventures of the Courland aristocracy came to an end late in the 17th century. Jacob's descendants showed little of his energy and creativity, and in 1795, the duchy became part of the Czar's empire following the Third Partition of Poland.

For much of 1918, the Duchy of Courland was revived as part of a German attempt to create a pro-German client state in the Baltic region, and the Baltic German residents of the area played a complex role in the Latvian war of independence. On the one hand, they fought actively to drive the Red Army from Latvia, but on the other hand, they had little interest in supporting the nationalist cause, and were closely allied to Rüdiger von der Goltz and the *Freikorps*. Consequently, many were expelled by the Latvian government at the end of the war. More left as part of the *Heim ins Reich* agreement with the Soviet Union following the Molotov–Ribbentrop Pact.

During the years of German occupation, some of the Baltic Germans returned to their lands, and in late 1944, they and the local Latvian population found themselves trapped with the German 16th and 18th Armies in the Courland peninsula. Hitler refused to regard the enclave as a 'pocket', and insisted that it be referred to as the Courland Bridgehead. This had a far more positive connotation, he told his subordinates, and once the Battle of the Atlantic was brought to a successful conclusion by the advent of the new Type XXI U-boats, it would be possible to resume offensive operations in the east; Courland would form an essential springboard for such an offensive. However, for the moment, the peninsula had to be held at all costs. On 21 October, the order of the day from Schörner for the two German armies made Hitler's views clear to the rank and file:

The Führer has ordered that Courland will be held and, initially, that the army group is to go over to the defensive in the present main line of resistance. Our mission is that not one single foot of ground in the area we hold will be given up. I cannot emphasise this enough. We are to pin the 150 major enemy formations facing us, to smash them wherever the opportunity appears and, in so doing, to aid in the defence of the homeland.

Effective immediately, all means are to be completely exhausted to strengthen our defence. The main defensive area must be developed to such a depth that it can withstand any and all attacks.

Accordingly, we must fortify and fortify again!

Every soldier who is not employed in positions with weapon in hand must work several hours a day with the shovel. It is impossible to do too much to adequately fortify the main defensive area, the road network and the trails!

The second and third positions, the road barriers, the ambush locations and the bunkers for quarters must be created in an extremely short time. Combat engineers must be pulled out of the main line of resistance and employed in building positions. It is important that the civilian population, without exception, also be used for this work.[2]

The construction of adequate defensive positions was a daunting task. Nearly 10 per cent of Courland is comprised of lakes, and the region has over 100 rivers, ranging from large streams to the Daugava. Generally, the area is fairly flat, especially nearer the coast, with modest hills inland. The swampy terrain made the digging of trenches difficult; in many areas, it was impossible to dig deeper than about a yard before the trenches began to fill with water. Construction materials such as concrete were in short supply, and the passive resistance of the local population made any mass mobilisation of manpower almost impossible, even if tools and materials had been available for them to use.

Despite their disparaging opinions about the German forces trapped in Courland, the Soviet High Command remained determined to seize the territory as soon as possible. Bagramian received orders from Moscow that a new offensive was to begin on 27 October, and in a conference with his army commanders on 20 October, he decided to attack between Pikeliai and Priekule. The attack would be led by 6th Guards Army and 4th Shock Army and a rifle corps from 51st Army. As the attack widened, 5th Guards Tank Army would join the advance. The railway line from Jelgava to the port of Liepāja was to be reached by the end of the second day. As Bagramian's armies advanced from the south, Yeremenko's 42nd army, 10th Guards Army and 3rd Shock Army would advance from the east, pushing into what was expected to be a rapidly collapsing German position.[3]

In addition to the forces he originally planned to use, Bagramian was pleased to have 61st Army assigned to him. However, the force was not as powerful as he might have expected. The army had been involved in constant fighting for several months, its commander reported, and its divisions were significantly weakened. Nevertheless, Bagramian decided to insert 61st Army between 4th Shock Army and 6th Guards Army, with the intention of attacking north from Vainode.[4]

The Germans were aware of the impending attack, and in order to disrupt Soviet preparations, X Corps ordered 14th Panzer Division to push the front line forward. The attack began on 24 October, catching the Soviet forces by surprise and making good initial progress. Seeing a possible opportunity to make further gains, X Corps ordered 4th Panzer Division to dispatch a company of tanks to support an advance by 30th Infantry Division. 4th Panzer Division was being held in a rear area, and it took until mid-afternoon for its armour to reach and cross the front line. By the time General Betzel joined his lead elements, he found that they were making minimal progress, and almost all of the tanks committed to the attack were bogged down in swampy ground. By the end of the day, the attack was abandoned, and the tanks laboriously hauled back.[5]

The first battle of Courland commenced on 27 October. The day started with dense fog, and the Soviet artillery and aerial preparation did not commence until the mist began to lift. By then, ground units had already commenced their attacks, seizing jumping-off positions in the sector held by *Nordland*. Assigned to support III SS Panzer Corps, 4th Panzer Division dispatched a panzergrenadier regiment, supported by the division's 37 operational Panther tanks, to the village of Audari, to the north-east of Priekule.

Commanders on both sides waited impatiently for hard news from the front; for 4th Panzer Division, information arrived from a small group of tanks led by Oberleutnant Gerlach. Deployed to support the original front line before the Soviet assault, the Panther tanks continued to hold out all day, helping to break up the Red Army's attacks. At first, the Soviet 67th, 51st and 75th Guards Rifle Divisions appeared to be making good progress, pushing back the western flank of 30th Infantry Division and penetrating perhaps three miles into the German positions to the east of Priekule. As the picture became clearer, 4th Panzer Division was ordered to counter-attack, in order to restore the front. Shortly after midday, Betzel's division attacked in two groups, and in heavy fighting, drove 51st and 67th Guards Rifle Divisions back towards their start line. Combat continued until long after nightfall, leaving the Soviet troops in possession of the eastern half of their gains. Even in this sector, the leading units were at least five miles short of their objective, the vital railway line running east from Liepāja.

4th Panzer Division's counter-attack epitomised the flexibilities of German operational doctrine that had played such a huge part in initial German successes in the war. Betzel was given a broad operational mission, and rapidly deployed his force in two groups. He accompanied the advancing battlegroups, and as their eastern flank became increasingly exposed, he was able to redeploy the division's reconnaissance battalion to deal with any threat. As was the case in all such operations, the division Chief of Staff, Peter Sauerbruch, took command of division headquarters and ensured coordination and communication between all elements, giving Betzel freedom to ensure that the combat formations of the division were used to maximum effect. According to the division's combat returns, the day's fighting cost it two Panther tanks destroyed (and several other tanks damaged, though repairable), 25 dead and 77 wounded; it claimed to have destroyed 23 Soviet tanks and assault guns and 24 anti-tank guns, and killed or taken prisoner over 400 enemy soldiers. Schörner acknowledged its efforts the following day in a personal message.[6]

At the same time that Bagramian's troops were struggling to make headway near Priekule, Yeremenko attacked the German 'bridgehead' from the east. 215th Infantry Division had only recently taken up positions defending the German line to the south-west of Dobele, and early on 27 October, spotted Soviet troops of 42nd Army assembling in their trenches. Artillery fire was immediately called down upon the Soviet preparation areas, at the same moment that Yeremenko began his own preparatory bombardment. Confused fighting raged all day, and during the afternoon, 215th Infantry Division's battalions began a fighting withdrawal to their secondary positions near Lake Lielauce. Here, with support from reserves – a battalion of assault guns and a battalion from 121st Infantry Division – the Soviet attack was first halted, then turned back. Towards dusk, as a single company of infantry, the last reserves of 215th Infantry Division, moved forward, they encountered a strong Soviet column moving in the opposite direction, and led by their energetic commander, Leutnant Werner Mozer, the Germans overwhelmed the Soviet troops in close-quarter fighting. The action earned Mozer the Knight's Cross, and brought the day's fighting in the sector to an end.[7]

The withdrawal of 215th Infantry Division towards Lake Lielauce also saw the first appearance of another new development on the Courland front. A military judge advocate was sent to the rear area by Schörner, accompanied by detachments of military police. Any soldiers found retreating without specific orders were marched before the judge advocate and faced charges of cowardice unless they were able to justify themselves. This practice became widespread under Schörner's command, first in Courland and later when he moved to Army Group Centre, and resulted in the execution of dozens of men, many of whom had done nothing wrong; in some cases, they were acting on verbal instructions, but this was not an acceptable excuse to the judge advocate. The rigidity of this attitude contrasts strongly with the German doctrine of operational orders being given in a fluid and flexible manner, often without resort to written instructions. The measure was intended to prevent panic and defeatism amongst the front-line troops, and its impact is hard to determine. Whilst the almost arbitrary execution of soldiers was repugnant to front-line troops, most appear to have regarded Schörner's hard-line attitude with approval; after all, they were still in the front line themselves, and had little sympathy for those who showed less resolve than themselves. Similarly, Schörner's insistence that rear area units be ruthlessly 'combed out' to release personnel for front-line service was a measure widely supported by combat soldiers.

On 28 October, Bagramian's forces attacked again, once more after a heavy artillery bombardment. The main effort fell on the German lines to the immediate east of Priekule, with heavy fighting raging all day in the woody and swampy terrain. 4th Panzer Division was involved in almost continuous combat until late afternoon; under pressure from four guards rifle divisions and at least two tank brigades, it was driven back in places, but barely a mile. The price paid by both the attackers and defenders was a heavy one. For his energetic leadership, Betzel was awarded the Oak Leaves to the Knight's Cross.

The following day, it was the turn of the Germans to mount an attack. 4th Panzer Division assembled a group consisting of its Panther battalion, a battalion of panzergrenadiers, and a battalion of combat engineers, supported by a regiment from 30th Infantry Division, and advanced on the village of Asīte from the north. Almost

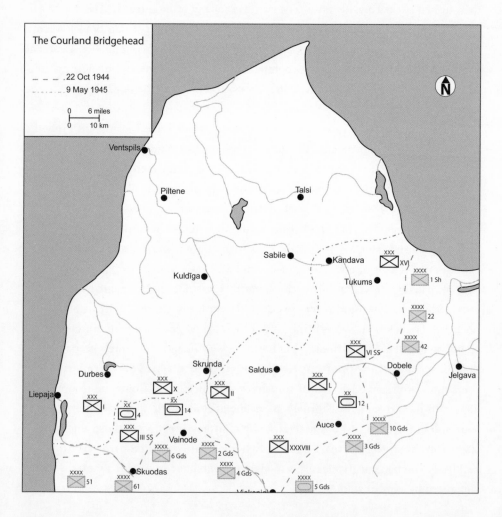

immediately, the assault group ran into the Soviet 29th Rifle Division, preparing to attack in the opposite direction. At close quarters, the two sides suffered further heavy casualties, and 4th Panzer Division was driven back to its start line. Here, it came under attack through the rest of the day, often having to improvise its defence: at one point, on the extreme eastern flank of the division, two Panthers, one towing the other, beat off an attack by seven Soviet assault guns and two tanks at close range.[8]

While bitter fighting raged north of Asīte, the German lines immediately east of Priekule came under fresh attack when a battalion from the Soviet 51st Guards Rifle Division, with supporting tanks, penetrated into the extended lines held by a battalion of 4th Panzer Division's panzergrenadiers. The situation was finally restored by a counter-attack late in the day. As darkness fell, Betzel's division reported that it had lost nearly 180 men dead, wounded or missing, but had accounted for 20 Soviet tanks, including a Josef Stalin, seven assault guns and eight anti-tank guns. The division's positions could only continue to be held, the division reported, if sufficient artillery support remained available, which would not be possible with the existing ammunition supply. The arrival of elements of 121st Infantry Division to relieve the battered panzergrenadiers to the east of Priekule was therefore particularly welcome.

The fighting continued the next day. The two infantry divisions on the flanks of 4th Panzer Division – 121st Infantry Division to the south-west, 30th Infantry Division to the north-east – came under heavy pressure, requiring repeated counter-attacks to restore the front line. Although the front line barely moved, the defence was at a heavy price. By the end of 30 October, the four panzergrenadier battalions of 4th Panzer Division had fallen from an aggregate strength of nearly 1,500 at the beginning of the battle to only 700. Betzel warned his corps commander that the ongoing shortage of artillery ammunition, losses from the constant Soviet artillery bombardment and a shortage of winter clothing were all combining to degrade the combat-worthiness of his division.[9] Fortunately for the Germans, the Soviet forces facing them were also approaching exhaustion.

On 31 October, there were only limited attacks on the German lines held by 121st Infantry Division, with most of the effort coming further east, on the seam between 30th and 263rd Infantry Divisions. Here, the Red Army attacked with the 415th, 23rd, 356th and 212th Rifle Divisions, with 13th Guards Rifle Division in support as a second echelon. The two German infantry divisions were forced back about a mile, but again a decisive breakthrough eluded the Red Army. The constant presence of a battlegroup from 14th Panzer Division did much to hold the hard-pressed 30th Infantry Division together. As intelligence reports came of a fresh Soviet build-up, this time to the west of Priekule, 14th Panzer Division was extracted from the front

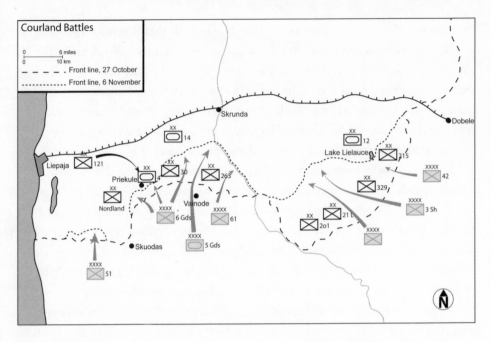

Courland Battles

0 ——— 6 miles
0 ——— 10 km
– – – – – . Front line, 27 October
. . . . Front line, 6 November

line and ordered west. It was replaced by elements of 263rd Infantry Division, but Soviet observers spotted the withdrawal of the German armour and immediately attacked. 14th Panzer Division was immediately ordered back to its former sector, where it restored the front in further costly fighting. Fortunately for the Germans, the anticipated Soviet attack to the west of Priekule did not materialise.

Fighting continued for the next few days. The Soviet 3rd Guards Mechanised Corps remained uncommitted, to the constant concern of the Germans, who were aware of its presence. The Latvians of 19th SS Waffen-Grenadier Division were ordered to launch an attack on their western flank to improve the front line, but discovered at first hand the perils of using penal battalions. The attack was intended for 4 November, but two soldiers from a penal battalion, employed in construction of fortifications, deserted to the Red Army on 2 November, and presumably acting on information provided by them the Soviets launched a spoiling attack the following day. But the weather was deteriorating, and finally, on 6 November, Bagramian decided that he had had enough, even without committing his reserves, and his armies sat back to lick their wounds and await the next round of fighting:

In three days, our troops managed to penetrate only six kilometres into the enemy's defences. The attack continued for a few more days, but every piece of ground in Courland could only be liberated after persistent and repeated attacks. Every farm, every height was contested bitterly. For the Fascists, this was a matter of life and death, while for the Soviet soldiers it was a military honour and duty to expel the Germans from the Homeland.[10]

Yeremenko, too, made almost no headway. His troops managed to gain perhaps a mile or two of ground, though again at a terrible cost. The price of stopping the Soviet attack had also been high. 215th Infantry Division, which bore the brunt of the onslaught of Yeremenko's troops, found that its fusilier battalion – effectively the division's reserve formation – was reduced to barely company strength. The three regiments of the division were in a similarly battered state.

Although Bagramian concluded from captured documents and prisoner interrogations that the Germans did not intend to evacuate Courland, Moscow remained concerned that even a piecemeal evacuation of Courland would release troops for the defence of the German homeland. Consequently, although Soviet troops were withdrawn from the area – 61st Army, 2nd Guards Army, and 5th Guards Tank Army from Bagramian's front, and 3rd Shock Army from Yeremenko's front – both Bagramian and Yeremenko were ordered to maintain pressure on the German lines, to prevent even a partial evacuation.

The failure of the Red Army in the first battle of Courland was due to several factors. Firstly, the assault was prepared in haste, assuming that the Germans were still reeling from Bagramian's surge to the Baltic. The strength of German defences therefore came as an unpleasant surprise. Secondly, the terrain that had played such a large role in holding up the German attacks in *Doppelkopf* and *Cäsar* proved to be equally difficult for the Soviet attackers. Thirdly, the deteriorating weather rapidly made any cross-country movement almost impossible, allowing the Germans to concentrate their anti-tank firepower on the few roads that were still usable.

Some of the fighting during the first battle of Courland resulted in Latvians fighting each other for their foreign masters. 19th SS Waffen-Grenadier Division took prisoner several individuals who informed their captors that they had only recently been conscripted into the Red Army from the eastern parts of Latvia. The general deterioration of the German position on the Eastern Front could not fail to have an impact on the Latvians still fighting with the Wehrmacht:

During this time, there was an apparent morale crisis … which manifested itself in increased desertion … [This] was caused by several reasons. After the vital defeats suffered by the Germans since summer 1944, and mainly [following] the loss of the Baltic area, many regarded the war as lost. Therefore, it was not worth sacrificing lives for. Others deserted hoping that as deserters they would get better treatment

when captured by the Communists. Several left their units [after] rumours that …
[19th SS Waffen-Grenadier Division] would be moved to Germany … Unwilling
to leave their homeland, these man joined the organisation 'Kureli'.[11]

The Latvian General Jānis Kurelis had started preparing an organisation to fight
against Soviet reoccupation of Latvia in the summer of 1944. Many of the Latvians
who were most strongly opposed to a resumption of communist rule had exhorted
their fellow Latvians not to flee the country – after all, they argued, a Latvia denuded
of Latvians would be easy for the Soviet Union to colonise. Kurelis started to establish
his first combat units around Riga in the late summer, and it seems that many of his
officers believed that, as had been the case at the end of the First World War, the
Western Powers would intervene to expel the Soviets from Latvia – therefore, keeping
up some level of resistance against the Red Army was essential. Whilst this may seem
a naïve point of view, it was a widespread one, with similar sentiments being expressed
not only in the Baltic States but also by the Polish nationalist fighters of the AK. The
eventual fate of the Kurelis Army is described later.

In damp conditions, occasionally broken by a night of frost, both sides continued
low-level combat while preparing for the next major battle. These preparations took
a variety of forms – raids, nuisance bombardments and, in the case of the Soviet
forces, repeated air attacks against German shipping using the ports of Liepāja and
Ventspils. In mid-November, another tactic was used in 4th Panzer Division's sector:

During one of the nights, the enemy slipped two German soldiers, who had been
prisoners for a while, into the front line. They brought with them letters from the
notorious *Nationalkomitee Freies Deutschland* ['National Committee for a Free
Germany'] to the commanders of the Army Group and the [18th] Army. Bearing
the signatures of senior German officers, it called for immediate capitulation and
promised excellent treatment and an immediate return home at the end of the war.
For the soldiers of the division, the proposal was incomprehensible. What pressure
could have compelled the signatures of the officers who had – really? – signed this?
But even then! Or were the reports or rumours of betrayal by senior officers true,
however unbelievable?[12]

As soon as German prisoners started to fall into Soviet hands in 1941, the Soviet
authorities tried to create a pro-communist movement that could be used to
undermine Hitler's control over the Wehrmacht, and might one day provide a nucleus
for a pro-Soviet administration, both military and civilian. At first, there was little

success, as even those who were taken prisoner by the Soviet Union remained convinced of ultimate German victory, and it was not until the disaster that befell the German 6th Army at Stalingrad that the mood changed. A large number of senior officers were captured at the end of the battle, many of them deeply embittered at what they perceived as Hitler's abandonment of their troops, and German communists who had fled to the Soviet Union to escape arrest in Germany began to promote the concept of patriotic German officers opposed to Hitler in much the same way that a previous generation of Prussian officers had refused to cooperate with Napoleon. At first, many senior German officers, from the ultra-conservative Prussian tradition, refused to be part of any organisation that included communists, and shunned the *Nationalkomitee Freies Deutschland* or NKFD. To improve recruitment, a parallel organisation, the *Bund Deutscher Offiziere* ('League of German Officers' or BDO) was therefore created, with General Walther von Seydlitz-Kurzbach as its first leader. Other senior officers, including Seydlitz's former commander from Stalingrad, Field Marshal Friedrich Paulus, soon joined the BDO, which ultimately merged with the NKFD.

Propaganda material produced by the NKFD was often dropped on German positions, particularly when troops were isolated or cut off. Whilst some soldiers may have believed the promises of good treatment and a swift homeward journey at the end of the war, most men serving on the Eastern Front can have had few illusions about what awaited them if they were to surrender; neither side had shown any inclination to treat prisoners well during the bitter conflict, and there was nothing to suggest that Soviet attitudes would change as victory over Germany drew nearer. Some of the numerous groups of soldiers sent back to German lines bearing messages from the NKFD were arrested by the Germans, and on occasion executed; other groups simply rejoined their comrades and resumed the fight against the Red Army. The fate of the two soldiers who returned to 4th Panzer Division in November 1944 is not recorded.

As the intention of the Germans to continue to hold Courland became clear, it seems that the mood of Germany's Latvian allies improved. The desertions of October came to an end, and many Latvians who had either fled to Courland as refugees, or were part of the local population, now volunteered for service. Included in their number were several who had previously deserted; in the main, they were allowed to rejoin their units without too many questions being asked. All along the front, Germans and Latvians laboured to improve their defences, creating a deep system of interlocking positions. The last line of defence, about three miles from the front line, was formed by fortified artillery positions, where the gunners deployed their weapons and prepared detailed fire plans. During the previous Soviet attack, a new artillery tactic had been used by the Red Army, with diagonal 'free lanes' left in the artillery barrage, allowing Soviet units to approach the German positions during the initial bombardment. To prevent any recurrence, German artillery planning now attempted to identify the probable locations of such 'free lanes', so that they could be subjected to a detailed counter-bombardment.

Bagramian's first failed attempt to break into the Courland Bridgehead was an operation intended to precipitate the collapse of the German defences; the second attempt, which began on 19 November, was explicitly intended to ensure that the divisions of Army Group North remained tied to their defensive positions, and could not be moved elsewhere. The Germans, too, wished to bind their Soviet opponents to this battlefield:

> An order of the day from the commander of the army group on the obligations of the soldiers in Courland was particularly effective: their mission in their remote positions was to bring relief to their hard-pressed comrades in East Prussia, to tie down the enemy with the utmost exertions and thus to help them overcome the Bolshevik assault against the Fatherland.[13]

On the eve of the second battle of Courland, the German High Command advised that a major Soviet attack was imminent, and would most likely be directed against X Corps, specifically 30th and 263rd Infantry Divisions. 4th Panzer Division was therefore ordered to prepare a powerful battlegroup behind the left flank of X Corps in preparation of the attack. On 19 November, the day dawned with frost, but temperatures rose rapidly during the day, reducing the roads and landscape to a swampy morass. In mid-morning, heavy artillery fire began to fall on the German lines, across a broad front. In addition to the positions of X Corps, shells also fell on the divisions of II Corps, further east. As the Soviet artillery attack lifted, the ground troops moved forward, across ground that was increasingly difficult to traverse. 103rd Rifle Division laboured through woodland in the sector held by the German 30th Infantry Division, to the east of Krote, and by dusk, 4th Panzer Division was ordered to dispatch a battlegroup to the area, consisting of one of its panzergrenadier regiments and a battalion of artillery. Overnight, the weather deteriorated further with more rain, greatly delaying the arrival of 4th Panzer Division's battlegroup in 30th Infantry Division's sector. Finally, in mid-morning, a counter-attack began, hindered as much by the terrain as by Soviet resistance. By the end of the day, most of the previous day's Soviet gains had been reversed.

Betzel and his commanders grew increasingly unhappy about the state of 4th Panzer Division. Elements of the division had already been detached and assigned to other formations, or were being held as corps- or army-level reserves, and Betzel protested that he had been left with too small a remnant to be able to intervene meaningfully on the battlefield. He need not have worried. The roads remained little more than rivers of mud, and although seven Soviet rifle divisions from 54th and 11th Guards Rifle Corps managed to push into the lines of II Corps, somewhat to the east of the original Soviet assault of 19 November, these new attacks gained little ground. Counter-attacks rapidly restored the front, with 4th Panzer Division being inserted into the front line between 32nd Infantry Division and 31st Volksgrenadier Division. Tanks became bogged down in deep mud, often requiring the combined power of three tractor vehicles to pull them free. 14th Panzer Division was also committed to the battle, shoring up the western flank of II Corps, though as was the case with 4th Panzer Division, the division commander, Oskar Munzel, complained bitterly that too much of his division was subordinated to other formations, leaving him with inadequate forces for the division to function effectively. Nevertheless, 14th Panzer Division succeeded in holding a three-mile sector of the front, repeatedly beating back attacks by the Soviet 311th Rifle Division.

Fighting gradually died down on 26 November; although Bagramian's divisions had made very little headway, they had succeeded in moving the front line forward just far enough to allow them to bring the vital railway line running east from Liepāja under artillery fire. Losses had been severe on both sides. The German 32nd Infantry Division reported that its 4th and 94th Grenadier Regiments could only muster 225 combatants between them.[14] Even if a Soviet breakthrough had been prevented, the cost was high.

Martin Unrein, who had commanded 14th Panzer Division until he was forced to return to Germany due to illness, resumed command of his division in the last days of the battle. In the lull that followed, together with 4th Panzer Division's Clemens Betzel, he made the opinions of the panzer officers about the fragmentation of their divisions very clear to the commander of 18th Army, Ehrenfried Boege. There was clearly a conflict between the need to respond rapidly to Soviet attacks at different points of the front line, especially as the German infantry divisions were, by the standards of their enemies, relatively weak in anti-tank firepower, and the desire of the panzer commanders to retain sufficient striking power to be able to mount decisive counter-attacks. Given the terrain, which made any such attack en masse almost impossible, and the increasing frailty of unsupported German infantry in the face of combined attacks by Soviet tanks and infantry, the dispersal of German

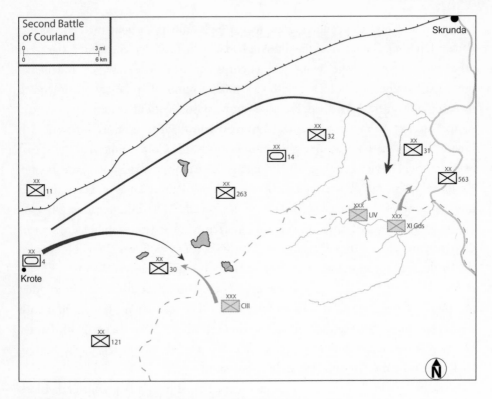

armoured forces was probably inevitable, though the unhappiness of the panzer commanders with this arrangement is understandable.

Throughout December, both sides attempted to reorganise their positions and rest their major units. Bagramian maintained pressure on the Germans by ordering constant air operations whenever the weather permitted. One of the heroes of the Soviet air effort was Nelson Gevorgi Stepanyan, an Armenian fighter-bomber pilot, whose 47th Fighter Division was in the forefront of the air effort. As was the case with leading personalities of all sides, his fame was enhanced by official propaganda efforts, and he was known as the 'Storm Petrel of the Baltic' by Soviet troops in the area. He had already been awarded the title 'Hero of the Soviet Union' when he flew his final mission on 14 December. His Il2 aircraft was hit by ground fire and badly damaged, and crashed into a ship in Liepāja harbour; the official Soviet report stated that he selflessly steered his plane into its target, but it is possible that the crippled plane merely continued along its attack path, and was unable to pull up due to damage. He was once more awarded the title of 'Hero of the Soviet Union' after his death. Unlike other air forces, the Soviet Air Force allowed women to fly combat missions, and another prominent figure in the air campaign over the Baltic was Lidia Shulaikina, who flew some 36 missions, mainly attacks against shipping. She was credited with sinking three transport ships, a patrol boat and a barge.

On 20 December, Betzel left for Germany, intending to combine a visit to Berlin for discussions with higher commands with some well-earned leave at home. Unlike on previous occasions, it seems that the Germans had not detected Soviet preparations for renewed fighting, at least not on any significant scale. On 21 December, heavy artillery fire fell on the lines of the German I Corps. By mid-morning, reports reached I Corps and 18th Army of pressure particularly on 218th, 132nd and 225th Infantry Divisions, around the villages of Laci, Stedini, Cubas and Zanenieki. The attacking forces were from 4th Shock Army, which deployed 15 rifle divisions in the assault, with substantial armoured support. At the same time, VI SS Corps came under heavy attack, where a shortage of reserves allowed the Soviet forces to penetrate right into the depths of the defenders' positions. In I Corps' sector, an immediate counter-attack at Laci eased the situation, and 4th Panzer Division was ordered to restore the front line at Stedini. For the moment, VI SS Corps would have to fend for itself.

In the absence of Clemens Betzel, 4th Panzer Division was under the command of Oberst Hans Christern, the commander of the division's 35th Panzer Regiment. He had served with armoured units throughout the war, including a time organising the training of tank crews when the Tiger tank was introduced in 1942. An ebullient, energetic leader, he was popular amongst his men, and constantly led from the front in the traditional style of all good panzer commanders. When he reached the headquarters of I Corps at 1150hrs, he was ordered to move an armoured battlegroup to a preparation area near Labdomas. Christern raised doubts about this plan:

> Oberst Christern objected that based on reconnaissance the previous day, the approach to the armoured battlegroup's preparation area would be most difficult and time-consuming. The terrain was mainly low-lying swamp with sandy ridges. The roads were partly dykes. He suggested that the entire division except for 33rd Panzergrenadier Regiment's commander's battlegroup [which had already been detached from the division] should assemble in the reconnoitred area north of Zanenieki, from where deployment in any direction had been reconnoitred. This was turned down.[15]

Christern's suggestion was entirely in keeping with the principles of *Auftragstaktik*, and his frustration at the restrictive nature of his orders can be imagined. Although the ground was relatively firm following recent frosts, it was badly rutted, making movement by wheeled units particularly difficult. To make matters worse for

Christern, his division was ordered to maintain strict radio silence during its movement. Early in the afternoon, 4th Panzer Division was ordered to move 12th Panzergrenadier Regiment to the same assembly area, putting further pressure on roads that he already regarded as unsuitable.

Christern's difficult time commanding a division for the first time steadily worsened. Although he was given control of *Schwere Panzer Abteilung 510* and its valuable Tiger tanks, they only added to congestion and degradation of the roads. As vehicles laboured through the mud and confusion, orders changed yet again. During the evening, I Corps ordered Christern to dispatch the armoured battlegroup to a new preparation area at Ozolini, where it would join with elements of 225th Infantry Division to mount a counter-attack. At this stage, only a single battalion of panzergrenadiers had reached the originally designated preparation area. Forbidden to use radio communication, Christern had to dispatch officers to locate the units of the armoured battlegroup, so that they could be informed of these new orders. To complicate matters still further, Soviet aircraft made harassing raids along all roads throughout the day.

At about 0130hrs on 22 December, Christern reached the headquarters of 225th Infantry Division. The division's commander, Walter Risse, had been out of contact with higher commands for most of the day, and the arrival of Christern and his staff would have provided a timely boost to his confidence. As the night drew on, with constant Soviet air raids and artillery fire, elements of Christern's division continued to struggle into their preparation area. By first light, the armoured battlegroup had managed to assemble, but had left large numbers of vehicles broken or bogged down in its wake. Only seven Pz.IVs and 24 Panthers were still running, out of 28 Pz.IVs and 40 Panthers that had set out on the difficult march. Half of *Schwere Panzer Abteilung 510's* Tigers had also failed to reach the preparation area. Nevertheless, as it grew light, a force of 20 Panthers and ten Tigers, supported by a few half-tracks of panzergrenadiers, formed up to launch a counter-attack.

Christern had been assured that the wooded area to the south-east of the area he would be attacking was still in German hands. There was considerable consternation, therefore, when the group came under heavy fire from that direction, especially as the battlegroup lacked the artillery and infantry required to clear the area. The attack faltered and ground to a halt, and all Christern could do was attempt to assemble a defensive line.

Early in the afternoon, General Theodor Busse, commander of I Corps, arrived in Christern's headquarters. He advised those present that he had been told by Boege, commander of 18th Army, personally to ensure that 4th Panzer Division and 225th

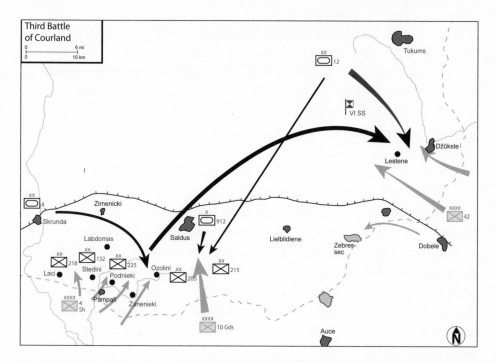

Infantry Division restored the former front line. Struggling across the impossible landscape, under constant aerial and artillery fire, the German units made little headway. 23 December saw further fighting, in which one of 4th Panzer Division's panzergrenadier divisions was almost destroyed, for little gain. Orders to retake positions continued to arrive, with no regard for the realities on the ground. During the afternoon, Busse appeared to lose patience, and ordered that 4th Panzer Division was now subordinated to 225th Infantry Division. Generalleutnant Risse was to take overall command.

For Christern and the officers of 4th Panzer Division, this must have come as a blow to their pride. 4th Panzer Division had served with great distinction on the Eastern Front, and had never been criticised in this manner before. It must have been particularly galling that the division's failures were in no way due to its personnel – despite Christern's objections, he had been forced by higher commands to deploy his forces in unsuitable terrain, and orders had been changed repeatedly. The requirement for urgent action was not compatible with an insistence on absolute radio silence, but again, the division's requests for this restriction to be lifted had been dismissed. However, several factors within the division worked against it. Had Betzel been present, he would probably have been far more assertive and might have had more influence on Busse and Boege, neither of whom appeared willing to take advice from a mere *Oberst*. Christern's temporary assignment as division commander also resulted in his panzer regiment – and therefore the armoured battlegroup – being commanded by Major Toelke, a newcomer to the division, which may have led to further friction in the chain of command. To compound matters further, the division's chief of staff, Peter Sauerbruch, had also been replaced recently. There were, therefore, a number of officers in key positions who were not familiar with their roles, and whom their superiors did not appear to regard with any great confidence.[16]

The newly formed *Gruppe Risse*, consisting of 225th Infantry Division and those elements of 4th Panzer Division not detached to other units, was now tasked with a further counter-attack to restore the front line at Podnieki. For the moment, though, a counter-attack was out of the question, as Risse struggled to prevent a powerful Soviet drive from splitting his forces in two. Just as it seemed that the Red Army might be able to achieve a significant breakthrough, the attack ran directly into 4th Panzer Division's combat engineer battalion, which threw it back in disarray. It is a measure of the severity of the German losses that by the end of the day, 4th Panzer Division was reduced to only 13 operational tanks, having started the day with over 30.[17]

The weather was cloudy and significantly above freezing on 24 December, ensuring a widespread softening of the terrain. The counter-attack by *Gruppe Risse* finally began, but ran into a further Soviet attack, scheduled for the same sector of the front at about the same moment. It was a wooded area, broken by tracks and firebreaks, and confused fighting continued all day. The Germans tried to push forward to the line of the small River Zana, while the Soviet forces struggled to break free of the woodland to the north-east of the river. Neither side was able to achieve its objective. The energetic efforts of 4th Panzer Division's combat engineers first to stop the previous day's thrust by the Red Army, then to reverse it and drive through the dense woodland towards the Zana, earned the battalion commander, Hauptmann Beukemann, the Knight's Cross. But exhaustion was setting in on both sides. As the day drew to a close, Risse cautiously suggested that the crisis was past, and that his combined group had survived.

The third battle of Courland was not confined to the sector held by Busse's corps. A little further to the east, Soviet forces made determined efforts to advance on Saldus, putting the 205th and 215th Infantry Divisions under great pressure. A panzergrenadier regiment from 12th Panzer Division was committed to shore up the line. Although 215th Infantry Division lost over 600 men killed, wounded or missing, Soviet losses were even higher. Like the men of 4th Panzer Division, the Soviet tank crews struggled with almost impossible conditions. By the end of the fighting, a guards tank regiment reported that it had been reduced to only five serviceable tanks.[18] In addition to breakdowns, the losses from German action were heavy. Major Josef Brandner's *Sturmgeschütz-Brigade 912*, deploying rapidly from its holding position in Saldus, ran straight into the advancing Soviet tanks, as Brandner described:

We moved widely dispersed to avoid presenting the Russians with a closed up target that would be easy to engage with artillery. But we also had to be ready for the oncoming Russian tanks.

I saw the muzzle flash of an enemy tank's main gun. The round burst just to the right of us. The driver grasped the situation in the blink of an eye. He pulled back the right lateral and we were then in firing position facing our opponent.

I gave a fire command to my gunner and give him the range.

'Identified!' he reported. Seconds later, the first round left the barrel. A jet of flame spurted from the enemy; the targeted T34 exploded.

Exactly 400m further away a second T34 broke through and reached the main supply route.

'Damn it! Misfire!' the gunner called out.

The loader cursed. All that took place within a few seconds. Both of the assault guns that were following me were already involved with other T34s. There was nothing they could do to help us. Why didn't the T34 fire? What was going on?

At that moment it fired and the round took off the top of a tree right above us.

I was glued to the enemy with the scissors telescope. He seemed that close to us already in the magnification of the optics. Then my assault gun bucked and I saw the brilliant rosette of flame marking the impact on the front of the T34. The Russian crew bailed out and disappeared into the underbrush.

Then there was a heavy artillery barrage on the stretch of road in front of us. The enemy had spotted the brigade's approach and wanted to put us out of action before we had really joined the fight.

A radio message from the second assault gun battery came in: 'Friendly infantry abandoning the position to the right of us and falling back before the Russians.'

But there was no way we could support the right flank. The tight-packed groups of armour were thundering toward us in two assault wedges. The duelling began. T34 and Josef Stalin tanks fired with everything they had. Nevertheless, we managed to knock out several of them right at the beginning.

The gunners and loaders worked like men possessed. The drivers took evasive actions. Rounds zipped past us. Tanks – tanks – tanks, wherever you looked.[19]

As he attempted to pull back with the retreating German infantry, Brandner received a radio message from his left flank, where one of his batteries was under heavy pressure. Under almost constant artillery and mortar bombardment, his battery continued to inflict losses on the advancing Soviet tanks, and the German infantry now rallied and counter-attacked, restoring the front line. For his efforts, Brandner was awarded the Knight's Cross.[20]

On Christmas Day, 4th Panzer Division beat off the last Soviet attacks in its sector, particularly the woodland where the division's combat engineers, now supported by the reconnaissance battalion, were in position. As the Soviet infantry attacked, the Germans called in artillery support, which proved effective at breaking up many of the attacks; however, the fire from one of the division's batteries fell on the positions of the Germans themselves. Unable to identify which battery was firing short, the defenders stoically endured. During the evening, orders arrived for the division to withdraw; it was to move to the sector held by VI SS Corps, further to the east.

VI SS Corps consisted at this stage of 93rd and 227th Infantry Divisions, 21st Luftwaffe Field Division, and 19th SS Waffen-Grenadier Division (2nd Latvian). Soviet forces had attempted to turn the left flank of the corps in order to capture Dzukste, and confused fighting had left the front line in a shambles, with neither side able to say with any certainty where their units were. One regiment of Latvians, operating in support of the neighbouring Luftwaffe Field Division, lost nearly 60 per cent of its personnel to artillery fire, but managed to pull back in some semblance of order. Ongoing attacks against the well-constructed positions of the Latvian division made little headway, but a considerable penetration was achieved on the seam between the Latvians and the Luftwaffe division, advancing most of the way to the village of Lestene. In their wake, a small group of Latvians was surrounded in Dirbas, but continued to fight on. But the advance marked the high tide of the Soviet effort, and attempts to push on over the next two days made almost no headway. Still encircled a mile or more behind the Soviet front line, the Latvians in Dirbas, under the command of Obersturmführer Ancans, continued to resist. Finally, late on Christmas Day, Ancans withdrew with 35 survivors, carrying many of their wounded with them back to Latvian lines. Ancans, who had himself been wounded, was awarded the Knight's Cross.[21]

Some elements of 12th Panzer Division had already been dispatched to the VI SS Corps' area, and 4th Panzer Division now followed. Wheeled elements would make their own way to the new sector, while tracked units were moved by train. When they arrived in VI SS Corps' area, the panzer officers were relieved to find that although the terrain was dotted with woodland and swampy areas, it was relatively more open than the landscape where 4th Panzer Division had laboured so strenuously in preceding days. By the end of 27 December, most of the division had arrived in Dzukste, with some elements already assigned to support 227th Infantry Division and 19th SS Waffen-Grenadier Division. Perhaps as further fallout of the criticisms directed at the division by Busse, the division was subordinated to Generalleutnant von Bodenhausen's 12th Panzer Division, forming *Gruppe Bodenhausen*. Counter-attacks made some headway the following day, but eventually ground to a halt due to inadequate infantry support; it seems that some of 227th Infantry Division's units were too exhausted or weakened to advance. To add insult to injury, three of 4th Panzer Division's Pz.IV tanks were shot up by German assault guns as they withdrew.

On 29 December, Betzel returned to Courland, and resumed command of his division from a relieved Oberst Christern. On the last day of the year, Soviet forces penetrated into the positions of 93rd Infantry Division, and 4th Panzer Division once more moved to a new area. Here, they found that the attack was led by the 308th Latvian Rifle Division, made up largely of newly recruited Latvian troops with Russian officers. The panzer division's reconnaissance battalion immediately counter-attacked, followed by other elements of the division as they arrived, led personally by Betzel. In a wild counter-attack that continued long into the night, 4th Panzer Division drove the Soviet forces back to their start lines. Fighting continued for the next two days before both sides came to an exhausted halt.[22]

The contrast between this successful counter-attack and the failed operation by 4th Panzer Division at the beginning of the third battle of Courland could not be greater. Many of the factors that led to a successful counter-attack on 31 December were the exact opposites of those on 21 December. Unlike Busse, Obergruppenführer Walther Krüger did not interfere with the panzer division's internal arrangements, and other than ordering a counter-attack to restore the front line, he left the details to Betzel. The terrain was more favourable for armoured operations, and the division was back under the control of its experienced commander; likewise, Christern was back with his panzer regiment. The Soviet forces facing 4th Panzer Division on 31 December also put up less determined resistance than those ten days earlier.

This was also one of the few occasions that Latvian troops faced each other across the battlefield. Generally, the Soviets tried to avoid such battles, especially when they involved relatively new Latvian battalions of the Red Army; these often contained men who had served the Germans in a variety of roles, and were regarded as politically unreliable. The longer established Latvian rifle regiments were a different matter, but of course they contained large groups of soldiers who might be Latvian in terms of ethnicity, but had been living in the Soviet Union when they were recruited. These regiments also contained significant numbers of non-Latvian soldiers and officers, another factor that made their possible encounters with pro-German Latvians less 'risky'. As soon as they realised that the 308th Rifle Division was up against 19th SS Waffen-Grenadier Division (2nd Latvian), the Soviet leadership swiftly arranged for the division to be relieved, and redeployed it elsewhere. The troops of 19th SS Waffen-Grenadier Division fought alongside the panzer divisions during the German counter-attack, and performed well, not least because they had the good fortune to capture Soviet prisoners on 28 December who revealed the intention of the Red Army to attack the following day. The Latvians were able to position their artillery accordingly, and inflict major losses on the Soviet forces with a timely bombardment.

To the rear of the front line, the Germans found that partisan activity in Latvia was, for the first time, a serious matter. Many divisions were required to form company- or battalion-sized groups that were sent into the hinterland to fight the increasingly active partisans. The make-up of these partisan bands was diverse. Their core was formed of Soviet soldiers, often specially parachuted into the area; many were members of the NKVD. Around this leadership there gathered a variety of men and a small number of women. These included deserters from both the Red Army and the Wehrmacht, and also Soviet soldiers who had been German prisoners of war. Some of this last group had succeeded in escaping captivity, but most were men who had volunteered to serve with the Germans as *Hiwis* (*Hilfwilliger*, or volunteers) in order to avoid continued detention in the terrible conditions that prevailed in prison camps for Red Army soldiers. In their role as *Hiwis*, they performed a variety of tasks, such as driving, cooking, and other rear area activities, but many also served as combatants. Now that it was clear that the Wehrmacht was headed for defeat, many *Hiwis* slipped away from the ranks and joined the partisans.[23]

As 1945 began, the outcome of the war was scarcely in doubt. But in order to ensure the success of the coming great offensive, the Red Army remained anxious to prevent any of the Courland divisions from returning to Germany, where they might strengthen the German defences on the Eastern Front. Even had a rapid transfer of all the Courland divisions been possible, it seems likely that the release of the Soviet forces from the Baltic would have offset any strengthening effect, so it is worth considering why Stalin was so keen to ensure a quick victory over Germany. The answer probably lies in his own past behaviour, and how he interpreted the possible intentions of others. During his rise to power, he was very adept at siding with more conservatively inclined members of the Communist Party in order to isolate and destroy radicals such as Trotsky; then, once the threat from the 'left' had been dealt with, he adopted the policies of the left and turned against his conservative allies from the 'right'. As he negotiated the shape of post-war Europe with the Western Allies, Stalin must have wondered whether Britain and the United States might at some point in the near future turn against him, just as he had turned against his former allies. Consequently, although Soviet occupation of much of Germany had been agreed at Tehran in November–December 1943 – and subsequently clarified in meetings of officials in Moscow in 1944 – Stalin was keen to get his troops physically into position before the Western Allies moved against him. As part of this strategy, the German forces in Courland were to be kept under attack, and ideally destroyed where they were; Stalin was determined to ensure that a restoration of pre-war frontiers was interpreted as a return to the *status quo* of 1941, at which time the Baltic States were part of the Soviet Union. Complete occupation of the three countries before the end of the war would ensure that there was no question of any other outcome.

Chapter 11
ENDGAME

The beginning of 1945 in Courland saw a continuation of the fighting that had smouldered on as the third battle of Courland passed its peak. *Gruppe Bodenhausen*, consisting of 12th Panzer Division on the eastern flank and 4th Panzer Division on the western flank, deployed to the west of Džūkste, and on 5 January attacked towards the south, with 12th Luftwaffe Field Division and 19th SS Waffen-Grenadier Division to their east and west respectively. Once again, Betzel was with the leading elements of his division. The objective of the attack was to secure a new, shorter front line, by advancing about two miles. The leading armoured elements achieved this on the first day of the operation, with infantry gradually following, clearing the pockets of woodland of Soviet defenders as they came. 4th Panzer Division now turned to the west in order to close up with the Latvians of 19th SS Waffen-Grenadier Division, attacking just after midnight. By first light, the assault formations had broadly achieved their objectives, but found themselves in an area overseen by Soviet defences further south. Fighting continued through 6 January, with Soviet counter-attacks from the south being beaten off. As darkness fell, 4th Panzer Division's combat engineers hauled away a large amount of Soviet materiel that the division had captured the previous night, including several T34 tanks.[1]

Although German combat losses in this latest operation were not severe, they reduced the strength of 4th Panzer Division to what the division commander described as 'barely supportable', with most of its Pz.IVs out of action; although several of the division's tanks, including three Panthers, had been knocked out in *Gruppe Bodenhausen*'s attack, most of the vehicles that were no longer available were disabled due to mechanical problems. Nevertheless, the German estimates of Soviet losses were considerable. Betzel's staff reckoned that since the start of the third battle of Courland, the division had accounted for half the tank strength of a tank brigade, almost half a regiment of assault guns, the anti-tank gun complement of a tank corps and a rifle division, and half the artillery complement of a rifle division. A further five Soviet infantry battalions were accounted for in terms of dead, with an unknown number of wounded.[2] In a similar manner, 19th SS Waffen-Grenadier Division calculated that it had destroyed or severely degraded ten rifle divisions and an armoured corps during the fighting of December and early January.[3] Whilst such claims have always been regarded as being prone to exaggeration, the German attack does seem to have caught the Red Army by surprise, resulting in many tanks and guns being captured as their crews fled. It should also be remembered that in almost every battle on the Eastern Front, Soviet losses were higher than German losses; but the ability of Soviet armaments production to replace these losses was also far greater than German industrial output. In earlier years, Soviet resources of manpower had also seemed bottomless, but by 1945, this had changed. The huge losses of earlier years had left much of the Soviet Union denuded of men, and the advancing Red Army was forced to recruit replacements, often forcibly, from the areas that it 'liberated'. The training and discipline of these replacements was poor, and as a result, may have contributed to the ease with which operations such as the attack by *Gruppe Bodenhausen* put the Soviet troops to flight.

There were further changes in higher commands. Generaloberst Hilpert and General Boege remained commanders of 16th and 18th Armies respectively, but it was time for Schörner, the commander of Army Group North, to move on. Whatever the views of his critics, both then and since, many front-line soldiers held him in high regard, as a junior NCO of 4th Panzer Division wrote:

> In Courland, apart from our camaraderie, which grew ever stronger, only iron orders to hold out kept us together. General Schörner was an iron commander. He was frequently with the combat troops. It was this man who prevented chaos for thousands of soldiers, by mobilising numerous rear area and administrative units for front line service.[4]

In recognition of their achievements, all soldiers serving in Army Group North were awarded a 'Kurland' badge or armband. For 4th Panzer Division, though, its time in Courland was coming to an end. On 9 January, orders arrived for the division to be withdrawn into a rear area, where it would form a reserve for the entire army group. On 17 January, as the final crisis in East Prussia and Poland began, the division was ordered to proceed to Liepāja, from where its personnel would be transferred by sea to Gdansk. It was to leave its heavy equipment behind, though at a later date, much of this equipment was sent to help re-equip the division. Although the division had sometimes failed to achieve its objectives – particularly during *Doppelkopf* and *Cäsar* – its personnel could be proud of their achievements. The total tank losses of the division since the beginning of *Doppelkopf* were 20 Pz.IVs and 12 Panthers, compared to an estimate of 215 Soviet tanks and assault guns destroyed. These figures include a distortion: they give the number of German tanks lost, i.e. unrecoverable, whilst the Soviet 'losses' would include knocked out tanks and assault guns that would subsequently have been recovered, repaired and returned to the front line. Nevertheless, even allowing for this, and for exaggerated claims of enemy losses, it was a remarkable achievement.

12th Panzer Division continued to be involved in fighting in the front line after the success of the attack near Džūkste. Operations continued until 15 January, with the division claiming the destruction of 81 Soviet tanks, many with close-range *Panzerfaust* and *Panzerschreck* weapons. But although the division's own losses were light, their impact on the thinning ranks of veterans was considerable. The commander of the division's 5th Panzergrenadier Regiment, Oberstleutnant Bischoff, was seriously wounded and had to hand over his command; he recovered and returned to the front line just a few days before the final surrender.[5]

The great Soviet offensive against the German defences on the Eastern Front began on 12 January, and spread from the Sandomierz bridgehead in southern Poland to East Prussia over several days. Bagramian's armies had already been depleted to ensure that the assault formations had the greatest possible advantage, but the forces assembled against the Courland Bridgehead remained formidable. Yeremenko was replaced as commander of 2nd Baltic Front by Leonid Alexandrovich Govorov, whose Leningrad Front had been disbanded. Together, he and Bagramian planned further assaults on Courland, in an attempt to prevent German forces from being withdrawn for use elsewhere. This strategy proved to be of limited efficacy. As has already been seen, 4th Panzer Division was transferred to Gdansk and thence to the Vistula valley, and several infantry divisions followed in the next few weeks.

In his memoirs, Bagramian reflected on whether he and his colleagues might have done more to destroy the Courland Bridgehead. He concluded that the Red Army faced several major difficulties:

> The first of these was that the Fascist high command succeeded in withdrawing the main forces of Army Group North from the Riga area into Courland, and deployed them there in compact formations, allowing a successful defence to be carried out in the wooded and swampy terrain with few metalled or non-metalled roads.

Besides, it should be said that before it decided on such a manoeuvre, the Fascist high command was clearly aware of the danger of the final destruction of the personnel of its two operational groupings in Riga and Courland, cut off from East Prussia. The only way to save the troops who had earlier been deployed in the Baltic States was to gather them together in Courland. There, they found the most favourable of conditions for the creation of a stable defence and were able to maintain maritime communications links.

Secondly, one needed substantial strength and resources to destroy such a strong grouping. But at precisely this time, our high command required powerful units in preparation for the final, definitive assault towards the west. Consequently ... soon after the liberation of the Latvian capital and again at the end of 1944, substantial forces were withdrawn from the Baltic region.

Thirdly, we had to attack in autumn and winter under difficult weather conditions, which greatly hindered the use of tanks, artillery and other combat equipment. In order to be able to advance, not only did we have to overcome the strong defences and bitter resistance of the enemy, but also literally had to force our way through every metre of overgrown woodland and swamp.

And finally, not only we at the front, but also our high command, believed that the forces in Courland were fully isolated from the main forces of the Wehrmacht. This circumstance, it seemed to us at the time, should have made the destruction of the blockaded divisions much easier.

But in contrast to Paulus' army [6th Army, which surrendered in Stalingrad in early 1943], which found itself encircled in a ring of iron in the truest sense of the words, it was possible for the troops in Courland, who were protected on three sides by the sea, to concentrate on a defensive sector of only 200km, where the operational demands were a mere 6km per division. In this manner, the enemy was able to create and thoroughly develop deep defences. His second – and in the most vital sectors, third – lines of defence allowed him to mount powerful counterattacks.

The Baltic was the door through which the [enemy] troops received everything required for their operations until the end of the war.[6]

Bagramian's closing sentence in this quotation immediately raises another question. Throughout the fighting for the Courland peninsula, the Soviet fleet based in Kronstadt made almost no significant intervention. Indeed, other than a small number of notable successes by its submarines, its ships made a negligible impact throughout the war. The fleet was considerable, both in numbers of ships and in fighting strength. At the outset of the war, it had two ageing battleships, the modern heavy cruiser *Kirov*, and a host of smaller vessels. Some were lost during the attempted naval evacuation of Tallinn, and others were damaged during the Siege of Leningrad, but the fleet remained a potentially powerful force. However, its surface units limited their voyages to the Gulf of Finland for the duration of the war. There are several possible reasons for this. Firstly, the long siege left many of the ships in a poor state, with a high likelihood of mechanical breakdown should they attempt a prolonged voyage. Secondly, Soviet warships had a poor maintenance record, even in peacetime, and there may have been serious concerns about their seaworthiness. Thirdly, many of their crews had been used as naval infantry during the Siege of Leningrad, and although some of these personnel returned to their ships after the end of the siege, they were short on training in their naval role, which would have further impaired the fighting power of the fleet. Fourthly, the Soviet navy had a poor historical record in surface warfare. During the wars that established the independence of Lithuania, Latvia and Estonia, a small squadron of British cruisers was able to prevent the Soviet fleet based in Kronstadt from making any major intervention, and inflicted repeated humiliations on the Soviet ships; two destroyers, *Spartak* and *Avtroil*, were captured by the British squadron and handed over to the Estonians, and the British naval officer Augustus Agar led two daring raids in 1919 on the Soviet naval base in Kronstadt with a group of flimsy coastal motor-boats armed with torpedoes, during which the British vessels succeeded in torpedoing the Soviet cruiser *Oleg* and – on the second raid – the battleship *Andrei Pervozvanny* at close range.[7] In late 1944 and 1945, faced with the possibility of a surface action against the experienced sailors of the Kriegsmarine, with their powerfully armed and strongly armoured cruisers, it is understandable that Soviet naval authorities were reluctant to risk their surface ships with their relatively inexperienced crews. Bagramian recorded in his memoirs that, as had been the case elsewhere, for example along the Black Sea coast and during the fighting around Lake Peipus, the Soviet High Command had intended to mount seaborne operations, including landings along the Courland coast, but the resources for such an undertaking were not available. Had even limited landings been possible, Army Group North would have been forced to deploy precious resources to protect the coast, which would have made assaults on the main front line much easier for the Red Army.

The fourth battle of Courland commenced on 23 January, and sought to tie down as much of Army Group North as possible. The first bombardment fell upon the ranks of the German 215th Infantry Division, near Saldus, and was followed by a swift Soviet attack, with infantry forces supported by tanks. Immediately, a penetration into the German positions was achieved near the village of Brammani, but despite repeated assaults by the Soviet 42nd Army, determined German counter-attacks consistently restored the front. 12th Panzer Division had been assigned the half-tracks left in Courland by the departing 4th Panzer Division, and used these to re-equip a battalion of its 5th Panzergrenadier Regiment; these troops found themselves deployed in counter-attacks to eliminate the Soviet penetrations.

Sturmgeschütz-Brigade 912 found itself in action near Priekule, where Soviet forces attempted to drive towards Liepāja. As had been the case in earlier battles, the assault guns proved to be formidable opponents, dealing with Soviet tanks and infantry alike. Major Brandner, the brigade commander, was credited with his 57th personal 'kill', and his brigade's overall claimed tally for the war passed the 500 mark. Fighting continued until 3 February, when, as had been the case in earlier Soviet assaults, the boggy ground rendered further combat almost impossible. Once more, the front line had barely moved.

By the end of the battle, the German forces in Courland were no longer designated Army Group North. As part of a general reorganisation of the German army groups on the Eastern Front, the former Army Group Centre, in northern Poland and East Prussia, became Army Group North, and 16th and 18th Armies became part of the new Army Group Courland. 215th Infantry Division, which had been so heavily involved in the fighting in the Courland Bridgehead, was withdrawn from the front line and ordered to proceed to Liepāja. From there, it was transported by sea to Gdansk, in an attempt to bring reinforcements to the shattered German 2nd Army. Like other men who served in Courland, many of its personnel had a generally positive view of their former army group commander:

> Our supply system functioned well, as did the mail from home. When it came to major fighting, there were always sufficient supplies of ammunition. In the times of greatest danger, tanks or assault guns rolled into our positions and forced the enemy out with their fire.
>
> This was no accident. At that time we were commanded by the future Field Marshal Ferdinand Schörner. His rigorous measures made him many enemies and caused bitterness. However, he always made sure that the rear-area services literally did everything to optimally supply the fighting troops. None of the staffs, right down to the battalion level, gave up a single position without good reason. There were no signs of deterioration on the front in Courland. All of that made it impossible for the enemy to conquer us.[8]

On 29 January, Army Group Courland received a new commander: Generaloberst Heinrich von Vietinghoff. The son of a military family, he had finished the First

World War with the rank of *Hauptmann*, and led 5th Panzer Division during the invasion of Poland. He was a corps commander in France and *Barbarossa*, before taking over command of 9th Army after Walter Model was wounded in June 1942. He had commanded 15th Army in the west, then 10th Army in Italy, and now found himself assigned to replace Carl Hilpert in Courland. As soon as he arrived, he ordered his staff to draw up a plan in cooperation with the Kriegsmarine for a complete seaborne evacuation of the army group. Codenamed *Laura*, the plan was presented to Hitler on 15 February by Guderian, Chief of Staff at OKH. By concentrating all its naval and transport assets, Guderian advised the Führer, it would be possible to evacuate the entire strength of 16th and 18th Armies, together with much of their equipment, in four weeks. Guderian commended the plan, but after two days, Hitler rejected it. There could be no question of a withdrawal from Courland, he insisted.

How practical would it have been to evacuate Army Group Courland at this late stage of the war? In late January, the Kriegsmarine evacuated the personnel of its U-boat training formations from the eastern Baltic, and used surplus shipping capacity to take wounded soldiers and civilian refugees to the ports of northern Germany and Denmark. As the days passed, the operation, codenamed *Hannibal*, became predominantly an attempt to rescue the hundreds of thousands of refugees who had fled the advancing Red Amy and were now packed into the ports of Pillau, Gdansk and Gdynia. Any diversion of shipping to rescue Army Group Courland would have brought *Hannibal* to a complete halt. The consequences of this for the trapped civilians would have been considerable. The use of almost every available ship allowed *Hannibal* to complete the civilian evacuation only days before the end of the war, so its suspension for several weeks would have resulted in tens of thousands of refugees being left in the east Baltic ports when they fell; given that the ports became fiercely contested battlefields, many of the trapped refugees would probably have died. The evacuation of Courland would also have exposed the ships involved to an additional day at sea, under hostile skies with the constant threat of Soviet submarine attack. Although Soviet attempts to interdict *Hannibal* had only limited impact, it is likely that a greater effort would have been made if the shipping had been carrying almost exclusively military personnel. Consequently, not only would the men of Army Group Courland have suffered losses from aerial and submarine attack, but the ships damaged and lost in such attacks would then no longer have been available for any resumption of *Hannibal* at the end of the Courland evacuation. One can conclude, therefore, that *Laura* would have been a hazardous enterprise, with inevitable consequences for German naval operations elsewhere.

Meanwhile, in Courland, fighting continued. A substantial number of Sherman tanks, supplied to the Red Army by the Americans, were delivered to the depleted Soviet armies in early February, allowing them to restore their combat strength. On 17 February, air operations against the ports of Ventspils and Liepāja intensified; it is possible that the Soviet High Command was aware to some extent of the plans for *Laura*.

The withdrawal of 4th Panzer Division from Courland substantially reduced the armoured assets of the army group. In an attempt to improve the flexibility of the remaining forces, a new formation, named *Panzer Brigade Kurland*, was created. Commanded first by Oberst von Usedom, then Major Graf von Rittberg, the brigade was initially termed *Panzer Aufklärungs-Gruppe Kurland* ('Armoured Reconnaissance Group Courland'), and consisted of the reconnaissance battalions of 12th and 14th Panzer Divisions. The group then received the personnel of *Grenadier Sturmbataillon Kurland* ('Grenadier Assault Battalion Courland'), another improvised formation, and a battalion of combat engineers. Two battalions of tank destroyers provided additional firepower. These were predominantly equipped with the excellent Jagdpanzer Pz.38(t) or *Hetzer*, a low-slung assault gun armed with a powerful 75mm gun mounted on the chassis of the Pz.38. This chassis had started life as the Czech Pz.38 tank, and was used by the Wehrmacht in the early years of the war. Although it had an excellent reputation for reliability, its relatively thin armour and small turret – which prevented the fitting of a gun powerful enough to deal with modern enemy tanks – rendered it obsolete. In its new role as a tank destroyer, equipped with a similar gun to the Pz.IV and *Sturmgeschütz III*, it was a capable vehicle. In addition to several *Hetzer* tank destroyers, *Panzer Brigade Kurland* also had a company of ten captured T34s. The creation of the brigade weakened 12th and 14th Panzer Divisions; their reconnaissance battalions had a powerful mixture of half-tracks and armoured cars, and were often used as independent battlegroups. However, the new brigade, effectively functioning as another battlegroup, was able to remedy some of the problems caused by the withdrawal of 4th Panzer Division.

On 20 February, the fifth battle of Courland commenced, with a heavy artillery bombardment of the German lines, using about 2,000 guns and mortars. There was little variation in either the tactics or objectives of the Soviet attack. As had been the case in previous bombardment, diagonal lanes were left clear during the preparatory bombardment, to allow the assault formations to move forward unobserved. The intention of this assault, as with previous attacks, was to separate the two armies of Army Group Courland, allowing for their destruction in detail. The attack, with about 21 rifle divisions with armoured support, fell either side of Priekule.[9]

On this occasion, there appears to have been confusion in the Soviet attack plans; many of the infantry units assigned for the initial assault failed to move forward during the artillery bombardment, resulting at first in isolated groups of tanks attempting to penetrate the German positions with little support. The German 126th Infantry Division had plenty of warning of the coming attack. Soviet forces attempted to secure jumping-off positions prior to their main assault, and the German 426th Grenadier Regiment found itself involved in desperate fighting. The regiment had been reduced to a single battalion prior to the battle, and despite receiving reinforcements in the form of *Sturmbataillon 18* ('18th Assault Battalion'), an improvised formation made up of training units and rear area personnel, the remnants of the regiment, reduced to about 200 men, found themselves surrounded by the end of the first day. On 21 February, the regiment came under repeated attack, but was able to hold its position, not least due to excellent artillery support. The following day, Oberst Henning Daubert, the regiment commander, was given permission to break out and retreat; his regiment had bought valuable time for a new defensive line to be established. As the Germans prepared themselves for a breakout, Soviet tanks penetrated into their positions. Confused fighting followed, but the majority of Daubert's men were able to escape to the new front line. Daubert was awarded the Knight's Cross for his role in the fighting.[10]

The town of Priekule was declared a fortress on 21 February, meaning that its garrison, 422nd Grenadier Regiment (part of 126th Infantry Division), was required to hold the town to the last man. Fortunately for the men of the regiment, they were ordered to fight their way back to the new front line, and abandoned Priekule in the early hours of 22 February. Led by a small group of assault guns, they succeeded in reaching German lines.

After the loss of its reconnaissance battalion, 14th Panzer Division organised itself into a heavy armoured battlegroup and a light, infantry-strong battlegroup. This latter group had defended the German positions near Priekule prior to the Soviet assault of 20 February, and the single company of Panther tanks attached to the battlegroup, commanded by Hauptmann Herbert Zimmermann, found itself facing repeated Soviet armoured attacks. It seems that the Soviet tanks failed to concentrate their numbers sufficiently, and attacked in small groups; these proved easy prey for the powerful guns of the Panthers, which claimed 26 kills in a little more than a day for no losses of their own. It is interesting to note that similar lack of coordination of Soviet armour was reported by German troops in the fighting in East Prussia after the initial Soviet drive to the Baltic coast came to an end, and this may reflect increasing numbers of second-echelon units, lacking the experience of the elite tank armies, being thrown into the battlefield.[11]

Brandner's *Sturmgeschütz-Brigade 912* was also thrown into the fighting in support of 11th Infantry Division. Despite having his personal assault gun knocked out – it was subsequently recovered and repaired, though hit at least twice more before the end of the fifth battle of Courland – Brandner's vehicles succeeded in stopping the Soviet assault from breaking through the German lines. Brandner received the Oak Leaves to the Knight's Cross for his brigade's repeated interventions in the most critical sectors of fighting.[12] Regardless of the achievements of Brandner and his brigade, his personal story highlights the perils of interpreting claims for the number of enemy vehicles knocked out. The two hits that forced him to abandon his assault gun were probably claimed as 'kills' by the Soviet unit involved – perhaps as two kills, given that two different Soviet tanks might have been involved – even though the assault gun was subsequently repaired and returned to action. The further hits it sustained may also have been claimed as 'kills', particularly if Brandner was forced to disengage from combat as a result, even if only temporarily.

Whilst most of the ships arriving at the ports of Liepāja and Ventspils carried munitions and other supplies, some brought reinforcements. The replacement battalion of 290th Infantry Division was in Denmark, and was ordered to Stettin, where it embarked aboard the steamer *Göttingen* on 21 February. The ship was carrying a total of 5,000 personnel to Courland, and its captain would have been aware of the threat of Soviet attacks. Late on 22 February, he received a radio warning that a Soviet submarine had been spotted in the area, but he calculated that it was sufficiently far from his course not to pose a threat. At 0430hrs on 23 February, two torpedoes struck the *Göttingen*, when she was 18 miles short of her destination, Liepāja. The ship sank rapidly, but not before a distress signal was sent. Several small vessels rushed to the scene from Liepāja, and about 2,000 men were saved and taken to Courland. The rest drowned.

At the beginning of March, the Red Army tried to force the lines of VI SS Corps. The weather had turned frosty, allowing for Soviet armour to manoeuvre with greater freedom on the frozen ground. By committing all available reserves to the fighting, including *Panzer Brigade Kurland*, the Germans were able to hold up the attack until a sudden thaw in the middle of the month brought major fighting to a halt again, and marked the end of the fifth battle of Courland. Casualties on both sides were heavy, but at least this time the Red Army had something to show for its assaults: the ruins of Priekule, in the west, and Dzukste, in the east, were in Soviet hands. At the end of the battle, Army Group Courland reported that since the isolation of the peninsula the previous October, the Red Army had lost 320,000 dead, wounded or taken prisoner, 2,388 tanks, 695 aircraft, and 906 heavy guns.[13] These figures could be little more than guesses, and are probably hugely inflated.

Von Vietinghoff's command of Army Group Courland proved to be a short one. He was sent back to Italy, and after a brief period when the group was under the command of Lothar Rendulic, Carl Hilpert became the last commander of the Courland armies. He was replaced as commander of 16th Army by General Ernst-Anton von Krosigk, who was in post for less than a week before he was killed in an artillery bombardment. His replacement was Friedrich-Jobst Volckamer von Kirchensittenbach.

Fighting did not exactly stop between the various Courland battles, but certainly reduced in intensity. The pause between the fifth and sixth battles was only a few days. On 18 March, 10th Guards Army attacked towards Saldus after another heavy artillery preparation. The depleted German infantry divisions of XXXVIII Corps struggled to hold the front line, and 14th Panzer Division was committed almost immediately to the fighting. Although 10th Guards Army was halted south of Saldus, the town remained under pressure, with the Soviet 42nd Army advancing from the east. A battlegroup of 24th Infantry Division held the railway station at Jostaji for four days while neighbouring units pulled back to relative safety. By the end of the month, the intensity of fighting died down again. Army Group Courland was still intact, though looking decidedly battered.

The attrition of the fighting – as heavy as any during the long, bitter campaigns of the Eastern Front – had taken a heavy toll on the German divisions. Hilpert prepared a detailed analysis of his formations on 1 April. He reported that only five of his divisions – 11th, 24th, 81st, and 121st Infantry Divisions, and 12th Panzer Division – could be graded as still being at a high standard. Five further infantry divisions were rated as good, but the rest were barely 'adequate', on account of their losses, both in absolute terms and in terms of experienced officers. 14th Panzer Division, one of the bulwarks of the German defence, had only a handful of armoured vehicles left, and amounted to barely more than a battlegroup.[14] However, the terrible losses of the Red Army during the fighting had greatly degraded the combat-worthiness of the Soviet formations that faced them. Here, in a corner of Latvia, the German and Soviet soldiers fought on in battles that were increasingly meaningless, neither able to prevail over the other, but neither willing to stop.

On 13 April, Hilpert ordered naval and Luftwaffe units in Courland to provide more manpower for his front-line units. Remarkably, the Luftwaffe managed to release sufficient men to create 17 infantry battalions, but the lack of heavy weaponry, and total lack of combat training, meant that these formations would be of very limited use, should a seventh battle of Courland commence. But it became increasingly clear that the Red Army had finally tired of the pointless fighting. From east to west, its lines were held by 1st Shock Army, 22nd Army, 4th Shock Army, 6th Guards Army, and 51st Army. The rest of the major formations were withdrawn from the front line. A further indication of the irrelevance of the Courland fighting came on 3 May. All along the front line, Soviet guns suddenly opened fire, lighting up the sky with tracers and flares. At first, the Germans prepared for yet another onslaught, but it rapidly became clear that the firing was more of a celebration than a bombardment. A few minutes later, Soviet loudspeakers confirmed this suspicion: the Red Army was marking the fall of Berlin, hundreds of miles to the west.

Of all the German forces still in the field, Army Group Courland was now perhaps the most coherent, and the one most capable of continued resistance, but there would be no further tests of its strength. Together with the German forces in the Vistula estuary and the Hela peninsula – *Armee Oberkommando Ostpreussen*, or 'Army High Command East Prussia' – the troops in Courland now became the focus of a last desperate effort to evacuate them to the west. Surrender to the Allies was inevitable, but, wherever possible, the Wehrmacht intended to surrender to the British or Americans rather than to the Red Army. The appalling treatment dealt out to Soviet prisoners of war by the Wehrmacht during the years of victory, and the long history of brutal atrocities by both sides, made the prospect of final surrender to the Soviet Union something to be avoided at all costs. Konteradmiral Conrad Engelhardt, who held the post of *Seetransportchef der Wehrmacht* ('Sea Transport Chief of the Wehrmacht'), had overseen the evacuation of hundreds of thousands of Germans, civilians and soldiers alike, as part of *Hannibal*. Now, the last civilians – or at least, the last of those who wished to leave – had been taken to the relative safety of north Germany and Denmark, and it was time to consider an evacuation of the last troops in the east.

Compared to previous proposals for the evacuation of Courland, such as *Laura*, the task was now far simpler. There would be no need to provide shipping space for equipment; the only consideration was to transport as many men as possible to the west. It would be possible, therefore, to evacuate both Army Group Courland and *AOK Ostpreussen* in a far shorter period than had previously been imagined – provided sufficient shipping was available. And here, Engelhardt found himself at the end of his resources. Although Soviet submarine and air attacks had sunk only a relatively small number of ships (though the losses of the *Goya* and *Wilhelm Gustloff* were probably the two worst losses of life at sea in history), many of the freighters, former trans-Atlantic liners and coastal vessels that he had cobbled together for his rescue fleet had been damaged, either as a result of Soviet action or simply due to mechanical breakdown. In the last days of the Third Reich, repairs for any of these ships were almost impossible. To make matters worse, throughout the course of *Hannibal*, Engelhardt had struggled to secure sufficient fuel oil and coal to keep his fleet running, and fuel supplies were now almost exhausted.

The negotiations that had begun with the Western Allies about a final surrender of the Reich were strongly influenced by the plight of the soldiers still fighting on the Eastern Front. Grossadmiral Karl von Dönitz, who had become leader of Germany after Hitler's death, was desperate to secure a ceasefire in the west, while continuing to resist the Red Army in the east, and on 3 May, his headquarters sent a signal to General Dietrich von Saucken, who was now commander of *AOK Ostpreussen*:

> The changed military situation in the Reich requires the urgent evacuation of numerous troops from East and West Prussia as well as Courland.
>
> Combat operations by the army in East Prussia and Army Group Courland are to reflect this requirement.
>
> Personnel with light infantry weapons are to be embarked for return. All other materiel, including horses, is to be left behind and destroyed. Army Group Courland is given operational freedom to pull back the front line to the planned bridgeheads at the ports of Windau [Ventspils] and Libau [Liepāja].
>
> The Kriegsmarine will dispatch all available transports to East Prussia and Courland.[15]

At the same time, Dönitz tried to obtain terms from the Western Allies that would allow operations, including evacuations, to continue on the Eastern Front, even after a ceasefire was signed in the west. At first, there seemed a prospect of achieving some such understanding; on 4 May, Admiral Hans-Georg von Friedeburg, one of the German emissaries negotiating with the Western Allies, reported to Dönitz that the British required any surrender to include the Netherlands and Denmark, but that Montgomery would issue orders that would prevent any interference with the ongoing evacuation from the east. A ceasefire was signed that evening, coming into force at 0800hrs on 5 May.

When Generaloberst Alfred Jodl, the leader of the German delegation, and Friedeburg proceeded to Rheims, where they met Eisenhower's staff, they had a somewhat different reception. The Germans insisted that the disruption of communications caused by the collapse of the Reich would make any immediate ceasefire in the east difficult to achieve. The Kriegsmarine had advised Dönitz that, provided sufficient fuel could be found, all the troops in Courland and the Vistula estuary could be brought west in three days. But unlike Montgomery and the British, Eisenhower refused to countenance any such arrangement. Although the Germans made repeated representations, they were all rebuffed, and early on 7 May, Jodl sent a message to Dönitz. Eisenhower insisted on immediate surrender on all fronts, he said, and any ships at sea would have to surrender to whichever Allied Power had been assigned control of that region. If the Germans were not willing to accept these terms, Jodl reported, Eisenhower threatened to prosecute the war to the very end. In order to prevent any prevarication, Jodl was given just 30 minutes to decide whether the terms were acceptable. He advised Dönitz that in his view, there was no alternative to accepting the terms.[16]

At 0130hrs on 7 May, Dönitz sent a radio message to Jodl, authorising him to agree to the terms offered by Eisenhower. The ceasefire would come into effect at 0900hrs on 9 May. At the same time, Engelhardt and his staff were ordered to redouble their efforts to bring as many personnel west as was possible in the few hours that remained. Inevitably, the main effort concentrated on the Vistula estuary, as its relative proximity to Denmark and Germany allowed for more journeys to be made. Nevertheless, ships were also dispatched to Liepāja and Ventspils, where they joined forces with vessels already present. Aware of the extreme time pressure under which they were operating, the commander of the German destroyers still seaworthy in the Baltic sent a signal from aboard one of his ships shortly before midnight on 8 May:

8 May 1945, 2323/AD/53 KR-Blitz [urgent-expedite]
To all units engaged in eastern transport: operate in the spirit of the assigned mission. Make haste![17]

A similar sense of urgency gripped the ships and men of the Kriegsmarine's 9th Security Division, which operated the minesweepers and torpedo boats active around Courland. Their orders also left no room for confusion:

As a result of the changed situation subsequent to the surrender, all sea and security forces, as well as all commercial shipping, must depart from the harbours of Courland and Hela [the naval base on the northern side of the Bay of Danzig, in German hands until the final surrender] by 0100 on 9 May. Ships and boats are to proceed to the harbour limits of Kiel, Eckernförde and Neustadt. Putting in at other harbours en route is prohibited based upon the situation.[18]

Hilpert and his staff in Army Group Courland had already started making arrangements for the final surrender. Front-line units were thinned out, then withdrawn from the front line that had been defended at such a terrible cost throughout the winter. The German troops were under orders to destroy as much equipment as possible as they retreated, but the shortage of explosives and in particular specially designed demolition charges made the destruction of the few remaining tanks almost impossible. Instead, the crews of 14th Panzer Division simply drove them into the swamps. Collection stations were created in rear areas, where radios, maps and other documents were left, and then set ablaze.[19]

Right to the last moment, the German military authorities were able to maintain discipline in the rear areas, particularly in the ports. Karl Roth, a *Stabsfeldwebel* from 14th Panzer Division, had been in Liepāja with other rear area units of the division since the end of the sixth battle of Courland, and had found a small sailboat. As the final surrender came closer, he provisioned it with food, water, and a map and compass. When the end came, he intended to try to sail across the Baltic to Sweden, but received a last-minute chance to escape. There was only a very limited number of spaces aboard the few ships available, and these were allocated mainly to wounded men, non-combatants, and soldiers who were fathers of young families or the last surviving sons of their families. Each division in Courland was ordered to draw up suitable lists, and Roth was included as he had a two-year-old daughter. He thus secured a place on board a torpedo boat, and gave his sailboat to less fortunate comrades. He later learned that they succeeded in sailing to Sweden.[20]

The torpedo boats that played such a large part in the evacuation were far larger than British or American vessels of the same appellation. They had a displacement of 1,400 to 2,300 tons, and were armed with four 105mm guns in twin turrets, with a number of smaller 30mm anti-aircraft guns, as well as six torpedo tubes; they were therefore more akin to small destroyers than torpedo boats. Large numbers of soldiers now crammed into their limited cabin space, with others crowding onto their decks. The crews tried, not always successfully, to ensure that the areas around their gun turrets were kept free, so that the weapons could be traversed and fired if necessary. Astonishing numbers of men managed to come aboard, with up to 2,000 being carried by a single warship with a displacement of barely 2,000 tons.

Some men made it aboard the ships through pure luck. Leo Schwartz, another member of 14th Panzer Division, was in the port of Liepāja on the last day of the war, and leapt aboard a small vessel to escape a sudden Soviet artillery bombardment of the area. To his relief, the captain allowed him to stay aboard. He and 120 others willingly endured a cramped voyage aboard a vessel intended to have a crew of only

12, in order to escape Soviet captivity.[21] 12th Panzer Division was granted permission to send its field replacement battalion (a formation used to complete the training of new personnel assigned to the division), an artillery battalion and a combat engineer company back to Germany. The division staff ensured that the personnel of these formations were made up entirely of those who conformed to the generally agreed selection criteria.[22]

Other men turned down opportunities to leave Courland. An infantry *Hauptmann* approached the captain of a torpedo boat and handed him a list of names; he asked if the naval officer would make their families aware that they had gone into Soviet captivity. The torpedo boat commander offered to take the *Hauptmann* with him, but the infantry officer refused. Although he would have qualified for a place, as he was the father of young children, he felt that his place was with those of his men who had to surrender to the Red Army.[23]

Just hours before the final ceasefire, the vessels gathered in Liepāja and Ventspils began to leave, forming five convoys. Between them, they carried about 23,000 troops away from Courland. The last convoy, commanded by Fregattenkapitän Karl Palmgreen, which left at the very last moment, succeeded in crowding over 11,000 soldiers into its ships. Soviet aircraft attacked the convoy with machine guns, killing many of those aboard, but almost all the ships managed to reach the north German coast. Three ferries were unable to make the long crossing, and instead made for the Swedish coast. Like other soldiers from Courland and the Vistula estuary, they were interned by the Swedes.

For a few of Army Group Courland's personnel, there was at least the possibility of escape by air. Several Ju52 transport planes arrived in Courland early on 8 May, landing at the Luftwaffe airfield at Grobiņa. They took aboard wounded and others nominated for evacuation, but as they attempted to fly to northern Germany, they were intercepted by Soviet fighters. Only two transports succeeded in reaching their destination; the rest were shot down. The last fighters of *Jagdgeschwader 54*, which had provided air support for Army Group Courland throughout the six great battles, had already left for Germany, and were unable to help. Many of the fighters had had their armour and other equipment stripped out, to make room to allow a ground crewman to squeeze in behind the pilot's seat.

The remnants of Army Group Courland – nearly 200,000 officers and men – prepared to go into captivity. Some chose alternatives. General von Bodenhausen, who had led 12th Panzer Division in Courland before briefly taking command of L Corps, chose suicide over surrender. Other members of his division attempted the long escape route through Latvia, Lithuania, East Prussia, and Poland; although most were captured, a small number succeeded in reaching German soil.[24] For the rest, there was only the prospect of surrender. Hilpert sent a signal to his units on 7 May that dispelled any last rumours of escape, or even that the British were about to intervene on the side of the Germans: 'According to the agreement with Soviet Marshal Govorov, the ceasefire takes effect at 1400. I request loyal compliance by the troops, since the future fate of the army group depends upon it.'[25]

Sturmgeschütz-Brigade 912 still had several operational assault guns, and on 8 May, Major Brandner thanked his men in a final parade for their service. He then positioned his remaining assault guns around the headquarters buildings and waited for the Soviet troops to arrive. A Soviet colonel approached the position and, via an interpreter, requested that the brigade surrender its weapons. Brandner replied that he had been ordered to respect a ceasefire, but had not yet received orders to surrender. The Soviet delegation withdrew, and Brandner and his officers proceeded to destroy their documents and equipment. The following morning, they surrendered formally and went into captivity.

The Latvians who had fought alongside the Germans were now faced with the bitter reality of surrendering to the Soviet Union. Some slipped away to join the anti-communist partisans, while a small number took their own lives. It is estimated that about 14,000 Latvian combatants surrendered; 19th SS Waffen-Grenadier Division had been reduced in strength to a little over 5,000 men. Obergruppenführer Krüger, commander of VI SS Corps, attempted to escape to East Prussia overland. When his group was intercepted by a Soviet patrol, he shot himself.

There were other Baltic citizens serving with the German forces, far from home. The men of 20th SS Waffen-Grenadier Division, the former Estonian 'volunteer' division, were evacuated from their homeland with other German forces. The division had suffered major losses, and was sent to Neuhammer to be replenished and restored to full strength. This process was incomplete when the final crisis on the Eastern Front developed, and the division was dispatched to Silesia in January 1945 in an attempt to repair the huge hole that Konev's armies had torn in the German front. The Estonians fought a constant rearguard action as they were driven west, and were encircled near Neustadt, to the east of Dresden. Several elements of the division managed to fight their way through the Soviet lines, and retreated west, though any overall coherence of the division had long since disappeared. Most of the men surrendered to the Red Army, though some succeeded in reaching the advancing Americans.

The Latvians of 15th SS Waffen-Grenadier Division, which was almost destroyed in the summer of 1944, were largely absorbed into 19th SS Waffen-Grenadier

Division, though the nucleus of the original division was evacuated to Zempelburg, in West Prussia. Like the Estonian division, 19th SS Waffen-Grenadier Division began the slow process of rebuilding, and was sent to the front line in February in a desperate attempt to stop the Red Army's drive into Pomerania. Near Schneidemühl, the division suffered heavy casualties, and retreated north-west with 33rd SS Waffen-Grenadier Division *Charlemagne*, a formation made up of French SS. When they reached the Baltic coast, the Latvians retreated west, finally reaching the Oder estuary. Here, the survivors were required to hand over their weapons to German units – which caused bitter resentment amongst the starving, exhausted men who had carried their weapons back during a long retreat – and were finally organised into a single regiment. Two battalions of this regiment found themselves facing the final Soviet assault on Berlin, and succeeded in avoiding becoming embroiled in the fight for the German capital. They skirted the southern edge of the city, and on 25 April the remnants of the division – a little over 800 officers and men – surrendered to the Americans. Other elements of the division surrendered to advancing elements of the Western Allies a few days later.

As fighting died down throughout Europe, the final surrender in Courland brought an almost unreal silence to the landscape, still strewn with the wreckage of the bitter battles. Here, the German capitulation had an added significance, in that it marked the end of centuries of German involvement in the region. For the three Baltic States, an uncertain future lay ahead.

Chapter 12
AFTERMATH

The end of the Second World War was marked in many ways. There were joyous celebrations in Britain, France, the United States, the Soviet Union and the other powers that had fought to defeat Germany. In many of the countries liberated from German occupation, there was quiet relief. For the three Baltic States, the end of the war merely marked the beginning of a new phase of rule by a foreign power.

Estonia, the first of the Baltic States to be wrested from German control, had already experienced attempts at mobilisation of its manpower for the Soviet war effort. Those who had worked with the Germans in roles not requiring them to bear arms were treated as being unreliable for front line service, but were required to perform labour duties both in Estonia and the Soviet Union; in order to avoid being sent to the bloody battlefields of Courland, many men therefore claimed that they had worked for the Germans. Similar patterns were seen both in Latvia and Lithuania. As has been discussed, subsequent Soviet punishment of those who had 'collaborated' with the Germans resulted in these individuals being arrested, and in many cases deported to Siberia.

The war had a huge impact on the economies of the three countries. Many industrial areas were devastated in the fighting, while others were deliberately destroyed, either by the retreating Red Army in 1941 or by the retreating Wehrmacht in 1944. As a result, Estonian industrial output at the end of the war amounted to only 55 per cent of pre-war figures. Transport was badly disrupted, with only 7 per cent the transport activity of 1939. Damage to major towns and cities had reduced housing to 45 per cent, and the amount of land under cultivation to 60 per cent.[1] In Lithuania, the Soviet authorities recorded that at least 21 villages had been completely destroyed by the Germans, often as part of anti-partisan operations, and 56 electricity-generating stations had been damaged or destroyed as the Wehrmacht withdrew.

Additional disruption was caused by the immense damage to the transport infrastructure, with over 1,140 bridges in Lithuania being destroyed in an attempt to hinder the Soviet advance.[2]

The three countries also experienced immediate changes to their borders. Even before the fighting had come to an end, in early 1945, Estonia was required to hand over the territory it had secured on the east bank of the Narva during its war of independence, and most of the county of Petseri, to the Soviet Union; this amounted to 5 per cent of its land area, and 6 per cent of its population. Latvia, too, was required to cede territory, about 2 per cent of its land area.[3] Lithuania had effectively lost territory already, as a result of the way that the Soviet Union handled the return of Vilnius in 1939, granting large parts of the former Vilnius territory to Belarus. The area known to the Germans as Memelland, stretching from Klaipėda to the line of the River Niemen, was returned to Lithuania.

Inevitably, in an area that had been the scene of such bitter fighting, there were plentiful supplies of weapons and munitions. There were significant numbers of former Axis soldiers at large in the countryside, both Germans and citizens of the Baltic States, and many of these now began to form anti-Soviet armed groups. During the unrest of 1905, many of those who took up arms against the Czarist regime in the Baltic States had hidden in the widespread forests, and the term 'Forest Brothers' – *metsavennad* in Estonia, *meža brāļi* in Latvia, *miško broliai* in Lithuania – was coined to describe both peasants who refused to cooperate with the authorities and those who fled to the countryside from the cities and towns.[4] The term reappeared during the first Soviet occupation of 1939–41, but became far more widespread following the defeat of Germany. As will be seen, the various groups fought against the Red Army units that occupied their countries, and against those they deemed as collaborating with the occupation; many held on to the hope that, as at the end of the First World War, the Western Powers would intervene to help them achieve independence.

In Estonia, many of those who sought to avoid conscription joined the widespread bands of Forest Brothers; when the Soviet-installed authorities took punitive measures against their families, this served merely to encourage others to take the same path. It is estimated that up to 15,000 Estonians fought against Soviet rule in the Forest Brothers groups, with the main areas of resistance in the south-east and south-west.

Richard Saaliste, who served as an officer in an Estonian border regiment, was wounded twice during the war, and in 1944 found himself on Hiiumaa Island. Here, he organised an escape route to Sweden for Estonians who wished to escape the German occupation. He was arrested by the Germans, but used personal contacts in the German military to secure his own release. In October 1944, when the Red Army landed on Hiiumaa, Saaliste fled to Sweden. In the summer of 1945, he attempted to return to Estonia, but turned back when he was nearly intercepted by a Soviet patrol boat. In October 1946, he tried again with three others. Although they landed successfully, they ran into a coastal patrol almost immediately. In the firefight that followed, two of the Estonians were killed, but Saaliste managed to evade his would-be captors. This encounter was no accident; an informer within Saaliste's organisation had informed the Soviet authorities of his plans, and it was only due to the poor execution of the Soviet ambush that Saaliste was able to avoid capture. He established contact with his brother, who was already an active member of the Forest Brothers, and helped them establish communications links with émigré groups in Sweden.[5]

By June 1947, Saaliste and others had united several disparate groups into a united and organised movement, the *Relvastadud Voitluse Liit* ('Armed Resistance League' or RVL). The movement continued to hope for western intervention, as its declaration made clear: 'The organisation is preparing an armed uprising against the Soviet regime at such a time when England and the United States go to war against the Soviet Union, or when a political coup occurs in the Soviet Union itself.'[6]

As a consequence of this aim, attacks on the Soviet authorities and pro-Soviet Estonians diminished, as the RVL attempted to preserve and develop further its network, in readiness for future action. Nor did the RVL attempt to absorb all the Forest Brothers into its ranks; rather, it tried to maintain links with resistance groups throughout the country. Nevertheless, combat against the Red Army continued. In Pärnumaa County, railway and other lines of communications were disrupted 22 times in just three months.[7]

Estonian resistance reached its maximum impact in 1947. In many parts of the countryside, the RVL and local Forest Brothers effectively controlled not only the forests, but also the villages and smaller towns, particularly at night. For much of the time, Soviet supply columns could only move if escorted by substantial bodies of troops. Some individuals in the resistance movement achieved considerable fame. One such person was Ants Kaljurand, known to ordinary Estonians as *Hirmus Ants* ('Ants the Terrible'). He was both a Forest Brother and a member of the RVL, and had fought for the Germans against the Soviet Union. He was one of many Estonians who chose to stay in their country as the Wehrmacht retreated. He was promptly captured, but succeeded in escaping and rapidly established a reputation for daring ventures. He allegedly rescued his girlfriend from captivity in Soontagana by visiting the town hall secretary in the middle of the night and demanding the keys to the cells at gunpoint, and was responsible for many attacks on Soviet and pro-Soviet Estonian personnel.[8]

With the country apparently slipping from their control, the Soviet authorities took stern measures. There were widespread arrests and sweeps of forests, and repeated attempts to infiltrate the RVL. Late in 1947, a failed attempt by a group of RVL fighters to seize a shipment of money resulted in the capture of a driver who had worked with many of the RVL's senior figures, and a series of attacks followed, in which many RVL hideouts and bunkers were destroyed, and a small number of RVL officers were either captured or killed; many took their own lives rather than fall into Soviet hands. Throughout 1948, RVL and Forest Brothers activity diminished, and General Boris Kumm, the Minister for State Security in the government of the Estonian Soviet Socialist Republic, declared – a little prematurely – that the RVL was no longer a functioning organisation. Fighting continued in 1949, and on 14 December, Richard Saaliste was killed when his bunker was overrun. Over the next two years, coordinated action by the RVL and Forest Brothers effectively ceased. Although a few individuals managed to continue to resist, the dreams of a mass uprising supported by the Western Powers rapidly faded. Ants Kaljurand was betrayed to the authorities in 1951. He was arrested, tried, and executed in Tallinn on 13 March.[9]

Soviet accounts tried to blame the resistance upon counter-revolutionaries, western spies and 'Kulaks', but the reality was that they enjoyed widespread support, though this fell away as Soviet arrests of all those who had any link with the resistance fighters detained ever-growing numbers of people. Partly in an attempt to destroy support for the Forest Brothers and the RVL, and partly to smooth the way for collectivisation of agriculture, the communist authorities in all three Baltic States took part in an operation codenamed *Priboi* ('Coastal surf' or 'Breaker'). The decision to implement a wave of mass deportations was taken in January 1949 by the Council of Ministers of the USSR, and additional forces were deployed specifically for the task. Arrests began on 25 March, and the operation lasted for three days. By the time it ended, nearly 20,000 Estonians had been deported to Siberia. Unlike the deportations of 1941, families were not forcibly separated, but all deportees were required to sign a declaration stating that they were 'special settlers' in Siberia, and faced arrest and hard labour if they attempted to return to their homelands.[10]

Like the Estonians, many Latvians also took up arms against the Soviet occupation. The total number of those involved may have been as high as 40,000, with perhaps a maximum of 10,000–15,000 active at any time.[11] In addition to Latvian nationals, the ranks of the resistance fighters included a small but significant number of German soldiers. Planning for a resistance movement began before the return of the Red Army. As has been discussed, the Latvians created the *Latvijas Centrālā Padome* ('Latvian Central Council' or LCP) in 1943, following the German defeat at

Stalingrad, to coordinate nationalist movements. From the start, the LCP opposed all foreign occupation, German or Soviet, and worked for a free and democratic Latvia.[12] The leader, Konstantīns Čakste, ensured that the organisation contained significant numbers of those who had been associates of the pre-war Ulmanis regime, but he also tried to incorporate all extremes of opinion. Previous sworn enemies such as the *Pērkonkrusts* and the Social Democrats, who had fought street battles during the 1930s, now found themselves within the same organisation. When the Red Army entered Latvian territory in 1944, many members of the LCP sought to leave the country, and despite German attempts to stop them, about 2,500 succeeded in fleeing to the Swedish island of Gotland. Here, they attempted to establish and build links with the Western Allies.

Back in Latvia, many of those who had hated the German occupation were now faced with a resumption of the even more hated Soviet occupation. General Kurelis created a volunteer force, initially with the approval of the Germans, who authorised *Frontaufklärungskommando 212*, a special part of General Gehlen's *Fremde Heere Ost*, the Wehrmacht's intelligence service in Eastern Europe, to train the Latvians.[13] Some of the Germans involved were impressed with their new recruits, with one describing them as 'most valuable ... many useful and satisfactory men, who sat purposelessly in the woods, [and now] once more could be involved in legitimate action'.[14] But as the 'Kurelis Army' developed, the Germans became increasingly aware of the anti-German sentiments of most of its personnel, and attempted to disband the Latvian force. This resulted in armed conflict between the two sides in mid-December 1944 in northern Courland, with German 'anti-partisan' sweeps that rivalled the brutality of similar operations in the territories to the east of the Latvian–Soviet border prior to the German retreat.

At the same time that the 'Kurelis Army' was developing, other elements of the German administration were taking part in Operation *Zeppelin*, a plan to establish anti-Soviet partisans throughout East Europe as the Wehrmacht fell back. The Latvian component of this plan, Operation *Wildkatze* ('Wildcat') was organised by the SS, using Latvian associates of the security police. The leader of the Latvians involved in *Wildkatze* was Boriss Jankavs, a former member of the *Arājs Kommando*. With many members of the *Pērkonkrusts* in its ranks, including a number specifically released from German imprisonment so that they could take part, the organisation run by Jankavs grew to incorporate groups such as *Latvijas Sargi* ('Latvian Guards'), which were then armed by the Germans in September 1944. It was a sign of the rapidly shifting political landscape that *Latvijas Sargi*, which was originally an anti-German group, was now armed by its former enemies.[15]

After the surrender of Army Group Courland, over 3,000 of the Latvians still serving alongside the Germans joined one or other of the active resistance movements in Latvia.[16] The movements had loose contacts both with each other and with similar organisations in Lithuania and Estonia. In addition to producing newsletters and other propaganda material, the groups attacked Latvian representatives of the communist authorities as well as Red Army and NKVD units. One such Latvian group, which included Talrids Krastiņš, a former member of a reconnaissance unit of 19th SS Waffen-Grenadier Division (2nd Latvian), attempted to assassinate Vilis Lācis, the head of the communist regime in Latvia. Acting on information from a Latvian woman who worked for the communist authorities, the group fired on a convoy of cars, but shot at the wrong vehicle. Undaunted, they recruited another female collaborator who also worked for the government to obtain intelligence that could be used in a future attack, but on this occasion, the woman turned out to be an agent of the NKVD. The group was arrested, and executed in 1948.[17] As in Estonia, activity in Latvia probably peaked in late 1946 and early 1947, and declined only after the mass deportations of *Priboi*, which resulted in nearly 42,000 Latvians being shipped to Siberia. Small groups continued to resist, both passively and actively, well into the 1950s, but with diminishing effect. The last fighters to surrender formally to the authorities handed themselves in as late as 1957; it is likely that others simply drifted back into civilian life.

Lithuania, which had provided the fewest combatants for the German cause during the war, proved to be the most active area for anti-Soviet resistance. In Estonia and Latvia, the Lutheran church tended to be identified with the Baltic Germans, and played little part in the resistance movements, but by contrast in Lithuania, the Catholic clergy were heavily involved, providing shelter and support to the fighters. The core of the movement came from personnel of the *Lietuvos Vietinė Rinktinė* ('Lithuanian Defence Force' or LVR) created by the Germans under the command of General Povilas Plechavičius in 1944. As was the case with the 'Kurelis Army' in Latvia, the LVR's strong nationalist tendencies had made the Germans increasingly nervous, and attempts were made to impose greater control on the group; at one stage it was proposed that it should become part of the SS, and in addition to taking a personal oath to Hitler, all members would have to use the Nazi salute. Plechavičius rejected these demands and pre-empted any German move to disband his group, ordering its members to disperse and take to the countryside; he was arrested in May 1944 and sent to a concentration camp, but about half of the LVR continued to function, mainly as small groups. Armed with a variety of weapons, ranging from small arms to mortars, the partisans established an organisation that extended throughout the country.

The LVR and other related groups fought against both the Soviet occupying forces and the local communist regime. The Soviet authorities reported that their own annual losses throughout 1945, 1946 and 1947 exceeded 8,700; during the same period, they claimed to have killed over 13,000 partisans, most of these during 1945. As was the case with anti-partisan operations conducted by the Germans during the war, this latter figure probably includes a significant number of civilians who were killed during Soviet anti-partisan sweeps. Over a thousand 'pro-Soviet civilians' also died during these years.[18] In 1949, with annual losses on both sides continuing to exceed 1,000, Jonas Žemaitis united the various Lithuanian groups under the title of *Lietuvos Laisvės Kovos Sąjūdis* ('Union of Lithuanian Freedom Fighters', or LLKS). The new High Command published a declaration calling for a restoration of democratic government and declaring the Communist Party an illegal organisation.

But the tide was turning against the anti-Soviet fighters throughout the region. As happened in Estonia and Latvia, *Priboi* greatly weakened the support base of the resistance fighters in Lithuania, with nearly 26,000 people being deported. Although the Western Powers showed interest in the resistance movements of all three countries, their attempts to provide support proved to be disastrous. Soviet infiltrators, both in the Baltic States and in the countries of the west, regularly provided detailed information to their controllers in Moscow, allowing the NKVD and its successor organisations to disrupt and destroy the partisan groups. Žemaitis suffered a stroke in 1951, and was captured in 1953; a year later, he was executed in Moscow. Adolfas Ramanauskas, his successor as commander of the LLKS, attempted to move the remnants of his organisation away from armed warfare and towards passive resistance. He was arrested in 1956 after he was betrayed by a former school friend, and brutally interrogated. In October, he was transferred to hospital, where a report was compiled showing how appallingly he had been treated. He had been stabbed at least six times through his right eyelid with a wire or nail, destroying the eye itself. His scrotum was badly torn, and both testes had been ripped out.[19] He survived until the following year, when he was sentenced to death and executed. His wife was sent to a labour camp in Siberia for eight years.

The last anti-Soviet partisan to be killed was Pranas Končius. In July 1965, he was involved in an exchange of fire with Soviet forces, and was either killed or shot himself. Remarkably, he was not the last partisan. In 1971, Benediktas Mikulis, who had been in hiding for an astonishing 27 years, during which he fought against both the Germans and the Soviets, decided to return to his family and attempted to slip back into normal society. A few years later, he was arrested and imprisoned. Other partisans, who escaped arrest, may have been active even later than Mikulis.

The scale and intensity of the resistance to Soviet rule, and its durability, was an unwelcome development for the Soviet regime. Stalin categorised all of the anti-Soviet partisans as 'fascists', and the attempts by the Western Powers to exploit the groups merely played into Soviet hands. But after Stalin's death in 1953, the Soviet authorities made attempts to bring the insurgency to an end. An amnesty was offered to all resistance fighters, and many took up the offer, a further factor in the weakening of the resistance movement.

Soviet control of the three countries was achieved through local communist parties, but although the First Secretaries of the three parties were local citizens, their deputies and other major figures were often Russians. As had been the case in previous occupations, a shortage of suitable local personnel at middle and lower tiers hamstrung the administrations of the three countries, a factor that was worsened by Soviet insistence that only those who had spent a minimum of 20 years in the Soviet Union undergoing 'Sovietisation' were entirely reliable. Although there were significant numbers of ethnic Estonians and Latvians who had lived in the Soviet Union prior to the war, they were regarded with contempt by their compatriots when they returned to take power under Soviet control. In the case of Lithuania, the pool of Lithuanians who were living in the Soviet Union was very limited, and in order to administer the country, large numbers of Russians moved into Lithuania; in 1947, 32 per cent of all government ministers were Russians. Similarly, the membership of the communist parties of the three countries was dominated by non-Balts. Until the end of the 1940s, only in Latvia did membership by Latvians approach 50 per cent, and this was largely due to the return to Latvia of large numbers of ethnic Latvians from the Soviet Union. Despite the use of Russians to try to ensure compliance in the three states, Moscow continued to be dissatisfied with arrangements, and in 1951, the Estonian Communist Party was heavily purged. The exact reasons are not clear, but widespread reluctance in the administration to embrace communist policies, particularly the collectivisation of agriculture, probably played a part.

The German and Latvian soldiers who surrendered in Courland in 1945 had been assured of good treatment and a swift return home at the end of the war. Like other Wehrmacht soldiers who surrendered to the Red Army in 1945, they were systematically robbed of their personal possessions, and in a few cases roughly treated. However, it appears that the determined resistance of the Wehrmacht in Courland had impressed the soldiers and officers of the Red Army, and there are many examples of the soldiers being treated with respect. The swift return to their homeland, however, did not materialise. The Soviet Union had suffered major losses, and was desperately short of manpower. The prisoners were transported east, and set to work in a variety of roles, ranging from clearing rubble to building factories and working in mines and fields. By 1949, many had been allowed to return home, but large numbers remained in captivity. Some, but by no means all, of these detainees had been charged with and convicted of a variety of crimes, and were no longer termed prisoners of war. The crimes they had allegedly committed varied hugely; in some cases, they included attacks on civilians and maltreatment of prisoners, but in other cases, the charges were absurd. One Luftwaffe pilot was sentenced to several years' hard labour for the crime of destroying Soviet state property – the property in question being the Soviet aircraft that he had shot down during the war. The death rate amongst those who were detained the longest was considerable, with fewer than 50 per cent surviving until 1956, when the German Chancellor, Konrad Adenauer, succeeded in negotiating their release during a momentous visit to Moscow.[20]

The German and Baltic soldiers who had succeeded in escaping to Sweden in the closing days of the war had an unpleasant shock awaiting them. At first, they were treated well, receiving payment for any work they undertook, but the Swedish government came under increasing pressure from Moscow. In June 1945, a formal demand was issued, requiring Sweden to hand over all former German combatants – including citizens of the Baltic States – who had fled to Sweden from the Eastern Front. The Swedish government was in a difficult position. Whilst many in Sweden, particularly the church and the military, were opposed to any such transfer, there were precedents for the handover of Germans. At the end of any war, former combatants were to be handed over to the controlling authority in their homeland, and as Germany had been divided into zones of occupation by the victorious Allies, this could be interpreted as requiring the Swedes to transfer Germans to whichever power they had fought against during the war. Consequently, some 3,000 Germans were handed over to the Soviet Union. Many attempted self-mutilation or even suicide as a means of avoiding extradition; once they had recovered from their injuries, they were extradited anyway.

The situation for the citizens of the Baltic States was somewhat more complicated, as they had not been fighting in the armies of their own nations during the war. There was also the difficult status of the Baltic States themselves. The Soviet Union viewed the soldiers as Soviet citizens, as Estonia, Latvia and Lithuania had become part of the Soviet Union prior to the German invasion, but this annexation had not been formally recognised by most other nations. Despite widespread protests against the extradition of any persons to the Soviet Union, about 150 Baltic soldiers – mainly Latvians who had escaped from the Courland Bridgehead or from West Prussia – were placed aboard the steamer *Beloostrov* in

Trelleborg on 25 January 1946. Two Latvian officers took their own lives rather than be handed over to the Soviet authorities.

Many of the Baltic soldiers who were returned to the Soviet Union, particularly the officers, were executed. The rest were sentenced to hard labour, and spent many years in captivity. In 1994, 44 of the group were still alive, and on 20 June, 40 of them – 35 Latvians, four Estonians, and a single Lithuanian – travelled to Stockholm, where they were received by King Carl XVI Gustaf. Margaretha af Ugglas, the Swedish Foreign Minister, acknowledged that the extraditions had been without legal justification, and stated the regrets of the Swedish government.[21]

The deaths in the Baltic States during the war, as a result of the fighting and the policies of the various occupying powers, resulted in a major change in the population. Accurate figures are hard to verify, but the total population reduction, as a result of Soviet deportations before and after the war, German extermination of Jews and others, and casualties from the fighting, was probably of the order of 20 per cent. This suggests that the Baltic States lost a greater proportion of their population than any other country in the Second World War, with the exception of Poland. It is striking that the countries that suffered the worst loss of population during and immediately after the Second World War were those that suffered occupation by both the Germans and the Soviets.

The few Baltic Jews who survived the Holocaust faced a difficult future. Samuel Esterowicz, one of those who owed his life to the efforts of Major Plagge, managed to find work in the new administration, but his past as a successful businessman meant that he was part of a class treated with suspicion by the communist authorities. A friend of his, Michal Girda, was arrested by the Soviets because he had served briefly with a White Russian unit in the Russian Civil War, and Esterowicz was forced to confirm this detail. When he was singled out for criticism when his department failed to achieve its performance targets, he concluded that there was no future for him in 'liberated' Lithuania. Along with over 90 per cent of other Baltic Holocaust survivors, he opted to emigrate to the west. He and his family left in a train of cattle-trucks in April 1945, travelling first to Poland, where they lived in Łódź. As anti-Jewish sentiment became more pronounced in the Polish population, the family travelled on to Italy before eventually emigrating to the United States.

Mascha Rolnikaite, who was taken from Vilnius after the liquidation of the ghetto to a work camp in Estonia, was later moved to Stutthof, near Gdansk. As the Red Army tore the German lines apart in the last winter of the war, she – like thousands of other concentration camp prisoners – was forced to leave the camp and set off on forced marches. Already malnourished, thousands of prisoners perished as they struggled through the snow, often clad only in their striped concentration camp uniforms:

> We went on and on, and there was no end in sight. Every day, a few women fell by the wayside. They collapsed and even with the help of others could no longer stand. The guards then shot them in the head, dragged them a pace or two, and another corpse rolled into the ditch. When we passed a village, the guards reported that a body lay a few kilometres back and would have to be buried.
>
> … I had a terrible hunger. They no longer gave us anything to eat. Sometimes the farmers, in whose barns we were locked at night, let us have a bucket of potatoes. Everyone got one or two potatoes.[22]

Eventually, Rolnikaite and her fellow prisoners were left in a barn. During the night, there were several large explosions, and the prisoners feared they were about to be killed. The following morning, there was silence. A Polish voice from outside the barn told them that the Germans had fled.

> Was it possible that the explosions had really frightened the Germans? That they had fled and left us here?
>
> Again the droning [of aircraft engines], coming nearer and nearer!
>
> … There were loud men's voices behind the barn. Russians? The Red Army? Was it really them?
>
> … The barn filled with soldiers. They came up to us, seeking out those still alive, helping them up. When they found those for whom help had come too late, they took off their caps.
>
> 'Do you need help, little sister?'
>
> I was pulled up onto my feet, but couldn't move, my legs were shaking. Two Red Army men took my hands, lifted me up and carried me into the open.[23]

Eventually, Rolnikaite returned to Vilnius. To her joy, she encountered her father, who she had not seen since immediately before the German occupation; he had escaped to the east with the Red Army. One of her sisters was also alive, but her mother and two youngest siblings had disappeared into Auschwitz, where they presumably died. Unlike the Esterowicz family, the Rolnikaite family chose to stay within the Soviet Union.

The Germans involved in the Baltic Holocaust also had diverse fates. Franz Stahlecker, whose *Einsatzgruppe A* oversaw so many of the killings in Lithuania and

Latvia in 1941, did not outlive his crimes by more than a few months. He was killed in March 1942 while leading an operation against Soviet partisans. Martin Weiss, who had played a major role in the killings in Vilnius, attempted to merge back into civilian life in Germany after the war. He was recognised and denounced, and in 1950 was sentenced to life imprisonment by a court in Würzburg. Karl Jäger, the author of the detailed report of the deeds of *Einsatzkommando 3* in Lithuania, assumed a false identity at the end of the war. He was working as an agricultural labourer when his report was first examined in public in 1959. He was soon recognised and arrested, and while awaiting trial, he committed suicide in prison in Hohenasperg.

Standartenführer Franz Murer, the man with overall responsibility for the Vilnius ghetto, during his time in command earned himself the nickname the 'Butcher from Vilnius'. He returned to his native Austria at the end of the war and attempted to pass himself off as just another returning soldier. Unfortunately for him, there was a displaced persons' camp near his hometown, and one of those living in the camp recognised him. He was arrested by the British occupation forces, and handed over to the Soviet Union, where he was convicted of murdering Soviet citizens – Vilnius was regarded as having been part of the Soviet Union at the outset of the German invasion – and sentenced to 25 years' hard labour. In 1955, when the Austrian State Treaty effectively re-established Austria as a sovereign state, he was released from prison. Although he was prosecuted again in Austria in 1963, he was acquitted. He died in 1995.

Bruno Kittel replaced Murer as the man with overall responsibility for the Vilnius ghetto, and supervised its liquidation. He personally killed several Jews in the ghetto, usually selecting his victims at random. At the end of the war, Kittel – who had been an actor before the war – simply disappeared. His fate is not known.

Erich Ehrlinger, who commanded *Sonderkommando 1b*, part of Stahlecker's *Einsatzgruppe A*, was involved in many killings in the Baltic States, playing a leading role in the massacre of Jews in Daugavpils. Later, he and his men were active in Belarus and Russia, killing Jews, non-Jewish civilians and suspected partisans. After the war, he adopted a fake identity, but in 1954 resumed using his real name. Four years later, he was arrested and charged with war crimes, and after his conviction was sentenced to 12 years' imprisonment. He was released in 1965 pending appeal, and his sentence was officially remitted on the grounds of ill health in 1969. Despite his apparent ill health, he lived until 2004.

Helmut Rauca, who was involved in the killings in the Kaunas ghetto, travelled to Canada after the war. Here, he was protected by the policy of the Canadian government to avoid investigating suspected war criminals, on the grounds that such investigations might be interpreted as promoting the opinions of particular special interests groups; the official policy of the Royal Canadian Mounted Police in 1962 stated:

> In view of the possibility that individuals or organizations may attempt to employ the Force as an investigational agency for groups engaged in locating and punishing individuals suspected of war crimes, unless otherwise instructed by Headquarters, Ottawa, investigations into allegations of this nature are not to be conducted by the Force.[24]

One of many to question this policy was Robert Kaplan, the Canadian Solicitor General from 1980 to 1984. He successfully encouraged the investigation and extradition of Rauca to Germany to face charges in connection with the deaths of up to 11,500 Jews in Kaunas. Rauca was sent to Germany in May 1983; he died in prison while awaiting trial the following October.[25]

Eduard Roschmann, who replaced Kurt Krause as head of the Riga ghetto in early 1943, was not as inclined as his predecessor to kill Jews on the spot; instead, he generally had them taken to the central prison in Riga for execution. It is thought that far more Jews died as a result of this than were killed by Krause within the ghetto. Although he subjected Jews returning to the ghetto from work details to searches in an attempt to prevent them from bringing in food, he often ordered that any food seized was to be sent to the ghetto hospital. He was also involved in German efforts to hide the evidence of the massacres around Riga, and helped organise work parties that dug up the corpses of earlier killings for disposal. The work parties were themselves executed every two weeks and replaced by new workers. After the war, Roschmann went to Austria, where he was arrested in 1945, though he managed to pass himself off as an ordinary prisoner of war and was then released. Two years later, he was recognised by a former concentration camp inmate and once more arrested. He was incarcerated in Dachau, which was now being used as a detention camp, but in 1948 he escaped and fled Germany, taking a ship from Genoa to Argentina, with the help of Alois Hudal, a Catholic Austrian bishop with strong pro-Nazi leanings. Hudal's involvement with escape routes for former Nazis resulted in increasing criticism of him, but he did not resign from his post in the church until 1952, and remained an active campaigner for former Nazis until his death. Roschmann set up a timber company in Argentina under the name Federigo Wagner, and from 1958 he faced repeated attempts to extradite him to Europe, where he faced charges ranging from bigamy to mass murder. In mid-1977, the Argentinian government stated that it would consider extraditing him, even though there was no formal extradition treaty with West Germany; it appears that there were numerous tensions between Argentina and West Germany at the time, and that this announcement might have been designed to placate the Germans. In any event, Roschmann fled Argentina for Paraguay. In 1977, a body was found in the capital with identity documents that suggested that the corpse was Federigo Wagner. The body had several wounds that were consistent with Roschmann's medical history, but some, including Simon Wiesenthal, were sceptical that it was Roschmann, and speculated that he had in some way fabricated the death in order to escape justice.

Friedrich Jeckeln was involved in organising many of the killings in Riga, and subsequently played a major role in the German administration in the Baltic States as head of police operations. By February 1945, he had risen to the rank of SS and Police General, and was assigned to the *SS-Freiwilligen Gebirgs-Korps* ('SS Volunteer Mountain Corps'). He was captured by the Red Army and tried in Riga in 1946. Convicted of war crimes, he was hanged in February. Hinrich Lohse, the *Reichskommissar* for Ostland, fled to Schleswig-Holstein in 1944, where he remained active as Reich Defence Commissar. The British occupation authorities arrested him, and in 1948 he was sentenced to ten years' imprisonment. Three years later, he was released on the grounds of ill health. He lived until 1964.

Jacob Gens, the Jewish head of the Vilnius ghetto police, who helped organise many of the 'actions' that were carried out to exterminate the population of the ghetto, was a controversial figure. It seems that he genuinely believed that by cooperating and being productive workers, the Jews of Vilnius might be able to prove themselves useful to the Germans and would thus survive. He often claimed that his deeds reduced the number of Jews who were executed. For example, an 'action' in July 1942 resulted in about 84 elderly Jews being shot, and Gens claimed that the original intention had been to kill several hundred, but he successfully negotiated a lower figure. After the *Judenrat* was dissolved by the Germans in July 1942, he became the sole Jewish authority in the ghetto. Although he was tasked with suppressing the anti-German resistance in the ghetto, he appears to have made and maintained regular contact with the resistance movement. In 1943, when it became clear that the ghetto was about to be liquidated, Gens resisted suggestions that he should attempt to flee – his Lithuanian wife lived outside the ghetto, and there was at least a possibility that he might be able to escape. He was summoned by the Gestapo on 14 September and accused of collaborating with the resistance movement, and executed the same day.

Viktors Arājs, whose paramilitary unit was involved in many killings in Latvia and elsewhere, was held in a British internment camp until 1949, after which he adopted the name Victor Zeibots, with the help of the Latvian government in exile in London. In 1979, he was prosecuted for war crimes in Hamburg and sentenced to life imprisonment. He died in prison in 1988. Another member of the *Arājs Kommando*, Herberts Cukurs, who had been a pioneering aviator before the war, was accused of involvement in several killings, but insisted that he had only worked as head of vehicle maintenance in Arājs' unit. He started a new life in South America after the war, where he was assassinated by Mossad agents in 1965, who lured him to Montevideo under the guise of wishing to collaborate with him in the creation of a new airline. After killing him, the agents sent an announcement to press offices in Germany and South America:

> Taking into consideration the gravity of the charge levelled against the accused, namely that he personally supervised the killing of more than 30,000 men, women and children, and considering the extreme display of cruelty which the subject showed when carrying out his tasks, the accused Herberts Cukurs is hereby sentenced to death. [The] accused was executed by those who can never forget on the 23rd of February, 1965. His body can be found at Casa Cubertini Calle Colombia, Séptima Sección del Departamento de Canelones, Montevideo, Uruguay.[26]

Another Latvian implicated in the killings of Jews and others was Kārlis Lobe. He fled to Sweden at the end of the war, and remained there until his death in 1985.

One of the Latvians to be involved in the Baltic Holocaust was Konrāds Kalējs, whose case caused controversy in recent years. He too served in the *Arājs Kommando*, and after the war lived first in Denmark, then in Australia, and eventually in the United States. In 1984, he was identified as a person who might have been involved in war crimes. He was arrested a year later as part of the elaborate 'Puño Airlines' operation – the United States Marshals Office created a fictitious airline, and then sent letters to suspects telling them that they had won airline tickets. When the suspects attempted to claim their tickets, they were arrested. After a prolonged legal process, he was deported from the United States to Australia, and attempted to enter Canada, only to be deported back to Australia. In 1999, he moved to England, but when the British government announced that he faced deportation, he once more returned to Australia. In 2000, the Latvian government opened proceedings against him, which were delayed due to Kalējs' ill health. He died in Melbourne in 2001, and in a last interview with Australian TV, he admitted his involvement in killings in Latvia.

The Estonian commander of the Jägala concentration camp, Aleksander Laak, moved to Canada after the war, where he started a new life under the name Alex Laak. In 1960, he was mentioned during Holocaust trials in Estonia, and subsequently tracked down by Russian and Canadian journalists. The exact circumstances of his death are unclear. He was found hanging in his garage in September 1960, and explanations have ranged from suicide to his being killed by Mossad. Karl Linnas, an Estonian who was in command of a concentration camp near Tartu, moved to the United States after the war. He was tried and convicted *in absentia* by the same trials that mentioned Laak, and in 1979 US officials charged him with making false statements to secure entry to the United States. In 1981, he was stripped of his US citizenship, and after a protracted legal process was flown to the Soviet Union in 1987. He died three months later in a prison in Leningrad. Ain Mere, who was also convicted as part of the Estonian trials of 1960, was living in England at the time. The British authorities refused to extradite him, as there was no treaty covering such arrangements between Britain and the Soviet Union, and he died in 1969.

Alfred Rosenberg, who had played such a large part in the creation of *Generalplan Ost*, was one of those who stood trial in Nuremberg after the war. He was convicted of crimes against humanity and helping to initiate wars of aggression, and was hanged in 1946.

The last commander of Army Group Courland, Carl Hilpert, went into captivity with his men. He died in the Soviet Union in 1948. Ernst Merk, commander of 18th Army, remained a Soviet prisoner until 1955, but survived to write about his captivity.[27] His opposite number in 16th Army, Friedrich-Jobst Volckamer von Kirchensittenbach, also survived imprisonment, and finally returned to Germany in 1955.

Many of the Latvian and Estonian soldiers who succeeded in surrendering to the Western Powers at the end of the war found themselves deployed in a surprising role, acting as guards during the Nuremberg Trials. Others served as guards of US facilities during the Berlin Blockade, and although the SS was condemned by the Allies as a criminal organisation, exceptions were made for men of non-German nationalities who were conscripted into its ranks. In September 1950, the United States Displaced Persons Commission declared that:

> The Baltic Waffen SS Units (Baltic Legions) are to be considered as separate and distinct in purpose, ideology, activities, and qualifications for membership from the German SS, and therefore the Commission holds them not to be a movement hostile to the Government of the United States.[28]

The long post-war struggle for independence in the Baltic States is beyond the scope of this book.[29] The trauma of the population losses from the fighting, mass executions and deportations scarred the three countries for decades. Despite the influx of large numbers of non-Baltic Soviet citizens, the countries were able to keep their distinctive cultures and languages alive throughout the years of Soviet occupation, and as the Soviet regime began to relax its hold during the era of *Glasnost* and *Perestroika*, demands for independence grew. Public acts of defiance began in 1987, and the following year, Estonia published the *Suveräänsusdeklaratsioon* ('Declaration of Sovereignty'), stating that Estonian laws superseded Soviet laws and that Estonia's government, not Moscow, had sole rights to the assets and territory of Estonia. In 1990, Estonia's government informed its citizens that conscription into the Soviet armed forces was no longer compulsory, and in March, Lithuania issued a Proclamation of Independence. A few weeks later, Latvia followed suit.

At first, the Soviet response was to impose an economic blockade. During 1991, there were attempts to assert Soviet control by force; in January, Soviet military and political units attempted unsuccessfully to establish a 'Committee of National Salvation' in Riga, and Soviet tanks advanced on the TV Tower in Vilnius, killing 14 civilians. Attempts by Soviet troops to move against key buildings in Tallinn were blocked by mass demonstrations, and as the short-lived coup attempt against Mikhail Gorbachev in August fell apart, the three states declared their independence. Iceland was the first foreign power to recognise any of them, and a plaque in Tallinn commemorates this event.

The years that followed the restoration of independence saw the three countries move swiftly away from their Soviet past. All three became members of both the European Union and NATO, and their economies flourished. In the second decade of the 21st century, the economic turmoil across the entire Western World has had a marked effect upon the three countries, but whatever financial pressures may face the three nations, it seems that they have firmly become part of the west, something to which they have aspired for nearly a century of struggle, and for which they have suffered so much loss and bloodshed. It seems that the fundamental question about the Baltic States – whether they can have an independent status, or whether they must be part of a larger political entity – has finally been resolved by their incorporation into both NATO and the European Union. Indeed, the vital role of these organisations in safeguarding the independence of much of Europe suggests that most nations have had to compromise the totality of their independence to some extent.

The nations involved in the war for the Baltic States have developed their own distinctive historiographies about the period. Soviet-era accounts are inevitably full of tales of heroic communists fighting the hated fascists, and reflect the doctrine of the period, that the three states had become part of the Soviet Union prior to the German invasion. Before Stalin's death, there was a deliberate policy of portraying the war – and the final victory – as a predominantly Russian affair, and the suffering and contributions of all other nationalities, including Soviet Jews, were reduced in significance. Much of the general understanding in the Western World of the Holocaust is based upon accounts written by Holocaust survivors in the west, who experienced and survived the horrors of the death camps, and inevitably these accounts make little mention of the mass killings that occurred before the Wannsee Conference in late 1941.

Since the end of the Soviet Union, a small number of Soviet veterans have written their own accounts of the war, and like many memoirs written so long after the events they describe, their accuracy and completeness is open to question. For example, despite widespread evidence of the almost routine rape of women in East Germany, Poland and the Baltic States as the Red Army advanced, almost no Russian-language accounts address this issue. Where authors acknowledge that such events occurred, they stress that their own regiments and divisions did not take part. Despite the acceptance of the independence of the Baltic States by the Russian Federation, there remains a strong point of view within Russia that the three states legitimately were, and perhaps still should be, part of the body of Russia, whether this body is the Czarist Empire, the Soviet Union, or the Russian Federation. Indeed, whilst the official attitude to the Latvian and Estonian Legions during the Soviet era was in keeping with the western viewpoint, that men coerced into joining the SS were not to be regarded in the same way as Germans serving in the SS, the attitude of Moscow today is quite the reverse. Soldiers who fought against the Red Army are frequently portrayed as also being the men responsible for the Baltic Holocaust and the killing of ethnic Russian civilians. Whilst it is true that many men within the legions were indeed guilty of such acts, it would be wrong to suggest that all were involved.

The legality – or otherwise – of the long Soviet presence in the Baltic States is itself a source of continuing controversy. Russian writers have made much of the expediency of Winston Churchill with regard to the borders of the Soviet Union. In March 1942, Churchill wrote to Roosevelt: 'In view of the increasing burdens of war, I have come to the conclusion that the principles of the Atlantic Charter should not be interpreted in such a way as to deprive Russia of the border that it had when it was attacked by Germany.'[30]

At the time, unable to offer the Soviet Union any aid by opening a second front in the west, Churchill may have felt the need to offer whatever political support he could to the country that was seen as bearing the brunt of the German war effort. Whilst Roosevelt may have been less willing to allow Stalin a free hand to annex the Baltic States, he ultimately had little choice; the Red Army was indisputably the master of the region, and nothing short of a war seemed likely to change matters. The inability of the Western Powers to dispute Soviet control of the Baltic States after the war, it is maintained, effectively legitimised the Soviet presence in the region, and as this presence was based upon the original Soviet occupation following the Molotov–Ribbentrop Pact, this in turn was in some way legitimised.

German accounts of the war began to appear during the 1950s, as veterans of the Wehrmacht began to compile histories of their regiments and divisions. Like Soviet accounts, these make almost no mention of war crimes; in a few cases, where the subject arises, attempts are made to blame the SS and its associated paramilitary formations. The unit histories instead concentrate on the years of dazzling victories, then the bitter resistance of the closing months of the war. The German soldiers are usually portrayed as patriots who fought to prevent their homelands from being overrun by the Red Army, with little or no discussion of the fact that it was the German invasion of the Soviet Union that ultimately brought the Red Army to Germany. When civilians are mentioned, it is usually in the context of jubilant Lithuanians, Latvians, and Estonians who welcomed the arrival of the Wehrmacht, or fearful refugees who attempted to flee the return of the Red Army. The casualties suffered in the face of the Red Army's advance are frequently described in German accounts; similar losses inflicted by the Wehrmacht in 1941 are almost completely absent.

The way that Germany has faced up to its past, particularly with regard to the Holocaust, is in many respects a remarkable achievement. Whilst the accounts of war veterans might shy away from the subject, other German writers have tackled the subject with, sometimes, painful honesty. Earlier accounts perhaps tended to be a little two-dimensional, with many of the German perpetrators portrayed as evil sadists; whilst such individuals undoubtedly existed, they were greatly outnumbered by those who appear to have treated their role in the machinery of the Holocaust in the same way that soldiers regarded their role in the fighting in the front line. In the last two decades, German writers have written some of the most detailed and comprehensive accounts of the crimes committed by the Wehrmacht and SS in the east. This is in stark contrast to the continuing silence of Russian-language writers about atrocities committed by the Red Army and the NKVD.

The nations that have struggled most with their accounts of the war years are, inevitably, the Baltic States themselves. On the one hand, the people of the Baltic States are proud of their resilience and their ability to survive so many occupations and the terrible loss of life that their nations suffered. On the other hand, they have a deeply ambivalent attitude to the events of the Second World War. Forced through circumstances to provide aid for Nazi Germany, they continue to struggle to reconcile their attitude to those they regard as nationalist patriots, with the unwelcome fact that they found themselves fighting for a regime that is generally reviled. Their historiography is further disadvantaged by the fact that, even if they try to address the crimes committed upon their people by the Germans and the Soviets in an even-handed way, they still struggle with the role that their own citizens played in those crimes. Many, though by no means all, of those who fought against Soviet occupation after the war were also extensively involved in fighting on the side of the Germans during the war, and some of those who are regarded as heroes are also implicated in some of the mass killings that occurred during the German occupation. Since 1990, many Latvians have celebrated 16 March as Latvian Legion Day, to commemorate the service of Latvians who fought against the Soviet Union. The date was chosen because it was the first occasion that the two Latvian divisions fought alongside each other against the Red Army, but the fact that the two divisions were part of the SS, and included in their ranks many men who had been part of the police battalions that helped carry out the Baltic Holocaust, has made this commemoration a controversial event. In 1998, the day was given official recognition, triggering protests from Russia, and the Latvian government withdrew the day's official status in 2000. For several years, the day became a flashpoint for trouble between right-wing and left-wing groups in Latvia, though it should be pointed out that the official organisations representing Latvian veterans have repeatedly distanced themselves from the more extremist bodies that have attempted to exploit the day. After serious trouble in 2005, the Latvian authorities attempted to fence off the Freedom Monument, the focal point of the clashes. This in turn attracted great criticism, highlighting the difficulties faced by Latvia and its neighbours in attempting to deal with their collective past.

The different interpretations of history in the nations involved have caused resentment and difficulties between them. The history of the Freedom Monument in Riga highlights many of these difficulties. The monument was first raised in 1935 to commemorate those who fell in the Latvian war of independence, and after the end of the Second World War, the Soviet authorities proposed the restoration of a statue of Peter the Great, which had been taken down to make room for the monument. It seems that the monument survived partly through a desire to avoid unnecessary provocation of Latvians, and partly because Vera Mukhina, a celebrated Soviet sculptor who was born in Riga, successfully argued that the monument had considerable artistic merits. Instead, attempts were made to reinterpret the nature of the monument; it is topped by a copper statue holding aloft three stars, originally intended to symbolise the three constitutional districts of Latvia (Kurzeme, Latgale and Vidzeme), but the Soviet authorities proclaimed that the statue and the stars represented Mother Russia, holding aloft the stars of Estonia, Latvia and Lithuania. By the late 1980s, official accounts accepted that the monument commemorated the liberation of Latvia from rule by the Czars and Baltic German barons, but failed to mention that most of the Latvian war of independence had been against the Red Army and its communist Latvian Rifle formations.

Many Russian writers, including those who have been active after the fall of the Soviet Union, have criticised what they see as Baltic 'ideology' or 'dogma', for example in connection with the Soviet deportations during 1941 and after the war.[31] Starting from the point of view that the Soviet occupation of the Baltic States was a legal event, Russian historians often regard the actions of the Soviet regime in safeguarding its rule as entirely legitimate. The deportations are seen as being no different in principle to the internment of civilians from Axis nations in Britain and the United States during the war.[32] Similarly, the widespread point of view throughout the Baltic States that those who fought against the Soviets, both during and after the war, were patriotic freedom fighters, is criticised as overlooking the crimes that some of those involved committed during the war, particularly when serving in auxiliary police units prior to the creation of Estonian and Latvian divisions.[33] It is felt in Russia that the growth in articles and publications about the 'Forest Brothers' began in the 1980s in Lithuania, largely due to the influence of Lithuanians living in the west, and then spread to Latvia and Estonia in the following years. Many of those fighting against Soviet authorities, it is suggested, were not doing so solely – or even primarily – for patriotic reasons. Some were deserters or were involved in plain criminal activities, but are now grouped together with other 'partisans' to give, from the Russian point of view, a misleading idea of the scale of the partisan movement.[34]

Another example of the tensions brought about by different interpretations of history is the case of Vassili Makarovich Kononov, who was a member of the pro-Soviet partisans operating in Latvia as part of the 1st Latvian Partisan Battalion; he was parachuted into Latvia in June 1943 as an explosives expert. In February 1944, a dozen partisans sought shelter in the village of Mazie Bati, and were allowed to stay in a barn. Early the following morning, German troops entered the village and set the barn ablaze, and any who attempted to escape were gunned down. Amongst the dead were the leader of the partisan group, Major Chugunov, his wife, and their child. Kononov was not present at the time, but after his battalion had held a field tribunal, without any of the villagers present at the proceedings, he was ordered to enter the village and seize nine villagers who were accused of collaborating with the Germans.[35] Kononov and several other partisans entered Mazie Bati dressed in Wehrmacht uniforms and killed the nine villagers, including three women, one of whom was pregnant. Kononov was charged with murder in 1998, and the following year, he was convicted and sentenced to six years' imprisonment.

In 2000, while he was appealing against his conviction, Vladimir Putin, President of the Russian Federation, offered Kononov Russian citizenship, which he accepted; shortly afterwards, the Latvian Criminal Affairs Division overturned his conviction, after Kononov's lawyers successfully argued that it was not clear whether the partisans were operating in occupied territory, and that the combatant status of both his partisans and the villagers – many of whom had been armed by the Germans – was also uncertain; consequently, the rules that applied to the conduct of soldiers and civilians in warfare could not be interpreted with any degree of confidence. The prosecution chose to continue proceedings against Kononov, pressing charges relating only to the killing of the three women, and in 2004, Kononov was once more imprisoned.

Four years later, the European Court of Human Rights ruled on Kononov's conviction. The court found that Kononov had only acted against the villagers after finding weapons provided by the Germans in their houses, and that it was not possible to argue unequivocally that the victims of Kononov's operation were civilians. When it came to the deaths of the three women, the court concluded that there were two possible explanations. The first was that the women had kept watch over Major Chugunov's group while the six male villagers travelled to a neighbouring village to alert the Germans, and had thus in effect become part of the anti-partisan and pro-German group; the second was that they were killed because Kononov's men exceeded their orders. In this latter case, it was argued, no evidence had been presented that Kononov had either directly taken part in their killings, or that he had ordered anyone else to kill them. As any prosecution under Latvian law as it existed in 1944 would have had to take place within ten years, Kononov could not be convicted by a prosecution in 1998. If the conviction was under the terms of the Latvian law relating to murder that was passed in 1961, the court ruled that the conviction was in contravention of Article Seven of the European Convention of Human Rights, which prohibits the retrospective criminalisation of activities.[36]

The Latvian government appealed against this judgement, and in 2010, a final judgement was issued. It was concluded that regardless of their status, the villagers of

Mazie Bati could not legally be murdered or ill-treated under existing laws in 1944. The use of Wehrmacht uniforms by Kononov and his group was ruled to be in breach of Article 23b of the Hague Convention, which states that it is forbidden 'To kill or wound treacherously individuals belonging to the hostile nation or army'.[37] The limitation under Latvian law that prosecution should have taken place within ten years was felt to be irrelevant, in that Kononov was deemed to have broken international laws, not Latvian laws, and as these international laws had been in force at the time of the killings, Article Seven had not been breached.[38]

Kononov died in 2011, aged 88, a controversial figure to the end, still attempting to overturn the ruling of the European Court. Throughout his legal process, the Russian Federation had provided legal, financial and moral support for his position. After his death, President Dmitri Medvedev of the Russian Federation declared: 'Vassili Kononov selflessly fought the Nazi invaders throughout the years of the Great Patriotic War. He remained loyal to the common bonds forged in battle and defended the truth about the events of those years throughout his entire life.'[39]

Many people in the Baltic States, particularly the significant non-Baltic populations that were left in the three countries as a result of Soviet post-war population movements, are uncomfortable with the denigration of the Red Army, which sacrificed so much to expel the Germans from the Baltic States. The large numbers of Russians in Estonia and Latvia, forming 26 per cent and 20 per cent of their respective populations, have had a particularly difficult time adapting to the new status of the three countries. Recently, the Russian population of Latvia tried unsuccessfully to have Russian recognised as an official language in the country.

Despite these ambivalent attitudes to the past, it seems that, for the moment at least, the three Baltic States are firmly embedded in the Western World. Recent economic events have shown that this is not always a blessing. Nevertheless, people living in Estonia, Latvia and Lithuania today can share a future with prospects of far greater liberty and safety from persecution than almost any preceding generation. For this future, the price that they pay – wrestling with a controversial and difficult past – is perhaps a small one.

APPENDIX 1: PLACE NAMES

In an area where borders have moved frequently, and even within each state there have been markedly different ethnicities, place names can be very confusing.

Wherever possible, the policy in this book has been to use current place names in preference to names that might have been used in the past. The exceptions to this rule have been where some locations have had names that were in almost universal use at the time. For example, the city currently known as St Petersburg was known as Petrograd at the end of the First World War, and Leningrad during the Second World War; given the resonance of the latter name, it would have been inappropriate to use the current name in preference.

Brest-Litovsk	Brest (Belarusian)
Daugava (river)	Düna (German), Western Dvina (Russian)
Gatchina	known during the Soviet era as Krasnogvardeisk
Gdansk	Danzig (German)
Jelgava	Mitau (German)
Jurbarkas	Georgenburg (German)
Kaunas	Kauen (German), Kowno (Polish), Kovno (Russian), Kovne (Yiddish)
Kingisepp	Yamburg (German)
Königsberg	renamed Kaliningrad (Russian) after the war
Liepāja	Libau (German)
Livonia	Livland (German)
Mežaparks	Kaiserwald (German)
Palanga	Polangen (German)
Paneriai	Ponary (Polish), Ponar (Yiddish)
Priekule	Preekuln (German)
Priekulė	Prokuls (German)
Pskov	Pleskau (German)
Rezekne	Rositten (German)
Schneidemühl	renamed Piła (Polish) after the war
Šiauliai	Schaulen (German), Szawle (Polish), Shavel (Yiddish)

Šilutė	Heydekrug (German)
Tallinn	Reval (German)
Tannenberg	Stębark (Polish)
Tilsit	renamed Sovetsk (Russian) after the war
Ukmergė	Wilkomierz (German)
Vilijampolė	Viriampol (German)
Vilnius	Wilna (German), Wilno (Polish), Vilna (Russian), Vilne (Yiddish)

APPENDIX 2: RANKS

Brigadeführer	SS rank equivalent to brigadier
Feldwebel	Wehrmacht rank equivalent to staff sergeant
Gefreiter	Wehrmacht rank equivalent to lance-corporal
Generalfeldmarschall	Wehrmacht rank equivalent to field marshal
Generalkommissar	senior rank in German occupation administration
Generalleutnant	Wehrmacht rank equivalent to major-general
Generalmajor	Wehrmacht rank equivalent to brigadier
Generaloberst	Wehrmacht rank equivalent to general
Gruppenführer	SS rank quivalent to major general
Hauptmann	Wehrmacht rank equivalent to captain
Hauptscharführer	SS rank equivalent to company sergeant-major
Hauptsturmführer	SS rank equivalent to captain
Kapitänleutnant	Kriegsmarine rank equivalent to lieutenant
Leutnant	Wehrmacht rank equivalent to 2nd lieutenant
Major	Wehrmacht rank equivalent to major
Oberfeldwebel	Wehrmacht rank equivalent to company sergeant-major
Obergruppenführer	SS rank equivalent to lieutenant general
Oberleutnant	Wehrmacht rank equivalent to lieutenant
Oberst	Wehrmacht rank equivalent to colonel
Oberstleutnant	Wehrmacht rank equivalent to lieutenant colonel
Obersturmbannführer	SS rank equivalent to lieutenant colonel
Rittmeister	Wehrmacht (originally cavalry) rank equivalent to captain
Rottenführer	SS rank equivalent to corporal
Stabsfeldwebel	Wehrmacht rank equivalent to regimental sergeant-major
Standartenführer	SS rank equivalent to colonel
Sturmbannführer	SS rank equivalent to major
Unterscharführer	SS rank equivalent to sergeant
Untersturmführer	SS rank equivalent to 2nd lieutenant

APPENDIX 3: ACRONYMS

AK Armia Krajowa ('home army'), the Polish resistance army supported by the Western Powers

AOK *Armee Oberkommando (*Army High Command), e.g. *AOK Ostpreussen*

BDO *Bund Deutscher Offiziere* (League of German Officers)

EVR *Eesti Vabariigi Rahvuskomitee* (Estonian Republic National Committee)

FPO *Fareynikte Partizaner Organizatsye* (United Partisans Organisation)

GPU *Gosudarstvennoye Politicheskoye Upravlenie* (State Political Directorate), Soviet, a part of the NKVD

HKP *Heeres Kraftfahr Park* (Army Freight Vehicle Pool), German

HSSPf *Höhere SS- und Polizeiführer* (senior SS and police commander), German

LAF *Lietuvos Aktyvistų Frontas* (Lithuanian Activist Front)

LCP *Latvijas Centrālā Padome* (Latvian Central Committee)

LKNS *Latviju Kareivju Nacionālā Savienība* (National Federation of Latvian Fighters)

LLA *Lietuvos Laisvės Armija* (Lithuanian Freedom Army)

LLKS *Lietuvos Laisvės Kovos Sąjūdis* (Union of Lithuanian Freedom Fighters)

LVR *Lietuvos Vietinė Rinktinė* (Lithuanian Defence Force)

NKFD *Nationalkomitee Freies Deutschland* (National Committee for a Free Germany)

NKVD *Narodnyy Komissariat Vnutrennikh Del* (People's Commissariat for Internal Affairs), the Soviet Secret Police

OKH *Oberkommando des Heeres* (German Army High Command)

OKW *Oberkommando der Wehrmacht* (Wehrmacht High Command)

RHSA *Reichssicherheitshauptamt* (Reich Main Security Administration), German

RVL *Relvastadud Voitluse Liit* (Armed Resistance League), Estonian

SA *Sturmabteilung* (Storm Detachment), German, the pre-war paramilitary wing of the National Socialist Party

SD *Sicherheitsdienst* (Security Administration), German

STAVKA Soviet High Command

TAR *Tevynes Apsaugas Rinktine* (Fatherland Defence Force), Lithuanian

TDA *Tautos Darbo Apsauga* (National Labour Service Battalion), Lithuanian

APPENDIX 4: FOREIGN TERMS

Abwehr the German military intelligence branch

Auftragstaktik military concept centered on achievement of a mission, which allowed junior officers to take decisions, in contrast to older, more rigid command and control systems

Freikorps volunteer military organisations assembled from former German army personnel in the Baltic States and Germany in the aftermath of the First World War

Judenrat lit. 'Jewish council', the Jewish administrative body responsible for organising the Jewish communities in the occupied territories

Komjautnatne Latvian youth organisation

Komsomol Soviet youth organisation

Ostministerium Common abbreviation for the *Reichsministerium für die besetzten Ostgebiete* ('Reich Ministry for the Occupied Eastern Territories')

Omakaitse Originally the Estonian 'Home Guard' after the First World War; re-established as a militia group after the German invasion in 1941

Pērkonkrusts lit. 'Thunder Cross', a Latvian extreme nationalist group, with links to the RSHA and to *Einsatzgruppe A*

SS-Führungshauptamt the headquarters of the non-combat elements of the SS, based in Berlin

ENDNOTES

Introduction

1. Misiunas, R., Taagepera, R. (1993) *The Baltic States – Years of Dependence 1940–1990*, London: Hurst, p.6
2. Henry Nevinson, quoted in Eksteins M. (1999) *Walking Since Daybreak*, New York: Mariner, pp.42–43
3. Bleiere, D., Butulis, I., Zunda, A., Stranga, A., Feldmanis, I. (2006), *History of Latvia: the 20th Century,* Riga: Jumava, p.68
4. Czernin von und zu Chudenitz, O. (1920) *In the World War,* New York and London: Harper & Brothers, pp.245–46
5. Davies, N. (2003) *White Eagle, Red Star: the Polish-Soviet War, 1919–20,* London: Pimlico
6. Volkogonov, D. (1994) *Lenin: Life and Legacy*, London: Harper Collins, p.482
7. Naumann, F. (1915) *Mitteleuropa*, Berlin: Georg Reimer
8. Madajczyk, C. (1961) *Generalna Gubernia w planach hitlerowskich. Studia*, Warsaw: Wydawnictwo Naukowe PWN, pp.88–89
9. Lower, W. (2009) *Empire, Colony, Genocide: Conquest, Occupation and Subaltern Resistance in World History*, New York: Berghahn, p.301
10. See Erichsen, C., Olusoga, D. (2010) *The Kaiser's Holocaust: Germany's Forgotten Genocide and the Colonial Roots of Nazism*, London: Faber & Faber
11. Holborn, H. (1969) *A History of Modern Germany*, New York: Knopf, p.429
12. Eidintas, A., (1997) *Restoration of the State*, in Eidintas, A., Žalys, V., Senn, A. *Lithuania in European Politics: The Years of the First Republic 1918–1940*, Basingstoke: Macmillan, pp.220–21
13. Davies, N. p.50
14. President Wilson's Message to Congress, January 8, 1918; Records of the United States Senate; Record Group 46

Chapter 1

1. Emelianov, Y. (2007) *Priybaltika: Mezhdoo Stalinim I Hitlerom*, Moscow: Izdatel' Bystrov, p.157
2. Emelianov, p.158
3. Nekrich, A., Ulam, A., Freeze, G. (1997) *Pariahs, Partners, Predators: German–Soviet Relations, 1922–1941*, New York: Columbia University Press, p.110
4. Sebag Montefiore, S. (2004) *Stalin, The Court of the Red Czar*, London: Vintage, p.40

5. Quoted in Sebag Montefiore, p.310
6. Resis, A. (2000) 'The Fall of Litvinov: Harbinger of the German–Soviet Non-Aggression Pact' in *Europe-Asia Studies 52 (1)*, p.35
7. Emelianov, p.161
8. Emelianov, p.163
9. Sebag Montefiore, p.314
10. Emelianov, p.165
11. Quoted in Sebag Montefiore, p.318
12. Halder, F., *Diaries*, Imperial War Museum, 22 August 1939
13. *USSR DVP*, 22/1, p.632
14. *Lietuvos Okupacija ir Aneksija 1939–40* (1993), Vilnius: Mintis, p.65
15. *Eesti NSV Ajalugui* III (1971), Tallinn, p.365
16. Sebag Montefiore, p.321
17. Hiden, J., Salmon, P. (1994) *The Baltic Nations and Europe* (revised edn), Harlow: Longman, p.110
18. Tarauskas, E. (1990) *Lietuvos Nepriklausomybės Netenkant*, Kaunas: Sviesa, p.74
19. Urbšys, J. (1990) *Atsiminimai*, Kaunas: Spindulys, quoted in Senn, A. (2007) *Lithuania 1940, Revolution from Above*, New York: Rodopi, p.17
20. Senn, p.18
21. Senn, p.20
22. The Winter War was fought between Finland and the Soviet Union between November 1939 and March 1940 in the narrow neck of land to the north and west of Leningrad.
23. Myllyniemi, S. (1979) *Die Baltische Krise 1938–41*, Stuttgart: Deutsche, pp.114–17
24. Felder, B. (2009) *Lettland im Zweiten Weltkrieg*, Paderborn: Ferdinand Schöningh, p.45
25. Zotov's telegrams form part (Reel 1, Container 1) of the Volkogonov Collection of the US Library of Congress
26. Quoted in Felder (2009), p.44
27. Felder (2009), p.79
28. Nollendorfs, V. (2005) *Battle for the Baltic. Yearbook of the Museum of the Occupation of Latvia 2004*, Riga, p.162
29. Štiemanis, J. (2002) *History of the Latvian Jews*, New York: East European Monographs, p.115
30. Komplektov, G. (1990) *Polpredy Soobshchaiut*, Moscow: Meshdunarodnye Otnosheniia, p.140
31. Rudis, G., quoted in Senn, p.74
32. Emelianov, p.167
33. Senn, p.97
34. Misiunas, R., Taagepera, R. (1993) *The Baltic States – Years of Dependence 1940–1990*, London: Hurst, p.201
35. Senn, pp.106–07
36. Felder (2009), p.32
37. *Brīvā Zeme*, 17/6/40
38. NKVD Report of 25/10/40 in Latvijas Valsts Arhīvs, Riga, PA-101/1/35, 3
39. Lejiņš, J. (1971) *Mana Dzimtene: Atmiņu un Pārdomu Atspulgā*, Vasteras: ICA bokförlag, p.180
40. Misiunas and Taagepera, p.21
41. *Third Interim Report of the Select Committee on Communist Aggression*, 83rd Congress, 2nd Session, Washington 1954, p.458
42. Misiunas and Taagepera, pp.28–29
43. Uustalu, E. (1952) *The History of the Estonian People*, London: Boreas, p.242
44. Nicholas, L. (2006) *Cruel World: The Children of Europe in the Nazi Web*, New York: Vintage, pp.194–205

45. *Third Interim Report*, p.471
46. Latvijas Valsts Arhīvs, PA-101/2/32, 35
47. Hoover Institution of War, Peace and Revolution Archive, Stanford, 89/18/1
48. Felder (2009), p.162
49. Misiunas and Taagepera, p.42
50. Felder (2009), pp.158–59, Misiunas and Taagepera, p.43
51. Pakalniškis, A. (1980) *Plungė*, Chicago: Spaudė M. Morkūno spaustuvė, p.45
52. Kuromiya, H., Pepłoński, A. (2009) *Między Warszawą a Tokio*, Toruń: Wydawnictwo Adam Marszałek, pp.470–85
53. Swain, G. (2004) *Between Stalin and Hitler*, London: Routledge, p.28

Chapter 2

1. Cecil, R. (1972) *The Myth of the Master Race: Alfred Rosenberg and Nazi Ideology*, New York: Dodd Mead, pp.42–43
2. Hitler, A. (1971) *Mein Kampf*, Boston: Houghton Mifflin, p.646
3. Rössler, M., Schleiermacher, S. (1996) '*Hauptlinien der nationalsozialistischen Planungs- und Vernichtungspolitik*' in *Central European History Journal*, Vol. 29, 2, pp.270–74
4. Speer, A. (1970) *Inside the Third Reich: Memoirs by Albert Speer*, London: Macmillan, p.115
5. Dallin, A. (1957) *German Rule in Russia 1941–45*, London: Macmillan, p.102
6. *Trials of the Major War Criminals before the International Military Tribunal 1947–49*, Vol. XXVI, pp.610–27, US Library of Congress
7. *Führer Naval Conferences* (1947) US Library of Congress, p.120
8. Quoted in Madajczyk, C. (1994) *Vom Generalplan Ost zum Generalsiedlungsplan: Dokumente*, Munich: Saur, p.24
9. Kay, A. (2006) *Exploitation, Resettlement, Mass Murder: Political and Economic Planning for German Occupation Policy in the Soviet Union*, New York: Berghahn, p.211
10. Snyder, T. (2011) *Bloodlands: Europe Between Hitler and Stalin*, London: Vintage, pp.161–162
11. Kay, p.164
12. *Trials of the Major War Criminals*, Vol. XXXVIII, pp.86–94
13. Raun, T. (2002) *Estonia and the Estonians (Studies of Nationalities)*, Stanford: Hoover Institution Press, p161
14. Quoted in Kangeris, K. (2008) *Latvijas Vēsturnieku Komisijas Raksti*, Riga: Latvijas vēstures institūta apgāds, p.241
15. Eberhardt, P. (2006) *Political Migrations in Poland*, Warsaw: Studium Europy Wschodniej UW, p.26
16. Shirer, W. (1960) *The Rise and Fall of the Third Reich*, New York: Simon & Schuster, p.647
17. *Führer Directive 21*, 18 December 1940: *Office of the United States Chief of Counsel For Prosecution of Axis Criminality*
18. Quoted in Widder, W. (2002) 'Auftragstaktik and Innere Führung: Trademarks of German Leadership' in *Military Review* Sept–Oct 2002, p.4
19. Rhodes, R. (2002) *Masters of Death: The SS-Einsatzgruppen and the Invention of the Holocaust*, New York: Alfred A. Knopf, p.9
20. Hillgruber, A. *War in the East and the Extermination of the Jews* in Marrus, M. (ed.) (1989) *The Nazi Holocaust Part 3, The 'Final Solution': The Implementation of Mass Murder*, Munich: Saur, pp.94–95
21. Rees, L. (1997) *The Nazis: a Warning From History*, London: BBC, p.177
22. Ries, T. (1988) *Cold Will: The Defence of Finland*, London: Brassey's Defence Publishers, pp.77–78

23. Glantz, D. (2002) *The Battle for Leningrad,* Lawrence: University of Kansas Press, p.22
24. Sewell, S. (1998) *'Why Three Tanks?'* in *Armor,* Jul–Aug 1998, p.24
25. Glantz (2002), p.23
26. Gorkov, I., Semin, N. (1996), 'Konets global'noi Ishi: Na sovetskom severozapade – Operativnye plany zapadhykh prigranichnykh okrugov 1941 godasvidetel'-stvuiut: SSSR ne gotovilsia knapadeniiu na Germaniiu' in Voenno-istoricheskii zhurnal 6 (Nov–Dec 1996): 2, pp.3–4
27. Quoted in Schneider, J. (1994) *The Structure of Strategic Revolution: Total War and the Roots of the Soviet Warfare State,* Novato: Presidio Press, p.178
28. Tukhachevsky, M. (1924) *Questions of Higher Command,* Moscow, p.88
29. Tukhachevsky, M. *New Problems in Warfare,* quoted in McPadden, C. (2006) *Mikhail Nikolayevich Tukhachevsky (1893–1937): Practitioner and Theorist of War,* Land Warfare Papers 56, Institute of Land Warfare, Arlington
30. Tukhachevsky, M. (1936) *Vremmenyi Polevoi Ustav RKKA,* Moscow, p.42
31. Lukes, I. (1996) *Czechoslovakia Between Stalin and Hitler: The Diplomacy of Edvard Beneš in the 1930s,* Oxford: Oxford University Press, p.95
32. Glantz, D. in Krause, M., Phillips, R. (eds) (2006) *Historical Perspectives of the Operational Art,* Washington: Center of Military History, p.247
33. Quoted in Sebag Montefiore, S. (2004) *Stalin, The Court of the Red Czar,* London: Vintage, p.341
34. Quoted in Sebag Montefiore, p.347

Chapter 3

1. Haupt, W. (1997) *Army Group North,* Atglen: Schiffer, p.28
2. Jones, M. (2008) *Leningrad: State of Siege,* London: John Murray, p.12
3. Conze, W. (1953) *Die Geschichte der 291 iInfanterie-Division,* Bad Neuheim: Podzun, p.119
4. Stolfi, R. (2003) *German Panzers on the Offensive,* Atglen: Schiffer, p.148
5. Haupt, W. (1987) *Die 8. Panzer-Division im Zweiten Weltkrieg,* Friedberg: Podzun, pp.136–37
6. Stolfi, p.150
7. *Kriegstagebuch 8. Panzer Division 22/6/41,* US National Archives, T315, Roll 483
8. Haupt (1987), p.139
9. Jones, p.19
10. Sebag Montefiore, S. (2004) *Stalin, The Court of the Red Czar,* London: Vintage, pp.369–70
11. Zolotarev, V. (1998) *Velikaeia Otechestvennaia Voina 1941–1945, I: Surovye Ispytaniia,* Moscow: Nauka, p.149
12. Richter, W. (1975) *Die 1. (Ostpreussische) Infanterie-Division,* Munich: Max Schmidt, pp.40–41
13. Zolotarev, V. (1958) *Boevye Dokumenty po Oboronitelnoi Zapadnogo Fronta* in *Sbornik Boevykh Dokumentov Velikoi Otechestvennoi Viony,* Moscow: Voenizdat, p.34
14. Haupt (1987), p.145
15. Quoted in Glantz, D. (2002) *The Battle for Leningrad,* Lawrence: University of Kansas Press, p.33
16. Quoted on http://www.axishistory.com/index.php?id=5281 insert accessed date
17. For accounts of the battle, see Raus, E. (2003) *Panzer Operations: the Eastern Front Memoir of General Raus, 1941–45,* Cambridge: Da Capo Press, pp.14–34 and Luttichau, C. von (1985) *The Road to Moscow: The Campaign in Russia,* Washington DC: Center for Military History Project 26-P
18. Glantz, D. (1998) *Stumbling Colossus: The Red Army on the Eve of World War,* Lawrence: University of Kansas Press, p.126

19. Ivnskis, Z., *Lithuania During the War: Resistance Against the Soviet and Nazi Occupants* in Vardys, V. (ed.) (1965) *Lithuania Under The Soviets*, New York: Praeger, pp.67–68
20. Manteuffel, H. von (1965) *Die 7. Panzer-Division im Zweiten Weltkrieg*, Krefeld: Schaberg, pp.137–38
21. Manteuffel, pp.138–39
22. Haupt (1987), pp.145–46
23. *Kriegstagebuch 8. Panzer Division 26/6/41*, US National Archives, T315, Roll 484
24. Haupt (1987), pp.150–51; Stolfi, pp.160–61
25. Stolfi, p.167
26. *Kriegstagebuch LVI A.K.(Mot)*, US National Archives, T314, Roll 1389
27. Zolotarev (1998), p.153
28. For Lasch's personal account of the battle, see Lasch, O. (2002) *So Fiel Königsberg*, Stuttgart: Gräfe und Unzer, pp.17–21
29. Glantz (2002), p.35
30. Pavlov was arrested and charged with treason; he was executed within days
31. Stolfi, p.170
32. Richter, p.63
33. Röngelep, R. et al. (2003) '*Tartu in the 1941 Summer War*' in *Baltic Defence Review* 9, Vol. 1, pp.165–82
34. Conze, p.219
35. Hubatch, W. (1961) *61. Infanterie-Division*, Bad Neuheim: Podzun, p.168
36. Hiio, T. (2006) *Estonia, 1940–1945: Reports of the Estonian International Commission for the Investigation of Crimes Against Humanity*, Estonian Foundation for the Investigation of Crimes Against Humanity, Tallinn: Kistler-Ritso, pp.424–25

Chapter 4

1. Quoted in Tauber, J., *14 Tage im Juni* in Bartusevičius, V., Tauber, J., Wette, W. (eds) (2003) *Holocaust in Litauen*, Cologne: Böhlau, p.40
2. Tauber, p.41
3. Levin, D. (1997) *Hidden History of the Kovno Ghetto*, Boston: United States Holocaust Museum, p.222
4. Pakalniškis, A. (1980) *Plungė*, Chicago: Spaudė M. Morkūno spaustuvė, p.45
5. Maslauskienė, N. (2001) *Lietuvos Tautinių Mažumų Įtraukimas į LSSR Administraciją ir Sovietinės Biurocratijos Tautiniai Santykiai 1940–1941* in *Genocidas ir Rezistencija*, I(9), p.38
6. Levin, D. (1995) *The Lesser of Two Evils. Eastern European Jewry Under Soviet Rule, 1939–1941*, Philadelphia: Jewish Publication Society, p.60
7. Hillgruber, A., *War in the East and Extermination of the Jews* in Marrus, M. (ed.) (1989) *The Nazi Holocaust Part 3, The 'Final Solution': The Implementation of Mass Murder*, Munich: Saur, pp.95–96
8. Orders of *Berück Nord*, 28 August 1941, Bundesarchiv-Militärarchiv, RH 22/6
9. *Richtlinien für die Durchführung der Sicherungsaufträge* ('Regulations for the Execution of Security Tasks'), 5/7/41, 9/7/41, Bundesarchiv-Militärarchiv, RH 26-281/4
10. Orders of Commander 3rd Panzer Group, 28 June 1941, Bundesarchiv-Militärarchiv, RH 26-20/19
11. Office of the United States Chief of Counsel For Prosecution of Axis Criminality, *Nazi Conspiracy and Aggression*, ('Red Series'), Vol. VII, pp.978–95, USGPO, Washington DC 1946, hereafter cited as 'Stahlecker Report'
12. Stahlecker Report

13. Stahlecker Report
14. Budreckis, A. (1968) *The Lithuanian National Revolt*, Boston: Lithuanian Encyclopedia Press, pp. 62–63
15. Levin (1995), p.222
16. Brandišauskas, V. (1996) *Siekiai Atkurti Lietuvos Valstybingumą*, Vilnius: Valstybinis leidybos centras, p.90
17. Ginaitė, S. (1999) *Atminimo Knyga*, Vilnius: Margi raštai, p.41
18. Evidence prepared for the trial of Karl Jäger in 1959, subsequently published in Wilhelm, H.-H. (1991) *Rassenpolitik und Kriegsführung. Sicherheitspolizei und Wehrmacht in Polen und der Sowjetunion 1939–1942*, Passau: Wissenschaftsverlag Rother, Document 18, pp.186–89
19. Jäger Report of 1/12/41, available in translation from the Jewish Internet Consortium, available at http://fcit.usf.edu/holocaust/resource/document/DocJager.htm, hereafter cited as 'Jäger Report'
20. Jäger Report
21. Jäger Report
22. Evidence of Fritz Bartmann, quoted in Wette, W. *SS-Standartenführer Karl Jäger* in Bartusevičius, V., Tauber, J., Wette, W. (eds) (2003) *Holocaust in Litauen*, Cologne: Böhlau, p.85
23. Evidence of Heinz Jost, quoted in Wette, W. in Bartusevičius et al, p.85
24. Jäger Report
25. Bundesarchiv-Militärarchiv, RH 26-403/4a
26. Arad, Y. et al (eds) (1989) *The Einsatzgruppen Reports. Selections from the Dispatches of the Nazi Death Squads' Campaign Against the Jews in Occupied Territories of the Soviet Union July 1941–January 1943*, New York: Holocaust Library, p.44
27. Bundesarchiv-Militärarchiv, RH 26-403/4a
28. Rolnikaite, M. (2002) *Ich Muss Erzählen*, Hamburg: Rowohlt, pp.40–41
29. Good, P. (2001) *Memoirs of Perella Esterowicz*, available at http://web.me.com/michaeldg/Site/Plagge_Documents_files/MemoirsP.rtf, p.2
30. Rolnikaite, pp.52–54
31. Rolnikaite, pp.59–64
32. Good, P., p.29
33. Rolnikaite, p.97
34. Good, P., pp.33–34
35. Good, P., p.35
36. Eckert, C. (2003), *Die Mordstätte Paneriai bei Vilnius* in Bartusevičius et al, p.133
37. Sackowicz, K. (1999) *Dziennik*, Bydgoszcz, p.46
38. Klee, E. et al (eds) (1988) *'Schöne Zeiten' – Judenmord aus der Sicht der Täter und Gaffer*, Frankfurt am Main: Fischer, p.48
39. Tomkiewicz, W. (2008) *Zbrodnia w Ponarach 1941–1944*, Warsaw: IPN, p.203
40. Langerbein, H. (2004) *Hitler's Death Squads: The Logic of Mass Murder*, Texas: A&M University Press, pp.67–68
41. Quoted in Eckert, p.137
42. Grossman, V., Ehrenburg, I. (1994) *Das Schwarzbuch. Der Genozid an den Sowjetischen Juden*, Reinbek: Rowohlt, p.504
43. Good, P., pp.40–42
44. Quoted in Lustiger, A. (2003) *Feldwebel Anton Schmid* in Bartusevičius et al, p.187
45. For an account of Schmid's activities, see Lustiger, pp.185–97
46. Inčiūrienė, J. (2003) *Rettung und Widerstand in Kaunas* in Bartusevičius et al, pp.202–03

47. Neumann, A. (2003) *Leben und Sterben im Ghetto Kaunas* in Bartusevičius et al, p.150

48. Dieckmann, C. (1998) *Das Ghetto und das Konzentrationslager in Kaunas 1941–1944*, Göttingen: Wallstein, p.448

49. Ganor, S. (1997) *Das Andere Leben*, Frankfurt am Main: Fischer, p.114

50. Inčiūrienė, pp.203–17

51. Neumann, A., p152

52. Rolnikaite, p.172

53. Good, P., pp.63–65

54. Good, P., pp.70–71

55. Good, P., p.75

56. Good, P., pp.77–89

57. See Good, M. (2005) *The Search For Major Plagge: The Nazi Who Saved Jews*. New York: Fordham University Press

58. For an account of the Kaunas ghetto, see Mishell, W. (1988) *Kaddish for Kovno: Life and Death in a Lithuanian Ghetto, 1941–1945*, Chicago: Chicago Review Press

59. Stahlecker Report

60. Incident Report 40, 1/8/1941, Bundesarchiv-Militärarchiv R-58/215, 129; see also Felder, B. (2009) *Lettland im Zweiten Weltkrieg*, Paderborn: Ferdinand Schöningh, p.212

61. Ezergailis, A. (1996) *The Holocaust in Latvia 1941–1944*, Riga: Historical Institute of Latvia, p.290

62. Stahlecker Report

63. Angrick, A., Klein, P. (2009) *The Final Solution in Riga: Exploitation and Annihilation 1941–1944*, New York: Berghahn, pp.133–50

64. Michelson, M. (2004) *City of Life, City of Death. Memories of Riga*, Colorado: University Press, p.112

65. Breitman, R. (1991) *Architect of Genocide. Himmler and the Final Solution*, London: Bodley Head, p.220

66. Report 51, 13/8/41, Bundesarchiv-Militärarchiv R-58/216, 4

67. Quoted in Felder (2009), p.211

68. Truska, L. (2003) *Litausiche Historiographie über den Holocaust in Litauen* in Bartusevičius et al., p.263

Chapter 5

1. Myllyniemi, S. (1973) *Die Neuordnung der Baltischen Länder 1941–44*, Helsinki: Suomen Historiallinen Seura, p.63

2. Report 13, 5/7/41, Bundesarchiv B, R 58/214, 75

3. Letter from KdS Lettland, Abt IIIB to the *Generalkommissar*, 11/3/42, Bundesarchiv B, R 92/6, 121

4. Note from *Generalkommissariat* in Riga, 27/8/41, Bundesarchiv B, R 92/6, 158

5. Felder, B. (2009) *Lettland im Zweiten Weltkrieg*, Paderborn: Ferdinand Schöningh, p.244

6. Felder (2009), pp.246–47

7. Kuusik, A., *Estonian Omakaitse in 1941–1944* in Hiio, T. (2006) *Estonia, 1940–1945: Reports of the Estonian International Commission for the Investigation of Crimes Against Humanity*, Estonian Foundation for the Investigation of Crimes Against Humanity, Tallinn: Kistler-Ritso, pp.797–806

8. Landwehr, R. (1999) *Estonian Vikings*, Halifax: Shelf Books, p.5

9. *Conclusions of the Estonian International Commission for the Investigation of Crimes Against*

Humanity, 2 available at http://www.historycommission.ee/temp/conclusions.htm

10. Letter from *Gruppenführer* Berger to Himmler, 2/10/41, National Archives Washington DC, RG-242, T175, Roll 22, frame 2527942

11. Jokipii, M. (1969) *Panttipataljoona*, Helsinki: Weilin+Göös, pp.115–116

12. Landwehr, pp.31–33

13. Landwehr, pp.39–42

14. Nash, D. (2002) *Hell's Gate*, Southbury: RZM, p.110

15. Press, B. (2000) *The Murder of the Jews in Latvia*, Evanston: Northwestern University Press, p.46

16. Felder (2009), pp.270–71

17. Internal communications of *Schutzmann-Bataillon 22*, Hoover Latvian Legion Collection, Box 1, Folder 9

18. See Kurzem, M. (2007) *The Mascot*, London: Ebury

19. Silgailis, A. (1986) *Latvian Legion*, San Jose: Bender, p.17

20. Silgailis, pp.19–20

21. Silgailis, pp.24–26

22. Silgailis, pp.30–39

23. Knezys, S. (2000) *Genocidas ir Rezistencija*, Vilnius: Lietuvos Gyventojų genocido ir rezistencijos tyrimo centras 1(7), p.133

24. Bubnys, A. (2009) *Lithuanian Police Battalions and the Holocaust*, p11, available at http://www.komisija.lt/Files/www.komisija.lt/File/Tyrimu_baze/Naciu%20okupacija/Instituciju,%20asmenu%20vaidmuo/Bubnys.%20Batalionai/ENG/Research%20by%20A.Bubnys%20(english).pdf

25. Knezys, pp.133–34

26. Browning, C. (2004) *The Origins of the Final Solution: The Evolution of Nazi Jewish Policy, September 1939–March 1942*, Lincoln: University of Nebraska Press, p.289

27. Gerlach, C. (2000) *Kalkulierte Morde*, Hamburg: HIS, pp.612–13

28. *Masinės Žudinės Lietuvoj*, pp.314–17, quoted in Bubnys, p.16

29. Evidence presented at the trial of A. Impelivičius, LYA, f. K-1, ap. 58, file 47386/3, Vol. 9, pp.378–79

30. Bubnys, p.32

31. Misiunas, R., Taagepera, R. (1993) *The Baltic States – Years of Dependence 1940–1990*, London: Hurst, p.65

32. *Nepriklausoma Lietuva* (1943) pp.11–12

33. Lester, D., Stockton, R. (2005) *Suicide and the Holocaust*, Nova, p.7

34. Budreckis, A. *Lithuanian Resistance, 1940–52* in Gerutis, A. (1984) *Lithuania: 700 Years*, New York: Manyland Books pp.347–48

35. Situation report of *Abwehrstelle Ostland* 1/7/42-30/9/42, Latvias Valsts Vēstures Arhīvs, Riga, P-70/5/37, p.75

36. Report on *Winterzauber* for Wehrmacht High Command Ostland, 20/3/43, Latvias Valsts Vēstures Arhīvs, Riga, P-70/5/36, pp.66–69

37. Felder (2009), p.331

38. Myllyniemi (1979), p.141

39. Swain, G. (2004) *Between Stalin and Hitler*, London: Routledge, p.140

40. Felder (2009), p.325

41. Štrauss, A. (1985) Autobiographical account, Latvijas Zinātņu Akadēmijas Centrālais Arhīvs Riga, P-40/5/22

42. Balashov, A. (2006) *Ystoriya Velykoye Otechiestvennoye Voinyi 1941–1945*, St Petersburg: Peter,

p.464

43. Report of *SS-Jagdverband Ost*, Latvijas Zinātņu Akadēmijas Centrālais Arhīvs Riga, PO 40/5/2, p.61

44. Hoover Latvian Legion Collection, Box 11, Folder 2

Chapter 6

1. See for example Glantz, D. (2002) *The Battle for Leningrad*, Lawrence: University of Kansas Press; Jones, M. (2008) *Leningrad: State of Siege*, London: John Murray

2. Glantz (2002), p.327

3. Glantz (2002), p.329

4. Ziemke, E. (2003) *Stalingrad to Berlin: the German Defeat in the East*, Honolulu: University Press of the Pacific, pp.248–51

5. Platonov, S. (1964) *Bitva za Leningrad*, Moscow: Voenizdat, p.304

6. Jones, p.284

7. Kardel, H. (1953) *Die Geschichte der 170 iInfanterie-Division*, Bad Neuheim: Podzun, p.88

8. Silgailis, A. (1986) *Latvian Legion*, San Jose: Bender, pp.39–40

9. Lohse, G. (1957) *Die Geschichte der Rheinischwestfälischen 126 iInfanterie-Division 1940–1945*, Bad Neuheim: Podzun, p.223

10. Seaton, A. (1971) *The Russo-German War 1941–1945*, New York: Praeger, p.411

11. Jones, p.283

12. Ziemke, p.256

13. Ziemke, p.256

14. Carius, O. (2003) *Tigers in the Mud*, Mechanicsburg: Stackpole, pp.46–47

15. Carius, pp.117–19

16. Platonov, p.359, quoted in Glantz (2002), p.353

17. Tieke, W. (2001): *Tragedy of the Faithful – a History of the III. (Germanisches) SS-Panzer-Korps*, Winnipeg: Fedorowicz, p.41

18. Platonov, p.373

19. Glantz (2002), p.364

20. Guderian, H. (1974) *Panzer Leader*, London: Penguin, p.336

21. D'Este, C., *Model*, in Barnett, C. (ed.) (1989) *Hitler's Generals*, New York: Weidenfeld & Nicolson, p.323

22. Mellenthin, F. von (1977) *German Generals of World War II*, Norman: University of Oklahoma Press, p.149

23. Misiunas, R., Taagepera, R., (1993) *The Baltic States – Years of Dependence 1940–1990*, London: Hurst p.70

24. Tieke, p.55

25. Krivoleev, E. (1984) *I Sraženie Dlinoj v Polgoda*, Tallinn: Eesti Raamat, p.87

26. Casualty figures: Tieke, p.64

27. Platonov, p.385

28. Zolotarev, V. (1999) *STAVKA VGK 1944–1945*, Moscow: Terra, p.44

29. Ziemke, p.262

30. Zolotarev (1999), pp.267–68

31. Carius, p.84

32. Carius, pp.89–90

33. Carius, pp.91

34. Carius, pp.94–95

35. Burnett, T. (2005) *Conspiracy Encyclopedia*, London: Collins & Brown, p.48

36. Carius, pp.103–10, 114
37. Haupt, W. (1997) *Army Group North*, Atglen: Schiffer, pp.212–13
38. Orlov, K. (1966) *Borba za Sovetsjuiu Pribaltiku v Velikoi Otechestvennoi Vione, 1941–1945*, Moscow: Liesma, Vol. I, p.120
39. For an account of the Latvian defence of the Velikaya, see Silgailis, pp.72–83

Chapter 7

1. Niepold, G. (1985) *Mittlere Ostfront Juni 1944*, Hamburg: Mittler, p.22
2. Newton, S. (1995) *Retreat from Leningrad: Army Group North, 1944/1945*, Philadelphia: Schiffer
3. Grigorenko, P. (1984) *Memoirs*, New York: Norton & Company, p.90
4. Erickson, J. (1999) *The Road to Stalingrad*, New Haven: Yale University Press, p.359
5. Manteuffel, H. von (1965) *Die 7. Panzer-Division im Zweiten Weltkrieg*, Krefeld: Schaberg, p.416
6. Report from 7th Panzer Division in Manteuffel, p.418
7. Plato, A. von (1978) *Die Geschichte der 5. Panzer Division*, Regensburg: Walhalla & Praetoria, p.353
8. Piotrowski, T. (1997) *Poland's Holocaust*, Jefferson: McFarland & Co, p.88
9. Piotrowski, pp.88–89
10. Report by Beria, L., to Stalin, Molotov and Antonov, 18 July 1944, available from http://www.doomedsoldiers.com/armia-krajowa-in-NKVD-NKGB-documents-pt-2.html
11. For a Polish account of Operation *Ostra Brama* and its aftermath, see Erdman, J. (1990) *Droga do Ostrej Bramy*, Warsaw: PWN
12. Silgailis, A. (1986) *Latvian Legion*, San Jose: Bender, pp.98–100
13. Carius, O. (2003) *Tigers in the Mud*, Mechanicsburg: Stackpole, pp.46–47, p.164
14. Carius, pp.166–71
15. *Tsentralnyi Archiv Ministertsva Oborony* f.3404, op.1, d.102, ll.55–56
16. After-action report of *Schwere Panzer Abteilung 502 4–27 July 1944*, quoted in Carius, pp.295–96
17. Carius, pp.183–84
18. After-action report of *Schwere Panzer Abteilung 502 4–27 July 1944*, quoted in Carius, pp.300–02
19. Silgailis, pp.108–15
20. Grier, H. (2007) *Hitler, Dönitz, and the Baltic Sea*, Annapolis: Naval Institute Press, p.121
21. Tieke, W. (2001): *Tragedy of the Faithful – a History of the III. (Germanisches) SS-Panzer-Korps*, Winnipeg: Fedorowicz, pp.88–94
22. Kattago, S. (2008) 'Commemorating Liberation and Occupation: War Memorials Along the Road to Narva' in *Journal of Baltic Studies* 39 (4), pp. 431–49
23. For casualty figures, see Laar, M. (2006) *Sinimäed 1944: II Maailmasõja Lahingud Kirde-Eestis*, Tallinn: Varrak, and Krivosheev, G. (1997) *Soviet Casualties and Combat Losses in the Twentieth Century*, London: Greenhill Books
24. Luck, H. von (2002) *Panzer Commander*, London: Cassell, p.249
25. Tieke, p.124
26. See Laar (2006). For an account of the battle, see Tieke, pp.111–35

Chapter 8

1. Niepold, G. (1987) *Panzeroperationen 'Doppelkopf' und 'Cäsar'*, Herford: Mittler, p.15
2. Bergstrom, C. (2007) *Bagration to Berlin: The Final Air Battles in the East: 1944–1945*, Weybridge: Ian Allan, p.82
3. Krivosheev, G. (1997) *Soviet Casualties and Combat Losses in the Twentieth Century*, London:

Greenhill Books, p.371

4. Neumann, J. (1989) *Die 4. Panzer Division 1943–1945*, Bonn: self-published, pp.437–45
5. Niepold (1987), pp.19-20
6. Spaeter, H. (1995) *History of the Panzerkorps Grossdeutschland*, Winnipeg: Fedorowicz, pp.389–90
7. Niepold (1987), p.21
8. *Vsemyrnaya Ystoriya Vtoroye Myrovoye Voynyi* (1999), Minsk, p.592
9. Bagramian, I. (1984) *So Schritten Wir Zum Sieg*, Berlin: Militärverlag der DDR, p.344
10. Schäufler, H. (1983) *So Lebten Sie und So Starben Sie*, Bamberg: Kameradschaft Ehemaliger Panzer-Regiment 35 eV, p.232
11. Plato, A. von (1978) *Die Geschichte der 5. Panzer Division*, Regensburg: Walhalla & Praetotia, p.358
12. Bagramian, pp.343–44
13. Bagramian, p.345
14. Manteuffel, H. von (1965) *Die 7. Panzer-Division im Zweiten Weltkrieg*, Krefeld: Schaberg, p.423
15. Bagramian, p.344
16. Quoted in Bagramian, p.346
17. Bagramian, pp.345–46
18. Plato, pp.358–59
19. Plato, p.359
20. Bagramian, p.348
21. Niepold (1987), pp.47–48
22. Bagramian, pp.352–53
23. Schäufler (1983), pp.232–33
24. Byrd, R. (2006) *Once I Had a Comrade: Karl Roth and the Combat History of 36th Panzer Regiment 1939–1945*, Solihull: Helion, p.133
25. Bagramian, p.354
26. Niepold (1987), pp.52–53
27. Neumann, J., pp.465–66
28. Plato, pp.360–61, Niepold (1987), p.68
29. Neumann, J., pp.469–71
30. Niepold (1987), p.73
31. Quoted in Niepold (1987), p.78
32. Neumann, J., p.474
33. Niepold (1987), p.81
34. Neumann, J., p.475, Niepold (1987), p.82
35. Bagramian, p.357
36. Kuznetsov, N. (2000) *Koorsom k Pobyedye*, Moscow: Golos, pp.411–18
37. Tieke, W. (2001): *Tragedy of the Faithful – a History of the III. (Germanisches) SS-Panzer-Korps*, Winnipeg: Fedorowicz, pp.157–58
38. Niepold (1987), pp. 87–88
39. Bagramian, p.360
40. Bagramian, pp.361–62
41. Bagramian, pp.363
42. Bagramian, pp.365–67
43. Neumann, J., p.487
44. Bagramian, p.368
45. Plato, p.361

46. Plato, p.361
47. Niepold (1987), p.94
48. Schäufler (1983), pp.234–35
49. Meckl, R., *Wartezimmer des Todes* in Schäufler, H. (1973) *Die Weg War Weit*, Neckargemünd: Vowinckel, pp.197–98
50. Meckl, p.198
51. Tieke, p.162
52. Hiio, T. *Combat in Estonia in 1944* in Hiio, T. (2006) *Estonia, 1940–1945: Reports of the Estonian International Commission for the Investigation of Crimes Against Humanity*, Estonian Foundation for the Investigation of Crimes Against Humanity, Tallinn: Kistler-Ritso, pp.1,035–1,094
53. Tieke, pp.171–72
54. Bagramian, pp.369–70
55. Kurowski, F. (2002) *Bridgehead Kurland*, Winnipeg: Fedorowicz, pp.19–20

Chapter 9

1. Eidintas, A, Žalys, V, Senn, A (1999) *Lithuania in European Politics: The Years of the First Republic, 1918–1940,* New York: St. Martin's Press, p. 86
2. Gerutis, A. *Independent Lithuania* in Gerutis, A. (ed.) *Lithuania: 700 Years (1984)*, translated by Budreckis, A., New York: Manyland Books, pp.247–49
3. Bagramian, I. (1984) *So Schritten Wir Zum Sieg*, Berlin: Militärverlag der DDR, pp.371–72
4. Bagramian, p.375
5. Bagramian, pp.377–78
6. Niepold, G. (1988) *12. Panzerdivision (2. Inf. Div.) Pommern 1921–1945*, self-published, pp.107–108
7. Tieke, W. (2001): *Tragedy of the Faithful – a History of the III. (Germanisches) SS-Panzer-Korps*, Winnipeg: Fedorowicz, p.175
8. Bagramian, p.381
9. Plato, A. von (1978) *Die Geschichte der 5. Panzer Division*, Regensburg: Walhalla & Praetoria, p.363
10. Bagramian, p.384
11. Bagramian, pp.387–88
12. Neumann, J. (1989) *Die 4. Panzer Division 1943–1945*, Bonn: self-published, p.505
13. Bagramian, pp.397–98
14. Plato, pp.363–64
15. Huber, J. (1994) *So War es Wirklich*, self-published, p.72
16. Huber, pp.72–78
17. Bagramian, p.389
18. Dieckert, K., Grossmann, H. (2002) *Die Kampf um Ostpreussen*, Munich: Motor Buch Verlag, p.31
19. Bagramian, pp.393–94
20. Plato, p.365
21. Spaeter, H. (1995) *History of the Panzerkorps Grossdeutschland*, Winnipeg: Fedorowicz, pp.389–90; Niepold (1987), p.413
22. Bagramian, pp.396–97
23. Neumann, J., pp.510–11
24. Bagramian, p.398
25. Bagramian, p.400
26. Bagramian, pp.400–01

27. Bagramian, pp.403–04
28. Silgailis, A. (1986) *Latvian Legion*, San Jose: Bender, pp.122–24
29. Bagramian, pp.405–06
30. Neumann, J., pp.520–22
31. Bagramian, pp.410–11
32. Uustalu, E. (1952) *The History of the Estonian People*, London: Boreas, p.350
33. *Latvijas Zinātņu Akadēmijas Centrālais Arhīvs*, Riga, P-40/5/22, P-40/5/26
34. Felder, B. (2009) *Lettland im Zweiten Weltkrieg*, Paderborn: Ferdinand Schöningh, p.337
35. Felder (2009), p.339
36. Winterton, P., quoted in Misiunas, R., Taagepera, R. (1993) *The Baltic States – Years of Dependence 1940–1990*, London: Hurst, p.72
37. Vīksne, R., Kangeris, K. (eds) (1999) *No NKVD Līdz KGB. Politiskās Prāvas Latvijā 1940–1986*, Riga: Latvijas Vēstures institūta apgāds, p.972
38. Dieckert and Grossmann, p.53
39. Christern, H., quoted in Schäufler, H. (1983) *So Lebten Sie und So Starben Sie*, Bamberg: Kameradschaft Ehemaliger Panzer-Regiment 35 eV, pp.238–39

Chapter 10

1. Plakans, A. (1995) *The Latvians: A Short History*, Stanford: Hoover Institution Press, p.50
2. Quoted in Kurowski, F. (2002) *Bridgehead Kurland*, Winnipeg: Fedorowicz, p.90
3. Bagramian, I. (1984) *So Schritten Wir Zum Sieg*, Berlin: Militärverlag der DDR, p.411
4. Bagramian, p.412
5. Neumann, J. (1989) *Die 4. Panzer Division 1943–1945*, Bonn: self-published, pp.522–23
6. Neumann, J., pp.524–28
7. Kurowski, pp.82–87
8. Neumann, J., p.533
9. Neumann, J., p.537
10. Bagramian, p.414
11. Silgailis, A. (1986) *Latvian Legion*, San Jose: Bender, p.134
12. Neumann, J., p551–52
13. Neumann, J., p.552
14. Kurowski, p.150
15. Neumann, J., p.571
16. For an account of these events, see Neumann, J., pp.570–77; Kurowski, pp.156–59
17. Neumann, J., p.579
18. Kurowski, pp.168–69
19. Kurowski, pp.170–71
20. Kurowski, p.173
21. Silgailis, pp.136–38
22. Neumann, J., pp.589–93
23. Felder, B. (2009) *Lettland im Zweiten Weltkrieg*, Paderborn: Ferdinand Schöningh, p.320–35

Chapter 11

1. Neumann, J. (1989) *Die 4. Panzer Division 1943–1945*, Bonn: self-published, p.596–600
2. Neumann, J., p.601
3. Silgailis, A. (1986) *Latvian Legion*, San Jose: Bender, p.143
4. Neumann, J., p.603

5. Niepold, G. (1988) *12. Panzerdivision (2. Inf. Div.) Pommern 1921–1945*, self-published, p.94
6. Bagramian, I. (1984) *So Schritten Wir Zum Sieg*, Berlin: Militärverlag der DDR, pp.430–31
7. For an account of the British naval deployment in the Baltic after the First World War, see Bennett, G. (1964) *Cowan's War*, London: Collins
8. Quoted in Kurowski, F. (2002) *Bridgehead Kurland*, Winnipeg: Fedorowicz, pp.175–76
9. Kurowski, p.186
10. Kurowski, p.187
11. See for example Buttar, P. (2010) *Battleground Prussia*, Oxford: Osprey, p.302
12. Kurowski, p.197
13. Silgailis, p.149
14. Kurowski, pp.259–61
15. Schramm, P. (1982) *Kriegstagebuch der Oberkommando der Wehrmacht*, Vol. VIII, Herrsching: Pawlak, p.1, 472
16. Schön, H (1983) *Ostsee 45*, Stuttgart: Motorbuch Verlag, p.606
17. Kurowski, p.269
18. Kurowski, p.270
19. Byrd, R. (2006) *Once I Had a Comrade: Karl Roth and the Combat History of 36th Panzer Regiment 1939–1945*, Solihull: Helion, pp.147–48
20. Byrd, pp.146–47
21. Byrd, p.147
22. Niepold (1988), p.96
23. Schön, p.627
24. Niepold (1988), p.96
25. Quoted in Kurowski, p.266

Chapter 12

1. Lentsman, L. (1977) *Eesti Rahvas Suures Isamaasõjas*, Tallinn: Partei Ajaloo Institut, p.439
2. Meškauskas, K., Januškevičius, V., Puronas, V. (1973) *Lietuvos Dabartis Ir Ateitis*, Vilnius: SN, p.12
3. Misiunas, R., Taagepera, R. (1993) *The Baltic States – Years of Dependence 1940–1990*, London: Hurst, p.74
4. Skultans, V. (1997) *The Testimony of Lives: Narrative and Memory in Post-Soviet Latvia*, Andover: Routledge, pp.83–84
5. Laar, M. (1992) *War In The Woods: Estonia's Struggle For Independence*, Washington: Compass Press, pp.106–07
6. Quoted in Laar (1992), p.108
7. Laar (1992), p.113
8. Laar (1992), p.119
9. For an account of Ants Kaljurand's activities, see Kiiver, V. (2010) *Hirmus-Ants. Bandiit, Kangelane, Legend,* Tartu: Kirjastus Aja Lood
10. Strods, H., Kott, M. (2002) 'The File on Operation Priboi: A Re-Assessment of the Mass Deportations of 1949' in *Journal of Baltic Studies* 33 (1), pp.1–36
11. Laar, M. (1992), p.24
12. Andersons, E., Siliņš, L. (eds) (2002) *Latvija un Rietumi. Latviešu Nacionālā Pretestības Kustība 1943–1945*, Riga: Latvijas Universitātes žurnāla 'Latvijas Vēsture' fonds, pp.14–126
13. Felder, B. (2004) *Das Unternehmen 'Wildkatze'* in *Totalitārie Okupācijas Režimi Latvijā 1940–1964*, Riga: Commission of the Historias of Latvia, Vol. 13, p.268
14. Leutnant Hasselmann's report from *Frontaufklärungskommando 212* dated 24/12/44, BA-MA, RH-2/2129, p.155

15. Felder (2009), pp.317–18
16. Strods, H. (1997) *Latvijas Nacionālo Partizāņu Karš 1944–1956*, Riga: Preses Nams, p.168
17. *Gazeta Kapitalist* (19/5/2004) *Zhizn' I Sudba 'Bolshogo Medvedya'. Sto Let Vilisu Latsisu*
18. Latišenka, A. (2001) *Lietuvos istorijos atlasas*, Vilnius: Vaga, p.25
19. Kuodytė, D., Tracevskis, R. (2004) *The Unknown War: Armed Anti-Soviet Resistance in Lithuania in 1944–1953*, Vilnius: Genocide and Resistance Research Centre of Lithuania, p.43
20. See Buttar, P. (2010) *Battleground Prussia*, Oxford: Osprey, pp.452–53
21. *Svenska Dagbladet*, 21/6/94 and 22/6/94
22. Rolnikaite, M. (2002) *Ich Muss Erzählen*, Hamburg: Rowohlt, pp.268–69
23. Rolnikaite, p.277
24. Matas, D., Charendoff, S. (1988) *Justice Delayed: Nazi War Criminals in Canada*, Toronto: Summerhill, p.77
25. Littman, S. (1984) *War Criminal on Trial: The Rauca Case*, Ontario: Paperjacks
26. *Time*, 19/3/65
27. Merk, E. (2005) *Schwere Jahre auf der Höhe des Lebens*, Norderstedt: Books on Demand
28. Baltais, M. (1999) *The Latvian Legion in Documents*, Toronto: Amber, p.104
29. For a good, concise account, see Misiunas and Taagepera
30. Quoted in Miagov, M. (2005) *SSSR, USA e Problema Pribaltikii v 1941-1945 Godah in Novaya e Novenshaya Istoriya*, Vol. 1 pp.50–59; see also Loewenheim, F., Langley, H., Jonas, M. (1990) *Churchill and Roosevelt: Their Secret Correspondence*, Cambridge: Da Capo Press, pp.217–18
31. See for example Djukov, A. (2007) *Meef o Genocheede: Repressii Sovietskiiy Vlasteii v Estonii*, Moscow: Yakovlev, pp.87–96
32. Emelyanov, V. (2007) 'Pribaltika vo Vtoroyi Mirovoyi' in *Nash Sovremmenik*, Vol. 6 pp.154–68
33. Yampolski, V. (2001) 'V Pribaltike Zhdali Furera ... e Furer Prishel!' in *Voenno-Istoricheskii Zhurnal*, Vol. 6, pp.36–43
34. Zubkov, E. (2007) '"Lesnyie Bratya" v Pribaltike: Viona Posle Vionyi' in *Otechestvennaya Istoriya*, Vol. 2, pp.74–90
35. Swain, G. (2004) *Between Stalin and Hitler*, London: Routledge, p.140, pp.247–48
36. European Court of Human Rights judgment in case Kononov v. Latvia, 24 June 2008
37. Hague Convention 1907, Article 23
38. Grand Chamber, European Court of Human Rights judgement in case Kononov v. Latvia, 17 May 2010
39. *Condolences to Family of Great Patriotic War Veteran Vassili Kononov*, Presidential Press and Information Office, Moscow, 1 April 2011

BIBLIOGRAPHY

Archives and collections

Bundesarchiv-Militärarchiv, Freiburg

Bundersarchiv, Berlin

Dokumenti Vneshnei Politiki (Foreign Affairs Documents), Ministerstvo Inostrannyk Del Rossiiskoi Federatsii (Foreign Ministry of the Russian Federation), Moscow

Hoover Institution of War, Peace and Revolution Archive, Stanford, California

Imperial War Museum, London

Jewish Internet Consortium

Latvijas Valsts Arhīvs (Latvian State Archive), Riga

Latvijas Zinātņu Akadēmijas Centrālais Arhīvs (Central Archives of the Academy of Sciences, Latvia), Riga

Records of the United States Senate, Washington DC

Tsentralnyi Archiv Ministertsva Oborony (Central Archive of the Ministry of Defence), Moscow

United States Library of Congress, Washington DC

United States National Archives

Journals, periodicals and newspapers

Armor, Fort Benning, Georgia

Baltic Defence Review, Tartu, Estonia

Brīvā Zeme, Riga

Central European History Journal, Cambridge University Press

Europe-Asia Studies, Central and East European Studies, University of Glasgow

Gazeta Kapitalist, Riga

Genocidas ir Rezistencija, Lithuanian Genocide and Resistance Research Centre, Vilnius

Journal of Baltic Studies, University of Washington, Seattle

Land Warfare Papers, Institute of Land Warfare, Arlington, Virginia

Military Review, Fort Leavenworth, Kansas

Nash Sovremmenik, Moscow

Nepriklausoma Lietuva (1943)

Novaya e Novenshaya Istoriya, Moscow

Otechestvennaya Istoriya, Moscow

Svenska Dagbladet, Stockholm

Time, New York

Voenno-Istoricheskii Zhurnal, Moscow

Books and articles

Andersons, E., Siliņš, L. (eds) (2002) *Latvija un Rietumi. Latviešu Nacionālā Pretestības Kustība 1943–1945*, Riga: Latvijas Universitātes žurnāla 'Latvijas Vēsture' fonds

Angrick, A., Klein, P. (2009) *The Final Solution in Riga: Exploitation and Annihilation 1941–1944*, New York: Berghahn

Arad, Y. et al (eds) (1989) *The Einsatzgruppen Reports. Selections from the Dispatches of the Nazi Death Squads' Campaign Against the Jews in Occupied Territories of the Soviet Union July 1941–January 1943*, New York: Holocaust Library

Bagramian, I. (1984) *So Schritten Wir Zum Sieg*, Berlin: Militärverlag der DDR

Balashov, A. (2006) *Ystoriya Velykoye Otechiestvennoye Voinyi 1941–1945*, St Petersburg: Peter

Baltais, M. (1999) *The Latvian Legion in Documents*, Toronto: Amber

Barnett, C. (ed.) (1989) *Hitler's Generals*, New York: Weidenfeld & Nicolson

Bartusevičius, V., Tauber, J., Wette, W. (eds) (2003) *Holocaust in Litauen*, Cologne: Böhlau

Bennett, G. (1964) *Cowan's War*, London: Collins

Bergstrom, C. (2007) *Bagration to Berlin: The Final Air Battles in the East: 1944–1945*, Weybridge: Ian Allan

Bleiere, D., Butulis, I., Zunda, A., Stranga, A., Feldmanis, I. (2006) *History of Latvia: the 20th Century*, Riga: Jumava

Brandišauskas, V. (1996) *Siekiai Atkurti Lietuvos Valstybingumą*, Vilnius: Valstybinis leidybos centras

Breitman, R. (1991) *Architect of Genocide. Himmler and the Final Solution*, London: Bodley Head

Browning, C. (2004) *The Origins of the Final Solution: The Evolution of Nazi Jewish Policy, September 1939–March 1942*, Lincoln: University of Nebraska Press,

Bubnys, A. (2009) *Lithuanian Police Battalions and the Holocaust*, p.11, available at http://www.komisija.lt/Files/www.komisija.lt/File/Tyrimu_baze/Naciu%20okupacija/Instituciju,%20asmenu%20vaidmuo/Bubnys.%20Batalionai/ENG/Research%20by%20A.Bubnys%20(english).pdf

Budreckis, A. (1968) *The Lithuanian National Revolt*, Boston: Lithuanian Encyclopedia Press

Burnett, T. (2005) *Conspiracy Encyclopedia*, London: Collins & Brown

Buttar, P. (2010) *Battleground Prussia*, Oxford: Osprey

Byrd, R. (2006) *Once I Had a Comrade: Karl Roth and the Combat History of 36th Panzer Regiment 1939–1945*, Solihull: Helion

Carius, O. (2003) *Tigers in the Mud*, Mechanicsburg: Stackpole

Cecil, R. (1972) *The Myth of the Master Race: Alfred Rosenberg and Nazi Ideology*, New York: Dodd Mead,

Conze, W. (1953) *Die Geschichte der 291. Infanterie-Division*, Bad Neuheim: Podzun

Czernin von und zu Chudenitz, O. (1920) *In the World War*, New York and London: Harper & Brothers

Dallin, A. (1957) *German Rule in Russia 1941–45*, London: Macmillan

Davies, N. (2003) *White Eagle, Red Star: the Polish-Soviet War, 1919–20*, London: Pimlico

D'Este, C. (1989) *Model* in Barnett, C. (ed.) *Hitler's Generals*, New York: Weidenfeld & Nicolson

Dieckert, K., Grossmann, H. (2002) *Die Kampf um Ostpreussen*, Munich: Motor Buch Verlag

Dieckmann, C. (1998) *Das Ghetto und das Konzentrationslager in Kaunas 1941–1944*, Göttingen: Wallstein

Djukov, A. (2007) *Meef o Genocheede: Repressii Sovietskiiy Vlasteii v Estonii*, Moscow: Yakovlev

Eberhardt, P. (2006) *Political Migrations in Poland*, Warsaw: Studium Europy Wschodniej UW

Eidintas, A., Žalys, V., Senn, A. (1997) *Lithuania in European Politics: The Years of the First Republic, 1918–1940*, Basingstoke: Macmillan

Eksteins, M. (1999) *Walking Since Daybreak*, New York: Mariner

Emelianov, Y. (2007) *Priybaltika: Mezhdoo Stalinim I Hitlerom*, Moscow: Izdatel' Bystrov

Emelyanov, V. (2007) '*Pribaltika vo Vtoroyi Mirovoyi*' in *Nash Sovremmenik*, Vol. 6

Erdman, J. (1990) *Droga do Ostrej Bramy*, Warsaw: PWN

Erichsen, C., Olusoga, D. (2010) *The Kaiser's Holocaust: Germany's Forgotten Genocide and the Colonial Roots of Nazism*, London: Faber & Faber

Erickson, J. (1999) *The Road to Stalingrad*, New Haven: Yale University Press

Ezergailis, A. (1996) *The Holocaust in Latvia 1941–1944*, Riga: Historical Institute of Latvia

Felder, B. (2004) *Das Unternehmen 'Wildkatze'* in *Totalitārie Okupācijas Režimi Latvijā 1940–1964*, Riga: Commission of the Historias of Latvia, Vol. 13

Felder, B. (2009) *Lettland im Zweiten Weltkrieg*, Paderborn: Ferdinand Schöningh

Ganor, S. (1997) *Das Andere Leben*, Frankfurt am Main: Fischer

Gerlach, C. (2000) *Kalkulierte Morde*, Hamburg: HIS

Gerutis, A. (ed.) *Lithuania: 700 Years*, translated by Budreckis, A., New York: Manyland Books

Ginaitė, S. (1999) *Atminimo Knyga*, Vilnius: Margi raštai

Glantz, D. (1998) *Stumbling Colossus: The Red Army on the Eve of World War*, Lawrence: University of Kansas Press

Glantz, D. (2002) *The Battle for Leningrad*, Lawrence: University of Kansas Press

Good, M. (2005) *The Search For Major Plagge: The Nazi Who Saved Jews*, New York: Fordham University Press

Good, P. (2001) *Memoirs of Perella Esterowicz*, available online at http://web.me.com/ michaeldg/Site/Plagge_Documents_files/MemoirsP.rtf

Gorkov, I., Semin, N. (1996), 'Konets global'noi Ishi: Na sovetskom severozapade – Operativnye plany zapadhykh prigranichnykh okrugov 1941 godasvidetel'-stvuiut: SSSR ne gotovilsia knapadeniiu na Germaniiu' in *Voenno-istoricheskii zhurnal* 6 (Nov– Dec 1996): 2

Grier, H. (2007) *Hitler, Dönitz, and the Baltic Sea*, Annapolis: Naval Institute Press

Grigorenko, P. (1984) *Memoirs*, New York: Norton & Company

Grossman, V., Ehrenburg, I. (1994) *Das Schwarzbuch. Der Genozid an den Sowjetischen Juden*, Reinbek: Rowohlt

Guderian, H. (1974) *Panzer Leader*, London: Penguin

Halder, F., *Diaries*, Imperial War Museum, 22 August 1939

Haupt, W. (1987) *Die 8. Panzer-Division im Zweiten Weltkrieg*, Friedberg: Podzun

Haupt, W. (1997) *Army Group North*, Atglen: Schiffer

Hiden, J., Salmon, P. (1994) *The Baltic Nations and Europe* (revised edn), Harlow: Longman

Hiio, T. (2006) *Estonia, 1940–1945: Reports of the Estonian International Commission for the Investigation of Crimes Against Humanity*, Estonian Foundation for the Investigation of Crimes Against Humanity, Tallinn: Kistler-Ritso

Hillgruber, A. *War in the East and the Extermination of the Jews* in Marrus, M. (ed.) (1989) *The Nazi Holocaust Part 3, The 'Final Solution': The Implementation of Mass Murder*, Munich: Saur

Hitler, A. (1971) *Mein Kampf*, Boston: Houghton Mifflin

Holborn, H. (1969) *A History of Modern Germany*, New York: Knopf

Hubatch, W. (1961) *61 Infanterie-Division*, Bad Neuheim: Podzun

Huber, J. (1994) *So War es Wirklich*, self-published

Inčiūrienė, J. (2003) *Rettung und Widerstand in Kaunas* in Bartusevičius et al (eds), *Holocaust in Litauen*, Cologne: Böhlau

Ivnskis, Z. (1965) *Lithuania During the War: Resistance Against the Soviet and Nazi Occupants* in Vardys, V. (ed.) *Lithuania Under The Soviets*, New York: Praeger

Jokipii, M. (1969) *Panttipataljoona*, Helsinki: Weilin+Göös

Jones, M. (2008) *Leningrad: State of Siege*, London: John Murray

Kangeris, K. (2008) *Latvijas Vēsturnieku Komisijas Raksti*, Riga: Latvijas vēstures institūta apgāds

Kardel, H. (1953) *Die Geschichte der 170. Infanterie-Division*, Bad Neuheim: Podzun

Kattago, S. (2008) 'Commemorating Liberation and Occupation: War Memorials Along the Road to Narva' *Journal of Baltic Studies* 39 (4)

Kay, A. (2006) *Exploitation, Resettlement, Mass Murder: Political and Economic Planning for German Occupation Policy in the Soviet Union*, New York: Berghahn

Kiiver, V. (2010) *Hirmus-Ants. Bandiit, Kangelane, Legend,* Tartu: Kirjastus Aja Lood

Klee, E. et al (eds) (1988) *'Schöne Zeiten' – Judenmord aus der Sicht der Täter und Gaffer*, Frankfurt am Main: Fischer

Knezys, S. (2000) *Genocidas ir Rezistencija*, Vilnius: Lietuvos Gyventojų genocido ir rezistencijos tyrimo centras

Komplektov, G. (1990) *Polpredy Soobshchaiut*, Moscow: Meshdunarodnye Otnosheniia

Krause, M., Phillips, R. (eds) (2006) *Historical Perspectives of the Operational Art*, Washington: Center of Military History

Krivoleev, E. (1984) *I Sraženie Dlinoj v Polgoda*, Tallinn: Eesti Raamat

Krivosheev, G. (1997) *Soviet Casualties and Combat Losses in the Twentieth Century*, London: Greenhill Books

Kuodytė, D., Tracevskis, R. (2004) *The Unknown War: Armed Anti-Soviet Resistance in Lithuania in 1944–1953*, Vilnius: Genocide and Resistance Research Centre of Lithuania

Kuromiya, H., Pepłoński, A. (2009) *Między Warszawą a Tokio*, Toruń: Wydawnictwo Adam Marszałek

Kurowski, F. (2002) *Bridgehead Kurland*, Winnipeg: Fedorowicz

Kurzem, M. (2007) *The Mascot*, London: Ebury

Kuusik, A. (2006), *Estonian Omakaitse in 1941–1944* in Hiio, T. *Estonia, 1940–1945: Reports of the Estonian International Commission for the Investigation of Crimes Against Humanity*, Estonian Foundation for the Investigation of Crimes Against Humanity, Tallinn: Kistler-Ritso

Kuznetsov, N. (2000) *Koorsom k Pobyedye*, Moscow: Golos

Laar, M. (1992) *War In The Woods: Estonia's Struggle For Independence*, Washington: Compass Press

Laar, M. (2006) *Sinimäed 1944: II Maailmasõja Lahingud Kirde-Eestis*, Tallinn: Varrak

Landwehr, R. (1999) *Estonian Vikings*, Halifax: Shelf Books

Langerbein, H. (2004) *Hitler's Death Squads: The Logic of Mass Murder*, Texas: A&M University Press

Lasch, O. (2002) *So Fiel Königsberg*, Stuttgart: Gräfe und Unzer

Latišenka, A. (2001) *Lietuvos istorijos atlasas*, Vilnius: Vaga

Lejiņš, J. (1971) *Mana Dzimtene: Atmiņu un Pārdomu Atspulgā*, Vasteras: ICA bokförlag

Lentsman, L. (1977) *Eesti Rahvas Suures Isamaasõjas*, Tallinn: Partei Ajaloo Institut

Lester, D., Stockton, R. (2005) *Suicide and the Holocaust*, Nova

Levin, D. (1995) *The Lesser of Two Evils. Eastern European Jewry Under Soviet Rule, 1939–1941*, Philadelphia: Jewish Publication Society

Levin, D. (1997) *Hidden History of the Kovno Ghetto*, Boston: United States Holocaust Museum

Littman, S. (1984) *War Criminal on Trial: The Rauca Case*, Ontario: Paperjacks

Loewenheim, F., Langley, H., Jonas, M. (1990) *Churchill and Roosevelt: Their Secret Correspondence*, Cambridge: Da Capo Press

Lohse, G. (1957) *Die Geschichte der Rheinischwestfälischen 126. Infanterie-Division 1940–1945*, Bad Neuheim: Podzun

Lower, W. (2009) *Empire, Colony, Genocide: Conquest, Occupation and Subaltern Resistance in World History*, New York: Berghahn

Luck, H. von (2002) *Panzer Commander*, London: Cassell

Lukes, I. (1996) *Czechoslovakia Between Stalin and Hitler: The Diplomacy of Edvard Beneš in the 1930s*, Oxford: Oxford University Press

Lustiger, A. (2003) *Feldwebel Anton Schmid* in Bartusevičius et al (eds), *Holocaust in Litauen*, Cologne: Böhlau

Luttichau, C. von (1985) *The Road to Moscow: The Campaign in Russia*, Washington DC: Center for Military History Project

Madajczyk, C. (1961) *Generalna Gubernia w planach hitlerowskich. Studia*, Warsaw: Wydawnictwo Naukowe PWN

Madajczyk, C. (1994) *Vom Generalplan Ost zum Generalsiedlungsplan: Dokumente*, Munich: Saur

Manteuffel, H. von (1965) *Die 7. Panzer-Division im Zweiten Weltkrieg*, Krefeld: Schaberg

Marrus, M. (ed.) (1989) *The Nazi Holocaust Part 3, The 'Final Solution': The Implementation of Mass Murder*, Munich: Saur

Maslauskienė, N. (2001) '*Lietuvos Tautinių Mažumų Įtraukimas į LSSR Administraciją ir Sovietinės Biurocratijos Tautiniai Santykiai 1940–1941*' in *Genocidas ir Rezistencija*, I (9)

Matas, D., Charendoff, S. (1988) *Justice Delayed: Nazi War Criminals in Canada*, Toronto: Summerhill

McPadden, C. (2006) *Mikhail Nikolayevich Tukhachevsky (1893–1937): Practitioner and Theorist of War*, Land Warfare Papers 56, Institute of Land Warfare, Arlington

Meckl, R. (1973), *Wartezimmer des Todes* in Schäufler, H. *Die Weg War Weit*, Neckargemünd: Vowinckel

Mellenthin, F. von (1977) *German Generals of World War II*, Norman: University of Oklahoma Press

Merk, E. (2005) *Schwere Jahre auf der Höhe des Lebens*, Norderstedt: Books on Demand

Meškauskas, K., Januškevičius, V., Puronas, V. (1973) *Lietuvos Dabartis Ir Ateitis*, Vilnius: SN

Miagov, M. (2005) SSSR, USA e Problema Pribaltikii v 1941–1945 Godah in Novaya e Novenshaya Istoriya, Vol. 1

Michelson, M. (2004) *City of Life, City of Death. Memories of Riga*, Colorado: University Press

Mishell, W. (1988) *Kaddish for Kovno: Life and Death in a Lithuanian Ghetto, 1941–1945*, Chicago: Chicago Review Press

Misiunas, R., Taagepera, R. (1993) *The Baltic States – Years of Dependence 1940–1990*, London: Hurst

Myllyniemi, S. (1973) *Die Neuordnung der Baltischen Länder 1941–44*, Helsinki: Suomen Historiallinen Seura

Myllyniemi, S. (1979) *Die Baltische Krise 1938–41*, Stuttgart: Deutsche

Nash, D. (2002) *Hell's Gate*, Southbury: RZM

Naumann, F. (1915) *Mitteleuropa*, Berlin: Georg Reimer

Nekrich, A., Ulam, A., Freeze, G. (1997) *Pariahs, Partners, Predators: German–Soviet Relations, 1922–1941*, New York: Columbia University Press

Neumann, A. (2003) *Leben und Sterben im Ghetto Kaunas* in Bartusevičius et al (eds), *Holocaust in Litauen*, Cologne: Böhlau

Neumann, J. (1989) *Die 4. Panzer Division 1943–1945*, Bonn: self-published

Newton, S. (1995) *Retreat from Leningrad: Army Group North, 1944/1945*, Philadelphia: Schiffer

Nicholas, L. (2006) *Cruel World: The Children of Europe in the Nazi Web*, New York: Vintage

Niepold, G. (1985) *Mittlere Ostfront Juni 1944*, Hamburg: Mittler

Niepold, G. (1987) *Panzeroperationen 'Doppelkopf' und 'Cäsar'*, Herford: Mittler

Niepold, G. (1988) *12. Panzerdivision (2. Inf. Div.) Pommern 1921–1945*, self-published

Nollendorfs, V. (2005) *Battle for the Baltic. Yearbook of the Museum of the Occupation of Latvia 2004*, Riga

Orlov, K. (1966) *Borba za Sovetsjuiu Pribaltiku v Velikoi Otechestvennoi Vione, 1941–1945*, Moscow: Liesma

Pakalniškis, A. (1980) *Plungė*, Chicago: Spaudė M. Morkūno spaustuvė

Piotrowski, T. (1997) *Poland's Holocaust*, Jefferson: McFarland & Co

Plakans, A. (1995) *The Latvians: A Short History*, Stanford: Hoover Institution Press

Plato, A. von (1978) *Die Geschichte der 5. Panzer Division*, Regensburg: Walhalla & Praetoria

Platonov, S. (1964) *Bitva za Leningrad*, Moscow: Voenizdat

Press, B. (2000) *The Murder of the Jews in Latvia*, Evanston: Northwestern University Press

Raun, T. (2002) *Estonia and the Estonians (Studies of Nationalities)*, Stanford: Hoover Institution Press

Raus, E. (2003) *Panzer Operations: the Eastern Front Memoir of General Raus, 1941–45*, Cambridge: Da Capo Press

Rees, L. (1997) *The Nazis: a Warning From History*, London: BBC

Rei, A. (1970) *The Drama of the Baltic Peoples*, Stockholm: Vaba Eesti

Resis, A. (2000) 'The Fall of Litvinov: Harbinger of the German–Soviet Non-Aggression Pact' in *Europe-Asia Studies 52 (1)*

Rhodes, R. (2002) *Masters of Death: The SS-Einsatzgruppen and the Invention of the Holocaust*, New York: Alfred A. Knopf

Richter, W. (1975) *Die 1. (Ostpreussische) Infanterie-Division*, Munich: Max Schmidt

Ries, T. (1988) *Cold Will: The Defence of Finland*, London: Brassey's Defence Publishers

Rolnikaite, M. (2002) *Ich Muss Erzählen*, Hamburg: Rowohlt

Röngelep, R. et al (2003) '*Tartu in the 1941 Summer War*' in *Baltic Defence Review* 9, Vol. 1

Rössler, M., Schleiermacher, S. (1996) '*Hauptlinien der nationalsozialistischen Planungs-und Vernichtungspolitik*' in *Central European History Journal*, Vol. 29, 2

Sackowicz, K. (1999) *Dziennik*, Bydgoszcz

Schäufler, H. (1973) *Die Weg War Weit*, Neckargemünd: Vowinckel

Schäufler, H. (1983) *So Lebten Sie und So Starben Sie*, Bamberg: Kameradschaft Ehemaliger Panzer-Regiment 35 eV

Schneider, J. (1994) *The Structure of Strategic Revolution: Total War and the Roots of the Soviet Warfare State*, Novato: Presidio Press

Schön, H. (1983) *Ostsee 45*, Stuttgart: Motorbuch Verlag

Schramm, P. (1982) *Kriegstagebuch der Oberkommando der Wehrmacht*, Vol. VIII, Herrsching: Pawlak

Seaton, A. (1971) *The Russo-German War 1941–1945*, New York: Praeger

Sebag Montefiore, S. (2004) *Stalin, The Court of the Red Czar*, London: Vintage

Senn, A. (2007) *Lithuania 1940, Revolution from Above*, New York: Rodopi

Sewell, S. (1998), 'Why Three Tanks?' in *Armor*, Jul–Aug 1998

Shirer, W. (1960) *The Rise and Fall of the Third Reich*, New York: Simon & Schuster

Silgailis, A. (1986) *Latvian Legion*, San Jose: Bender

Skultans, V. (1997) *The Testimony of Lives: Narrative and Memory in Post-Soviet Latvia*, Andover: Routledge

Snyder, T. (2011) *Bloodlands: Europe Between Hitler and Stalin*, London: Vintage

Spaeter, H. (1995) *History of the Panzerkorps Grossdeutschland*, Winnipeg: Fedorowicz

Speer, A. (1970) *Inside the Third Reich: Memoirs by Albert Speer*, London: Macmillan

Štiemanis, J. (2002) *History of the Latvian Jews*, New York: East European Monographs

Stolfi, R. (2003) *German Panzers on the Offensive*, Atglen: Schiffer

Štrauss, A. (1985) Autobiographical account, Latvijas Zinātņu Akadēmijas Centrālais Arhīvs Riga, P-40/5/22

Strods, H. (1997) *Latvijas Nacionālo Partizāņu Karš 1944–1956*, Riga: Preses Nams

Strods, H., Kott, M. (2002) 'The File on Operation *Priboi*: A Re-Assessment of the Mass Deportations of 1949' in *Journal of Baltic Studies* 33 (1)

Swain, G. (2004) *Between Stalin and Hitler*, London: Routledge

Tarauskas, E. (1990) *Lietuvos Nepriklausomybės Netenkant*, Kaunas: Sviesa

Tauber, J. (2003), *14 Tage im Juni* in Bartusevičius et al (eds) *Holocaust in Litauen*, Cologne: Böhlau

Tieke, W. (2001): *Tragedy of the Faithful – a History of the III. (Germanisches) SS-Panzer-Korps*, Winnipeg: Fedorowicz

Tomkiewicz, W. (2008) *Zbrodnia w Ponarach 1941–1944*, Warsaw: IPN

Truska, L. (2003) *Litausiche Historiographie über den Holocaust in Litauen* in Bartusevičius et al (eds) *Holocaust in Litauen*, Cologne: Böhlau

Tukhachevsky, M. (1924) *Questions of Higher Command*, Moscow

Tukhachevsky, M. (1936) *Vremmenyi Polevoi Ustav RKKA*, Moscow

Urbšys, J. (1990) *Atsiminimai*, Kaunas: Spindulys

Uustalu, E. (1952) *The History of the Estonian People*, London: Boreas

Vardys, V. (ed.) (1965) *Lithuania Under The Soviets*, New York: Praeger

Vīksne, R., Kangeris, K. (eds) (1999) *No NKVD Līdz KGB. Politiskās Prāvas Latvijā 1940–1986*, Riga: Latvijas Vēstures institūta apgāds

Volkogonov, D. (1994) *Lenin: Life and Legacy*, London: Harper Collins

Wette, W. (2003) *SS-Standartenführer Karl Jäger* in Bartusevičius et al (eds) *Holocaust in Litauen*, Cologne: Böhlau

Widder, W. (2002) '*Auftragstaktik and Innere Führung: Trademarks of German Leadership*' in *Military Review* Sept–Oct 2002

Wilhelm, H.-H. (1991) *Rassenpolitik und Kriegsführung. Sicherheitspolizei und Wehrmacht in Polen und der Sowjetunion 1939–1942*, Passau: Wissenschaftsverlag Rother

Yampolski, V. (2001) 'V Pribaltike Zhdali Furera … e Furer Prishel!' in *Voenno-Istoricheskii Zhurnal*, Vol. 6

Ziemke, E. (2003) *Stalingrad to Berlin: the German Defeat in the East*, Honolulu: University Press of the Pacific

Zolotarev, V. (1958) *Boevye Dokumenty po Oboronitelnoi Zapadnogo Fronta* in *Sbornik Boevykh Dokumentov Velikoi Otechestvennoi Viony*, Moscow: Voenizdat, p.34

Zolotarev, V. (1998) *Velikaeia Otechestvennaia Voina 1941–1945, I: Surovye Ispytaniia*, Moscow: Nauka

Zolotarev, V. (1999) *STAVKA VGK 1944–1945*, Moscow: Terra

Zubkov, E. (2007) '"Lesnyie Bratya" v Pribaltike: Viona Posle Vionyi' in *Otechestvennaya Istoriya*, Vol. 2 pp.74–90

Eesti NSV Ajalugui III (1971), Tallinn

Lietuvos Okupacija ir Aneksija 1939–40 (1993), Vilnius: Mintis,

Sbornik Boevykh Dokumentov Velikoi Otechestvennoi Voiny, Moscow: Voenizdat

Totalitārie Okupācijas Režimi Latvijā 1940–1964, Riga: Commission of the Historias of Latvia

Vsemyrnaya Ystoriya Vtoroye Myrovoye Voynyi (1999), Minsk

Reports and documents

Conclusions of the Estonian International Commission for the Investigation of Crimes Against Humanity, 2, available at http://www.historycommission.ee/temp conclusions.htm

Condolences to Family of Great Patriotic War Veteran Vassili Kononov, Presidential Press and Information Office, Moscow, 1 April 2011

European Court of Human Rights judgement in case *Kononov v. Latvia*, 24 June 2008

Evidence presented at the trial of A. Impelivičius, LYA, f. K-1, ap. 58, file 47386/3, Vol. 9

Führer Directive 21, 18 December 1940: Office of the United States Chief of Counsel For Prosecution of Axis Criminality

Führer Naval Conferences (1947) US Library of Congress, p.120

Grand Chamber, European Court of Human Rights judgment in case *Kononov v. Latvia*, 17 May 2010

Hague Convention 1907, Article 23

Incident Report 40, 1/8/1941, Bundesarchiv-Militärarchiv R-58/215, 129

Internal communications of Schutzmann-Bataillon 22, Hoover Latvian Legion Collection, Box 1, Folder 9

Jäger Report of 1/12/41, available in translation from the Jewish Internet Consortium, available at http://fcit.usf.edu/holocaust/resource/document/DocJager.htm, hereafter cited as 'Jäger Report'

Kriegstagebuch 8. Panzer Division 22/6/41, US National Archives, T315, Roll 483

Kriegstagebuch LVI A.K.(Mot), US National Archives, T314, Roll 1389

Letter from Gruppenführer Berger to Himmler, 2/10/41, National Archives Washington DC, RG-242, T175, Roll 22, frame 2527942

Letter from KdS Lettland, Abt IIIB to the Generalkommissar, 11/3/42, Bundesarchiv B, R 92/6, 121

Note from Generalkommissariat in Riga, 27/8/41, Bundesarchiv B, R 92/6, 158

Office of the United States Chief of Counsel For Prosecution of Axis Criminality, Nazi Conspiracy and Aggression, ('Red Series'), Vol. VII, pp.978–95, USGPO, Washington DC 1946 (= 'Stahlecker Report')

Orders of Berück Nord, 28 August 1941, Bundesarchiv-Militärarchiv, RH 22/6

Orders of Commander 3rd Panzer Group, 28 June 1941, Bundesarchiv-Militärarchiv, RH 26-20/19

President Wilson's Message to Congress, January 8, 1918; Records of the United States Senate; Record Group 46

Report 13, 5/7/41, Bundesarchiv B, R 58/214, 75

Report 51, 13/8/41, Bundesarchiv-Militärarchiv R-58/216, 4

Report by Beria, L., to Stalin, Molotov and Antonov, 18 July 1944, available from http://www.doomedsoldiers.com/armia-krajowa-in-NKVD-NKGB-documents-pt-2.html

Report by Leutnant Hasselmann from Frontaufklärungskommando 212 dated 24/12/44, BA-MA, RH-2/2129

Report of SS-Jagdverband Ost, Latvijas Zinātņu Akadēmijas Centrālais Arhīvs Riga, PO 40/5/2

Report on Winterzauber for Wehrmacht High Command Ostland, 20/3/43, Latvias

Valsts Vēstures Arhīvs, Riga, P-70/5/36

Situation report of Abwehrstelle Ostland 1/7/42-30/9/42, Latvias Valsts Vēstures Arhīvs, Riga, P-70/5/37

Third Interim Report of the Select Committee on Communist Aggression, 83rd Congress, 2nd Session, Washington 1954

Trials of the Major War Criminals before the International Military Tribunal 1947–49, Vol. XXVI, pp.610–27, US Library of Congress

USSR DVP *Gazeta Kapitalist* (19/5/2004) *Zhizn' I Sudba 'Bolshogo Medvedya'. Sto Let Vilisu Latsisu*

Extract from Prit Buttar's *Battleground Prussia: The Assault on Germany's Eastern Front 1944–45* – out now in paperback and eBook.

BATTLEGROUND PRUSSIA

THE ASSAULT ON GERMANY'S EASTERN FRONT 1944–45

PRIT BUTTAR

CHAPTER 4
THE LAST CHRISTMAS

The Ostfront must help itself and make do with what it's got.
– Adolf Hitler

Fighting died down along the East Prussian front as autumn turned to winter. Both sides were exhausted by the battles that had moved the frontline hundreds of kilometres west, from the heart of Belarus and Ukraine onto German soil. Only in Hungary, and in the north around the embattled Courland pocket, did fighting continue at high intensity.

Stalin only agreed to a downturn in Soviet attacks with reluctance. He was keen to continue offensive operations, but Zhukov was adamantly opposed, and his advice prevailed. In November 1944, 1st Belorussian Front and Ivan Konev's 1st Ukrainian Front to its south were designated as the main forces for the coming offensive. They would exploit along the 'Warsaw–Berlin axis' in order to deal a decisive blow to German forces in the east. To prepare for this, Zhukov insisted that his battered units needed time to reorganize, incorporate new drafts, repair damaged equipment and to prepare for what should be the decisive battle.

In most respects, it had been a stunningly successful year for the Soviet Union. The prospect of final victory now lay ahead, and the disjointed nature of the fighting on the Ostfront increased the likelihood of Soviet success. The battles in Courland and Hungary tied down German forces some distance from the critical sector of the front, the main axis for the Soviet offensive. Such matters were first discussed in detail in early November. Zhukov's and Konev's fronts would receive massive armoured reinforcements in preparation for their key role. Their northern flank posed considerable concerns for the Soviet planners: as Zhukov's forces moved west, they would skirt the southern side of the heavily fortified German line in East Prussia.

Isolation of East Prussia and its elimination, therefore, would be critical for the main Soviet drive into the heart of the Reich.

Meanwhile, German units were redeploying. The Grossdeutschland Division was withdrawn from Memel and began to reform in East Prussia. In conjunction with the recently created Panzergrenadier Division Brandenburg, it was to form a new Grossdeutschland Corps. The 83rd Infantry Division, which had an illustrious record of service on the Ostfront, was transferred from Courland and dispatched to Thorn, where it received reinforcements. The fighting in Courland had reduced the division to about 7,000 men; the division medical officer reported to Generalleutnant Wilhelm Heun, the division commander, that at least 10 per cent of replacement drafts were simply not fit for frontline service, and should be discharged immediately.

Towards the end of November, 7th Panzer Division was withdrawn from the Memel bridgehead, and Huber and his comrades sailed south aboard a freighter called the Volta. The ship made the overnight run down the coast of the Samland peninsula to Pillau, and from there continued up the channel to Königsberg, where the crews and tanks of 7th Panzer Division's 25th Panzer Regiment were unloaded. From the docks, the men travelled the short distance to the nearby barracks, where they were to spend the night:

> We are all shocked during our short drive through the inner part of Königsberg. There are only ruins there. Rubble and empty darkness lie to left and right. There must have been a heavy air raid on the city in recent times. The bombers have reduced everything to soot and ashes. Beautiful Königsberg! The strong smell of smoke surrounds us as we drive through the streets. Everyone thinks of his own folk at home. Does it look the same as this? They have written to us so often about the bombing attacks – although we haven't had to face this at the front, we are nevertheless familiar with the problem.

Apart from some minimal bombing by a few Soviet aircraft in 1941, Königsberg had survived unscathed until August 1944. On the night of 26–27 August, 174 RAF Lancasters – allegedly violating the airspace of neutral Sweden – struck the city, followed by a heavier raid three nights later. This second raid by 189 Lancasters could only deliver 487 tonnes of bombs, as the aircraft were operating at maximum range, but the damage was considerable. The planes delivered a lethal mix of high-explosive and incendiaries, striking the historic city centre and reducing the Teutonic castle, the cathedral, the university and many other famous landmarks to rubble. About 3,500 people were killed, and many more were left with their homes at least partially damaged. Alerted by the previous raid, in which four Lancasters were shot down by flak, the defenders put up better resistance, destroying 15 bombers.

In anticipation of possible attacks, some of the city's residents had been evacuated to the countryside. Gretel Dost, the girl from Friedrichstein who had been overawed by Marion Dönhoff's visit to her school, was now a nurse working in a private clinic in the city, and in midsummer the clinic was relocated from Königsberg to Fischhausen, a small town to the west of the Prussian capital. Dost and her colleagues were delighted with the move, because they found themselves next to a military hospital, with plenty of time to fraternize with the army personnel. Erika Morgenstern, who had been born in 1939, was sent to a farm in the village of Almenhausen with her mother and younger sister:

> On a wonderful summer's day, when there was nothing to suggest death or suffering – at least not in Almenhausen – a few women were standing in the village street with their children in their arms or holding their hands. It was between breakfast and midday, the sun was high in the sky and this gathering was an unusual sight at this time of day. My mother too joined the group of women with we children. Silent and saddened, everyone stared in one direction, in which normally there was nothing to see but fields. But on this day, there was something else. A large part of the sky from the horizon upwards was deep, dark red. A grisly image, as if blood was rising into the sky. A woman said, 'Königsberg is burning.'

Air raids struck other parts of East Prussia, too. Tilsit was bombed several times by Soviet planes, as were other towns along the frontier. For much of the war, the citizens of East Prussia had been envied by their fellow Germans who lived further west, within range of British and American bombers; now, the long arm of the Allies' air fleets could reach even to here, and Soviet aircraft were close enough to threaten air attacks at any time.

Despite this, East Prussia at the end of 1944 was still relatively untouched by the war, compared to other parts of Germany. Its farms continued to work productively, albeit relying on workers from prisoner of war camps. In some cases, these prisoners had been captives since the opening months of the war, and some had worked on the same farms for years. Many were regarded almost as family by the German women who struggled to keep their farms functioning while their men were away at the front. The Party issued strict orders that the Poles and others were to be kept in isolation from the German population, but the realities of farm life were such that most farmers simply ignored such instructions, as one such farmer related to a girl sent to work on his farm:

Jan is not allowed to go to the next village, not even to church. He is not supposed to listen to the radio or read a newspaper. He must not sleep under the same roof as us and should take his meals in the shed where he lives. They told us not to get too chummy with him; there are hefty penalties for that sort of thing. But I say 'bullshit'. He's more like a member of the family; out here a man is as good as his work and I will not have a man treated like an animal on my property. Mind you, when Herr Stiller is here – he's the rural inspector, a Party man, a real Hitler fanatic they say; you know, 'Heil Hitler' here, 'Heil Hitler' there – I shout a bit at Jan to make Herr Stiller think I'm keeping Jan on a tight rein!

The East Prussian farms were a vital part of the Reich's ability to continue to function, with an annual productivity of several million tonnes of agricultural produce – the farms produced more food than all of Holland. Meat, dairy products and fish (from the productive fleets of small boats operating from the Baltic ports) ensured that even with widespread rationing the people of East Prussia continued to be comparatively well fed.

The mood of the German people at this time is difficult to assess, particularly by those who have never had the misfortune to live in a totalitarian state where all forms of communication are firmly under government control. People had abundant evidence of the perilous state of German fortunes – cities right across the Reich had been bombed repeatedly, and every family had lost men on the various fronts. The eastern edge of East Prussia itself was now occupied by the Red Army, and of course everyone knew about Nemmersdorf, and feared further advances by the Bolsheviks. In Berlin, a city that had never enthusiastically embraced Nazism, the grim joke in circulation this Christmas revolved around the eternal question of what to buy as a Christmas present: 'Be practical,' suggested the wags, 'send a coffin.' Others, such as the dissident Marion Dönhoff, could see only one outcome, but how freely they were able to discuss such matters is open to question. The ever-increasing death toll of the war, though, left few unscathed:

Frau Duttke was … a self-confident, but at the same time modest, outstanding woman. She looked after the pigs and was proud that she hadn't missed a day's work for many years. She and her husband had simply worked all their lives so that their children should have something better. The younger son was killed in France, and the older was an NCO – a magnificent, straightforward, reliable chap, that any army in the world would have regarded with pride: he was certain to become an officer one day, and then all the drudgery would be worthwhile.

But this day didn't come; instead, a day came in autumn 1944, when I saw Frau Duttke crossing the estate yard, a bucket in each hand. The handsome woman looked old, absent-minded, a ghost of her former self. 'In God's name, Frau Duttke, what's happened?' She looked at me with staring, dead eyes, put down the buckets – and suddenly threw her arms around my neck, and cried and cried: 'Karl is dead, the news came today. Now everything is at an end. Everything was for nothing – our whole lives.'

Many soldiers in the frontline, too, were under little illusion about what lay ahead:

It was therefore not surprising that confidence in military leadership … from the front to the highest levels of the Wehrmacht, was deeply shaken, given the completely false evaluation of the facts by these leaders. All that remained now was to save innocent victims of the senseless war from the retaliation of the Red Army, driven on by the revengeful Soviet demagogues.

To speak publicly of such things was to invite court-martial for defeatism, so most soldiers remained cautious, even when discussing matters amongst themselves. Some, though, while aware that things looked grim, continued to hope for a favourable outcome:

We receive a startling report on 18 December. Our forces on the Western Front, in the Ardennes, have launched a counter-offensive. Strong army formations and tank units have hurled back the Americans. We hope for a decisive victory by our side on the Western Front. Our own morale rises. That must be why we have received so few supplies and have had to give up so much ground on the Ostfront – the units in the west were being prepared for an attack!

Days later, the radio reports the success of the Luftwaffe. Six hundred enemy aircraft were shot down yesterday! So, the fortunes of war are turning.

The Ardennes offensive broke as an enormous surprise for both the Allies and most of Germany. In a final burst of productivity, German armaments production reached record levels in the autumn of 1944, and several divisions were completely re-equipped and prepared for action. Guderian and others wanted these divisions deployed in the east to shore up the fragile front, but Hitler gambled on a last offensive in the west. Under heavy skies, which grounded the Allied air forces, the German assault formations made good initial progress, but from the earliest stage stubborn pockets of

American resistance delayed them. Ultimately, the offensive came to a standstill some distance short of the River Meuse, the first major objective, and as the skies cleared, Allied air power was brought to bear with lethal effect. The offensive cost the Germans 80,000 casualties for no tangible gains.

The Luftwaffe attack on New Year's Day, 1945, was also far from a great triumph. A secret airstrike was planned against Allied airfields, with the intention of destroying as many planes as possible on the ground. Most German aircrews were unaware of the exact mission until the morning of the attack. The German pilots struck shortly after dawn, and appeared to be devastatingly successful; more than 460 Allied aircraft were destroyed or damaged. But the flak defences of the airfields were stronger than anticipated, and British and American fighter patrols inflicted heavy losses on the German fighters as they flew home. Even worse, the mission had been prepared in such secrecy that the German flak defences had not been alerted. Seeing large numbers of planes flying out of the west, they opened fire on their own pilots, adding to their casualties. The Germans lost more than 270 planes, but most importantly 211 pilots were killed. The Allies, on the other hand, suffered serious material losses, but their aircrews escaped almost unscathed. Once replacement aircraft were brought forward, albeit over several weeks, they were able to resume operations without difficulty. The Luftwaffe, by contrast, suffered irreplaceable losses of experienced pilots. It would never mount an operation on this scale again.

In his New Year message to the German nation, Hitler characteristically showed no sign of doubt:

Millions of Germans of all callings and backgrounds, men and women, youths and girls, right down to the children, have laboured with spades and shovels. Thousands of Volkssturm battalions have been raised or are being formed. Divisions have been re-equipped. People's artillery corps, rocket brigades and assault gun brigades as well as armoured formations have been deployed, fighter squadrons once more refreshed and supplied with new machines, and above all the German factories have through the efforts of their male and female workers achieved singular results. In this way, whatever our enemies destroy has been restored with superhuman diligence and heroic courage, and this will continue until one day our enemies will find their end. That, my fellow countrymen, will be regarded as the wonder of the 20th century! A people, who labour so endlessly at the front and in the homeland, who endure so much ill fortune, will never be ground down. They will come out of this furnace tested and stronger than ever before in their history.

To some extent at least, Hitler spoke the truth. Tank production peaked in December 1944, with 1,854 tanks and assault guns being completed, equivalent to almost half the entire production of 1941, sufficient to re-equip several Panzer divisions. But this was the last surge of production, and Hitler's armaments minister, Albert Speer, was well aware that raw materials were running out. There was no longer sufficient brass to manufacture the huge quantities of cartridges required, and in some cases steel was being used. These steel cartridges were more prone to jamming, causing additional problems. There was also a shortage of tungsten, resulting in armour-piercing ammunition being of a poorer quality, and sometimes not even available.

Everywhere, German soldiers and civilians held on in the hope of the promised Wunderwaffen ('Wonder Weapons') – the miraculous new weapons that would turn the tide of the war. New assault rifles were now in widespread circulation, and official reports had made much of the advent of new Luftwaffe aircraft, particularly the jet-powered Me 262 and rocket-powered Me 163. Large parts of London had felt the power of V-1 and V-2 missile bombardments, and there were constant hints that other, even more potent weaponry would soon be available. But would it come in time?

All along the Ostfront, senior officers used what little time they had available, organizing training for their new drafts, preparing defensive positions and contemplating a grim future. Günter Emanuel Baltuttis was a member of a replacement draft sent to bring the former 16th Parachute Regiment, now renamed 3rd Regiment, of the Paratroop-Panzergrenadier Division Hermann Göring back to something approaching full strength. The draft consisted of a number of former airmen as well as new recruits like Baltuttis. When they assembled near Insterburg, they were surprised by the greeting they were given by a stony-faced Oberleutnant: 'Take note, I will not hesitate to drag any laggard or coward before a court martial!'

Baltuttis and his comrades were sent straight into the frontline, where they endured muddy, rainswept conditions – in order to keep their loads to a minimum, they had been sent forward in summer clothing, with the assurance that winter uniforms would follow in due course. These garments didn't actually appear for two months. Within days, Baltuttis had developed a form of trench foot from constant immersion in water and damp earth.

Baltuttis' regiment was holding the frontline in the area where the Führer-Grenadier Brigade had run into Soviet armour, west of Daken, and the landscape was dotted with burnt-out wrecks. From time to time, the soldiers came across the corpses of men who had fallen in the fighting, and had been left to sink slowly into the mud. Desertions to the enemy were a regular feature. Soldiers faced draconian punishments for other misdemeanours. Baltuttis' company commander, Leutnant Saul, was assigned to a court-martial, and recounted the story to Baltuttis when he returned to the company:

> An 18-year-old soldier, whose father was an Oberst in our corps, was condemned to death for the capital offence of plundering, because he had taken an abandoned wristwatch that he found in some ruins during a counter-attack. Leutnant Saul objected to the case being brought, and finally refused to take part, forcing an adjournment, probably saving the life of the accused. The chairman accused Leutnant Saul of 'refusing to follow orders', and reported the events to the regiment commander, resulting in an immediate summons for Leutnant Saul. But contrary to expectations, the commander, Oberstleutnant Rebholz, issued not the slightest rebuke, but just gently shook his head, and made it clear that he regarded the procedure as unnecessary and pointless. Leutnant Saul escaped any punishment.

During the winter, Baltuttis' company suffered a steady stream of casualties. These included two suicides, two executions (one for desertion, one for self-wounding) and two deaths as a result of attempts at self-wounding that went badly wrong. Baltuttis noted that all of the casualties, including those from enemy snipers, involved new drafts rather than the company's small number of veterans. Alarmed by the poor performance of new recruits, both the division and corps commanders recommended that the division be pulled out of line and allowed to undergo intensive training; the almost non-existent reserves available on the front effectively precluded any such action.

The German soldiers worked hard to improve their bunkers, which served as homes as well as fortifications. They would need all the protection they could get; German intelligence made force estimates that gave the Red Army an advantage of 11:1 in infantry, 7:1 in tanks and 20:1 in artillery. Hitler dismissed these estimates, deriding them as 'the greatest bluff since the time of Genghis Khan'. For the moment, though, Hitler had other concerns in the east than Army Group Centre.

August 1944 was a bad month for the Reich in the Balkans. Bulgaria first declared itself neutral, and then – under pressure from the Soviet Union – declared war on Germany. Bulgarian contributions to the Reich's war effort had always been modest, but the political impact of Bulgaria's defection was considerable. Romania also defected, in a much more dramatic manner. After secret negotiations with the Soviet Union, Romania switched sides and the two armies guarding the flanks of the German 6th Army allowed the Red Army unrestricted passage. In 1942, the failure of Romanian armies guarding the German flanks at Stalingrad had resulted in the envelopment of the 6th Army, and now the same result ensued, with the remnants of no fewer than 20 divisions being encircled near Kishinev. Few men succeeded in breaking out of the envelopment. In October, as Hungary's government was finalizing secret arrangements to surrender to the approaching Red Army, Germany engineered a coup, putting the Crossed Arrows Party, the nearest Hungarian equivalent to the Nazi Party, into power. Most of the last remaining Jews in Hungary, about 70,000 individuals in and around Budapest, were gathered together into an area of about 0.3 square kilometres and were force-marched to the Austrian border during November and December. Many perished in the cold.

The 337th Volksgrenadier Division was ordered on 16 October to take over a sector of the front from the Hungarian 5th Reserve Division, near Warsaw. The Hungarians were to be disarmed, a task that Hans Jürgen Pantenius and his fellow officers found deeply distasteful, as they had established very close relations with the Hungarian division:

Without any major fanfare, I travelled to Natolin, and explained the situation and my mission to the [Hungarian] commander, and asked him for his pistol, not out of any sense of danger to my own person, but because I wanted to prevent a suicide attempt. The commander was completely helpless, tears filled his eyes, and he could not and did not want to issue orders; he handed his weapon to me silently. The adjutant ... issued the orders I wished, concerning the replacement, disarmament, and internment. Due to previous discussions about replacement and the positional maps that had been prepared, the action was carried out comparatively swiftly and without difficulty. Naturally, the Hungarians could see no reason for their disarmament and like their commander were concerned and agitated. This did not prevent the officers and NCOs from taking care to list what weapons and equipment they handed over.

I never found out who at army, corps or division level actually issued the order for the disarmament of the Hungarian reserve division. Did those in higher commands really think that the division would desert to the Poles? If they had asked the 'frontline', in other words our general or 337th Volksgrenadier Division's regimental commanders, for our advice beforehand, we would have told them that we never doubted the camaraderie of the Hungarians. But the views of subordinates were not sought. But the very same day came a counter-order. The Hungarian division was to be given back its weapons immediately, the internment was to be stopped, and the division was to prepare for transport to Hungary the next day. The whole affair was a mess. I was now tasked to make my 'colleagues' who remained in Natolin aware of the new situation and to return their weapons to them with expressions of regret. The Hungarians were delighted with the prospect of returning to their homes in Hungary ... our general was almost speechless with anger.

Meanwhile, the Red Army was approaching Hungary from the east. Stalin may have agreed to a pause in offensive operations into Poland and Prussia, but he urged the powerful Ukrainian Fronts forward towards Budapest. His Front commanders asked in vain for an opportunity to pause and gather their strength, but the disjointed nature of their attacks actually proved to their advantage. A single, well-organized thrust at Budapest would probably have been successful, and Hitler would have been forced to accept the inevitable, but the succession of drives against the Hungarian capital resulted in a steady transfer of German forces to this sector, stripping Poland and East Prussia of vital armoured reserves. By mid December, the Hungarian capital lay in a salient, with both its flanks threatened. The SS Dirlewanger Brigade, which had acquired a grim reputation for its part in the suppression of the Warsaw Rising, was routed north of the city. As the diminishing defenders were frantically reshuffled to restore the front, the pincers of 2nd and 3rd Ukrainian Fronts turned towards each other.

On 26 December, they met at Esztergom, northeast of Budapest. The Hungarian capital, containing about 188,000 German troops, was surrounded. Refusing to accept the loss of the city, Hitler ordered the garrison to continue to resist, and IV SS-Panzer Corps, currently deployed as armoured reserve in Poland, was sent south. Much of the Ostfront had already been denuded to shore up the defences, and this latest move left the critical Warsaw–Berlin axis dangerously weak.

Worse was to come in January. After the Ardennes offensive was abandoned, the SS divisions that might have provided a vital reserve for Army Group Centre were sent to launch another relief attempt in Hungary. For the moment, though, the diversion of IV SS-Panzer Corps left Reinhardt's Army Group Centre only one Panzer division and two Panzergrenadier divisions as armoured reserves. To make matters worse, the army group's frontline, which bulged dangerously to the east, inviting strikes against either flank, was rendered less defensible as the winter frosts froze the marshy land around the Narew and Bobr, terrain that had previously been impassable to Soviet tanks. Hossbach found that the Masurian Lakes to his rear were now ideal landing areas for airborne troops, and his engineers had to improvise obstacles, using farm machinery and tree trunks embedded vertically into the frozen surface of the lakes.

The fighting around Goldap and Gumbinnen had been complicated by the inability, or unwillingness, of the Wehrmacht and the local Party officials to cooperate and arrange a timely evacuation of civilians, and to arrange appropriate deployment of the Volkssturm. Now, there was a third entity, raising the possibility that matters would become even more complex. General Otto Lasch had been appointed as commander of Wehrkreis I (Defence District I), the military administrative authority that oversaw most of East Prussia. Rather than being subordinate to Reinhardt's army group, Lasch was answerable to Heinrich Himmler in his role as commander of the Replacement Army. Lasch was from Silesia, but was married to an East Prussian, and had spent most of his life in the province, serving as a police officer in Lyck and Sensburg before rejoining the army in 1935. He was serving in France, about to take command of LXIV Corps, when he received the news over the telephone that he was to go to East Prussia:

'Why me, a frontline solder?'

'Precisely because of that, things are now hotting up in East Prussia.'

I had the gravest misgivings, particularly with respect to Gauleiter Koch, with whom I had had few personal dealings, but about whom I had unpleasant memories as a fanatical National Socialist from the years of peace. I also was aware that two Wehrkreis commanders had already been replaced at his insistence, as he did not regard them to be working in a sufficiently National Socialist manner. Whether I would be able to succeed in my military role in the face of the inconsiderate interference of someone who unfortunately was so well connected seemed more than questionable.

INDEX